THE WHALING CITY

VIEW OF NEW LONDON, CONNECTICUT, FROM THE SHORE ROAD.

From Gleason's Pictorial Drawing Room Companion, 1855.

The Whaling City

A History of New London
By Robert Owen Decker

Globe
Pequot

Guilford, Connecticut

Published by Globe Pequot
An imprint of The Rowman & Littlefield Publishing Group, Inc.
4501 Forbes Boulevard, Suite 200, Lanham, Maryland 20706
www.rowman.com

Unit A, Whitacre Mews, 26-34 Stannary Street, London SE11 4AB

Distributed by NATIONAL BOOK NETWORK

Copyright © 1976 by Robert Owen Decker
Published for The New London County Historical Society
First Globe Pequot paperback edition 2017

British Library Cataloguing in Publication Information Available

Library of Congress Cataloging-in-Publication Data
The hardback edition of this book was previously cataloged by the Library of Congress as follows:

Library of Congress Catalog Card No. 74-30794

ISBN 0-87106-053-1

ISBN 0-87106-053-1 (cloth)
ISBN 978-1-4930-1561-0 (paper : alk. paper)
ISBN 978-1-4930-1562-7 (electronic)

∞™ The paper used in this publication meets the minimum requirements of American National Standard for Information Sciences—Permanence of Paper for Printed Library Materials, ANSI/NISO Z39.48-1992.

Printed in the United States of America

*I wish to dedicate this
volume to my Wife, Margaret
Harris Decker, whose New
London and Preston ancestors
were a part of much of the
history of this area from
1645 on—the Robinson's,
Tracy's, Rix's and Kimball's..*

TABLE OF CONTENTS

LIST OF ILLUSTRATIONS

LIST OF APPENDICES

PREFACE

The author has written the story of New London with a strong maritime flavor for which he makes no apology as New London owes its very being to the sea. The oceans of the world brought it wealth and—at least in the "age of sail"—fame as well as fear. One might say that New London's greatness was in response to its dangers. As with any seaport community, the town had to fear for the lives of her sons while at sea. Much wealth came from fishing, whaling, coastal and foreign trade. On the other hand the sea often provided sadness—losses of men, goods and ships to disease, pirates, privateers and storms. With its fortunes and future so at the mercy of the seas, it is small wonder that one finds so many maritime reminders at the port—the "Whaling City" on signs as one enters town, the names of streets, business titles, statutes and monuments.

Originally this study was planned to deal primarily with the period from 1860 to 1970. At that time it appeared that Frances M. Caulkin's *History of New London* which covered various families in detail and several topics in less depth of the town's development to 1860 might contain enough material so that only a brief account would be needed of pre 1860 days. Unfortunately, it became apparent to the author early in the research that her work does not provide the firm basis which would be needed for such a study and which could only be provided through several in depth chapters covering the early years of the town. This is not meant as an unfavorable reflection upon that fine study which has proven so valuable to historians since its printing. Thus the first chapters were developed on a chronological basis to relate the story from John Winthrop, Jr.'s founding of the town to the year 1819.

Since the history of the town appears to fall into two major periods, pre 1819 and post 1819, the main portion of the work carries the exciting story of New London from the end of the War of 1812 to the 1970s. Each chapter is built about a significant topic. While the author recognizes that some readers will expect to see chapters on the Civil War, World War I or World War II, they will find such topics are covered within each chapter as it affects the subject under discussion. Attention should be directed to Chapter VII where the town's history is interwoven with the town's business history.

I had great pleasure in researching and writing these pages and even at times a sense of being a part of the town's history. I hope the reader will receive a little of the great pleasure I have enjoyed.

I wish to thank the New London County Historical Society for the opportunity to do this study—especially John Winthrop, Elizabeth Knox and Carol Kimball. In the parlance of today's youth—they are beautiful people. I can only hope that this work justifies their faith in my ability to write it.

The price paid by my wife, Margaret Harris Decker, and daughter, Terry Lynn Decker DeIulis, has been great. I thank them both for accepting the hours of neglect as well as hours of listening to different drafts of materials for this study. My wife has typed, edited, criticized and encouraged this history from beginning to end.

My deep felt thanks to all others, far too numerous to mention, who gave of their time and materials to help.

September, 1975

Robert Owen Decker
Rocky Hill, Connecticut

P.S. I never could have gotten through the long hours of research at the Shaw Mansion without Mrs. Hamel's coffee and cookies.

FROM A PHOTO BY BOLLES & FRISBIE N.L. CONN.

PEQUOT HOUSE, NEW LONDON CONN.

INTRODUCTION—A New Puritan Settlement

Droves of cattle, hogs and horses moved through the narrow streets driven by groups of dusty, rough talking men. The din was deafening and became more so as one approached the wharfs. Several taverns doing an excellent business could be identified by their signs or even more quickly by the sounds of men "cutting the dust" of the trail from Springfield to the port with a little liquid refreshment or having a last drink before heading back home. Others, already refreshed, had taken to the streets in noisy gangs, seeking entertainment. Along the docks a variety of vessels received or relinquished cargoes. Seamen, from boys fired with excitement and dread to seasoned mariners fresh from the town's "entertainment section", prepared to ship out. Usually the port would be West Indian, but coastal ports from Newfoundland to Georgia often were sailed for as well as South American ports and less often African or European ports became the destination. This was New London, one of the chief Connecticut port towns during the colonial period.

For a town which came to figure so prominently in the maritime history of the American Colonies, proved so vital during the American Revolution, became a world important whaling and sealing port, and whose seagoing sons would make its name known world wide, New London's beginning seemed to promise little. Despite possessing one of the best natural harbors on the eastern coast of North America, settlement did not begin until later. Europeans visited, charted and examined the area as early as 1614, but considered it less attractive than other parts of the coast until 1637. The agricultural possibilities left much to be desired, the area lacked meadows, contained numerous swamps and would-be settlers could see that much hard physical labor would be required to clear the forests and cultivate the hilly, rocky terrain.

Still, it was only a matter of time before the beautiful green hills of Eastern Connecticut adjacent to Long Island Sound where the Thames flows into the Sound would attract settlers. The harbor possesses a hinterland of 2,050 square miles, the New England Upland.[1] In the long run the harbor, one of the deepest and largest on the Atlantic Coast, determined the history of the area. Sheltered by Fisher's Island, a natural breakwater, New London Harbor's strategic location near the entrance of Long Island Sound offered shelter when storms swept the "Devil's Belt" as the Sound had once been known. Additional advantages included being free from swift currents and almost always ice free, as well as, being on the direct route between Boston and New York. The harbor provided an excellent anchorage with its soft muddy bottom and sufficient depth of water for any size ship to enter safely as the tide rises and falls only two and one-half feet. In the age of sail it was estimated that from three to five hundred vessels could be anchored at one time in the harbor. A report of 1680 stated that:

> . . . a ship of 500 tunns may go up to the Town, and come so near the shoar, that they may toss a biskitt on shoar, ...[2]

Adrian Block became the first European to visit what is now Connecticut and to sail up the Thames River while representing a group of Amsterdam merchants in 1614. He explored and charted the future site of New London in the *Onrust (Restless),* the first decked vessel to be constructed within what is now the United States.[3]

Although New London calls May 6, 1646 its natal day, the actual beginning of a settlement should be credited to 1637 when the first house was built on Fort Neck.[4] Roger Williams, religious leader and founder of Rhode Island, aroused the interest of John Winthrop the Elder in the area when he sent a map of the Connecticut shore to him in 1636. The Massachusetts Governor sent his son, John Winthrop, the Younger, on an exploratory expedition to the region.

By 1644 the son had decided to establish a colony in "Pequot Country." He received from Massachusetts "leave to make a plantation at Pequot" in 1644 and already claimed Fisher's Island for which he acquired grants from Massachusetts in 1640, Connecticut and Saybrook in 1641 and New York in 1668.[5]

John Winthrop, the Younger, represented a new generation of leaders which emerged to replace the original Puritan leadership which began the

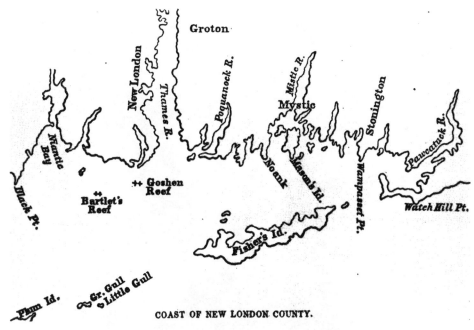

COAST OF NEW LONDON COUNTY.

From Frances Caulkin's History of New London, 1866.

settlements in New England. The seventeenth century settlers were Puritans who saw the colony as a divine mission to establish a "city upon a hill". John Winthrop, the Elder, battled every sinner and wayward saint who threatened his world. A shift of New England conscience took place and by the eighteenth century the "Yankee" replaced the "Puritan". His son's generation was more wordly, less concerned with religion and more involved with economic opportunitites.

The younger Winthrop led an extremely active life. He never pursued a single task, but tackled several at once and rarely finished any. This proved to be the major weakness of his long career. An excellent planner and organizer, Winthrop just seemed to lack perseverance in handling the day-to-day details of a project. On the other hand his activities in science and technology earned him a membership in the Royal Society of London, probably the first colonist so honored.[6] Winthrop made the first systematic astronomical observations in the colonies. He possessed great charm which attracted the older generation rather than his own and an inquisitive mind which resulted in a rather unconventional circle of friends which included

John Winthrop, Founder of New London. Governor of Connecticut, 1657-1676.

John Davenport (New Haven Colony), an orthodox Puritan, Roger Williams (Rhode Island Colony), a radical Puritan, and Sir Kenelum Digby (London), a Roman Catholic.

A busy thirty-eight years preceded John Winthrop's founding of New London. He attended Trinity College, Dublin, studied law, took part in the Duke of Buckingham's campaign of 1627 and served aboard a Levant Company vessel in the Mediterranean—all before John Winthrop, the Elder, left for the New World. Family affairs in England were wound up by John Winthrop, the Younger, before he followed his father to Massachusetts in 1631. Once there, he joined the Boston Church, became a freeman and was elected an assistant in 1632.[7] The New World saw a continuation of his activity as he founded settlements and engaged in numerous business enterprises. None of Winthrop's projects enjoyed much success until he became involved with the New London settlement. In the thirty-one years remaining to him, John Winthrop, Jr., served the people of Connecticut as doctor, diplomat and governor,—becoming one of the most highly respected men in the history of the colony.[8]

Winthrop's group began to settle at New London in the summer of 1645 when Robert Hempstead, Cary Latham, Thomas Miller, William Morton, Jacob Waterhouse and Isaac Willey along with Winthrop, his sister-in-law, Margaret Lake, and Thomas Peters, minister, arrived. Although land grants appear to have been made before the spring of 1646, none were recorded until the following year.

The first settlers, many of Pilgrim stock, possessed deep religious convictions, gave strong support to law and order, and strove to live without sin in a sinful world. Unfortunately the rocky and hilly land failed to exert a strong hold on many of the people who arrived. Departures became so common that New London in its early years, especially after the loss of the minister, Thomas Peters in the fall of 1646, acquired a reputation as an unsteady community where rules of the church were not well observed. Until 1650 the future of the plantation appeared shaky, only the financial support of Emmanuel Downing, a friend of the Winthrop family and a wealthy distiller in Salem, Massachusetts, allowed the colony to keep going. In 1650, the town received a new impetus and needed religious guidance when fourteen families from Gloucester arrived under the leadership of the Reverend Mr. Richard Blinnman.

Direction of town settlement remained in John Winthrop's hands until 1648 when the townspeople met and organized a government. John Winthrop then shared the leadership with others until 1651 when personal business and colonial obligations required most of his attention. At an annual meeting held on the last Thursday of every February town officials were selected. These positions included a constable, five townsmen, (selectmen), two fenceviewers, two clearers of highways and two overseers of weirs. It was not usual for office holders to remain in their posts for a number of years, such as Obadiah Bruen who served as recorder for sixteen years.

From its very settlement New London began to develop as a port. Once begun, the development continued until by the American Revolution it ranked as a major colonial port. The area possessed the three prerequisites necessary to become a leading seaport—a good natural harbor, a large productive hinterland and an enterprising merchant class. In an attempt to stimulate its rate of growth, the Governor and Council requested that a free port be established at New London. Connecticut claimed that such a grant would attract men of substance and increase the value of the colony, but no favorable response came from the English government. Even without special status, development of the port proceeded at such a pace that by 1680 it ranked as one of the principal Connecticut towns and in 1702 the Connecticut Assembly selected it as one of eight legal ports for the colony. By that date it had become one of the principal market towns of Connecticut.[9]

New London grew along the three mile crescent shaped waterfront between Winthrop's Cove and Shaw's Cove. The first houses were built on the shoreline between these coves at the base of hills which reached an elevation of 250 feet. Main (Town) Street and Water (Beach) Street became the early business centers of the seventeenth century with Bank (the Bank) Street becoming the site of business in the eighteenth century. Winthrop's Cove became an important part of the settlement early as the Winthrops located themselves there on Winthrop's Neck in 1645 and the town mill was built near their home in 1650. By 1670 shipyards, shops and warehouses began to dot the west side of the Cove and the town ferry landing was located near the southwestern edge of the Cove where the town wharf was built in 1703.

Before 1700 new homes were simple and were furnished with items made by the owners or local craftsmen, usually with tools of their own making. A householder owned house, garden and orchard. Upon the hill behind the harbor was the town square where the meeting house was erected in 1655 and a courthouse in 1724.

By 1756 one could travel from the town mill on Winthrop's Neck to Captain Nathaniel Shaw's stone house on Bank Street and in the process have passed the town wharf, shipyards, merchant wharves, warehouses,

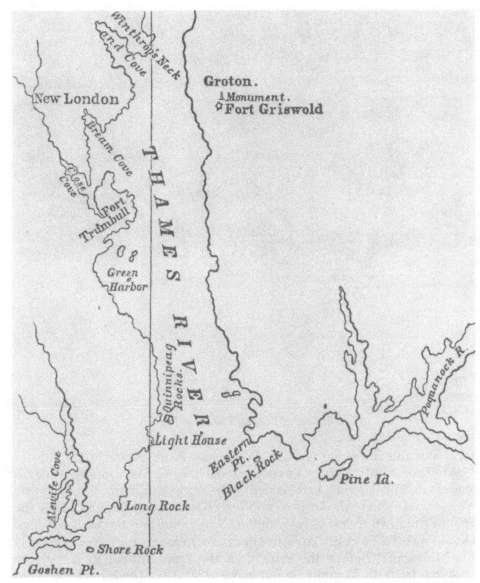

New London Harbor. Long. W. from Greenwich, 72° 5′ 44″. From Frances Caulkin's History of New London, 1866.

Old Town Mill and Winthrop House.

ferry slip and stores along Main, Water and Bank Streets.

Winthrop's Indian policy was not calculated to win the support of Indian leaders in Southeastern Connecticut. The settlers organized a plantation without payment to the Indians and forced those not willing to accept the rule of the town to leave. In addition, New London followed a policy of extending influence and harrassment against neighboring tribes, especially the Mohegans. Before the settlement the main Indian group of the area had been the Pequots—a fierce, war-like tribe whose influence held sway from Rhode Island to New Haven. The Pequot War of 1637 ended their predominance. After that date there existed little threat of an attack from Indians in the New London area.[10]

Pequot Indians served the new settlement as guides, messengers, assistants and servants. Their cooperation with John Winthrop's plantation angered Uncas, Chief of the Mohegans. He had been given control over all Pequots in the area as a reward for allying himself with Captain John Mason's forces during the Pequot War.

Difficulties developed which lasted for several years between the settlers and Uncas who resisted the attempts to undermine his authority. In an attempt to achieve his goal of control, Winthrop constantly made charges against Uncas to the Colony of Connecticut and the Court of Commissioners of the United Colonies. The chief constantly met with provocations designed to force actions supporting the complaints.

A number of serious incidents occurred before peaceful relations developed. Some Pequots, while on a hunting trip for the Reverend Mr. Thomas Peters, were ambushed and driven back to New London. The battle resulted in the wounding of several Indians, the destruction of some English property, a few Indian cattle being driven off and the threatening of the settlement. The town in turn seized Uncas' followers, Mohegan lands, their fort and once even the leader himself. Peace came only when the colonists, fearful of a united attack, began to back Uncas against his Indian enemies—even aiding him in some battles.[11]

At the outbreak of King Philip's War New London feared an attack and rumors of large gatherings of hostile Indians led to a plan to establish six fortifications. Governor Winthrop at Hartford received appeals for aid from New London and Stonington, as both believed attacks were imminent. He sent troops to eastern Connecticut and called the Assembly into special session. As it happened, no attacks took place and New London became a staging area base for troops, a storehouse for supplies and a hospital for the sick and wounded. Although Major Fitz-John Winthrop, son of the Governor, had charge of the base, illness prevented his taking part and Major Edward Palmes, his brother-in-law, directed military affairs. Captain Wait-Still Winthrop, brother of the Major, took part in the negotiations and treaty signed July 15, 1675 with the Narragansetts. One agreement promised a British coat for each head of a Wampanoag surrendered. New London officials received three such trophies with less than pleasure. New London volunteers served in the Narragansett territory defeating large numbers of Indians. Southern New England's Indian menace ended with the war.[13]

Once the settlement began, a struggle over jurisdiction took place between Connecticut and Massachusetts. Both colonies had sent soldiers into the area during the Pequot War and laid claim to it. In 1641, the Connecticut General Court authorized a survey of "Pequot Country" and the following year made a grant of land. At the same time the Massachusetts Bay General Court issued a commission to settle the area. After several years of controversy the Commissioners of the United Colonies determined in September of 1646 that Connecticut should have control.[13]

The original boundaries of the town as established by the Connecticut General Assembly included an area eight miles along the coast and eight miles inland. A dispute with Lyme over an area claimed by both towns reached a settlement in a most unusual way. Neither settlement would accept the decision of the court or legislature so they decided to reach a final decision by combat. The colonial authorities did not look kindly upon this method of settling disputes and charged Hugh Mould, John Keeny and Clement Minor with causing a disturbance and fined New London, which lost the fight, nine pounds and Lyme fifteen pounds—later remitted. The town diminished in size when several sections were detached to form independent towns. No less than five towns were carved out of the original grant—"Granted that the bounds of the plantation of Pequot shall be foure myles on each side of the River".[14] Half of the area became separate in 1705 when all east of the river became Groton, named after the Suffolk County seat of the Winthrop family. In 1836 the northern section of Groton, known as Groton North Society, became a separate town—Ledyard. The North Parish of New London became Montville in 1786. Waterford was set aside in 1801 leaving New London three-quarters of a mile in width and less than four miles along the Thames. New London kept all town property and record books. Groton had the right to send their children to the free grammar school and ferry costs were taken care of by New London.

At first, Winthrop's settlement continued to be known by the Indian name for the area, Nameaug—then in 1652 it became Pequot. The people of the area chose the name New London as early as 1649 but several of the colonial officials felt that name pretentious and insisted upon the name of Fair Harbor. Not until 1658, when John Winthrop sat in the governor's chair, would the assembly agree to accept New London as the official name. The river at New London was called Pequot or Mohegan until the name, changed naturally enough, became the Thames.[15]

1 Colonial New London: Its Leaders 1645-1763

New Londoners played a prominent role in Connecticut colonial affairs. Of the first ten governors three were from the port town—John Winthrop (18 years), his son Fitz-John Winthrop (10 years) and Gurdon Saltonstall (17 years)—close friend of Fitz-John. They served for a total of thirty-five years of the Colony's first eighty-six. John Winthrop also served one year as Deputy Governor and Gurdon Saltonstall served as Chief Justice of the Supreme Court of Errors.[1]

Winthrop, Palmes, Hempstead, Saltonstall, Rogers, Christophers, Deshon, Shaw, Mumford and Coit are among the names appearing most often in trade, political, religious and social history of the town during the colonial period.

Winthrop paid little attention to New London after 1656 when he moved to New Haven Colony. He was elected governor of Connecticut while living there and returned in 1657 to accept that post. With the elevation of John Winthrop to leadership of the colony, his sons and son-in-law became the leaders of the settlement—Fitz-John and Wait-Still Winthrop and Edward Palmes. The sons, born in 1638 and 1642, grew to manhood in New London. Neither desired political preferment but their name forced posts upon them for which they had no interest and little talent. The sons' primary interest concerned their own fortunes. They proved susceptible to flattery and manipulation, lacked the charm of their father, were self-indulgent, created enemies over trivial affairs and nourished grudges for years. Both possessed their father's drive to accumulate real estate and to engage in business enterprise, but their lack of capabilities led to numerous legal hassles.[2]

In Edward Palmes the brothers had a worthy opponent. A strongwilled merchant, originally of New Haven Colony, he became one of New London's most powerful merchants and husband of Lucy Winthrop. Ill feelings existed between Palmes and the Winthrops from the time of the marriage. Edward Palmes felt his wife's dowry—the original Winthrop homestead, garden and orchard, six acres of land and a home along the Thames—was too small. In most disputes concerning New London, Palmes and the Winthrops found themselves on opposing sides.[3]

John Winthrop left a widow and seven children when he died in 1676. His vast estate created many problems due to the claims and counterclaims of the family members. A number of debts had to be liquidated and funds had to be raised to pay the cash bequests of Winthrop. Business operations of the father had proved less profitable than anticipated when several grain crop failures were followed by the loss of a number of vessels and cargoes to privateers during the Dutch War of 1664-1667. To secure necessary capital, large sums of money had been borrowed and as a security for part of the amount, fifteen hundred pound mortgage on Fisher's Island and five hundred pound mortgage on a property known as Ten Hills existed.

Enough property was disposed of to pay the debts of the estate and meet the cash bequests of Winthrop. Of the five daughters, four received cash—Anne, Elizabeth, Margaret and Martha. Lucy Palmes, the fifth, received nothing and this began a quarrel which lasted forty years. The mother received the income from several properties during her lifetime.[4]

The property went to the two sons and even after selling some for the cash needed, amounted to considerable holdings. It included 1,590 acres in New London, Fisher's Island, Goat Island, 3,600 acres just outside New London, 13,000 acres in other parts of Connecticut, and holdings ten miles in circumference in Massachusetts Bay. The brothers never divided the estate. It passed intact to John, son of Wait-Still, as Fitz-John had no children.[5]

The eldest son, Fitz-John Winthrop (1638-1707) held the post of Major General of Militia and several civil offices, but he took little interest in the responsibilities. His major activity involved the management of the family property in and around the port. One can imagine the shock with which people must have viewed Fitz-John's living with Elizabeth Tongue without benefit of clergy. Even more dismay must have existed when the New London girl bore him a daughter out of wedlock. Whatever might have been the view of the town, the ties ended when he left New London in 1690.[6]

Wait-Still Winthrop (1642-1727) left New London in 1670 and lived out his life in Boston. He failed to take the covenant, did not join the church and lived as a second class citizen. Wait-Still handled the family property in the Boston area where he married Mary Brown, daughter of a prominent Salem merchant in 1677.

Edward Palmes, already angry over the dowry his wife received upon marriage, became incensed upon learning she would not share in her father's estate. He went so far as to appeal to the King in Council for a share of John Winthrop's property. To no avail.[7]

A merchant of the town, John Liveen, died in 1689 and a will was presented leaving the entire estate to the New London ministry upon his wife's death. During her remaining lifetime, she would have the use of one-third of the estate and the ministry two-thirds. The executors of the estate were Fitz-John Winthrop, Edward Palmes and the widow. The will contained several surprises and created doubt about the manner in which it may have come into being. Liveen who resided for twelve years in New London and had never attended any religious service left all his property to the ministry. Yet he made no provisions for his two step-sons despite the great affection Liveen had always shown towards them. Nor had he taken any notice of a sizeable estate of his wife, who had been the widow of a Barbados merchant, which had passed into the hands of Liveen. As a result the writer of the will, Daniel Taylor, was suspected by many of having pressured Liveen into signing the will. Fitz-John Winthrop accepted the will, but Edward Palmes and Mrs. Liveen refused.

The town brought suit against the executors and won. The provisions of the will were carried out during the widow's lifetime, but upon her death the sons, backed by Edward Palmes, contested the will. They lost in the New London court and the Hartford court. After receiving permission from the Lord Commissioners of Trade and Plantations, they took the case before the King's Council where in 1704 the Council upheld the decisions of the Connecticut courts.[8]

A case which had far reaching implications for the colony had its origin in New London. John Winthrop IV (1681-1747) son of Wait-Still, inherited the family property upon the death of his father in 1727. Mrs. Thomas Winthrop Lechmere, his sister, contested his right to sole possession of the estate. Unfortunately, although a will had been drawn up it had never been recorded and all the witnesses were either dead or their whereabouts unknown. In this situation the Connecticut courts upheld the sister's claim to one-half the estate. Winthrop went to England to plead his case and appealed to the King in Council and won a reversal of the Connecticut

Hempstead House, about 1891.

decision in 1728. The results of the appeal alarmed Connecticut for it was feared that the rule of primogeniture would be forced upon the colonists. Connecticut's agents managed to make an arrangement in which Winthrop received his inheritance but the Connecticut law of inheritance continued in effect.[9]

Joshua Hempstead provided much information about life in colonial New London. His family settled in the area at an early date and the house in which Hempstead was born is the oldest building in New London today. He kept a diary which presented a picture of the town in particular, and colonial life in general, from September 8, 1711 to November 7, 1758. Hempstead appeared to have been a part of all activity which took place in the area. He held three to four public offices at a time serving as justice of peace, judge of probate, executor of wills, overseer of widows, guardian of orphans and a number of many occupations. He acted as friend and confidential agent to the Winthrop family and worked as farmer, surveyor, house and ship carpenter, attorney, stone cutter, sailor, trader, merchant and public servant. His diary provides much information as to living conditions, political and social events, and wages and prices of the day.[10]

The Saltonstall family connection with New London dates from 1687 when Reverend Gurdon Saltonstall began preaching at the First Church of Christ. With the death of Governor Fitz-John Winthrop, a close friend, he became governor of Connecticut (1708 to his death in 1724). Two of his

Gurdon Saltonstall by Joseph Blackburn.

sons entered into merchant activities at New London—Roswell Saltonstall, a sea captain, died in 1738, while the other son, Gurdon, enjoyed a flourishing business at New London for thirty years. He sent out many ships—primarily in West Indian trade. His daughter, Elizabeth, married merchant, Silas Deane. Gurdon married Rebecca Winthrop, daughter of John Still Winthrop, and became involved in a dispute over land he claimed as part of his wife's dowry. For fifty-five years (1733-1788) he pressed his claims until the Winthrop family signed over land in 1760, 1772 and 1788 as well as making cash payment for services claimed by Saltonstall. He became a general in the Connecticut Militia and a leader in the opposition to the Acts of Trade and Navigation.[11]

When Reverend Gurdon Saltonstall became governor the town of New London often played host to the meetings of the governor and council. His selection caused displeasure among some who disliked a minister holding the post. Besides, he was not eligible for the post as all governors had by law to serve first as a magistrate. A special session of the General Assembly, January 1, 1708, repealed that restriction and Saltonstall received the appointment in January and was elected in May. John S. Winthrop, son of Wait-Still, did not like the governor of Connecticut—Gurdon Saltonstall. He referred to him as the great Hogen Mogen, two faced, Judas, and fallen angel.[12]

Saltonstall introduced the printing press into the colony. The first, at New London in 1708, was run by Thomas Short.[13] Reverend Saltonstall was very strict and tried to return to the conservative church of an earlier day. Many in New London opposed his role, but he had the power. A few examples of those punished for their sins while he was minister, indicates his viewpoint:

1. A woman taken before the court and fined for not attending public worship with her children;
2. John Lewis and Sarah Chapman charged with setting together on the Lord's Day under an apple tree;
3. A man living alone, in idleness and for not attending religious service;
4. A man who disagreed with his ministry and was taken to the General Court to be counseled for discipline;
5. A number of others who objected to these actions were suspended until they acknowledged their offenses.[14]

As can be imagined, he opposed the Rogerenes—a religious group. Saltonstall had them put out of church and charged their leader, John

Rogers, from whom he won a six-hundred pound settlement.

He decided that New Haven should house Yale rather than Saybrook and the General Assembly agreed in 1718. He called the Congregational Clergy to Saybrook in 1708 and the Saybrook Platform resulted—all churches in the colony to be united in doctrine, worship, discipline and to be established by law.

He died suddenly September 20, 1724 at the age of 59. Dr. Cotton Mather preached a commemoration service the following October.[15]

James Rogers settled in New London shortly after 1656. A baker, he leased the town mill from the Winthrops and supplied townspeople and military with bread and biscuits. Success appeared to have been Rogers from the start of the business and he bought several hundred acres of land on Great Neck, a tract at Mohegan and several town lots as well as 2,400 acres east of the river together with Colonel Pyncheon of Springfield. His tax rate was twice that of any other property holder in town and three times that of John Winthrop. Of course one must remember that much of Winthrop's holdings paid little or no tax and thus the conclusion several writers have come to—that this proves that Rogers' holdings greatly exceeded those of Winthrop's—is hardly valid. After several prosperous years, Rogers retired in 1666.[16]

New London merchants emerged as the leaders in the financial, political and social life of the port during the late seventeenth and early eighteenth centuries. Four men emerged as the important merchants during the second half of the seventeenth century—Christopher and Jeffrey Christophers, Charles Hill and John Pickett. They began to buy vessels, build wharves and warehouses and to open stores. The Christophers brothers shared in the expense of outfitting several vessels before Christopher and Charles Hill formed a business partnership, the first in New London, in 1665. They purchased land on Mill Cove with warehouse and wharfing. Christophers' son, Richard, ranked as a leading citizen and held many offices in the town and colony. Adam Pickett and Christopher Christophers owned jointly the ship *Adventure*.[17] John Pickett developed a profitable business and when he died in 1667 he left an estate of £1,140. His widow, Ruth, married Charles Hill in 1668 thus all four of the early merchants had connections.[18]

In the eighteenth century a new name entered the merchant class—Deshon. Daniel Deshon moved to town sometime after 1715 and married Ruth, daughter of Christopher Christophers. Their daughter married merchant Joseph Chew while three of their six sons entered the merchant service—Daniel, John and Richard. John Deshon (1727-1792) spent between twenty-five and thirty years at sea becoming a captain in the West Indian trade.

In the years leading to the American Revolution, John Deshon led the opposition to the British trade restrictions. His name is included on most committees prior to the Revolution and he provided continued leadership during the Revolution itself.[19]

A stone house set back off Bank Street represents many of the historical events in New London. Now the home of the New London County Historical Society, it once was the home of the Shaws, one of the leading and important families during the colonial period. As the family fortunes improved Captain Shaw had a home built which became a landmark in New London. When three-hundred French Acadians arrived at the port during the French and Indian War, Shaw hired a number of them to build a house from rock blasted off his property.[20]

Nathaniel, the first member of the Shaw family to settle in Connecticut moved to Fairfield from Boston sometime before 1703, after marrying Margaret Jackson of Virginia. A son, Nathaniel Shaw, Sr. (1703-1778), moved to New London as a young man, where he engaged as a seaman in the Irish trade, advancing to the post of captain by 1732. On a return trip from Ireland that year, he lost five of the fifteen man crew to smallpox, including his brother. As late as 1738 Shaw still sailed as a master of other people's vessels.[21]

In 1730, Shaw married Temperance Harris and they had eight children—six sons and two daughters. By 1765 Nathaniel Shaw, Sr., established his own business and met with considerable success as he was referred to as a wealthy shipowner. However, it was his second child and first son who really developed the successful business.[22]

After the French and Indian War one man emerged as *the* New London Merchant leader—Nathaniel Shaw, Jr. Until his accidental death in 1782, no colonial port had a more outstanding businessman. He figured prominently in New London, New England and American affairs. Nathaniel Shaw, Jr. (1735-1782), merchant, banker, supporter of the patriot cause, supplier of goods during the Revolution, outfitter of privateers, local, state, Continental office holder, friend of the leading Americans and contributor to the growth of New London, represents leadership at its height. In July of 1758 he married Lucretia Harris Rogers, widow of Captain Josiah Rogers who had died of smallpox in 1757 leaving her with a small child.[23]

Nathaniel Shaw, Jr., became manager of the family business, handling shipping interests and property, as partner in the firm known as Nathaniel

Shaw Mansion, Headquarters of the New London County Historical Society. Built in 1756 by Arcadian exiles.

Shaw & Son. Upon the retirement of his father, Nathaniel, Jr., ran the firm as Nathaniel Shaw, Jr., Merchant. A letter book kept until his death shows an extensive mercantile business involving coastal, European and West Indian ports. Shaw had a reputation as a kind and helpful neighbor, considerate employer and an ardent patriot. He was also considered shrewd, close, a man of his word, a curt letter writer and one who adhered rigidly to the ethical code for commercial dealings of the day.[24] The lucrative West Indian trade represented the major interest of his firm. Shaw possessed many business connections with the Constant family in Guadeloupe, Gaignard in Cape Haitien, as well as Charrier, Delcasse, Desmoulins, Goban, Mase, Pouquet and Texier families.[25]

He not only had business interests and connections with the leading merchant families in the colonies but through marriage the Shaw-Perkins family established a relationship with important Connecticut families— Bingham, Griswold, Haven, Mitchell, Mumford, Nevins, Williams and Woodbridge.[26]

The Mumfords were of Groton, but operated their shipping business out of New London and belonged to the Episcopal Church of the town. Thomas and David were active in the various maritime activities of the port. The Mumfords leased Fisher's Island in 1735 from the Winthrops.

As merchant activity grew at the port, shipping needs increased. Early New London possessed plenty of timber and shipbuilding became common. American vessels cost one-fifth to one-half less than English bottoms so the market for colonial craft proved lucrative. Since the early settlers lacked money, tools and means to build large vessels, shipbuilding at New London originally consisted primarily of small craft. A vessel would be begun after the fall harvest and finished in the spring before planting time. Its sale would provide an income until harvest time. Many New London built craft sailed with a cargo to a foreign port where both would be sold.

By 1651 New London with a population of not more than fifty males carried on trade with Barbados and Virginia. The population doubled by 1660 and included three master shipbuilders. Vessels up to seventy tons had been launched by the end of the seventeenth century.[27] The sloop represented the most often built vessel at New London with the snow quite popular. A small crew could handle either of these craft.[28] As demand for larger vessels came New London shipbuilders produced the brig, brigantine, schooner, bark and ship. Although New London yards did not produce a schooner until the eighteenth century, barks were built from 1660 and ships as early as 1666.[29]

John Coit established the first New London shipyard at Sandy Point on Close Cove. Associated with him were Joseph Coit, his son, and Hugh Mould and John Stevens his sons-in-law. The building of vessels began in 1660 and by 1664 three barks had been launched at a cost of fifty to eighty-two pounds each. These included the fourteen ton *Speedwell* built for Thomas Beebe, the *Hopewell* of between twelve and twenty-three tons constructed for William Keeny and the twenty ton *Endeavor* built for Matthew Beckwith.

The Coit Yard constructed three vessels for Christopher Christophers and Charles Hill—the *New London*, 1666, a ship of seventy tons for the European trade, the *Regent*, 1668, a bark and the *Charles*, 1672, a twenty ton sloop. John Liveen contracted for two vessels, the *Success*, fifty-four tons, used in the coastal and West Indian trade and the *Liveen*, a ship costing six-hundred pounds. The Coit Yard launched the largest of the seventeenth century vessels at New London in 1678, the *John and Hester*, built for John Prentis, Sr. It weighed one hundred tons and cost four hundred and forty-five pounds.[30]

Joseph Coit's son took over the business in 1697 and moved it to Point of Rocks on the Bank opposite the Pickett lot. Until 1735, the Coit Yard remained the major New London shipbuilder. No fewer than twenty vessels were recorded as having been produced by the yard from 1660 to 1735 and probably a number of others were constructed for which no record remains.

The Coit family not only built ships, but operated them. Joseph Coit (1698-1787) spent his early years as a sailing master. After a number of successful voyages, he established a firm and sent out his own vessels. Joseph Coit led an active public life. In 1744 he headed a committee which petitioned the King for proper defense against a feared French attack. At the time of the Townshend Duties, he served as a member of the Committee to enforce non-consumption of English goods. Another member of the family, Nathaniel Coit, sailed for many years as a master in the West Indian trade before operating an inn, the Red Lion, at New London. Captain Russell Hubbard (1732-1785), son of Martha Coit and Daniel Hubbard, graduated from Yale before earning a master's berth. After several voyages he set up his own shipping business at the port.[31]

The largest bottom built in the 1660's appeared to have been the *New London Tryal* whose tonnage has not been recorded, but exclusive of iron work, spikes and nails, cost about £200. John Elderkin produced it for Daniel Lane of New London and William Brenton of Newport in 1661 and it appears to have been lost at sea in 1664.[32]

John Leeds built the brigantine *Tryall*—eighteen tons—at a cost of eighty pounds in 1683 and also the *Swallow*. James Bennett constructed the bark *Endeavor*—fifty-two tons—in 1690. Captain John Hutton kept a shipyard on the lower end of the waterfront and built a snow in 1714 and a ship in 1716 for the West Indian trade.

Captain John Jeffrey established a yard on the east side of the Thames in 1720. His chief claim to fame came from a seven hundred ton vessel built in 1725 referred to as the great ship. Ordered by Captain James Sterling, it was the largest vessel built in America up to that time. Jeffrey constructed a number of other vessels, but none as large, although his five hundred and seventy ton *Don Carlos* considerably exceeded most of the others produced during the period. Proof that he continued to build ships through 1736 is in Hempstead's *Diary* which records that Captain "Jeffers (sic) launched his pink Sterned Ship" December 1, 1729 and mentions a new ship at New London harbor, November 28, 1736, built by Jeffrey. Other shipbuilders included: Samuel Edgecomb, and Ralph Stodder.[33]

Although wages and costs are not always available for shipbuilding,

Joshua Hempstead gave several details concerning shipbuilding. He recorded that he received five shillings per day for his work in the Coit Shipyard. Hempstead's son, Stephen, received four pounds per month from working on a vessel. Joshua Hempstead also constructed several vessels. For a man named Arnold, he built a sloop costing sixty-five pounds.[34] Frequently, shipbuilders retained a share in the ownership of the vessel and shared in its expenses and profits.

2 Colonial New London:
Its Commerce 1645-1763

From the six reports made by Connecticut to the Board of Trade, 1680 to 1774, one can construct a picture of conditions present at the port by the end of the colonial period.[1] The grand list of 1774 reached £35,528 which was less than one-half of New Haven's but over one-half of Norwich's. Groton, across the river, had reached a grand list of 26,902. Population totaled 5,888 including 316 Negroes and 206 Indians. Not until 1850 did the population again reach or exceed this figure.[2]

The reports show that maritime commerce was New London's only major industry. The seven vessels registered at the port in 1680 increased to seventy-two by 1774. This represented forty percent of Connecticut's one hundred and eighty vessels, while in 1680, New London's registration made up just under twenty-five percent of the Colony's total. When one considers the tonnage of the vessels, New London's share in 1680 was about thirty-three percent and in 1774 just over thirty-three percent. The reason for New London's percentage of tonnage remaining fairly stable while the percentage of the number of vessels increased fifteen percent is explained by the nature of the port's trade. New London concentrated on coastal and West Indian trade which involved smaller vessels. The trans-Atlantic trade utilized larger vessels. New London's vessels averaged forty-five tons while the total Connecticut fleet averaged fifty-seven tons.[3]

An examination of the marine list in the *New London Gazette* and the *New London Summary,* 1758 to 1767, indicates the nature of New London's trade. During the period under scrutiny 1,010 vessels cleared from New London while 714 entered for a total of 1,724 entrances and clearances. The shipping of the port falls into three categories—coastal, West Indian and foreign. Coastal shipping with 411 entrances and 573 clearances or a total of 984 or nearly fifty-eight percent, ranks first. Altogether, twenty ports made up the coastal trade which extended from Newfoundland to Georgia. Two of the ports dominated, New York and Boston. Two hundred and sixty-nine cleared for New York and 157 cleared for Boston while 169 entered from New York and 128 entered from Boston. Thus, 426 of 573 or nearly seventy-four percent of the clearances in coastal trade were for just two ports, value 297 of 411 or nearly seventy-two percent of entrances were from the same.[4]

West Indian trade consisted of commercial relations with twenty-two areas for a total of 708 or nearly forty-one percent of all entrances and clearances. Four areas—Antigua, Barbados, Jamaica and St. Kitts—had 284 or nearly sixty-nine percent of West Indian clearances, but represented only 122 of 295 or nearly forty-one percent of the entrances. Antigua, Barbados, Jamaica, Turks Island, St. Kitts, St. Martin and Saltortuda had 224 of 295 or nearly seventy-six percent of the entrances at New London, and represent 287 of 413 or nearly seventy percent of the clearances.[5]

Foreign trade totaled only twenty-four clearances or nearly two percent of the total and entrances totaled only eight or nearly one percent. The thirty-two entrances and clearances for the foreign trade also represent nearly two percent of the total.[6]

Unfortunately, the rig of the vessel is not indicated except for 1,089 of the voyages, so that any attempt to trace the types of vessels in New London trade in general in a particular area is limited. Of the 1,089 rigs identified, 805 were sloops which clearly indicated the dominance of sloops in the New London trade. The records showed 1,082 were made by schooners, sloops and brigs. Thus, it can be seen that small vessels with few men carried on most of the trade in and out of New London.[7]

During the colonial period New London shipyards constructed vessels primarily for the coastal trade which represented the major emphasis of shipping. Early maritime activity centered on trade between New London and Boston while a smaller trade developed with Rhode Island, Long Island and New Amsterdam. Clothing, household goods, farming implements and military supplies comprised the main imports from Boston while peltries and wampum represented the main exports. In the early 1660's trade began with Virginia for wheat and tobacco. Later Connecticut tobacco became a valuable export at the port.[8]

A triangular trade also evolved with New London goods being carried to Newfoundland and exchanged for fish which were then carried to the

West Indies where they could be bartered for sugar, molasses and rum which made up the cargoes on the return trip to the port. By 1700, trading activity with Newfoundland had declined and New York maritime relations had begun to increase.[9]

Although engaged in ferrying local produce to all the large markets from Newfoundland to the Carolinas in exchange for manufactured goods, two ports, Boston and New York dominated. Boston monopolized the port's trade for most of the colonial period but in the closing days of this period New York carried on more business with New London while Boston remained a close second.[10] Although New London vessels eventually carried local products to all parts of the world, coastal shipping remained dominant during the colonial period. As one author expressed it:

> ...New London must be content with coastwise shipping because Boston is the New England link between foreign lands and the interior of our own.[11]

West Indian trade became an important factor in the growth of New London as it provided much of the goods, specie and bills of credit required to pay for needed imports. Captain Samuel Chester, master of the *Endeavor,* is believed responsible for beginning the West Indian trade in 1661. He transported a cargo of beef, cooper's stock and ponies to the area and returned with sugar, molasses and one cask of rum. The trip took less than two months and opened what became the most lucrative trade of the port.[12]

While direct trade between New London and the West Indies remained the rule, a triangular trade emerged where New London products would be carried to the West Indies and exchanged for goods which would be taken to New York or Boston where English manufactured goods would be secured and carried to New London. Single decked vessels carried livestock, horses and timber usually making two round trips a year although three might be made. A crew consisted of a captain, who usually owned part of the vessel and cargo, a man and a boy or two. As many as six vessels loaded with horses sailed for the West Indies at a time. So many horses made up cargoes that the masters often received the name "horse-jockeys". The years from 1720 to 1770 represented the major period of West Indian trade during which a number of New London fortunes were made.[13]

At times, as many as twenty sail lay at anchor in the harbor with most either preparing to clear for or having just entered from the West Indies. About one-fourth of the tonnage of the port involved itself in West Indian trade during the 1720-1770 period. A number of vessels owned at other ports operated out of New London.[14]

Some unusual voyages took place as when three captains—Christophers, Prentis and Pickett left New London on the same day and arrived together in the West Indies. They sailed from there again at the same time and arrived back in port on the same day.[15]

West Indian trade could be hazardous. The *Success* lost twenty-six horses from the deck when caught in a storm after sailing for the West Indies in 1677. A sloop, under Captain Collins ran aground while on the same trip, suffering heavy damage. Captain Denison's brig also ran aground while leaving the harbor and lost thirty to forty sheep and hogs plus sixteen horses. After being refloated the brig sank in the harbor. A storm hit Captain Edward Roher's sloop and carried away the rigging and ten prize horses. Several vessels, such as the *John and Lucy* in 1671 and the *Providence* went aground on Fisher's Island.[16]

To help guide the vessels safely to the harbor the merchants decided a lighthouse needed to be built. They organized a lottery to pay for one. Among the directors were Nathaniel Shaw, Joseph Chew, Thomas Mumford and Joseph Coit. A list of winners listed in the *New London Summary* on June 30, 1761 showed prizes ranging from four to four hundred pounds on a sale of 4,583 tickets.

To lessen the merchants risk, insurance frequently covered the cargo or vessel and sometimes both. No one individual assumed the total responsibility. A number of men would agree to assume a percentage of the risk and would receive a like percentage of the premium paid. Rates depended upon conditions at the time. If wartime existed the rates might reach ten percent or more. In normal times two to six percent represented the usual rate.[17]

Another hazard of the West Indian trade, fever and disease, cost the lives of many New London seamen. John Crocker died in 1747 of yellow fever which he contracted on a trip to the West Indies. Nathaniel Shaw, Sr. lost three sons at sea in the West Indian trade on different voyages—John, Joseph and William T.—all before they reached the age of twenty-one. The Christophers family also suffered a number of losses in the trade. Jeffrey Christophers died in 1690 of smallpox contracted in the West Indies. John Christophers died at Barbados in 1703 and another John Christophers drowned in 1719 while returning from Barbados.

Often vessels brought sickness to the town when seamen returned ill and others contracted the illness. New London suffered from periodic outbreaks of smallpox and yellow fever. Joseph Coit's vessel arrived with outbreaks of smallpox and distemper in 1719.[18]

Pirates presented still another hazard of the trade. They preyed upon vessels from the Sound to the West Indies. In 1716 "George Buttolph arrived (November 1) from St. Kitts after having been taken by a pirate who took away his clothes and some other items".[19] The following year a pirate operating in the Sound looted several vessels. Usually clothing and cargo were seized and sometimes the crewmen themselves. In 1728 pirates seized the Isle of Wight. Expeditions of Connecticut and Rhode Island vessels set out to clear the Sound when pirate activity became too bold. A number of craft carried guns for protection well into the nineteenth century.[20]

A particularly bad period for West Indian trade came during the French and Indian War 1754-1763. With its end a brief revival of commerce took place, but by 1768 business had slowed. A number of merchants reported the market for goods in the West Indies was not good and by 1774 merchants could not sell West Indian products in New London. Merchant Nathaniel Shaw, Jr., wrote to Peter Vanderwoort & Company, New York, October 14, 1774, "Markets are very dull in all the Islands, unless the times alter we had better do nothing than Import melasses".[21]

Direct European trade eluded the merchants of New London although they made sporadic attempts to develop it up to the time of the American Revolution. A small number of large craft were especially constructed for European trade. However, these pass quickly from New London records indicating the lack of success. John Wheeler, a successful West Indian trader, made an early attempt with a vessel built under his supervision in 1689-1690. Although he succeeded in sending off the vessel with cargo under Captain Samuel Chester, Wheeler died before the craft returned. Another try took place in 1704 when the *Adventure* was outfitted for the European markets. Bad luck "dogged" the venture from the beginning. The captain died just prior to the planned departure and the new captain missed meeting with a convoy and sailed alone. A French privateer seized the vessel ending its voyage.[22]

Such failures did not lessen the hope for direct trade. New London merchants wanted to become less dependent upon Boston and New York and desired the lower prices which European goods would cost if shipped directly to the port. Unfortunately, New London merchants found themselves in an unfavorable position in trying to deal directly for European goods. Boston and New York merchants had established close relationships with the English merchants and enjoyed their confidence and credit. In addition, Hartford and New Haven merchants enjoyed a favored position with the Boston and New York merchants and received European goods at a lower price than that charged New London merchants.[23]

In an effort to get the capital necessary to compete for European trade the New London Society for Trade and Commerce was organized. It applied unsuccessfully for a charter under the leadership of Solomon Coit, requesting the power to issue bills of credit.[24] A 1732 request by some eighty individuals under the direction of Coit made no mention of the right to issue bills of credit and received a charter. Capital came from bills of credit to be redeemable in twelve years secured by the property members put up as security. The Society became a land bank when the notes began to circulate as money. Members planned an ambitious program of activity to include not only the main goal of direct trade with Europe, but building, purchasing and operating vessels, trade with other colonial ports, fishing ventures and whaling expeditions.[25]

Although the organization undertook a number of maritime activities, none proved successful. Several vessels were built and others purchased. At least two attempts at whaling took place. One whaling schooner returned empty on November 17, 1733 and another valued at three thousand pounds suffered a similar fate. After a successful voyage another merchant vessel went on the rocks in a storm while on its way back to New London. Several fishing vessels sent out by the Society returned empty. Finally, the loss of a merchant vessel to the Spanish ended the ventures of the Society.[26]

During the time these unsuccessful enterprises took place, the colonial government moved to end the operations. Governor Joseph Talcott, concerned about the issuance of bills of credit and pressure from merchants outside New London who feared the success of the Society, called a special session of the General Assembly in February 1733 which ordered the corporation dissolved. The colonial government assumed all responsibility for the £15,000 of notes issued by the Society and authorized £30,000 in state currency to meet all the financial obligations of the group. Members found their property mortgaged to the colony as security for the state in assuming the debts.[27]

A number of the members unsuccessfully tried to keep the Society going by petitioning the government for a loan of £25,000 at three percent interest. An application for a new charter and a loan of £30,000 took place in 1734 when the merchants offered to accept any restrictions the assembly might choose to apply. Not only did the petition receive a rejection, but the colonial government demanded new mortgages. Joshua Hempstead received orders, as agent of the colony, to seize the plates of the company and deliver them to the government. All notes had to be burned. Finally, in 1735, the company held a meeting and dissolved itself. Former members of the Society drew up petitions requesting the release of their property from the mortgages for a number of years after the organization came to an end. The last of these appeared in 1749.[28]

As late as 1772 Nathaniel Shaw, Jr., continued efforts to increase direct trade. He informed agents in England that he was sending the sloop *Dove*, loaded with goods which were in abundance at New London and asked that European goods be sent in exchange. Shaw stated that he could use three or four cargoes a year. Still, direct trade never flourished. At best, occasionally cargoes of flour, lumber and provisions were shipped to Europe and Africa in exchange for European goods. The most successful European trade involved a triangular arrangement in which New London goods carried directly to Europe were exchanged for commodities desired by the West Indians and the usual West Indian produce was brought back to New London.[29]

Several European merchants moved to New London during the colonial period due to the commercial growth of the port. The most notable of these, the Sistera (Sistare) family engaged in the European-West Indian commerce from Barcelona, Spain until 1771 when Gabriel Sistare and his son moved to New London. They became an active and vital part of the port's life as did several other merchants who chose to resettle in New London.[30] During the most lucrative period of West Indian trade a number of New London merchants established members of their families in the Islands to act as agents. West Indian families who acted for New London merchants also established representatives at New London Port. Barbados had the most extensive exchange of persons with the town. Many of these settled permanently at the port and married local girls. Still another merchant source of new blood came about as New London served as a gathering spot for agents from a number of Connecticut River towns such as Springfield, Hartford and Middletown. Vessels from these ports stopped at New London to take on produce before sailing for the West Indies. Many would also pause on their return voyages to lighten their cargoes enough to cross bars in the Connecticut River.[31] On the other hand the toll of New London masters and sailors was high. Disease, storms and shipwrecks cost the lives of many—particular younger sons of merchants.

One usually became a merchant by going to sea as a young man. For boys from the Puritan farming settlements the sea exerted a strong attraction. An ambitious lad would be drawn to New London and sail on its vessels. Advancement could come early to those with promise and masters in their late teens or early twenties were not uncommon. Even if the young man remained a seaman during his career a sizeable estate could be established. Peter Browley, a seaman, died in 1662 leaving an estate which included a house, four acres, a separate tract of twenty-eight acres, and miscellaneous property worth sixty-nine pounds and one shilling.[32]

As a master, a young man had to become a competent businessman. Success or failure of a venture depended upon the wisdom of the many decisions made by the captain on each voyage. Without telephone, telegraph or radio, it was up to the master to seek out markets and cargoes which would produce the best profits. He also controlled the crew and arranged for the minimum of necessary repairs while away from home port. Owners, at the mercy of the decisions of the master, shifted matters more in their favor by having the captain as part-owner of the vessel and cargo as well as possessing the right to part of the cargo space to ship his own goods.

A capable master could acquire enough capital and knowledge to become a merchant. Since business operations did not tend to be specialized, a merchant would settle at New London, build a store, a warehouse, a wharf and send out his own vessels. His sons and sons-in-law would usually go to sea on the former master's vessels and learn the business prior to becoming members of the firm. Although the merchants doing business at New London represented a large number of individuals and many family names, an examination of the merchants shows that marriage alliances made their individuality more apparent than real.[33]

Captains tried to keep in touch through letters entrusted to masters of vessels sailing to New London and owners sent instructions on vessels clearing New London for areas where their vessels had gone. Most often these merely brought the other up to date on decisions which had already been made. In 1766, Captain Samuel Welch of the *Hartford* wrote the owner, Ebenezer Grant, that the cargo had proved to be difficult to sell as the horses shipped were not heavy enough for the needs of the West Indians. To make matters worse, the over-supplied market forced prices down. To top it all off, the vessel needed extensive repairs to enable it to reach New London and no one would purchase it due to its age. In a like vein, Nathaniel Shaw, Jr. received the unpleasant news from Captain William Packwood that his vessel had been damaged while in the West Indies and would require refitting.[34]

Frequently, owners received letters from their representatives in other ports which kept them abreast of conditions there. Not uncommon complaints against certain captains were made by the agents. One wrote Shaw that a captain of his was a rascal and a villain and warned him not to send the master back or he would be placed in jail.[35] Another master, Shaw learned, had been accused of dishonest business dealings and must pay a fine or go to jail.

Although few figures are available, it is obvious from the activity at the port that fishing provided much of the food, employment and produce for export at New London. It appears that forty to seventy fishing craft found employment in the industry each year. Probably this became the nursery for seamen of the deep sea trade of the port.[36]

The Navigation Acts did not affect New London until 1673, since little direct trade with England existed. At that date Parliament passed an act levying a plantation duty, payable at the colonial port of clearance on enumerated goods unless the captain had taken out a bond to carry his goods directly to England. To enforce this the English government began to appoint customs officials at the major ports and in 1707 John Shackmaple received the post at New London. He became the first English official in Connecticut owing his office directly to the Royal government. Although the appointment found little favor, no opposition appeared for two years. The Treasury declared in 1709 that any vessel sailing from a Connecticut port to another colony or to a foreign port must have its papers signed by a Royal Collector of Customs. Since the only official who signed the papers of a vessel resided in New London, it became the entrance and clearance port for the colony.[37] In opposition to this the General Assembly issued a resolution in May of 1710 declaring:

> That whatsoever masters do enter and clear their vessels with the naval officers in any of the ports within this Colony, have free liberty to sail directly from such port . . . to any port. . . .[38]

Vessels could move safely from port to port within Connecticut, but were in danger outside the waters of the colony without the proper papers. Shackmaple had several vessels seized for lack of papers only to find that Connecticut courts would not find the vessels guilty. When he tried to use a Vice-Admiralty Court, Connecticut refused to allow it to operate. Shackmaple resorted to having the vessels seized without taking the cases to court. Connecticut officials then questioned the validity of Shackmaple's authority since the officials of the Treasury had not signed his commission. Connecticut capitulated in 1718 when the English government issued a new commission granted by the Treasury and New London became the official port of entry and clearance.[39]

The colonial wars (1689-1763) greatly hampered New London mer-

chants with the seizure of New London vessels, the threat of port attack
and the demands for men and supplies. To protect the town, a fort with a
battery of six cannons of four and six pounders was erected at the foot of
State Street covering the space where the railroad depot and the Soldiers
and Sailors Monument now stand. Townspeople feared that the fort
offered scant protection against an attack and petitioned the colonial
government for a better defense. Forty militia men were detailed to duty at
the fort—ten to be present at any one time. Despite many alarms and
rumors of impending attacks none came.[40]

Often the town served as a gathering station for English and Colonial
forces. An unusual event occurred in June of 1756 when three hundred
French families arrived from Nova Scotia. The following May another
vessel landed with Acadian families and possibly others arrived. They were
scattered among the Connecticut towns for the duration of the French and
Indian War. After the war Captain Richard Leffingwell sailed to Nova
Scotia carrying two hundred and forty of the French people back home.
The wars from 1689 to 1763 meant disrupted businesses, bankruptcies,
losses of vessels to privateers or to the British for illegal flag of truce trade
and moving of some merchants from the town.[41]

Robert Sloan and Matthew Steward are examples of two businessmen
who lost so many vessels to privateers during the French and Indian War
that they had to cease business operations. Other merchants could not pay
their creditors and faced imprisonment for debt. In 1762 Thomas Allen
requested a declaration of bankruptcy as he had suffered a number of
losses by privateers and had been imprisoned for twelve months by his
creditors. Before the war, Allen had been a leading West Indian trader.
Merchant Joseph Chew asked the court to appoint a committee to handle
the affairs for the business losses suffered would not allow him to satisfy his
creditors. Chew complained that any money his business activities brought
in had been seized by his creditors and he could not support his family. An
investigation revealed that he had turned all his property over to creditors,
but still owed over £16,000. Still another once successful merchant, John
Braddock, became insolvent. Losses at sea, failure to collect debts due him
and illness combined to force him to offer all his property to his creditors
in return for freedom of imprisonment for debt. William Adams and Alexander Pygan received release from debtors prison after signing over all
their property to their creditors.[42]

Merchants in general faced a number of difficulties in their trading
activities. The collection of bills of credit, overdue accounts, the scarcity of
specie and depreciated currency commonly plagued businessmen. Girard

Beekman, a New York merchant who had extensive dealings with New London traders, provided an excellent picture of those difficulties in business papers of his firm. In a letter to a merchant of Stratford, David Lewis, he referred to the difficulty facing him in collecting New London accounts and wanted them brought to suit. Beekman revealed that an agent of his, Thomas Allen at New London, had collected cash on Beekman's accounts, but failed to send it to the firm.[43]

Extension of credit sometimes created problems for the merchant. Beekman extended credit to a Captain Robert Stanton upon recommendation of New London merchants, Joseph Chew and Thomas Mumford. When Stanton failed to pay, Beekman sent the bonds signed by the Captain to the merchants requesting some form of security or court action. In another case, Joseph Chew brought about an angry correspondence with Beekman when he sent a note in place of cash for money due. Beekman indicated his critical shortness of money and the uselessness to him of a note.[44]

By the 1770's a variety of merchant shops had been established in New London. An examination of the advertisements carried by the *New London Gazette* identifies the source and type of goods available. Two ship-chandlers advertised, Samuel Loudon and David Gardiner. The latter stated that he sold ship chandlery wares, rum, sugar and molasses and that he would purchase beeswax, small furs and ox horns. Samuel Belden sold European goods in a shop next to the Court House, while Roger Gibson's shop near the Customs House sold European and West Indian goods. Other shops included a clothier, drug shop, linen and pewter shop, fulling mill and a drink shop. Several merchants offered to take flax, grain or provisions in exchange for goods.[45]

Solomon Coit obtained the first license in the colony for distilling molasses. It became a major business as rum prices increased rapidly after 1721. Richard Rogers established an extensive business with eight looms making duck or canvas.[46]

A buisness which attracted several craftsmen, some fifteen in the colonial period, was silversmithing. Mostly spoons and buttons were produced in the Boston style. Few could make enough from this skill to provide an adequate income so they also operated general stores, made clocks and watches, did engraving, held public office or entered the merchant trade. Samuel Gray had the first silversmith business in New London. From 1705 to 1713 he carried out his trade—marrying Lucy Palmes, daughter of Edward Palmes in 1707. A second silversmith arrived upon the death of Samuel Gray—John Gray, his brother, moved to New London and carried on his brother's business. He married Mary Christophers in 1714. Daniel Deshon, who had studied under John Gray, arrived in town by 1719 and became a leading silversmith. He married Ruth Christophers.

At least eight silversmiths were in business by the American Revolution. A hazard of the business seemed to be the lure of counterfeiting. Many silversmiths let themselves become involved in this. By and large those of New London were a highly respected group and only one seems to have run into trouble as a result of counterfeiting. One of the finest silversmiths, Captain Pygan Adams—son of Reverend Eliphalet Adams, also had a successful career as a merchant. His public service was outstanding. He was overseer of the Mohegan Indians and a representative to the General Assembly 1735-1765.[47]

The most unusual incident of colonial New London occurred in 1752. The results of the event caused an international incident between England and Spain and reportedly cost Governor Roger Wolcott re-election. A disabled Spanish ship entered New London harbor in November of 1752 carrying a cargo of gold, silver and indigo worth $400,000. The Spanish claimed that New London mariners deliberately disabled the vessel while piloting it into the harbor. The cargo, removed so repairs could be made, became the responsibility of Gurdon Saltonstall. Part of the ship's contents, the gold and silver, was placed in Saltonstall's cellar under a guard of six men while the rest was stored in Robert Sloan's warehouse under a four man guard. Unfortunately, when the Spanish requested the return of the cargo, part of the gold, silver and indigo had disappeared. The English, Spanish and Colonial governments sent men to investigate the theft, but all efforts proved unsuccessful. Officials did arrest eight men suspected of the crime—four of them guards—and placed them in jail, but all escaped and were never recaptured. Supposedly the $5,100 in gold gradually came into circulation in later years.[48]

Silver Porringer by Daniel Deshon,
18th century.

Silver Pepper Pot by Daniel Deshon,
18th century.

Silver Creamer by Pygan Adams,
18th century.

Three Tine Fork by Pygan Adams,
18th century.

3 New London's Role in the American Revolution 1763-1784

New London never accepted British officials or trade regulations easily or willingly. While it is true that businessmen tend to be conservative and try to avoid activities which might disrupt their commercial dealings, merchants at the port took the lead in resisting the mother country. They knew themselves to be particularly susceptible to British retaliation for any actions taken in opposition to the Navigation Acts, especially in light of the ease with which New London harbor could be blockaded by the powerful English fleet.

Several factors accounted for the aggressive nature of the merchants at the town. Chief among them was New London's location in the eastern radical section. The Connecticut River created two sections—to the east an area politically and religiously radical, while to the west an area politically and religiously conservative. A second factor originated with the resentment of New London merchants to the favored trading position enjoyed by Hartford and New Haven with Boston, New York and the English ports. A third factor involved the short lived prosperity at the end of the French and Indian War. A final factor resulted from the English determination to enforce the Navigation Acts after 1763.

Merchant apprehension increased towards the end of 1763, when word arrived that His Majesty's Ship *Cygnet* would be stationed at New London. Concurrently a report arrived that 10,000 troops would be stationed in America at the expense of the colonies. On the "heels" of this information came the arrival in New York of General Thomas Gage, to be military commander of all British troops in North America. The first concrete action under the new English policy, which affected the New London merchants, took place in December, 1763. A regulation went into effect requiring all vessels to report to the Customs House upon arrival and before clearance, where the papers could be checked to determine if all cargo carried had been listed and all duty paid.[1] Failure to comply meant severe penalties if caught. Although the period of "salutory neglect" had ended, New London resistance had not. Illegal trade represented a way of life in eastern Connecticut, and trade regulations besides being unpopular, proved difficult to enforce. Smuggling was a fairly simple matter. One could use forged papers, bribery, misrepresentation of illegal goods as legal, or take advantage of the irregular coast line to land illegal goods undetected.[2]

The American Revenue Act of 1764 (Sugar Act) only further aroused the merchant opposition at New London. While the act decreased duties by fifty percent, the English made it clear that they intended to collect the up till then largely ignored duties. The merchants insisted that payment, even at the new lower rates, would ruin them. Nathaniel Shaw, Jr., assumed a position of leadership among the merchants. He did not believe that foreign sugars could be imported if the government collected the duty. His captains received instructions on methods of landing illegal sugars.[3]

Up to the time of the Stamp Act, the merchants had not received general backing from the population. That act proved to be the catalyst which united the merchants in particular and the population in general and provided the mass support which the merchants utilized to oppose English trade restrictions. News of the impending passage of the Stamp Act for the American colonies reached New London in May of 1763. Interestingly, New Londoners seemed to take scant interest in the prospect of the passage of such an act. Not until the passage of the bill would opposition manifest itself among New London merchants. A Londoner wrote the town calling the proposed legislation unconstitutional. He claimed the English could not levy such a tax upon the colonies. Months before the passage of the Stamp Act, a letter appeared in the *New London Gazette* warning that the bill would receive approval at the next session of Parliament unless the Americans came up with a better proposal. The writer commented that all well wishers to America considered it a fair act.[4]

The recently improved economic conditions for New London declined abruptly with the Stamp Act. Angered public opinion prevented the use of the stamps and the "radicals" seized and burned them. Men from the port joined other "radicals" and forced Jared Ingersoll of New Haven to resign

Anno quinto.

Georgii III. Regis.

C H A P. XII.

An Act for granting and applying certain
Stamp Duties, and other Duties, in the
British Colonies and Plantations in America, towards further defraying the Expences of defending, protecting, and fecuring the fame ; and for amending fuch
Parts of the feveral Acts of Parliament
relating to the Trade and Revenues of
the faid Colonies and Plantations, as direct
the Manner of determining and recovering the Penalties and Forfeitures therein
mentioned.

WHEREAS by An Act made in the laft
Seffion of Parliament, feveral duties were
granted, continued, and appropriated, towards defraying the Expences of defending, protecting, and fecuring, the Britifh
Colonies and Plantations in America : And whereas it is
juft and neceffary, that Provifion be made for raifing a
further Revenue within Your Majefty's Dominions in America, towards defraying the faid Expences : We, Your Majefty's moft dutiful and loyal Subjects, the Commons of
Great Britain in Parliament affembled, have therefore
refolved to give and grant unto your Majefty the feveral Rates
and

Preamble.

Stamp Act.

his commission as seller of stamps. By January 1766 the lack of stamps had
made itself felt in merchant circles. Shaw reported that "Their being no
Courts . . . on account of the Stamp Act which has put a Stop to all
Bussiness. . . ."[5]

In order to get commercial activities moving once again, merchants sent out vessels without stamped papers. Principle appears to have given way to financial consideration as Shaw instructed his masters to have the officials note on the clearance papers that no stamped paper could be had and ordered the captains to request stamps if seized and taken into port.[6]

Repeal of the Stamp Act in 1766 provided an occasion for rejoicing in New London. Merchant activity flourished again, but English efforts to prevent evasion of the Act regulating trade increased. His Majesty's Ship *Cygnet* became a part of New London's life from 1764 to 1767. While the officers provided quite a boost for the social life of the port, the merchants feared the dangers its cruises represented for their shipping. Shaw warned his agents to take care in the selection of their cargoes when the *Cygnet* lay at anchor in port.[7]

Word arrived in the fall of 1766 of the recruitment of troops in Hanover for service in the American colonies by the English government. The first German troops arrived at New York in January of 1767. Connecticut received a request to billet them for the winter. The Governor and Council met and decided to quarter them.[8]

Many British sailors and soldiers decided they liked New London and its people better than the service. A number of the crew from the *Cygnet* deserted while stationed at New London. At least one of the deserters, William Weaver, remained at the port where he became a respected shipmaster. Hardly an issue of the *New London Gazette* failed to contain at least one notice of an army deserter. Some indication of the numbers of those deserting can be gained from the offering of general pardons from time to time to all British soldiers who would return, excepting those who had committed serious crimes.[9]

After a period of quiet, the Townshend Duties (import duties on glass, lead, paints, paper and tea) led the New London merchants to again exert their leadership against English policy. A letter reached the port in December, 1767, from Boston, containing the resolutions adopted by the Boston selectmen in October. New London merchants accepted the idea of non-importation of British goods and selected a committee of fifteen to handle the matter. Those serving on the committee included: Samuel Belden, Daniel Coit, Joseph Coit, Ezekiel Fox, Titus Hurlburt, William Hillhouse, Russell Hubbard, Richard Law, Jeremiah Miller, James Mumford, Guy Richards, Gurdon Saltonstall, Winthrop Saltonstall, Nathaniel Shaw, Sr. and Nathaniel Shaw, Jr. They drew up a list of European goods and circulated it among the townspeople urging them not to purchase any. Most townspeople agreed and signed a pledge to observe non-importation.[10]

New London went through a quiet period for the next several months. In fact not until 1769 did affairs begin to warm up. Reports reached New London during the summer of 1768 that force might be used if the Americans failed to acknowledge the right of Parliament to tax them.[11] New arrivals of soldiers began.

A letter in the *New London Gazette* stated that:

> I Am glad the troops are come, and believe their arrival will be for the health of this country . . . I imagine we are now convinced of necessity of leaving off trade with the people of Great Britain, . . . [12]

The *Cygnet* left New London but a new revenue vessel, the *Liberty*, replaced it. It sailed between New London and Newport checking the papers of all vessels it encountered. Shaw, quite upset over the activities of the new craft, referred to it as "Our cruising pirate". The *New London Gazette* called it the armed sloop *Slavery*.[13] Alarmed over the close surveillance of the port's shipping, Shaw warned that smuggling had become too dangerous. His vessels received particularly close scrutiny as the British suspected Shaw of smuggling. He had his revenge after the *Liberty* seized and took into Newport a brig of Shaw's under the command of Joseph Packwood. The owner and master went to Newport where a mob handled the British officials roughly, burned the *Liberty* and freed both Shaw's brig and its cargo. William Reed, commander of the British sloop, complained to officials that Nathaniel Shaw and Joseph Packwood acted as the "principal abetters in these illegal proceedings". Despite British insistance, Shaw escaped arrest and trial for his alleged part in the affair. He maintained his innocence of the charges and Connecticut officials refused to take action against him. The only action against him came when Duncan Steward, Customs official at the port, seized a sloop of Shaw's as the vessel involved in the affair and refused for a long time to release it.[14]

As tension mounted between the colonies and England, a number of new officials arrived at the port. In August of 1769 Thomas Botenau arrived to become the Surveyor and Searcher for the port of New London. His appointment brought the number of new officers to five and the total to fourteen. The merchants felt the office unnecessary and the large number of officials caused suspicion and unrest.[15]

Resistance at the port became general. Mobs frequently broke into buildings where goods had been stored from seized vessels and carried them off.

This is to give Notice That . . . the Store of Mr. Nathaniel Shaw, Jun. was broke open and Twenty-Eight Hogs-heads of Rum carried away . . . (which) had been seized . . . for being illegally imported, . . . [16]

In no colony did the general population better support non-importation than in Connecticut. A Committee of Inspection checked to make sure that all abided by the agreements. It uncovered several violations. Discovery meant ostracizing for the culprits regardless of their positions in the society. Usually those caught became cooperative. A shopkeeper detected purchasing British goods by way of Newport turned over the goods to the Committee. Some merchants from outside the colony attempted to import British goods from Newport and New York. To deal with this threat the General Court levied a tax upon goods brought into Connecticut for sale by non-residents. In addition when outside merchants attempted to land and sell British goods the people of New London would not allow it. Individuals making such attempts learned that the merchants and traders of New London ". . . at all times heartily approve of the . . . Resolves, to discourage . . . the Importation and Sale of British Manufactures . . . until all Revenue Acts imposed on the American colonies were repealed."[17]

Some regarded non-importation as a blessing. They believed that the American colonies would be forced by non-importation to develop their own industries. Connecticut merchants, under the leadership of Silas Deane, Colonel Gurdon Saltonstall and Nathaniel Shaw, Jr. formed an association to promote American industry. Members agreed to keep prices competitive and offered bounties in an effort to increase native production. Some in New London considered the British ministry the best friend American industry possessed. As one expressed it, those who are for repeal of the duties are really against America. He saw the tax as ruining England while enriching the colonies through the production of their own goods.[18]

Despite these views, non-importation ended when the Lord North ministry withdrew all of the Townshend Duties, except that on tea, in 1770. New London and Groton decided to continue the policy at a meeting on August 2, 1770 and established a new Committee of Inspection. Several attempts were made by New London merchants to make agreements with other Connecticut towns to keep non-importation going. William Manwaring, Gurdon Saltonstall and Nathaniel Shaw, Jr., represented New London at a September 13, 1770 meeting of merchants at New Haven and these same merchants attended a grand convention of Connecticut merchants the following December, in a vain attempt to keep non-importation a fact. Despite all efforts, non-importation ended as New London merchants could not, alone, refuse to handle British goods while Boston, New York and merchants of other ports dealt in them.[19]

Some found it difficult to understand the change in the merchants position towards American and British goods. One such person complained that during non-importation the merchants claimed Americans could produce all the goods needed, but now these same merchants sold British goods cheaper than colonial goods and spoke of their superiority over American goods.[20]

Revenue vessels continued to be based at New London after the ending of the Townshend Duties. In October of 1771, two British sail arrived, the *Beaver,* sloop of war, and the *Halifax,* armed schooner. The latter remained at the port until 1772 when replaced by the ship *Swan.* Matters went along smoothly at the port after the repeal of the Townshend Duties, until the beginning of 1772. Trouble in that year mainly took the form of letters to the *New London Gazette,* attacking the growing "Whig's" patriot power, although in February, British officials seized a schooner at Boston for having sugar on board which had not been cleared at the Custom House when the vessel left the port of New London. One New Londoner wrote to the *New London Gazette* complaining that the people suffered from the "Tyranny of Patriotism"

> . . . True Liberty is the uncontrolled exercise of every privilege which we derive from the Laws of our Country. . . . Bad as our present Ministers are . . . they still allow us some degree of Freedom; they suffer us to think, to talk, and to write as we please, but the Patriots allow us no such indulgence.[21]

Another writer, identifying himself as an "Old Whig", lamented that although a Whig he received the misnomer Tory because the Tories now called themselves Whigs. Still another writer bemoaned the uselessness of petitioning the King for action against the Whigs.[22]

The Tea Act brought things to a head at New London. Shaw expressed the merchant (Whig) view:

> In regard to the Tea that is expected from Great Britain, I pray heartily that the Colonies will not Suffer any to be landed. . . . The people with us are determined not to purchase any that comes in that way.[23]

When tea did arrive at New London the "radicals" seized it and burned it upon the Parade. The next action took place after the "Intolerable Acts".[24] On the twenty-seventh of June, 1774 a Committee of Correspondence which included Richard Law, Samuel Parsons, Guy Richards, Gurdon Saltonstall, and Nathaniel Shaw, Jr., began to operate. A mass meeting of townspeople, November 27, 1774, resulted in resolutions which expressed

Nathan Hale School in original location, corner of State and Union Streets. From a drawing by L.L. Gardner, 1880.

Nathan Hale School in present location, Captain's Walk, 1975.

Nathan Hale Statue, Williams Park.

sympathy for Boston and indignation against the "Intolerable Acts"—
(Boston Port Bill, administration of Justice Act, Massachusetts Government Act, Quebec Act and Quartering Act).

On the 20th of April 1775, news of the Lexington engagement reached
the port. New London's guidance during the Revolution came from the
same merchants who had provided leadership before the war, Captain
John Deshon, William Hillhouse, Richard Law, Thomas Mumford, Gurdon Saltonstall, Nathaniel Shaw, Jr., and Thomas Shaw. They served in a
number of town, state and Continental posts.[25]

New London contributed to the land as well as to the sea war. Men from
the port served at Bunker Hill and in most other engagements of the
Revolution. Nathan Hale, a teacher at New London, when the news of
Lexington arrived, closed the school and spoke in favor of the patriot
cause at Miner's Tavern before joining the troops headed for Boston.
Residing with John Richards, Hale taught from March, 1774 to July, 1775.
His reputation as a firm disciplinarian does not mean his pupils failed to
like him. Hale taught a class of young ladies which met from 5 A.M. to 7
A.M. before the regular school day began. Gilbert Saltonstall appeared to
have been his closest friend while John and Edward Hallam, Stephen
Hempstead and David Mumford also had close contact with Nathan Hale.
Hale and Thomas V. Fosdick of New London were among 120 volunteers,
chiefly from Connecticut regiments, who formed a corps of Rangers
commanded by Captain Thomas Knowlton.[26]

A New London militia unit existed before the Revolution and it took
part in the Bunker Hill battle under command of William Coit. An independent militia company organized by Major Jonathan Latimer also took
part in the battle.[27] Efforts to provide an adequate defense system at the
port continued throughout the war. Shortly after hostilities began the
town became alarmed when at sundown three vessels began to head
towards the harbor. By midnight a group of men women and children had
used picks and shovels to dig a breastwork from Bank Street to Prison
Street only to discover that the visitors were merchantmen seeking shelter.[28]

A number of inspections of the area and an inventory of its armament
took place, but except for some repairs and voluntary efforts of the people,
little had been accomplished by early 1776 except for the rebuilding of the
fort at the foot of State Street under the direction of Gurdon Saltonstall.
Captain Nathaniel Saltonstall took command of the strengthened fort with
twelve to twenty men. At that time the Governor and the Council of Safety
recommended the building of three new fortifications at the port.[29]

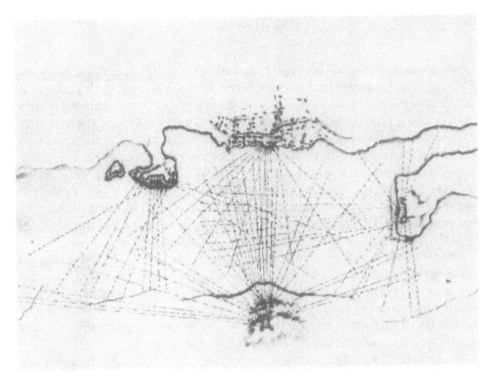

Plan of New London Harbor, 1776. Drawn by John Trumbull for his father, Governor Trumbull.

Fort Trumbull.

Fort Griswold, picture taken 1892.

Fort Trumbull (named after the Governor) at Mamacock (Fort Neck) protected the southern approach to the harbor and its building became the responsibility of Nathaniel Shaw. Fort Griswold (named after the Lieutenant-Governor) on Groton Point, overlooked the center of the harbor from the Groton side and had its building directed by Ebenezer Ledyard. The third fort at Winthrop's Point, provided a defense on the northern side of the harbor and Gurdon Saltonstall supervised its preparation. The fort at the foot of State Street was abandoned at this time and its cannons moved to the other forts. The area at the foot of State Street has been known as the parade ever since. Another fortified spot existed on the town square where an earthworks had been thrown up and a single cannon protected the town from the land side. The port appeared reasonably safe from British attacks by the summer of 1777 when the forts were considered complete. In fact, the posts lacked men, cannon and proper defensive positions for a good defense. Fear of an attack led to the stationing of two regular army companies at the town in 1777. Two years later Colonel Dearborn arrived to take charge of Fort Trumbull.[30]

The British did not test New London defenses until 1781 even though naval vessels became a frequent sight anchored near the town. Primary interest of the British lay in securing provisions from islands off shore which had become popular for the raising of livestock as no Indians or wolves threatened and expensive fences were not needed. Fishing and coastal vessels from New London also became targets.[31]

So many had joined the military by August of 1776 that Nathaniel Shaw wrote Governor Jonathan Trumbull that ". . . this Town has been drain'd of men already, so that their is Scarsly Sufficiency of hands left to get in the Harvest, . . ."[32]

The port's position became both valuable and precarious at the same time. The patriot cause needed the provisions, military supplies and West Indian goods which the merchants could supply while British naval vessels posted a dual threat of blockade and invasion. An emergency embargo against exporting of provisions from Connecticut went into effect August 1775.[33]

West Indian goods became so scarce in May of 1776 that the Assembly established an embargo against exporting them except for the use of the Continental Army. Just a year earlier Nathaniel Shaw, Jr. complained:

> . . . I have Considerable Large Quantities of West Indian Goods in Store both at Boston, N. York & Philadelphia but Cannot Raise a Shilling.[34]

New London became one of the most active ports in the activity of the Revolution. Many craft of the State and Continental navies operated out of New London. The great demand for vessels meant a seeking out of suitable merchant craft until new sail could be constructed. New London furnished vessels, captains and seamen.

A committee appointed by the Governor and Council procurred Connecticut's Navy, one of the first established after the authorization of

Congress. Its members—John Deshon, Giles Hall, Nathaniel Wales and William Williams—commissioned three vessels in 1775, the brigs *Minerva*, the *Old Defense* and the schooner *Spy*.[35]

The *Minerva* left state service in December of 1775, the brig *Defense* replaced the *Old Defense* in 1776 and the British captured the *Spy* in 1778. The galley *Crane*, added in 1776, sailed out of New London for New York and fell into British hands. A new ship, the *Oliver Cromwell*, authorized by the General Assembly and outfitted at New London had a very successful career. In one four day period it took four prizes and sixty-one prisoners. The British captured it in 1779. The *Defense*, rebuilt into a ship, ran aground on a reef off New London and was lost in 1779. Three other galleys became part of the fleet in 1776—the *Whiting* captured that year, the *Shark* captured the next year, and the *New Defense* captured in 1780.[36]

Three more vessels joined the fleet in 1777—the brig *America*, the sloop *Schuyler*, and the schooner *Mifflin*. The *America* lay at anchor in New London in 1777 but no other record of it exists, the *Schuyler* ran aground and was captured in 1777 and the *Mifflin* was sold in 1778. The sloop *Guilford* (a former British vessel), last to be added to the fleet, fell to the British in 1779 along with the *Oliver Cromwell*, ending the Connecticut Navy. Eight of the thirteen had been captured, one wrecked at sea, three removed from state service and of one no record exists. During its existence the Connecticut Navy took forty-one prizes worth over $1,000,000.[37]

When war came, privateering won quick approval from the Continental Congress. The May 1776 session of the Connecticut Assembly authorized the Governor to sign "Commissions for private ships of war and Letters of Marque and Reprisal". Privateers were vessels armed and fitted out at private expense for the purpose of attacking enemy ships. Privateering proved popular because all who took part—owners, officers, sailors and government—shared in the spoils. Men, especially merchant seamen, would rather serve on privateers with the possibility of high return, rather than accept the low pay and hardship of the army or navy.[38]

Privateering proved more attractive among the merchant seamen than service in the Connecticut Navy and proved more damaging to the British economy. Prizes for the Americans amounted to over $39,000,000, increased the prices the British paid for imports, decreased sugar prices and can be directly attributed to the failure of several British firms. New London played no small role as over three hundred prizes came into the port including the *Hannah* richest prize of the war and perhaps the most costly, as it may have led to Arnold's attack.[39]

Connecticut had 297 privateers in action during the American Revolution of which New London owned 59 or one-fifth. These 297 privateers captured nearly 500 British sail; while New London's one-fifth captured 157, one-third of the prizes. This record indicates the initiative and aggressiveness of New London merchants and seamen. Such activity established the port as one of the leading American privateering centers and famous for injuring British trade.[40]

Three merchants, Nathaniel Shaw, Jr., Thomas Mumford and John Deshon, sent out the majority of privateers and took the major share of prizes. Shaw owned ten vessels and had investments in at least two more. These twelve brought in fifty-seven prizes. Thomas Mumford also owned ten privateers and invested in two others. Thirty-three captures were made by his twelve. John Deshon owned eight vessels and invested in one other. His nine privateers took eight prizes.[41]

Ninety-seven of the 157 prizes brought in by privateers of the port or nearly sixty-two percent were by the sail of these three gentlemen—Shaw, Mumford and Deshon. The thirty vessels of these merchants averaged 3.2 prizes per vessel, while the twenty-nine vessels of the other merchants averaged just 2.0 prizes per privateer. The total number of privateers at New London, fifty-nine, averaged 2.7 prizes each.[42]

Most privateering ventures had the backing of three investors who shared the cost of outfitting. Usually these included the owner, the captain and one outsider. Typical of arrangements under which a privateer sailed is the agreement for the *Hibernia*. It called for the owners to supply the vessel, armament and provisions in return for a one-half share of prizes taken. The other half would be for officers and crew divided as follows: Captains to receive eight shares; senior officers four shares; other officers two shares; gentlemen volunteers one share; and boys one-half a share. In addition special money awards went to the seaman who first sighted a prize (one-hundred pounds) and the first seaman to board the prize (three-hundred pounds). Even those who became disabled profited—one thousand pounds for those who lost a limb or suffered other permenently disabling wounds.[43] On November 20, 1778 the *Connecticut Gazette* carried an advertisement for privateering crewmen:

> The fine new ship Governor Trumbull, Henry Billings, Commander, Now laying in the Harbour of New London mounting 20 Carriage Guns, will sail in 8 days on a six Months Cruize against the Enemies of AMERICA. A few more Volunteers are wanting to compleat her Complement of Men. Those who are desirous of serving their Country and making their Fortunes, are desired to apply immediately on Board the Ship . . . .[44]

While the success of a voyage depended upon the number of prizes taken, too much of a good thing could be fatal. Each capture required removal of the original crew while the privateer put a prize crew on board. Several captures could reduce the privateer to a small crew with many prisoners. The *Eagle,* a privateer sloop out of New London under Captain Edward Conkling, took seven quick prizes. While carrying a large number of prisoners from the captures, the privateer crew of fifteen men suffered an attack by the confined men and all lost their lives except for two boys.[45]

Two of Shaw's privateers had outstanding careers. The *American Revenue* took fifteen prizes, 1776-1779, before falling victim to the British frigate *Greyhound.* In a thirteen month period the *General Putnam* set a record, May 13, 1778 to June 26, 1779, when fourteen prizes were seized.[46]

New London privateers launched some daring raids on British bases. In 1778, Captains Ebenezer Dayton and Jason Chester, with twenty-four men, sailed to Long Island, transported their craft overland and launched them again. They attacked Fire Island where five British vessels lay at anchor, seized and sailed them back to New London. On another occasion, the *Middletown, Eagle* and *Beaver* attacked Sag Harbor where they seized a Tory privateer and returned to New London with it. Privateers disposed of their prizes and cargoes at New London so that advertisements for their sale appeared often in the port's newspaper.[47]

Benedict Arnold requested Shaw's aid in 1780 in settling a claim against one of Shaw's captains. Just a month before Arnold fled to the British, he wrote Shaw asking him to dispose of all his (Arnold's) property in Connecticut and to transfer the funds to him at West Point.[48]

Continental Naval Vessels also found New London's harbor a valuable base. John Deshon and Nathaniel Shaw, members of the Marine Committee of the Eastern Department acted as agents for the outfitting and supplying of Continental Naval Vessels and naval affairs at the port. The *Trumbull,* a Connecticut built Continental ship, outfitted at the port and recruited its crew from the area. Elisha Hinman and Richard Law, two well-known New London captains, served aboard the ship. The Continental brig *Resistance,* also prepared for the sea at the port and sailed under Captain Samuel Chew of New London. Captain John Barry of the Continental frigate *Alliance* had to put down a mutiny while the vessel lay in New London harbor.[49]

If New London had done no more than furnish Nathaniel Shaw, Jr., to the patriot cause, its name would always be a valued part of American history. Shaw, the leading merchant patriot of New London, played a role of vital importance in the American victory. He served as a member of the

Committee of Correspondence, the only one to serve continuously during the war, and acted as Naval Agent for the Continental Congress, Colony of Connecticut and the State of Connecticut. Additional appointments placed him on committees to oversee the building of forts to protect the port and on the Marine Committee of the Eastern Department.[50] At the same time he attempted to carry on his commercial activities. Using his home as an office, Shaw carried out his official and private duties from New London during the war. He left the port only to transact business with various Continental and State officials at nearby sites or upon his private yacht the *Queen of France*.[51]

As war became imminent Shaw instructed his masters to ship in as much in the way of military supplies as possible. Through correspondence one sees war approaching. On April 6, 1775, he wrote:

> But as to trade for the future, the Whole Depends on the British Parliament Repealing the American Acts. I have Sent you sum of our News Papers by wich you'l see that we are Determin'd and Unanimous to Abide by the Resolutions of the Continental Congress.[52]

Two days later Shaw recorded:

> I think by ye best acct from England matters seem to draw near when ye longest sword must decide the controversy.[53]

The twenty-fifth of April he noted:

> We have no further News from the Eastward only that there is Thirty Thousand Provential Troops in the Neighbourhood of Boston . . . .[54]

Although powder and lead received priority as imports as early as April 6, 1775 when Shaw stated that nothing "but Molas. and Powder" will command cash, he expressed alarm at the lack of supplies for the defense of the Colony after Lexington and Concord. He urged the purchasing of 400 to 500 barrels of powder which he promised he could deliver within ten weeks as he had a fast sailor ready to go. The Colony did place an order, but only for 600 half barrels. Even before this order came Shaw on his own searched out sources of supply. He ordered a small amount from New York and requested that Thomas and Isaac Wharton, merchants of Philadelphia, secure fifteen tons of lead for which he would ship sugar and rum. The twenty-fifth of April he wrote Peter Vandervoort, a New York merchant, seeking 500 pounds of powder, 1,500 flints and 1,800 weight of lead.[55]

As he had anticipated, Shaw began to receive requests for military supplies. In August of 1775 he delivered powder and ball to Lieutenant Nathan Hale for his company and as he had feared arms and munitions became scarce when the British began to restrict the amount which could be shipped from Europe. Shaw informed Governor Trumbull of this difficulty as early as February of 1776.[56]

Nathaniel Shaw was on intimate terms with most of the leaders of the Revolution. George Washington stayed at the Shaw Mansion in April of 1776 while moving his forces from Boston to New York. During his previous visits to New London in 1756 the General had also visited the Shaws and had kept in close contact throughout the following years. He made use of Shaw several times during the Revolution. The General requested expert and trusted pilots to be recommended who could guide French vessels in the Sound when needed. Alarmed about the British fleet and where it might appear, Washington decided to station relays of dragoons every fifteen miles between his headquarters and Tower Hill. Unfortunately, he could spare only enough men to establish the line to New London and had to ask Shaw to hire men and horses to extend the line from the port to Tower Hill (Rhode Island). Apparently the plan proved to be of value for after several days of operation Washington wrote Shaw and thanked him for information gathered and requested that the contact be continued. General LaFayette also received aid from Nathaniel Shaw. In September 1778 he was supplied with horses to carry dispatches between New London and New Haven.[57]

Governor Jonathan Trumbull and Shaw worked extremely well together. The Governor received detailed reports from Shaw concerning port conditions, supplies and naval and military activities. Even before receiving any official appointment, Shaw informed the Governor of the military supplies at New London and the means to transport the same.[58]

The first naval engagement of the colonies took place in March and April of 1776 when an expedition sailed to seize British naval stores at New Providence (Nassau) Bahamas. New London furnished eighty members of the crews including Captain Dudley Saltonstall, Lieutenant Elisha Hinman, midshipmen Charles Bulkeley and Peter Richards. On its return the expedition put into New London harbor, where guns, powder and cannon, prisoners, sick seamen and wounded were landed. All came under the supervision of Shaw, while Washington who happened to be in New London at the time, examined the captured British supplies and boarded one of the American naval vessels.[59]

As Naval Agent, Nathaniel Shaw faced a variety of problems. Allotment of materials and provisions and arrangements for their delivery led to many pressures. Behind each referral to the Naval Agent for supplies lay the implied threat of terrible consequences if not honored. All prizes brought into port became the responsibility of Shaw and he had to dispose of them. In addition, he had to handle the prize money and pay it to those entitled to share in it. Often those paid disagreed with the amount. Another duty involved the paying of bills presented to him as Naval Agent for which he had to request repayment from the State or Congress. Sums from $5,000 to $80,000 were paid to Shaw upon presentation of bills to the Continental Congress.[60]

Prison ships, very unpleasant and undesirable no matter which side owned them, were commonly used at this period of history. Since Shaw had charge of sailors taken prisoner, New London became the site of prison ships. Actually his brother, Thomas Shaw, as deputy commissioner, handled the duties concerning the prisoners. The first prison ship at the port, a prize ship rented from Samuel Aborn of Warwick, Rhode Island, saw use for only a short time in 1778. The schooner *Penquin* and sloop *Pease* apparently saw use as prison ships since in 1780 Shaw provided bread for men held aboard the two vessels. For a time no craft became available and the prisoners had to be confined in various places in the New London area or placed on parole. The merchants of New London provided a new prison ship the *Retaliation* in 1782. Some excitement developed when eighty of the prisoners escaped in June of the same year. Twenty-six eluded capture, while the rest suffered recapture. Thomas Shaw charged Captain John Chapman, commander of the prison ship, with negligence and the Militia Guard with inefficiency. Captain Chapman lost his post as a result of the escape.[61]

Prisoner exchanges took place from time to time as a result of Nathaniel Shaw's negotiations. The Committee of Safety instructed him to work out an exchange as early as 1777. Possibly Shaw carried on negotiations in New York City with the British. In early exchanges American prisoners arrived at New London in poor condition, while British prisoners left in much better shape. By the middle of 1779 conditions had improved in British prisons so that prisoners arriving at New London appeared in better condition. New London made every effort to have its townspeople released from prison ships. One prisoner claimed: "all New London men are exchanged by virute of their townspeople. . . " Officers had more of a chance to be exchanged than seamen and Shaw often received requests to arrange for such.[62]

He took care of exchanging French prisoners as well as American. The French government promised to pay all expenses involved in the transporting, feeding, outfitting and medical assistance for the French prisoners. In 1779 the French paid Nathaniel and Thomas Shaw £3,779 12s. 2 d. for prisoner expenses.[63] Prisoner exchange could result in dangers. Returned Americans often suffered from disease and caused a number of others to become ill. Also British prisoners suffered from illnesses which could spread. Lucretia Shaw, wife of Nathaniel, spent a great deal of time nursing them, even taking prisoners into her home to care for them. As a result of such kindness, she fell ill with a malignant fever and died December 11, 1781.[64]

During the Revolution Shaw continued to look after the members of West Indian families who had been sent to New London for education. Among those entrusted to his care was a son of John Giddis. In August of 1777, Giddis sent a letter with one of Shaw's captains expressing concern because he had not received any word of his son nor bills for the son's expense. He requested information about his son's progress in education and asked that he be put to work in a firm if he showed an interest in business. Actually Shaw had drawn at least a thousand livers on the Giddis account and had written in December of 1775 about the boarding school, clothing and supplies arranged for the boy. Shaw also made provisions for schooling and board for a young man named Sargenton and arranged for the expenses to be paid through his agent, William Constant, in the West Indies.[65]

Among the other prominent merchant families which played a major role in New London during the Revolution was the Coit family. Daniel, Joseph and Thomas Coit, three cousins, actively supported the patriot cause. Daniel, Justice of the Peace and innkeeper, held several civic and Congregational Church posts. Thomas served the town for thirty years as a doctor. Joseph became the merchant of the family. He learned the shipbuilding business in Boston and New York, before entering the family business at New London. An injury ended his shipbuilding career and he turned to the sea. After eleven successful voyages, Joseph Coit set himself up as a merchant. His vessels engaged in the West Indian, coastal and foreign trade. He owned a warehouse and store at the port. Smuggling seemed as much a part of his activity as Shaw's.[66]

Daniel and Joseph served on the Non-Importation Committee with Nathaniel Shaw in 1767. Joseph moved his business operations to Norwich during the war to escape British attacks. His son, Joshua, a Harvard graduate of 1776, returned to New London in time to represent the family business there for the rest of the Revolution except a period in 1779 when he was at Philadelphia serving in a minor Continental Post. Joshua had been admitted to the Bar in 1779 and served the war effort as merchant and lawyer. The firm shipped munitions and supplies to aid the war and Coit used his legal services to handle privateers and their prizes. He served in the defense of the town when the British attack came during which the firm lost two stores, a wharf and other properties. By 1782 Joshua served as clerk of the Probate Court, the port's only notary public and Justice of the Peace.

Another merchant family, the Saltonstall, committed its fortunes to the patriot cause. Gurdon Saltonstall had opposed the Stamp Act and took a leading part in civic affairs. After service on most of the town committees from 1740 to 1776, he became a Brigadier General early in the war with the responsibility of providing for the defense of the port. The war years cost him heavily—fifteen vessels and in the burning of New London, the loss of his home, two warehouses, a wharf, a barn full of horses, papers, books and other belongings.[67]

Dudley, Gilbert and Winthrop, Gurdon Saltonstall's three sons, played important roles in the war effort. Dudley, a captain—later commodore in the Navy, served as second in command to Commodore Esek Hopkins on the first American Naval Expedition. Captain Saltonstall as master of the *Trumbull* had the honor of first flying the national flag on the high seas. The lack of success of the expedition resulted in his reduction from first to fourth captain in seniority. He had charge of a fleet sent to attack the British post on the Penobscot River but his fortunes did not improve. A superior British fleet trapped his force in the river and Saltonstall received a dismissal from the service. Success finally came to Dudley Saltonstall as a privateer captain. After making some excellent captures of prizes, he returned to the West Indian trade at the end of the war. Gilbert served as captain of the Marines on the *Trumbull* and Winthrop held a number of civic posts before the war. He also served as registrar of the Court of Admiralty during the Revolution.[68]

One other Nathaniel Saltonstall took part in New London's Revolutionary War effort. He does not appear to have been directly related to the Gurdon Saltonstall family. At the start of the war he commanded the garrison at the fort on the Parade. Later he took charge of several privateers for Nathaniel Shaw.[69]

New London's merchant activity continued but unevenly to put it mildly. Some merchants managed to keep businesses going by having their captains keep away from New London for several years. Captain Lamb of the *America* sailed from New London in 1774 and did not return until 1777. Others found themselves detained in foreign ports for long periods such as Captain James Rogers who did not return to New London until six years had passed. A few captains managed to ship out of the harbor and returned safely. Captain William Rogers made such a voyage to France and back in 1779. Even a few foreign vessels entered port such as the French sail *Lyon* under command of Captain Michel.[70]

Nathaniel Shaw's commercial activities slowed during the American Revolution and he voiced concern over the future of his private business activity in several letters to merchant associates. In general what he said personified the general merchant feelings at the port. To an associate in Newport in 1775, he wrote:

> . . .for in short the Times are such that I Scarcely know what to Do or what Plan to Persue . . . .[71]

By the following year he felt trade had come to an end:

> . . . God knows wether we shall ever be in a situation to Carry it on Again, no Bussiness now but preperation for Warr, Ravaging Villages, Burning of Towns & c.[72]

Still while normal trading could not be carried on, Shaw kept several sail active. If one would risk a vessel, needed goods could be purchased in Europe. From Amsterdam, John de Neuville & Son, agents of Shaw, informed him in 1781 that goods could be secured cheaply, in large amounts and that warships were scarce in the North Sea.[73]

Several New London merchants decided to sell all or some of their vessels when war came. Captain Joshua Hempstead received orders to sell the sloop *Lizard* for £220 lawful money, cash or six months credit at six percent. If a sale could not be arranged the owner, Meredith Steward, desired to lease it at six shillings per ton per month.[74] Nathaniel Shaw tried to dispose of sail in various ports. Instructions to his captains often included orders for them to sell the vessel ". . . *if* you Can Sell her for (the price varied) . . . Sell her, . . ." He sold a vessel in 1778 and showed his support of the patriot cause by putting all the funds into the Loan Office at six percent interest.[75]

Gerard Beekman sold a new vessel at New London in 1778 at a price which pleased him considerably:

> I have Sold my New Ship at New London for Eleven Thousand pounds Shea Cost me in Centenel Dollars But 4300 pounds I thinck Shea is Well Sold and I Shall Cleare a Bout £300 for My half of her freight.[76]

Another blow to merchant activities during the war resulted from many captains engaging in naval and privateering duty. Three of the leading captains who did so—Charles Bulkeley, Elisha Hinman and Michael

Melally—provided outstanding service.

Bulkeley had been in the West Indian trade before the war. The family's connection with New London dated from 1661 when Gershon Bulkeley became the third minister to serve at the port. When war came Bulkeley's vessel was at sea and unaware of the situation until seized by a British tender while preparing to enter New London harbor. Bulkeley jumped overboard and swam to Fisher's Island where he gathered a force which retook the vessel.[77] After militia duty at the port he joined the Continental Service and took part in the first United State naval action. While serving on the *Alfred,* Bulkeley suffered capture by the British and imprisonment in England. He escaped and went sightseeing in London before crossing to France. When off the American coast on his way home, he again fell victim to the British, but they released him. He became a privateer captain in charge of the *Randolph, Marshall* and *Active.* In 1777 once again the British seized Bulkeley and imprisoned him for three months at New York before releasing him through exchange.[78]

Elisha Hinman went to sea at the age of fourteen and rose to the rank of captain at nineteen while serving in the West Indian and European trade. He became one of the first captains in the Continental Service. In 1778 while commander of the *Alfred,* he was captured and imprisoned in England. Escaping, he returned home and became a privateer captain.[79] Hinman commanded the sloop *Hancock,* ship *Deane,* and the *Marquis de LaFayette.* The last named ended its service August 13, 1783, the last of New London's privateers.[80]

Captain Michael Melally, friend and business associate of Nathaniel Shaw, had a long and successful career as master sailing out of New London. He entered State service for a short time during the Revolution and received an assignment to the *Oliver Cromwell.* Unfortunately, the vessel underwent several delays while being outfitted and when the prospect of a wait of several more months faced Melally without pay, he requested and received a discharge from State service from Governor Trumbull. He spent the war years sailing privateers for Shaw and working at Shaw's headquarters between cruises. Captain Melally commanded the *Lady Spencer, Nancy, Le Despencer* and *Rochambeau,* seizing at least seven prizes. He invested in each of these vessels plus the *General Putnam.* The British captured the *Le Despencer* in 1780 and took the captain into New York where he must have been exchanged quickly for in 1781 he commanded the *Rochambeau.*[81]

New London had a number of suspected Tories including some important merchants such as Roswell Saltonstall. Several families had members who fought on the British side. At least one New Londoner served in the British Navy, Robert Winthrop, son of John Still Winthrop, born in New London in 1764, who attained the rank of vice admiral before his death. The Reverend Mr. Matthew Graves, Anglican minister in New London from 1748 to 1779, continued to read the prayers for the King and Royal family after the Revolution began. Many members of St. James Episcopal Church became angered by his insistance on prayers for the monarchy and finally, during a church service, Thomas Mumford, a prominent merchant and his brother David, each seized an arm of the clergyman and removed him from the pulpit. He was not allowed to preach in New London again and left for New York in 1779 where he died the following year. St. James burned during General Arnold's raid in 1781.[82]

Duncan Stewart, Collector of Customs, served at New London from 1764 until the Revolution. He had become well liked and suffered no harm during any of the disturbances after the struggle began. Stewart's only difficulty came when some English goods arrived for him and a mob seized and burned them. In July of 1777 Stewart decided to leave and permission for his departure to New York was permitted.[83]

Beginning in 1776, a large number of Tories were arrested and confined in New London from Connecticut and other colonies. One of the more famous was Governor William Franklin. Shaw probably expressed the merchant viewpoint and general patriot feeling when he wrote Peter Vandervoort: "I think it now high time that all the Tory Party should be made to be Silent." War split the Chew brothers—Joseph and Samuel. Joseph, a Tory, finally left town for Canada while Samuel supported the patriot side.[84]

Tories from Long Island proved more troublesome than the local people as they carried out activities which included smuggling, marauding, plundering and kidnapping along the Connecticut shore. Gangs from the lower Hudson, called Cowboys and Skinners, used small sloops and boats named Shaving-Mills for their raids along the Connecticut coast. The lure of British gold attracted those known as Long Island Traders who had livestock or other goods sought by the British.[85]

Apprehension of the merchants at New London came not from the hit and run tactics of the Tories, but from the fear of a British attack which existed from the beginning of the war. Despite many alarms about impending attacks, none came until 1781.

After years of alarms which resulted in the hasty removal of the ill, children, women and valuable goods only to have no attack occur, the British finally struck September 6, 1781. Success as a privateering port probably led to the attack. The port had just seen the arrival of the richest prize, the *Hannah,* and its capture appeared to have so angered General Henry Clinton that he ordered General Benedict Arnold, a native of New London County, to attack New London.[86]

A warning reached the port concerning the imminent attack and the merchants requested troops. Arnold planned to strike early in the morning but a shift in the wind slowed the fleet's movement and troops did not land until 10 A.M. Still many were caught by surprise as New London had arranged a warning of two cannon shots if an attack came. Unfortunately, when the alarm sounded, the British fired a third shot which converted the warning into a notice of a visitor or prize. About nine hundred troops, British regulars, American Tories and Hessians, landed on each side of the Thames from twenty-four transports.[87]

As the alarm spread about the town, most of the inhabitants fled and several vessels moved upstream. A number of merchants and sea captains organized a defense force under Captain Nathaniel Saltonstall. Fort Trumbull fell quickly as its defenses were so weak that the men fired one volley and then fled across the Thames to fight from Fort Griswold. The town's battery on the Square fared no better as it was abandoned as Arnold and his troops arrived.[88]

When Arnold's raid began the *Hannah's* goods were in a warehouse and frantic attempts to load them on lighters and wagons saved very few. Only one lighter of several got away and most wagons were intercepted and the goods destroyed.[89]

The British burned 143 buildings, including 65 houses, 31 stores, 18 shops, 20 barns, 9 public and other buildings. Nearly all the shipping of the port burned except for 16 schooners and sloops which fled upstream. Most of the houses on Bank Street suffered destruction. A neighbor saved the Shaw Mansion by putting out the fire. Nathaniel Shaw had gone fishing early that morning and had to hide to escape capture by the incoming British troops. Guy Richard's home escaped burning when spared due to his daughter's illness. A number of the homes burned belonged to suspected Tories, destroyed many believed to divert attention from them. Even the home of James Tilley, a friend of Arnold's and in whose home he ate that day, received the torch.[90]

Tilley who had not contributed to the revolutionary cause, resulting in suspicion on the part of his neighbors about his loyalty, invited Arnold to eat and drink at his table. The group had just raised their wine glasses when a slave ran in exclaiming "Massa Tilley, them d———d redcoats be setting fire to this here house!" Arnold explained that if he failed to

Benedict Arnold.

destroy the house, Tilley's life would be worthless and besides the King would take care of him.[91]

Mrs. Elisha Hinman reportedly tried to shoot General Arnold, a one time friend of Captain Hinman as he passed their house. Among the most serious losses were the Customs House with all of its records, the courthouse, and a wooden building of Shaw's in which he had stored papers, letters and account books.[92]

Across the river a very bloody battle on Groton Heights took place. After twice refusing British demands to surrender, the fort succumbed to a brutal attack in which the commander, Colonel William Ledyard, suffered a fatal thrust with his own sword after surrendering the fort. The British reportedly raced through the fort, bayoneting the Americans, many of whom were already wounded or dead. A number of badly wounded suffered additional wounds and even death when the British loaded them upon a wagon which ran down a hill out of control smashing into a tree. A number of defenders lost clothes and possessions when the enemy departed with thirty prisoners.[93] Governor Jonathan Trumbull, upon learning of the raid, sent out a request for aid to Major General William Heath which proved unnecessary as the attack had been a hit and run affair.

Damages amounted to $485,980 and the port had a large number of homeless people to care for. The British lost ten officers and 183 enlisted men. Several of the men of Arnold's expedition believed the raid could have been carried out without losses or burning the town. General Arnold claimed there had been no plan to burn private dwellings, but gunpowder stored in some caused them to burn. He carried off a number of New London residents. Roswell Saltonstall, merchant of the port and a suspected Tory, aided the residents while they were prisoners. The grateful townspeople allowed goods to be landed for Saltonstall. Most returned to the port in November after Shaw opened negotiations for their release. Death claimed four while the British held the group.[94] While several courts-martial were held after the British raid, most dealt leniently with those who had failed to respond to New London's call for help. Some officers were dismissed from the service as unsuited.[95]

Although the raid represented a terrible blow to the port, another incident possibly even more serious took place on April 15, 1782 when Nathaniel Shaw, Jr. died. Death removed the logical and dynamic leader who might have directed the rebuilding and post war merchant development of New London. Shaw had been accidentally shot while on a hunting trip and died after suffering for three days. Before he died his will was drawn up and signed.[96]

The will indicates the wealth of Shaw, even after suffering a £12,000 loss in Arnold's raid. The bulk of the estate went to his brother, Thomas Shaw; a £300 annual grant to his mother, Temperance Shaw; lavish gifts of real estate to his sister's children, Nathaniel Shaw Woodbridge and Lucretia Shaw Woodbridge, named after the Shaws. He freed all his slaves except one, Solah, who was to be set free at the age of twenty-one.[97]

4 New London Seeks Prosperity 1784-1819

By the end of the war, New London no longer possessed a flourishing commerce. The port does not appear to have grown "rapidly under the stimulus of privateering and periods free from blockade" as one author believed.[1] While facilities had been built to take care of increased shipping activity during the Revolution, these hardly compensated for the lack of schools and teachers, shortage of able-bodied men, clergymen and fathers or for the loss of population. Further the presence of British armed vessels, movement of several merchants to the safety of Norwich and the burning of the town, left it lacking in leadership, port facilities and capital. In 1793 New Londoners received land grants in the Western Reserve to pay for losses incurred during Anrold's Raid and Congress confirmed the grants in 1800.[2]

As New London merchants returned to peacetime commercial dealings, the old rivalries with Hartford and New Haven appeared again. The town no longer enjoyed the position of being the official port of entrance and clearance. Officers and seamen returned to the merchant trade rapidly and by 1784 vessels cleared from New London for the West Indies, London, Liverpool, Ireland and Cadiz. Most foreign vessels could not navigate the Connecticut River and they landed their goods and picked up cargoes at New London. To aid in the economic recovery of the town, it was declared a free port in 1784. Foreign and United States merchants, who established their business at New London, could carry on commerce tax free. In addition, to encourage foreign trade, merchants who imported £3,000 sterling worth of goods annually would be exempted from taxes on such transactions, while goods from other states paid an import tax of five

by W. Leney, 1814.

percent. Merchants would also receive a tax exemption for their vessels if they engaged in European, Asian or African trade for four or more months a year. Whaling and fishing sail received the same tax exemption status and the men paid no poll tax if involved for the same period of time.[3]

Prosperity failed to return to the port after the Revolution despite a return to commercial trade in 1784. West Indian trade, formerly the corner-stone of economic well being at New London, just could not overcome a number of handicaps to once again maintain the pre-war level of maritime activity. By the mid 1790's depresseion set in at the port, brought about by heavy losses of men and vessels and financial difficulties of many merchants. At least twenty-two captians and unknown scores of seamen plus many vessels were lost during this period to disease, climate, pirates, privateers and imprisonment. Add to this the dumping of English goods at the port and the harrassment at foreign ports and one can see why hard times came to New London in the 1790's.[4]

A number of merchants had to end their operations due to these difficulties. The important families of the colonial maritime leadership had their ranks considerably reduced in the post war period. General Gurdon Saltonstall had to file bankruptcy as early as 1785, after thirty years as a merchant. At seventy-seven he suffered from poor economic and physical health and found it impossible to recoup from his Revolutionary War losses of fifteen vessels and £1,440 worth of property. The family lost several members in the West Indies—three sons of the General, Thomas in 1795; Dudley in 1796; and Winthrop in 1802; and Captain Gurdon Saltonstall in 1795, son of Winthrop. The Saltonstalls never played an important merchant role again at the port.[5]

The leadership provided by the Shaw family came to an end in 1795 with the death of Thomas Shaw. He had been overshadowed by Nathaniel during his early years, but appeared to have been a very active participant in the family business. Thomas' leadership first became evident during the Revolution when he handled shipments of supplies for the military, repairs for Continental vessels, distribution of prize cargoes and kept the State government informed as to shipping losses.[6]

After the war Shaw prospered and engaged in new enterprises as well as old. One new venture appeared to have been a trading voyage to China. A letter from Richard Platt to Thomas Shaw requested a chance to invest in Shaw's "China Venture" as he had made a thirty-three and one-half percent profit on a previous investment in a Shaw venture.[7] Much time and energy had to be spent by Thomas Shaw settling his brother's estate. He lacked the documents necessary to close out his brother's Continental accounts as a result of Arnold's raid. From Shaw's correspondence one can see how difficult accounts were to collect and why many merchants were forced into bankruptcy.[8] He wrote Dr. Silvester Gardiner of Providence requesting payment for money owed by Philip Dumarty which the Doctor had guaranteed. Dr. Gardiner claimed as lies any promise that he would make good the sum and rejected the demand for payment. In another case Shaw wrote a "Mr. Textier":

> Sir
> I am informed that you are in good circumstances & happy, while I am poor and much reduced by the late war, my unfortunate brother Nath'l Shaw's Estate has suffered much by the burning of this Town Sept. 6, 1781 by the British Savages.
> . . . Your note in my hands is dated 12th Nov. 1772, for 576 Livers, In your Note and Receipt of same Date for an Execution against Mr. Castaignet for 3915 lb. 12 s.
> I should be happy that you would inform me in what manner it would suit you to remit me the amount together with the Interest.

Thomas Shaw requested payment on June 15, 1784. Apparently "Mr. Textier" failed to pay for in an undated letter Shaw assigned the power of attorney to a Mr. Dousset to collect the debt. He found it necessary, in still another case, to have the sheriff in Hartford attach the farm of Peter

Thomas Shaw by Ralph Earl.

Vanderwood for debts to his brother of £556 5 s. 9 d. Obviously, unless a merchant had enough capital to carry such a bad debt he would go under.[9]

In the face of such slow and difficult collections Shaw proved cautious in recognizing debts owed by his brother. John Chenward wrote demanding payment for debts owed which Shaw promised to pay if proper papers proved the sum represented a legal debt. Thomas Shaw refused to honor what Esek Hopkins claimed were promises made by brother Nathaniel to pay him sums of money. A legal action by Hopkins finally forced Shaw to pay £300 in 1792.[10]

Thomas died in 1795, leaving an estate of £56,136 15 s. 5 d. divided evenly between his sister's children Nathanial Shaw Woodbridge and Lucretia Shaw Woodbridge Perkins. These same two had received lavish property gifts from Nathaniel Shaw and shared £3,194 15s. 6d. estate of their Grandmother Shaw. Thus ended the Shaw leadership.[11]

Two other once prominent families ceased to play leading roles at the port but for a far different reason. Roswell Saltonstall's family and the Winthrop family although remaining for a number of years after the Revolution found that their real or imagined Tory sympathy made their presence in New London uncomfortable.

After the Revolution Roswell Saltonstall at first prospered. The family operated sumac factories in New London and Groton and a horse mill on Water Street. He built a residence on Federal Street in 1786, the most aristocratic block in town and was a prominent member of St. James Episcopal Church. Bishop Samuel Seabury died while visiting at Saltonstall's home. In 1801 Roswell Saltonstall declared bankruptcy and faded from the scene.[12]

The substantial mainland Winthrop land holdings were sold by Francis Bayard Winthrop, last of that name to operate the town mill, shortly after the end of the American Revolution. James Stewart (British Consul) became owner of the Winthrop homestead on the Cove in 1810. Some people mistakenly link this Winthrop Mansion, built in 1752-1755 by John Still Winthrop, with John Winthrop, Jr. William H. Winthrop, brother of Francis Bayard, owned and continued to live on Fisher's Island and their sister, Mary Winthrop Parkin, lived in a mansion at Federal and Huntington Streets until 1834 when William H. Winthrop purchased it.[13]

Only Mrs. John Winthrop and her five daughters appeared to have remained in New London during the American Revolution. Francis Bayard Winthrop spent the war years in New York. He returned under a flag of truce in 1777 in the sloop *Union* and was permitted to land with packages for people at New London. These were inspected by officials. F. B. Winthrop was permitted to go ashore in day time and visit his mother and sister at Thomas Harris' under the direction of commanding officer of the fort, the civil authority and selectmen of New London.[14]

When the prisoners from Arnold's Raid reached New York, Francis Winthrop spent nearly £100 aiding them. In return the town allowed goods sent by him to be landed at New London for his mother and sisters.

Winthrop property and goods were attached and seized by mobs at the port upon at least one occasion in 1777. In 1778 Mrs. Winthrop sent her sons Benjamin and Robert to their Uncle in New York so that he could send them to London for schooling. She, herself, was in England by 1783 for her son William received permission to go to New York to collect funds due his mother to be sent to her in England.[15]

Another son, John, became ill and received permission from the Connecticut authorities to seek medical help in New York. William and Robert returned to New London after the war and entered business together, but in 1790 Robert returned to the British navy.[16]

The Coit family continued to provide leadership. Joseph and his sons, Daniel and Joshua, were all quite active. Much of the rebuilding received money and direction from them, especially the First Church and the New Library Company. Joshua began a political career in 1784 which led to Congress. As a Federalist member of the Assembly from 1784 to 1793, excepting the years 1786, 1787 and 1791, Coit aided the port with legislation such as a shipping tax used for the repair and maintenance of the lighthouse at New London and a tax abatement for New London people who suffered losses during Arnold's Raid.

Coit gained passage of a bill which established Connecticut's first turnpike to connect New London and Norwich, of which company he served as commissioner. He backed passage of a charter for the Union Bank of New London in which the Coit family had invested heavily. The brothers, Daniel and Joshua Coit, became directors while John Hallam, brother-in-law of Joshua, became cashier. Hallam, an early silversmith, formerly served as engraver for Connecticut.

Joshua Coit became a member of Congress in 1793 and served until his death in 1798. He made a number of enemies at New London including Charles Holt, owner of the Republican newspaper, the *New London Bee,* for backing Federalist measures. Several merchants lost vessels to the British in the West Indies and wanted strong action taken to protect American shipping and provide adequate protection for the port. Coit opposed their desires by helping defeat bills which provided for the arming of merchant vessels, which provided for coast defense galleys and which provided for coastal defense. He backed a limited naval bill and opposed strong action against the British. During the Quasi War with France, he cast the deciding vote against privateering. In spite of his opposition for better defenses at New London, he believed the threat of a British attack real enough to make plans to move his family to a farm in Montville if one came.

On the more popular side he worked for a bill which provided Western

Reserve land for New London people who had lost their property during Arnold's Raid. He also backed a bill which passed providing for buoys at the entrance of New London harbor. Coit died of yellow fever in 1798 when an epidemic swept the town. Ironically, he had returned to New London to attend the funeral of a friend, victim of yellow fever.

Robert Coit (1785-1874), son of Joshua, carried on the family merchant business. He began as a supercargo to the West Indies and then operated a ship chandlery business as well as a number of other merchant interests.[17]

WAR OF 1812

With the advent of the British-French conflict in 1793, a period of prosperity developed for some New London merchants as neutral trade in the West Indies became important. This period of economic improvement lasted until the Embargo Act of 1807. Three families in particular recovered from wartime losses as a result of the neutral trade—Billings, Deshon and Williams. They gained a dominant position in New London merchant activity which carried over to the whaling era. By 1805 the port had recovered to the degree that it had two banks in operation—the first town in Connecticut to have the financial demands for such facilities.[18] Until 1807, port activity increased each year. A look at the customs duties collected at New London indicates that from $78,478 in 1801, the duties reached a high of $214,940 in 1806. After the passage of the Embargo Act the duties dropped to $201,940 in 1807 and by 1808 fell to less than $100,000. In 1811 the duties reached a low of $22,343.[19] An unusual case which came up as a result of the Embargo Act was the United States vs. Thirty-seven Sacks of Coffee. The coffee had been imported at New London and seized after court action. An appeal to the circuit court of the United States reversed the decision and the coffee recovered its freedom![20]

It was a very difficult period for New London merchants as so many privateers of several nations sought prizes in the world's waters and often they were careless in their seizures. An excellent example of these difficulties can be seen from a voyage made by Captain Richard Law, Jr. In 1810 he sailed for St. Petersburg in the *Egeria* only to be seized by a Norwegian privateer as a British ship. Taken into Farksand, Denmark, it took three months for the case to be decided in the courts in favor of Law. Then the privateer owners appealed the decision to Copenhagen and Law had to travel three weeks to reach that court. It took from September 1810 to January 1811 to obtain the release of the vessel and this only after Law agreed to pay the privateer owners £100. Expenses totaled $33,000 by this time and the cargo had a value of only $45,000. Upon leaving port to continue to St. Petersburg and while still in Danish waters with a pilot aboard, French privateers seized the vessel and Law found himself back at Copenhagen.

By December of 1811, Law once again won freedom of the vessel and decided to sell the cargo in Denmark. Since he could not take the full amount realized by the sale of the cargo out of the country, he sent the *Egeria* back under the mate with a new cargo while he arranged to get the funds out of the country. Off the coast of the United States, the *Egeria* fell victim, the first of the war of 1812, to a British privateer. On its way to Halifax with a prize crew it ran aground and sank.

Law had not yet finished out his trials. Leaving Denmark on a small vessel he became shipwrecked when it sank off the coast of North Carolina. He managed to reach shore and set out overland for Connecticut. Finally, in the winter of 1812-1813 he reached home. The final blow came when insurance claims were refused although the vessel carried insurance against loss or seizure.[21]

The loss of one vessel could involve many people—the owners, crew, shippers and insurers. A case in point is the *Lovinia*, a sloop of New London seized in 1798, while on a voyage to the West Indies. Insurance papers list the value of the vessel at $779.88, owned equally by three men—Samuel Hurlbut, Joseph and Samuel Tabor. The cargo carried insurance to the value of $3,970.12. The total of $4,750 value and the high risk of West Indian shipping meant a $950.00 premium at twenty percent. Nine individuals divided the risk:

David Greene	$1,000	Nathan Bond	$500
William Stackpole	500	William Smith	500
Perez Morton	500	Tuthill Hurlbut	500
Cromwell Hatch	500	Daniel Sargent	400
		Nathaniel Pellow	350[22]

During the years before the War of 1812 impressment existed as a problem for New London. It was not uncommon for notices such as the following to appear:

It having been represented to the Secretary of State, that, Henry Jessop, a native of the State of Connecticut, has been impressed into the British service, and that he was, not long since, on board the Cambrian frigate—his friends are requested to furnish the subscriber with proof of the citizenship of said Jessop, and a description of his person, in order to procure his enlargement.

J. Huntington, Collector[23]   New London

As conditions worsened between Great Britain and the United States, New London became worried about the lack of protection from attack. Only the inadequate earth forts from the Revolution remained as protection. The State and a number of individuals made efforts from 1781 to 1812 to improve the fortifications, but to no avail. News of the war arrived on the twenty-fourth of June 1812, which apparently could not have come wholly as a surprise for the merchants of the port had been advertizing swords, books on military tactics and regulations for sale.[24]

Troops began to arrive at the port shortly after war came and by October 1812, one regiment had arrived and by June of 1813, three more regiments settled down in New London. After the experience of September 6, 1781, New London became understandably apprehensive of another attack. Beginning in April of 1813 a British fleet under Sir Thomas Hardy blockaded the Sound. The presence of Commodore Decatur and his squadron added to the fears of an attack. Decatur attempted to slip through the Sound from New York and was detected and fled into New London Harbor for safety. Although there were several alarms about impending British attacks which resulted in removal of women, children and specie from the town, Decatur's taking his squadron upstream for safety and the rushing of volunteers to defend the port, none came.[25]

Finally Decatur, after several false alarms, began to plan a dash for the open sea. The squadron moved downstream and on December 12, 1813 began to slip out of the harbor. However, blue lights appeared on both banks of the river and Decatur, believing these were signals to warn the British fleet, moved back into port. With the exception of the *Hornet*, which made its way out the following November, the squadron remained on the Thames for the duration of the war. A strong suspicion developed that an officer at Fort Trumbull had played a part in the "Blue Light" alarm. Major General William Williams' aide de camp, a Captain Anter of Newport, was arrested at Fort Trumbull. Not enough evidence could be produced and authorities had to release him. The last news available indicated that he had gone on board one of the vessels in the British Fleet after release from the fort.[26]

Alfred Carpenter of Norwich lost his son, James, to British impressment in 1810 and when the father learned that James was a member of Commodore Hardy's squadron, he travelled to New London seeking aid for a request that the British release his son. To the surprise of many at the port, the Commodore quickly agreed to release the son and gave him a voucher for $300 in wages due and $2,000 prize money.[27]

The British treated the New London area people kindly at first. Commodore Hardy pledged his word that he would not interfere with fishermen. However, the British seized supplies from the islands off shore and paid only what they wished. This angered many. The break in relations came when the editor of the local paper, the *Gazette*, received a note sent him by the British Commander at New London, Jirah Isham, to be published for the information of the community.

> I am under the necessity of requesting you to make it publicly known that I cannot permit vessels or boats of any description, (flags of truce of course excepted,) to approach or pass the British Squadron, in consequence of an American vessel having exploded yesterday, three hour after she was in our possession.[28]

This came as a result of the schooner *Eagle* being rigged to blow-up after having been allowed to fall into British hands—a second lieutenant and ten men were killed and several others badly wounded.

Little privateering took place out of New London during the war. Vessels which did become privateers included schooner *General Armstrong* (Guy Champlin), *Joel Barlow* (Champlin) *Saratoga* (Champlin), *Mars* (Charles Bulkeley), brig *Anaconda* (Middleton), *Jacks Favorite* (Miller). The *Mars* while on a hundred day cruise (November 1812 to February 1813) took eleven prizes—brought rum, sugar, brandy, wine, dry goods, iron, fish, fruit and such into New London with not a man lost.[29] By May Captain Charles Bulkeley prepared to sail again:

> Notice to Sailors
> The Sch. Mars Charles Bulkeley, Esq. commander, is intended for a cruise and wants 100 men, for which 20 dollars in advance will be paid each able seamen, and in proportion for ordinary seamen, landsmen and boys that go sail cruise. Apply on board or at the store of Daniel Deshon.[30]

A number of prizes taken by privateers from other ports arrived at New London. The privateer brig *Anaconda* took the British packet *Express* with $15,000 in gold. Disaster overtook at least two of the privateers. The *Anaconda* mistakenly fired on the United States schooner *Commodore Hull* wounding the master. Naval officers had the master of the privateer arrested. The *Mars* was lost at Hempstead, Long Island on March 1814. Most of the officers and crew became prisoners.[31]

Quite a few New London vessels themselves fell victim to British vessels. On at least one occasion the British kept their prize for a very small period of time. A sloop the *Fox* of Groton was taken by the British. Captain A. Burrows with thirty volunteers in the sloop *Hero* decided to take it back. They sailed from New London, April 14, at 1:30 P. M. and sighted the *Fox* in the Sound with a prize crew on board. It was seized with the crew and

500 barrels of corn and taken into Mystic by 11 A. M.—just nine and one-half hours later.[32]

Recruiting was carried on at New London by both the navy and the army.

NAVY DEPARTMENT

Wanted for the Navy, forty able bodied seamen, ordinary seamen and lands-men. A handsome bounty and good wages will be paid. Apply to the sub-scriber, commanding officer of the Gunboats at New-London.

William Coit[33]

If you enlisted in the army for five years a bounty of $16.00 would be paid.

When the welcomed end of the war came, New London held a Grand Ball and invited all the British officers of the blockading ships. The courthouse, built in 1784 at the head of State Street to replace the one burned in 1781 on the Parade, was the site of the "peace ball".[34]

New London's shipping can be traced in the period between the end of the American Revolution and the start of the War of 1812 by insurance policies and the French Spoilation Claims. These records show that from 1790 to 1801, 799 sail can be documented in the West Indian trade. Of these, 702 or nearly eighty-eight percent were brigs, schooners and sloops, with 613 or nearly seventy-seven percent being schooners and sloops. There is small room for doubt that small craft and crews dom-inated the New London-West Indian trade.[35]

Insurance rates paid by the New London merchants indicated the areas of greatest safety and risk for trade. Checking the rates from 1802 to 1818, one readily sees that rates varied from as low as three-quarters of one percent to twenty percent depending upon the designation and whether it was peacetime or wartime. In 1813-1814 the blockade worked so effi-ciently that no policies were found.[36] Risk in the coastal trade, usually light, involved mostly New York and Boston. New York voyages paid as low as three-quarters of a percent, but more usually two percent. European trade, usually safe, cost three percent, although one year—1809—the rate reached seven percent. South American trips could be risky for Spanish officials often seized vessels for illegal tradings and the insurance cost seven to twelve percent.[37] The West Indian trade with the danger of storms, shipwrecks, fevers, pirates and privateers ranked as fairly danger-ous. Peacetime rates ranged from two percent to thirteen percent, while wartime highs reached twenty percent.[38]

For the years 1794-1819 total New London tonnage declined although not necessarily year after year. For one seven year period the increase of the fishing fleet offset the decline of the merchant tonnage and an overall

Court House, erected, 1784 soon after the burning by Arnold.

Corner of Broad and Huntington Streets. Public Library, left. Court House and Firemen's Monument, right.

increase is recorded. Foreign trade (includes West Indian) represented the main shipping activity, 1794 to 1808. Coastal and foreign shipping were about equal from 1808 to 1817. Coastal shipping dominated in 1818 and 1819. Fishing tonnage represented a large fleet from 1805 to 1807 and even exceeded coastal shipping during those years. By 1819 New London's tonnage had dropped to less than one-half that of 1794. In fact the total tonnage of 1819 represented less than the foreign tonnage of 1794.[39] The future of New London's maritime activity appeared dark by 1819.

5 New London In Whaling Days 1718-1909

Oh fare you well, we're homeward bound,
Goodbye, fare you well.
We're homeward bound for New London town,
Hoorah my lads, we're homeward bound.[1]

Following the War of 1812, New London merchants once again attempted to revive their sea going commerce. Visions of a renewed prosperity based upon West Indian trade as in the pre-Revolutionary period led many merchants to enter that industry. Little success met their efforts and not even coastal, African, European or Asian voyages stimulated business at the port.

Not until 1819 did the merchants come upon the enterprise which would provide the basis of New London's prosperity for fifty years— Daniel Deshon and Major Thomas Wheeler Williams each sent out whaling vessels that year and rapid development of the industry followed. Interestingly, the port had been active in whaling much earlier but this involvement had been very minor compared to its other maritime endeavours.

"The first ship bringing settlers to New London reportedly ran into a whale outside the harbor which so shook the ship as to cause "anxiety and the loss of a hogshead of vinegar which was staved by the impact."[2] References to hunting the whale appeared early in the town's history. A "Mr. Skillings" became associated in 1668-69 with a company organized for the purpose of whaling in boats along the coast.[3] Joshua Hempstead reported in his *Diary* that "Comfort Davise hath hire my whale boart to go a whaling . . ." in 1718.[4]

The first New London outfitting of a vessel to engage in whaling outside of Long Island Sound appeared to have taken place in 1718 when the sloop *Society* made a whaling voyage off the coast of the Carolinas. Several attempts were made to establish companies for whaling at the port following this voyage.[5]

Although one or more whalers sailed most years following 1718 no large scale operation developed as most capital and interest went into other ventures. Operation of a company organized mainly for whaling came in 1804, when Dr. Samuel H. P. Lee, the hero of the port's 1798 yellow fever epidemic established a company. He began with the ship *Dauphin* in 1805 and added the ships *Leonidas* and *Lydia* the following year. A number of successful voyages were made before the Embargo Act, Non-Intercourse Act and the War of 1812 brought a halt to maritime activity.[6]

Deshon and Williams are credited with having opened the main period of the industry at New London. In 1819 Deshon outfitted two vessels, the ship *Carrier* and the brig *Mary Ann* while Williams sent out the brig *Mary*. Although Deshon ceased operations in 1824, Williams began a company operation which continued until 1892 when it was the last whaling firm in existence.[7]

When whaling became the major industry of New London, it quickly monopolized the population and directed the way of life of nearly every family while almost all businesses became partly if not wholly dependent upon it. A few families controlled the major industries connected with whaling. Agents handled all the details of a venture—procured capital, outfitted the vessels, signed on the masters and crews, arranged for insurance on vessels, equipment and cargoes, handled all paperwork, provided funds to pay for necessary repairs and supplies in foreign areas, collected amounts owed by the investors for expenses incurred by the venture and disposed and distributed the profits to the investors and lays to the crews. Such responsibility meant the possibility of large rewards, which usually could be increased by a controlling interest in the undertaking and the operation of businesses in conjunction with whaling, such as candle and soap manufacturing, warehouses, wharves, freight lines and supplies. Additional profits might be realized by the agent through the selling of supplies to himself and his partners and by disposing of the cargo through his own firm. In short, they conducted commission and general merchandising businesses which extended to all types of commercial activity. Most agents became wealthy and prominent New London citizens, making numerous business investments, filling civic posts, often holding political offices and setting the social pace of the town.

The docks became the focal point of the town during the days of whaling. Thousands of barrels of whale oil and sperm oil, large piles of whale bone, stacks of supplies and swarms of men covered the wharves. Numerous wagons and one horse drays carried loads onto and off the docks. When whalers returned additional crowds gathered to welcome fathers, brothers, sons and husbands who had been gone for months or even years. The building of ships and whale boats; the manufacturing of casks, barrels and ship's hardware; the making of sails and the baking of bread, crackers and biscuits furnished employment to many at the port. Caulkers, riggers and ship carpenters were also in demand. Most young men were trained for occupations necessary to whaling. During the years 1718 to 1908 over sixty agents sent out 1000 vessels on 260 voyages which places New London second only to New Bedford among American whaling ports.[8]

The major firms were Williams and Haven, Williams and Barns, Lawrence and Miner, N. and W. W. Billings, Perkins and Smith, Frink-Chew-Prentis, Fitch-Learned-Stoddard and Benjamin Brown. These interests formed thirty-four different companies.[9]

The Williams' family played the most active role in the New London whaling business. This merchant family had been involved in the maritime activity of New London since the eighteenth century. Major Williams received his early business experience in New York City, Russia and England. After sending out the *Mary* in 1819 he increased his fleet rapidly in the years which followed, adding the ships *Ann Maria, Connecticut* and *Jones* in 1822; the bark *Neptune* and the ship *Stonington* in 1824; and the ship *Chelsea* in 1827; while withdrawing the *Mary* in 1824. When New London's fleet of seven vessels went out in 1827, six belonged to the William's firm.

By 1838 great success attended the firm and Williams developed quite an interest in politics. His political activities, particularly during his two terms in Congress, led to the removal of his name from the firm (1838-1846) while he remained as a silent partner. Havens and Smith, the firm which replaced T. W. Williams, included as partners—Henry P. Haven, Parker H. Smith and T. W. Williams.[10]

"Could you use a boy?" With these words, one of New London's most successful merchant careers began. Fifteen year old Henry Phileman Haven approached Major Thomas W. Williams in 1830 seeking work and became indentured for a period of six years. Although Haven contracted to work for $90 the first year, $120 the second and $150 for the rest of his indenture, hard work, ambition and shrewdness led to rapid promotion.

At fifteen, Henry Haven had already set a pattern of application of his energy and talent which led to success and wealth. Shortly after beginning work, Major William's bookkeeper's contract ended and Haven hoped to secure the post. He suffered his first and only setback in the firm when rejected. However, he applied two years later when the post once again became vacant. The firm still considered eighteen year old Haven young for the post, but offered him a trial period at the job if he did it in addition to the one he already had. This meant working until 2 A. M. and getting up at 4 A. M. to begin the next day's work. At nineteen he received the bookkeeper's post at a salary of $400 rather than $150 for which he contracted. When his apprenticeship ended at the age of twenty-one, Haven advanced to confidential clerk and two years later (1838) became a partner in the firm. He directed the outfitting of whaling vessels for the next thirty-eight years.[11]

Parker H. Smith also became a partner in 1838. He belonged to a very successful family of whaling captains. His income from whaling and other business activities allowed him to live most comfortably and to engage in an active role in civic affairs.[12]

Havens and Smith lasted only from 1838 to 1846 when Thomas W. Williams resumed active participation in the firm which became Williams and Haven. Five major partners appear to have been involved—Williams, Haven, Richard H. Chapell, Charles A. Williams and Ebenezer Morgan.

Richard H. Chapell as a young man attracted the attention of Haven who took him into his home to live and into the office of the firm to train. Chapell with the training and backing of Henry Haven became an active partner in the firm by 1855. Much of the world wide activities of the Williams and Haven firm can be directly traced to the skill and hard work of Chapell. Williams' son, Charles Augustus Williams, became a partner in 1856 and acted as agent for the firm in Hawaii for a number of years.

Another very active member of the firm, Ebenezer Morgan, began his career in whaling on a Greenlander at the age of ten. By twenty-one his skill netted him a master's berth. He made several outstanding voyages before becoming a partner. Morgan made a number of business trips around the world for the firm, especially in relation to the Alaskan seal operation.

One can imagine the pride Henry Haven must have felt in 1869 when the firm became Williams, Haven and Company as Thomas Williams Haven joined as a junior partner. Haven's son proved to have his father's energy and ability while handling the company's affairs. Unfortunately, he picked up a fever while on a business trip and died at just twenty-three in

565 tons.

296 tons.

1870. Although reorganized in 1871, the firm kept the same name Williams, Haven and Company until 1875. Thomas W. Williams died suddenly in 1874, elevating Haven to senior partner in a reorganization of the firm to Haven, Williams and Company. At the demise of Henry P. Haven, 1876, C. A. Williams took over the direction of the firm and by 1878 it became the C. A. Williams Company. This was the final successor to Thomas W. Williams and ended operations in 1892.[13]

William Williams, Jr. (1787-1870), older brother of Thomas, began his merchant career in 1806, when eighteen, as supercargo for his father. By 1827, he engaged in commercial activity in Europe and South America as well as the coastal trade. He joined with Acors Barns to form a partnership in 1827. Barns was born in Westerly, Rhode Island, son of a mariner. He

Ship Corinthian, *505 tons.*

turned to the sea and by the War of 1812 owned and operated his own vessel. After the war he operated merchant vessels out of Stonington before joining Thomas W. Williams in New London whaling activities. This led to the partnership with William Williams, Jr., which appeared rather speculative until 1832 when they established permanent facilities for their business.

In 1836, Williams, his son Thomas W. Williams II and Barns formed the firm of Williams and Barns. Although the firm continued operations until 1875, Williams and Barns left the firm in 1841 and 1858 respectively while T. W. Williams II died suddenly in 1855. William Barns and Charles Barns, sons of Acors, joined the firm in 1847 and 1856 respectively while Henry R. Bond joined in 1856.[14]

Two brothers formed a partnership in 1823 and built their firm into one of the leading whaling operations. Their father, Coddington Billings, active in the merchant trade in Stonington became connected with the Williams family in merchant and whaling ventures as well as through marriage. Coddington Billings married Eunice Williams, sister to Thomas and William Williams, Jr. William Williams Billings graduated from Yale in 1821 and entered a counting house for a time. He made a number of trips to Europe as a supercargo before joining his brother, Noyes Billings, a Yale graduate of 1819 to form a partnership. They sent out vessels from 1824 to 1851.[15]

Guiseppe Lorenzo (1788-1872) arrived at Baltimore at the age of sixteen from his native Venice. He entered the East Indian and China trade as a seaman, shipping out of Baltimore. Advancing rapidly to captain, he prospered enough to establish his own grocery and shipping business at

Savannah, Georgia. In 1814 while on one of his periodic trips to New York City for supplies, Lorenzo or Joseph Lawrence as he anglicized his name, visited New London. Impressed with the possibilities of the port, Lawrence moved to the port in 1818 and began a grocery business on John Street. He sent out a sealer in 1829 and the following year bought a wharf. Joseph Lawrence did not enter the whaling business until 1833, but despite the late date, the firm became a major one in short order. Lawrence and Company operated from 1833 to 1844, when Joseph retired and in 1845 Miner, Lawrence and Company began as a partnership of Sidney Miner (1805-1881), Francis Watson Lawrence (1821-1895), and Sebastian Duffy Lawrence (1823-1909) sons of Joseph Lawrence.[16]

Miner, from one of the oldest New London area families, worked as a clerk in the Joseph Lawrence Company offices and worked his way up to an associate member of the firm prior to joining the partnership. Very active in business and civic affairs, Miner retired from the firm in 1855 and engaged as a merchant in the coastal trade.[17]

The brothers reorganized the firm as Lawrence and Company and kept business active until 1892, although their last whaling voyage took place in 1887.[18]

One of the most interesting and for a time highly prosperous firms consisted of a partnership of Elias Perkins, Nathaniel Shaw Perkins and Captain Franklin Smith. The Shaw-Perkins brothers, brought to the firm position, contacts and the Shaw wharves, while Captain Franklin Smith possessed considerable whaling experience. He sailed for N. and W. W. Billings until several excellent voyages provided sufficient capital to join the partnership. By 1846 the firm succeeded so well that he retired from the sea. Elias Perkins represented the firm in Hawaii and N. S. Perkins ran the home office. A very successful business operation resulted. The Panic of 1857 began to undermine the firm which ceased all operations by 1861.[19]

Another important partnership included Adam Frink (1781-1859), Andrew Miner Frink (1793-1867), Ephriam M. Frink (1777-1837), Coleby Chew (1802-1850) and Adam F. Prentis. The Frinks—E. M. and A. M.—sent out whalers in 1827 and 1829 respectively before forming a partnership in 1830. The brothers—Adam, Andrew and Ephriam Frink became partners in E. M. Frink and Company 1833-1837.[20]

Coleby Chew, Ezra Chapell and John Dickinson organized the firm, Coleby Chew and Company in 1834 which lasted until 1837. In 1837 Chew joined with E. M. and A. M. Frink and Adam F. Prentis to create Frink, Chew and Company. This partnership ended with the death of Coleby

Whaling Fleet in New London Harbor, 1863.

Chew in 1850, after having already lost E. M. Frink in 1837. The last members of this firm—Frink and Prentis consisted of A. M. Frink, Adam F. Prentis, John H. Frink and Ezra C. Smith. They ended business operations in 1863.[21]

The Fitch, Learned and Stoddard interests operated whalers from 1841 to 1863. Thomas Fitch, II and Edward H. Learned sent out the *Peruvian* 1841-1843. Apparently each decided to remain in the business but separately as they ended their association in 1843. Fitch sent out whalers from 1843 to 1863. Learned sent out the *Peruvian* 1843-1844 before forming a partnership with Enoch V. Stoddard, 1844-1848. Stoddard operated alone from 1848 to 1863.[22]

The last of the major agents, Benjamin Brown operated a firm from 1830 until his death in 1849. His three sons joined the firm and after his death carried on as Benjamin Brown's sons. The sons continued the business until 1861.[23]

Regardless of the financial ability or shrewdness of the owners, the master of the vessel determined the success or failure of the voyage and therefore the success or failure of the firm. The demand at other ports for New London captains indicated the proven ability of men from the port.

No one had a more successful career as a whaling captain than Ebenezer "Rattler" Morgan (1817-1890). His long career in whaling covered forty-one years from his first voyage at the age of ten to his last at the age of fifty-one. Morgan's drive netted him a captaincy at twenty-one, while his rapid speech and "rattling" good voyages led to the name "Rattler." Captain Morgan sailed for several New London companies bringing in a number of excellent cargoes and gradually worked up to a partnership in the Williams and Haven firm. He made the best whaling voyage on record—1864-1865 in which the investment amounted to $35,800 and the cargo brought in after fifteen months sold for $150,000. Another honor for Morgan was the command of the first American steam whaler, the *Pioneer* in 1866. As a partner in the Alaskan Commercial Company, he raised the first American flag on Alaskan territory when he began the American seal fishery there. The success of Captain Morgan's career can be seen by the large—nearly $1,000,000—estate he left.[24]

John Rice (1798-1873), known as "Boney" because of a great admiration for Napoleon, spent forty years whaling—thirty-seven of them as a captain. Rice began as a greenhand in 1819 and in three years became a captain. His career paralleled the major period of New London whaling and his rise from greenhand to captain indicated the rapidity with which success could come. In his long career Rice sailed for all major New London merchants.[25]

A family record was established by five brothers all of whom became whaling captains. The Smith brothers—Franklin (1803-1874), James (1800-1877), Parker (1795-1851), Richard (1809-1884), and Robert (1794-1828) set several individual as well as a family record for whaling. They made at least thirty-five whaling voyages during the 1821-1862 period with a total return of $1,237,417.36. Two of the brothers became whaling agents—Parker in the Havens and Smith firm and Franklin in Perkins and Smith. James became owner and captain of packets between San Francisco and Hawaii. Robert died at sea and Richard appears to have retired after leaving whaling.[26]

Incredible is the only term possible for the forty-one year career of Captain John Orrin Spicer (1835-1903). On his first voyage as captain, he returned after only four months with a cargo which yielded a three hundred percent profit. Spicer became an expert on Eskimoes after spending many years living and working among them. He once won a court case by having an Eskimo family travel to New London to testify for him.

Captain Spicer hired his friend, Eskimo John Bull, and crew to kill and store blubber and bone for him. The captain caught in the ice failed to return for several months. Meanwhile two New Bedford ships arrived and informed Bull that Spicer had been lost and they wanted the cargo. When Bull refused they took the bone and blubber. Spicer returned and learned of the development. He approached the New Bedford owner and asked for payment which Spicer put at $20,000 to $25,000. The New Bedford agent said it never happened and that Spicer could go to court if he wished as there was plenty of money to fight him.

Captain Spicer hired a lawyer, brought Bull, his wife and daughter to testify as well as two Revenue Cutter officers who had been on the New Bedford vessel. The court awarded Spicer $18,000 and then the lawyer told him that he, the lawyer, had an investment in the voyage and lost by the decision but he had considered the captain in the right. When Spicer thanked the owner, he replied that there was no need to thank him "for I would not have paid it, if I was not obliged to." The Eskimoes disliked the limits of free movement in modern civilization and returned home. Never did the two men of different cultures meet again.[27]

Captain Christopher Chappell lost his vessel in Hudson's Bay in 1863. As fate would have it he was rescued by Captain J. O. Spicer, the man whose promotion to officer he had prevented some years earlier. They became fast friends on the voyage home.

Spicer's success led to a partnership in the Williams and Haven firm. After long years of service Spicer made the final voyage out of New London on a vessel owned at the port the *Era* of C. A. Williams in 1892. Upon retirement he created quite a stir with his Eskimo boots, a big sombrero, and around his neck a small vial of seal blood, which he said, lessened the pain of a series of heart attacks he suffered in his declining years.[28]

Running away to sea has passed into folklore for most boys today. James Monroe Buddington (1817-1909) began his long maritime career doing just that at the age of seventeen. While sailing for Perkins and Smith, he became world famous when he discovered the *Resolute* in the Davis Straits, one of several vessels searching for the vanished British explorer, Sir John Franklin. It had been abandoned in the ice sixteen months earlier and eleven hundred miles from where Buddington found it. He sailed it into New London harbor on Christmas Eve, 1855. The United States government decided to purchase the vessel and paid Perkins and Smith $40,000. Unfortunately, the firm failed before payment could be made to the crew and in the handling of the firm's affairs the trustees—Henry Haven, Charles Prentis and Thomas W. Perkins—apparently failed to pay Captain Buddington his share of the $40,000. In an article in *The New London Day* he blamed Henry Haven. Nevertheless, the *Resolute* was repaired, outfitted and returned to England as a gift from the United States.[29]

Buddington had the dream of many a sailor to retire to a farm and he did it not once but twice. In 1853 and again in 1860, he farmed in Illinois, but each time he returned to whaling. In fact, he did not retire until he reached the age of seventy-three.[30]

James Waterman Buddington began his career as a cabin boy on his father's famous voyage in 1855. He became a captain in 1866 and closed his long career in 1909 when he brought in the *Margaret* clean (empty), last of the vessels to whale out of New London.[31]

In its role of outfitting whaling vessels, many businesses catering to supplying the fleet, flourished; skilled craftsmen provided the tools and weapons needed; and hotels and saloons provided for the comfort of sailors. New London was a wide open town and sailors in from a trip took over. Their particular area was Water Street where plenty of entertainment existed. On the heights overlooking the harbor stood the handsome houses of the captains and agents, those elite created by oil.

Many happy reunions were held as a crowd of women and children gathered to meet returning vessels. However, returns were both happy and sad. Vessels seldom returned with all who had sailed on them and the master would often be required to report a husband's or son's death. Some, such as James A. Rogers, seemed to be doubtful about the sincerity of the reception. "All folks glad to see me, they pretended." [32] This was written March 28, 1841 after he had been away nineteen months and one week. One captain, William Hobbs, returned to port after a whaling voyage only to be informed of his wife's death. It so shocked him that he refused his pay and left the vessel, never to sail again. For many years Captain Hobbs was a part of the waterfront doing odd jobs and some fishing. Once when caught gathering milk by the owner of a herd of cows, he explained that he was just removing the overflow as "Old Billy Hobbs

HMS Resolute, *Melville Island, May 1854, caught in the polar ice and abandoned, later discovered by James Buddington.*

would never steal."[33]

Whaling agents operated other businesses especially those for dispensing of the whale products. The T. W. Williams firm sold oil and candles in the United States as well as in Europe. They generally sold to companies who retailed the products. Augustus Durand & Co. and Walles and Co. of Paris, I. & H. Rose of Charleston and J. Bradlee & Co. of Boston appeared to have been the major customers of Williams. Competition could drive the price down such as when the average price per gallon for whale oil was thirty cents and T. W. Williams was informed:

> New Bedford people anxious to sell, few gals. have been disposed here at 26 cents a gal. Whale oil is a dull seller. Yours being in very large casks we shall find them hard to sell at more than 25¢.[34]

Lyman Allyn owned a hardware store and sold parts for vessels, Abner Bassett and Williams and Barns directed iron and ship chandlery businesses, N. and W. W. Billings and Benjamin Brown manufactured soap and candles, and of course they all sold oil and bone.[35]

Sometimes crews of whalers entertained townspeople before departing as when the crew of the *Nile* marched through Main Street to a damaged drum.[36] The crews included men of all nationalities, racial backgrounds, varying social levels and educational attainments. No particular racial difficulty appeared in the records. In fact so unusual were the whalers that the presence of women meant good luck. Quite a few of the captain's wives went along with their husbands and took their children. This resulted in a number of New London Captain's children being born all over the world. On at least one occasion the practice of having a wife along led to tragedy. Captain William Beck died at sea of fever and his wife was so unhappy that she jumped overboard and drowned during a gale.[37]

Families with difficult sons often would send them on a whaling voyage. If one trip failed to cure them, a second usually took care of it. John Ross wrote to Sebastian Lawrence: "I am sorry to inform you that my son is giving me a good deal of unnecessary trouble by his bad habits, so much so that I am determined to send him on a long voyage to sea in a whaling vessel or something of the kind. . . ."[38]

One reads about slavers disguised as whalers plying their trade between Africa and America. Understandably, little evidence exists to substantiate such stories. Only one New London whaling vessel can be pointed out as a slaver. The *Fame* owned by William Tate became a slaver in 1846. While on a whaling voyage the captain died and according to law, that ended the ships articles the crew had signed. Anthony Marks, second mate, took charge as the first mate had been lost at sea and decided to undertake a slaving voyage. His brutality led many of the crew members to leave the vessel before it began its illegal operations. A whale ship averaged $16,000 a year while slavers could earn $150,000 to $200,000 on one voyage and a captain who averaged $900 a year on whalers could realize $9,000 on a slave voyage.

Marks took the vessel to Rio de Janeiro for repairs and supplies, aided by an unsuspecting United State Consul who believed the vessel would go whaling. The *Fame* went to the East coast of Africa where 530 slaves were picked up. Only three died and 527 were delivered at Cape Frio, Brazil. A five month voyage grossed Marks $40,000. The last time anyone saw the *Fame* was when it appeared at Paranagua where its appearance was altered.[39]

A suspected conversion of a whaler to a slaver took place in New London port. The bark *Laurens* became the object of suspicion when Captain Charles Prentis reported to federal officials that some rather unusual activity had been going on concerning the outfitting of the vessel. Although supposedly preparing for a whaling voyage, the crew quarters were more comfortable than usually found on a whale vessel and the food much better—beef, pork, tea, coffee, sugar, ham, butter and whiskey— items which normally were carried in very small amounts, if at all. A Boston ship broker purchased the vessel from Perkins and Smith and no Captain or mate was on board when United States agents seized it under suspicion of preparing for a slave voyage. The following March the District court dismissed the case for lack of evidence.[40]

Crews received a share of the profit rather than wages. Each signed for a lay (percentage) which depended upon his experience and number of men available. Profits would be divided in a similar fashion as listed below:

Captain	1/8	Cooper	1/60
1st Mate	1/8	Boatsteerer	1/80
2nd Mate	1/28	Steward	1/90
3rd Mate	1/36	Cook	1/100
4th Mate	1/60	Foremost Hand	1/150

A crew member's lay would be figured after all costs and owner's profit were deducted. Thus, this usually meant that 2/3 of the cargo would be required for the owners leaving 1/3 for the crew. Anything each owed the ship for money advanced, clothing, tobacco or supplies would be taken from his share. Months of hard labor could result in a very small return. Anthony Jerome sailed on the *Julius Caesar*, September, 1844 and returned three years later. His share of the 6,860 barrels of oil taken was a suit of clothes worth $8.00. Antone J. Ramis went out on the *Pearl*, Williams and Haven, for twenty-two months. He received $2.50 while his next voyage netted him nothing.[41] A voyage cost $12,000 to outfit in 1790 and $65,000 in 1850.[42]

An unfortunate event occurred in 1846 when a young whaler arrived home. He had shipped out at seventeen but upon his return he owed money and immediately shipped out again. On his second return he carried a large sum of money for his mother. That evening his shipmates found him in a bar drunk and carried him to his rooming house where he died about 11 P. M.[43]

A number of vessels had outstanding careers among the 260 of the New London fleet. The finest vessel sailing from New London and largest except for the *Atlantic* of Lawrence and Company was the *Morrison*. It was the last of Stephen Girard's vessels, built for the East Indian trade.[44] The *Pioneer*, which had been sailing out of New London on whaling voyages since 1855, was converted to a steamship in 1866 and sent out by Williams and Haven. After a successful voyage to the Davis Straits in 1866, the steamship was crushed in the ice at Hudson Bay the following year.[45]

Charles Colgate *Whale Ship.*

One of the most unusual voyages of New London was that of the *Nile,* a bark owned by Williams and Haven. It sailed May 5, 1858 and did not return until April 1869. Eleven different captains served during the eleven years. In 1865 it had to pay a sum of $45,000 to the Confederate Raider *Shenandoah* to prevent destruction.[46] Captain Slate in the *McClellan* took only one whale on a voyage but returned with 362 barrels of oil and 4,000 pounds of bone.[47]

How valuable a vessel could be can be seen from the record of the *Charles Colgate,* named after a soap manufacturer, purchased for $8,000 by Lawrence.[48] It cost $10,000 for outfitting on eleven voyages from 1860 to 1884 which grossed $423,777.

Conditions aboard whalers became unpleasant after 1830 as the greed of some owners and captains allowed for little attention to the comfort of the men. Jestin Martin quit whaling at New London and moved to Chilicothe, Ohio. When he learned his brother Charles wanted to go whaling he wrote him on November 29, 1844, describing whaling as terrible and maintained:

> . . . that it would be better . . . to be painted black and sold to a southern planter rather than be doomed to the forecastle of a whale ship. . . .

Further the brother received the warning that he would miss girls so much that the first one he would see after a voyage ". . . will look so pretty that you will bite a piece out of her cheek before you know it. . . ."[49]

Many if not most New London vessels were strictly temperance vessels, well supplied with choice and selective libraries. Thomas W. Williams, a pioneer temperance leader in New London, met with a great deal of opposition when he tried to eliminate liquor from his vessels. His shipping articles prohibited any liquor, profane language and sheath knives.[50] Beliefs in temperance received a boost when one captain arrived in port after fishing an unusual cargo out of the sea—three barrels of whiskey. Unfortunately, other than that catch the voyage proved unprofitable as few whales were taken. When the captain reported to the owners upon his return, his lack of success, unsteady hands, reddened eyes, and a number of missing entries in the log book strengthened their conviction that whiskey had no place on a whaling voyage.[51]

One captain brought back his vessel after a voyage of four years and upon being asked how much oil he brought replied "None, but we had a hell of a good sail."[52]

Letters usually reported problems or success, however, one contained a request "Dear _____, Send me by outboat Indian Chief gallons more of that cider brandy—same as you sent before—and great will be your reward"! It was signed Jones, Master of the Bark *North Star*.[53]

The industry failed to enjoy a sustained period of prosperity. After a rapid development from 1819 to 1844, the years 1845-1848 saw it reach its zenith and become second only to New Bedford. Then a series of developments from 1849 to 1871 combined to undermine the whaling business. No evidence exists that anyone perceived that trouble lay ahead for the whaling industry as 1849 began, but by the end of 1871 all could look back and see that the industry had suffered its decline from events which began that year. The gold rush of 1849, panic of 1857, Civil War, populization of kerosene, attraction of Western lands, the adoption of steam for use in vessels and the Arctic disaster of 1871 collectively sounded the end for New London whaling.

Gold caused the first decline when the rush to California attracted at least twenty-five captains and uncounted seamen from New London. So great was the demand for transportation that a number of whaling vessels were diverted to carrying passengers and supplies to California. The *Charles Carroll, Mentor, Palladium, Robert Bourne* and *Sarah Lavinia* all took part in the gold field traffic, while another six appeared to have taken part before being sold to other ports.[54] Next, the industry suffered from a lack of capital which resulted from the financial crisis of 1857 and the investment of much capital in the cotton textile industry. Perkins and Smith failed with a suddenness that shocked the town. The firm had prospered so much that nothing seemed likely to harm it. In 1857, Captain Franklin Smith brought in a cargo worth $130,000 and no less than thirteen vessels were reported on their way home with excellent cargoes. The partners held stocks, considerable real estate, a recently built hotel—Pequot House—in addition to vessels, a wharf and shipyard. The financial crisis of 1857 occurred and the firm did not have the cash resources to survive as much of the profit had gone back into the business or into other investments. Hope for recovery of the firm continued for some time, especially during 1858 when the port believed that whale and sperm oil were going to be in greater demand and the prices appeared to foretell that the future of oil was excellent.[55]

Unfortunately, kerosene began to replace oil, real estate prices fell, the hotel went bankrupt and stocks held dropped in value. When conditions failed to improve during 1858 and 1859 the firms closed down and trustees appointed by the court began to sell off its assets. Shares in various whaling vessels were sold. Thirty-five lots, a wharf and shipyard brought in $10,515.[56] Sixteen thousand dollars worth of New London, Willimantic and Palmer Railroad bonds had to be sold at a few cents on the dollar. The Railroad had never prospered and trustees had taken over in January of 1859.

To Adam Prentis	$ 1,500 @ 34 cents on the dollar
Melville Chester	1,500 @ 34 cents on the dollar
Thomas Fitch	2,000 @ 33 cents on the dollar
Acors Barns	10,000 @ 33½ cents on the dollar
S. D. Lawrence	1,000 @ 33¼ cents on the dollar[57]

A mysterious event occurred when Captain Fisher Kibbling arrived in New London with $35 but minus the bark *N. S. Perkins*. He had sailed from the port in May of 1857 for Perkins and Smith. They learned that he made a Pacific whaling voyage and entered San Francisco where he sold the cargo and whaling gear for between $8,000 and $9,000. He then signed the vessel over on charter for a year, collecting the money and took passage for New London. No one appeared to know what happened to the money. After he was arrested, Kibbling signed over his property to answer the claims against him and took a debtor's oath. After five months in jail at Hartford awaiting trial, all charges were withdrawn and he reportedly paid a sum over to the firm. He died at the age of seventy-three in 1895 and one of the local newspapers spoke of him as a plain old fashioned New England shipmaster.[58]

By 1861 the firms assets were all sold. Friends tried to put Captain Smith on the path of success again by outfitting a vessel for him. Unfortunately, the vessel was wrecked in 1862 and Captain Franklin Smith's whaling career ended.

Conditions during the Civil War hurt whaling as the shortage of capital, men and ships offset the impact of the price rise. Confederate raiders hit the industry hard as New London lost five vessels—the *Catherine, General Williams*, the *Peria*, and *William C. Nye* to the *Shenandoah* while the *Alabama* burned the *Alert*. A sixth vessel, the *Electra* went down as a result of a collision with the *Nile* of New London.[59] Gideon Welles became convinced that a rapid method of blockading southern ports could be found in the sinking of vessels loaded with stone in the channels of major ports. In seeking out vessels, Richard H. Chapell and Henry Haven suggested idle whalers and Chapell acted as agent in purchasing vessels and stone. Eleven of the forty-five whaling vessels in the two stone fleets came from New London. However, only seven had been outfitted from New London before the Civil War.[60]

By 1859 New London's Fleet had been reduced to 59 vessels. New London sold or withdrew eighteen vessels from whaling 1859-1865, another sixteen were wrecked or condemned in that period and Confederate Raiders and the Stone Fleet took care of twelve. Thus, the fleet had been reduced by forty-six vessels while adding twelve. As a result of this rapid decline, the New London fleet of eighty-one in 1845, numbered only twenty-five in 1865.[61]

After the war, crews were scarce, costs of outfitting had increased greatly, and three new factors had entered the whaling picture—kerosene, steam whalers and the shift of whaling to the Pacific. New London's sailing vessels could no longer compete and its days were numbered. A final blow for many came in 1871 when thirty-nine captains ignored warnings from Eskimoes and lost their vessels, outfits and cargoes to the amount of

$2,000,000. New London lost three vessels—the *J. D. Thompson*, *Monticello* and *Paiea Kohola* (New London owned-Hawaiian Registry), one-third of her whaling fleet.[62]

As whaling declined two other closely connected industries became important. Williams and Haven began a new line of business when a partner of the firm discovered guano deposits on the Phoenix Island. Haven organized a new firm, the Phoenix Guano Company, with headquarters at New London to handle the guano business in 1859. Southern markets were large until the Civil War, but Haven, always aggressive,, ordered the guano to Europe where it took an investment of $100,000 before a market began to develop. When Europeans accepted guano the European market then absorbed all that could be shipped. A total of 70,000 tons were shipped to Europe for a gross return of approximately $2,000,000.[63]

Sealing, long engaged in by New Londoners, became of major importance with the purchase of Alaska. Unlimited world killing of the seals had left only the Russian Islands of St. Paul and St. George with large numbers of fur seals. Henry Haven, Richard H. Chapell, Ebenezer Morgan and Charles A. Williams organized the Alaskan Commercial Company and received a lease for exclusive sealing operations. A Pacific headquarters for the company was opened at San Francisco with a fleet based at Honolulu for freight connections with New London. From 1870 to 1890 the company paid the United States government over $10 million.[64]

By 1878 decay and idleness prevailed along the once active wharves as whaling days drew to a close. Just a few vessels docked in the harbor and those remained a sad lot. New London did outfit *Ponces* and *Fanny* for the Chilean War but not for whaling. The decline did not come upon everyone as a surprise. In 1855 the *New London Star* expressed fears of the declining whaling industry of New London in reporting about the growing importance of the Pacific as the center of industry. *The New London Chronicle* rejected this and pointed out that New London agents had established branches in the Pacific but continued to operate from the port. Whale products were collected and shipped from the Hawaiian Islands. Two other articles in the same paper denied the decline.[65] However, despite any denial by 1891 the city was in deep depression with ships rotting at its wharves. Whaling, which made New London world famous, had been abandoned by 1892. Most fortunes at the port came from whaling and as it declined, the families failed to branch out into other industries.

Captain James W. Buddington bought the *Rosa Baker* in 1899 and made an attempt to renew the industry. Hopes were high, the voyage appeared

Mariner's Bank
"Whaling Exhibit", 1920's.

to be going well when misfortune struck and the vessel was lost. The last whaling vessel to sail from New London was the *Margaret* (October 12, 1909). It made voyages from New Bedford after that, but no more from New London. Admiral Billard Academy was able to try 250 barrels of oil from a whale washed ashore on Pequot Avenue, March, 1944. Perhaps the last "whaling" done in New London.[66]

The closing years of the nineteenth century found the old whaling captains setting out on their final voyages. Each year one read of the exploits of one or more of these men from a once glorious period of New London history now only a memory. Snug Harbor on Staten Island became the final port for most. It had been established by Captain Robert R. Randall for "aged, decrepit, and wornout sailors." Alexander Hamilton drew up Randall's will providing for this home.[67]

At least one merchant tried to provide for his employees in their old age. T. W. Williams established a fund in 1870 which paid $10 a month and later $15 to ex-whalers. In 1930 fifty were receiving these checks. Few outside those concerned were even aware that the fund existed.[68]

A proud era ended for New London with the close of the whale industry. Still many monuments of those once proud days can be seen about the port—the public library (Henry P. Haven), Lawrence Hospital (Sebastian Lawrence), Williams Park (Williams Family), Lyman Allyn Museum (daughter of Captain Lyman Allyn), and Soldiers and Sailors Monument (Sebastian Lawrence). A reminder of the whaling past could be found at the Mariners Saving's Bank until it closed its doors. Captain Thomas Peterson executed paintings showing the industry and a collection of whaling items represented a small museum open to the public during business hours. At present whaling murals can be seen in the lobby of the New London post office.

A sad reminder for many years was the rotting hulk of the *Charles Colgate* in Winthrop's Cove. A sad spectacle of a once fine sailing vessel.

6 Financial and Insurance Institutions 1791-1973

Merchant activities at the port necessitated the development of a financial system which would be capable of meeting the day-to-day requirements of the New London business community. It was natural that the need would be met by the organizational ability of the merchants themselves. Between 1792 and 1972 no fewer than seventeen financial institutions were organized and chartered with merchant leadership and monetary backing:

1791-1811	Union Bank
	New London Bank
1812-1860	Savings Bank of New London
	Whaling Bank
	Pequot Bank
	Bank of Commerce
	New London County Savings Bank
	Mechanics and Farmers Association & Bank
1861-1900	First National Bank
	Equitable Trust Company
	Mariners Savings Bank
	Dime Savings Bank
	New London Trust Company
1901-1929	New London Trust and Safe Deposit Company
	New London Building and Loan Association
	Winthrop Trust Company
1930-1973	New London Federal Savings & Loan Assoc.

Maritime and industrial developments of the port required institutions to handle the financing needed as well as to handle the large sums accruing to the firms accounts.

1791-1811

Merchants dominated as stockholders and officers of the institutions chartered. They established one of the earliest banks in the United States and the first in operation in Connecticut. Only five other banks were then operating in the country:

> Bank of North America (Philadelphia) 1782
> Bank of Massachusetts (Boston) 1784
> Bank of New York (New York City) 1784
> Providence Bank (Providence) 1791
> Bank of the United States (Philadelphia) 1791[1]

Since the State of Connecticut would allow only one bank in the New London County, the merchants of New London and Norwich established the Union Bank at New London because they considered it the best location. Three Connecticut banks received charters from the General Assembly in 1792—the Union Bank, the Hartford Bank and the New Haven Bank—only the New London Bank was in operation prior to the granting of the charter.[2]

On February 1, 1792, an organizational meeting took steps to acquire a charter and chose a committee to solicit subscription for $100,000. This amount had been pledged by 157 individuals by March 5 and at a meeting in Ephrian Minor's Tavern a board of directors was chosen consisting of New London and Norwich merchants—General Jedidiah Huntington, Marvin Wait, Guy Richards, William Steward, Edward Hallam, Joseph Perkins, Joshua Lathrop, Joseph Howland, Joseph Williams, Daniel L. Coit, Samuel Woodbridge, George Phillip and Samuel Wheat.[3] General Jedidiah Huntington, president, launched the bank on a very successful career. It operated out of a rented room at Hallam and Water Streets until 1818 when the bank constructed a stone building at 61 State Street for its growing operations.

John Hallam, a silversmith and jeweler, became the bank's first cashier. In the early years of American banking the cashier became the most important official of the institution. He received deposits, approved loans, collected interest and protected funds of the banks. Depending upon the amount of funds in his keeping, the treasurer kept them on his person,

*General Jedediah
Huntington,
1743-1818.*

*The Union Bank,
State Street.*

under his pillow or in a chest.[4] Union Bank cashiers must have been extremely astute as dividends were paid beginning March of 1793. By 1892 some 832 and ¾% had been returned on the original investments with 261 regular and extra dividends paid by 1921.[5]

Success could have an unfavorable side also. Banks issued their own currency and unfortunately these notes did not always prove difficult to copy. A ring in New York City passed counterfeit $5.00 bills on the bank in 1857 and again in 1859. In 1865 the institution became a national bank and operated as the Union National Bank until 1882 when it returned to a state charter. The bank received permission to engage in a Trust business in 1913 and it became the Union Bank and Trust Company.[6] No history of New London's oldest bank would be complete without mentioning the names of J. Lawrence Chew, Alfred Coit, Carlos Barry and Joseph A. Stanners all of whom assisted in the growth of this financial institution. On August 5, 1963 the Union and Trust Company merged with the Connecticut Bank and Trust Company becoming the Union New London office of Connecticut Bank and Trust Company.

Successful operation of the first bank and expanded merchant activity led to the formation of a second bank. In 1807 a number of New London merchants announced that the need for new capital to conduct the West Indian trade and to aid in the development of whaling required another bank. Elisha Denison and Captain Edward Chappell directed the application for a charter. The Union Bank agreed that it would not oppose the move. New London with a population of 3,000 became the first Connecticut town to have two banks with the granting of a charter in May of 1807 to the New London Bank. There were only five others in the state —one each in Bridgeport, Hartford, Middletown, New Haven and Norwich.[7]

Included among the first merchant directors were: Edward Chappell, Elisha Denison, William Williams, Edward Hallam, Elias Perkins, Isaac Thompson, Jacob B. Gurley, Cushing Ellis and William Noyes. Under Elias Perkins' presidency the bank began operations in rented quarters. In 1820 a bank building was constructed.[8]

As early as 1811 counterfeit five dollar bills on the New London Bank were being passed. These appeared to have been thicker and much darker than legal bills but apparently succeeded.[9] On November 14, 1855, five men were surprised in the bank by two citizens. The robbers fled yelling

*Two-shilling and six-pence printed
by Timothy Green, June 1780.*

*Paper five-cent piece issued
by the Whaling Bank.*

fire and leaving behind their kit of tools. Three more robbers in an office above the bank also fled. Only one of the eight was caught—John William.[10]

In 1861 the New London Bank offered the Governor $25,000 to be used during the war. The Bank received a charter as a national bank in 1865 and became the New London City National Bank.[11] Located at the corner of Bank and Golden Streets, the Bank served the public until 1953 when it merged with the Hartford National Bank and Trust Company. After the merger with the Hartford National Bank and Trust Company permission was obtained from the banking authorities to move the so-called New London City Office to a new building located at the New London Shopping Center off Vauxhall and Colman Streets,' thus vacating the structure at the corner of Bank and Golden Streets. Later, this building was purchased by the First New London Savings and Loan Association since they desired larger quarters.

1812 - 1860

During the War of 1812 the banks moved their records and funds to Norwich for safety.[12] After their return at the end of the war, renewed merchant activity, especially the whaling industry required additional banking facilities. No safe or convenient place existed for the deposit of savings, especially small amounts. Seamen, having no safe place for their funds, were often robbed or spent their money for drink and then could not buy food or lodging. They had no encouragement to save for their old age. To meet with those needs, New London became the home of a third bank, The Savings Bank of New London, the fourth savings bank established in Connecticut.[13] The incorporators, connected with the whaling business, included William P. Cleaveland, Robert Coit, Isaac Thompson, Archibald Mercer, Nathaniel Shaw Perkins, Ebenezer Learned, Ephrain Cheeseborough, Jirah Isham, Nathaniel Saltonstall, Peter Richards, Increase Wilson, Thomas West, Guy Turner, Ezra Chappell, William P.

The Savings Bank of New London.

Cleaveland, Jr., Charles I. Stockman, Thomas Williams, Jacob B. Gurley and Edward Learned.[14]

Ebenezer Learned became the first president and the bank opened for business using rooms of the Union Bank, July 1, 1827. Robert Coit, treasurer, accepted deposits of $2.00 to $200.00 from each person on the first and third Mondays from 10 A.M. to 12 Noon only. Interest was paid beginning in 1828—5%, but one had to have at least $5.00 on deposit to receive this. Coit's first depositor, July 2, 1827, Robert Jones, a Black, deposited $10.00. The first loan was made in July of 1827 for $195.[15]

Although operating very cautiously the bank suffered a large loss when the New London, Willimantic and Palmer Railroad underwent reorganization and the $10,000 worth of bonds held could only be redeemed for fifty cents on the dollar.[16]

An attempt to rob the bank took place in January of 1877. Four men arrived in town during late December 1876 and aroused suspicion when they began to examine the Savings Bank. One was observed opening a door of the bank with a key. Bank officials when apprized of the situation hired Captain James F. Smith to keep watch. He decided that the four men planned to rob the bank on January 10 and he hid in the office at noon that day. Smith had only an old gun which would not fire. Only Charles Brown was seized when the four attempted to rob the bank. Captain Smith later received a card postmarked New York City—"Beware how you testify a word to the wise is sufficient if you ever come to New York you will get a head put on you".

An attempt to "break" Brown out of jail occurred when John Preston of New London was offered $25.00 for wax impressions of the jail keys. After he delivered the impressions, he informed police who were waiting when Brown used the keys to get out of jail. William MacKay, supposedly Brown's New York counsel, visited New London several times. It turned out that he was Canada MacKay, a notorious forger, who probably had been one of the original four robbers. Brown (Shell Hamilton) received a sentence to Wethersfield Prison in September of 1877.[17]

Over its long history as a part of the town's business community, the Savings Bank could always be counted on to support financially the country, state and town. During the Civil War, World War I and II the bank purchased government securities, war bonds of the states, victory bonds, liberty bonds, savings bonds and defense bonds. Also the Bank supported the town by buying municipal bonds.

The Savings Bank moved into its own building in 1852 on Main Street, where in the following years, additions were made until 1903-1905 when the entire building was enlarged and remodeled. A school Savings Department began in 1917 and a Savings Club in 1920.[18] An unusual development took place in 1924 when twenty businessmen each put $10.00 in the Savings Bank at 4% interest, compounded semi-annually as a fund for the town. It is not to be removed until the $200 reaches $20,000,000 in 2214.[20] From these small beginnings and under the capable leadership of such presidents as William H. Chapman, William Belcher and Charles E. White, the bank developed into a sound financial institution with deposits of $20,000,000 by July 2, 1927.

Another expansion of the building began in 1930 with new vaults and teller area. The improvements completed in 1931 took care of its needs through World War II and the Korean War. By 1972 increased business requirements led to three branch offices and a three level addition costing $1,000,000. At the distinguished age of 145 years assets totalled $118,805,421.55.[19] Today the magnificent building represents an institution which has grown with the town, providing increased services as New London and vicinity had need of them.

Increased whaling activities led the leading whaling agents and investors to organize a new banking institution in 1832. Appropriately named the Whaling Bank of New London, it opened for business in 1833. The organizers of the new bank included: Peter C. Turner, W. Weaver, Abner Bassett, C. Wilson, Lyman Law, S. Ingham, J. Lawrence, John Brandegee, Noyes Billings and William W. Billings.[21] The bank operated from a building on Bank Street beginning under the guidance of Coddington Billings as president and Peter C. Turner as treasurer.[22] The Lawrence family appeared to have control of the institution with Joseph and his sons Joseph Jeremiah, Sebastian and Francis serving as directors. Sebastian served for over forty-five years as president of the bank and planned that it would end with his death. However, the officials decided to remain in business and continued operations until 1943. After 110 years of service the stockholders voted to place the bank at 42 Bank Street in voluntary liquidation January of 1943.[23]

A notice appeared in the *New London Daily Chronicle*, February 7, 1851 that a new bank, Pequot, would be seeking power of incorporation from the General Assembly with a capital of $500,000 and the right to increase it to $1,000,000. Nothing more appeared.[24]

Whaling interests also established the fifth financial institution—The Bank of Commerce—in 1852. It proved to be an undertaking in which many had confidence. Originally planned to be capitalized at $50,000 that amount was reached in just four days and subsequent figures of $100,000 and $150,000 were also easily realized so that by July of 1853 the capitalization was established at $200,000. The first board included: Acors Barns, Henry P. Haven, Daniel Latham, F. W. Holt, G. L. Ford, Lyman Allyn, Martin K. Cady, Benjamin F. Brown and Charles W. Strickland.[25]

Control of the bank appeared to have been by the Williams and Barns firm in general and the Barns family in particular. From 1852 to 1902 the presidents of the institution were of that family:

Acors Barns	1852-1862
William H. Barns	1862-1886
Charles Barns	1886-1902[26]

Charles Butler, the cashier, opened business in the Williams and Haven Offices. The first day's business amounted to $11,000. Later the Bank moved to the second story of the Union Bank building and remained there until 1872 when the business relocated in the Crocker House building. There a fire and burglar proof vault protected securities.[27] The Bank of Commerce became a national bank as a result of the passage of the National Bank Act of 1863. It received from the Comptroller of the Currency on January 2, 1865 papers authorizing it to commence business under a new charter and also under a new name—The National Bank of Commerce. A new building costing $150,000 became the bank's home in 1922 at 250 State Street. The National Bank of Commerce in 1953 with assets of over $17,000,000., and a branch office in Mystic, Connecticut, merged with the Hartford National Bank and Trust Company to become its Commerce Office in the City, which office became its headquarters for the Southeastern Connecticut area.[28] Much of the success and growth of this bank may be attributed to such men as William H. Reeves and Earle W. Stamm who served as presidents for many years.

A new savings bank, the New London County Savings Bank appeared to have had the same personnel as the Whaling Bank and shared its quarters. With a capitalization of $125,000 it was organized in 1855. Joshua Bolles served as president, Albert Ramsdale—vice president and Joseph C. Douglas—secretary-treasurer. Joseph Lawrence later became vice-president and still later, president. The directors included: Robert Coit, Jr., Francis W. Lawrence, S. D. Lawrence, W. W. Billings, W. A. Weaver, J.

N. Harris, Acors Barns, Sidney Miner, W. Miner, Lyman Allyn, Augustus Brandegee, John Brandegee, Andrew Lippitt, Joshua Bolles, Peter Turner, William H. Starr, and Thomas Ramsdale. It appeared to have ceased operations around 1857.[29]

The Mechanics and Farmers Association and Bank started April 7, 1855 with a capital of $100,000. Deposits were to be handled by the treasurer of the Bank of Commerce. Officers handling the bank's business were E. Chappell—president, William B. Benjamin—vice president, and Charles Butler—secretary-treasurer. Directors included: E. Chappell, H. P. Haven, Philip Morgan, William Stearne, M. K. Cady, Daniel Lathrop, Increase Wilson, A. M. Frink, Henry Hobart, William P. Benjamin, N. S. Perkins, Cortland Starr, J. N. Harris, Charles Prentice, Thomas Fitch II, Acors Barns and E. V. Stoddard. The organization appeared to have remained in operation until 1858.[30]

1861 - 1900

No new major developments in New London's financial history came until the Civil War. Northern financial developments had been hampered by a lack of a stable currency. To remedy this the National Bank Act created a system of national banks which would issue currency, printed at Washington, signed by the president and cashier of each bank. Although a Connecticut group was the first to apply and receive a charter, it was from New Haven not New London. New London's first bank to be chartered under the new act was the First National Bank in 1864. That same year the Bank of Commerce received a national charter. In 1865 the Union Bank, New London City Bank and the Whaling Bank all gave up their state charters for national charters.[31]

The First National Bank stayed in operation only thirteen years. Its directors and officers included: Frank B. Loomis (president), Henry Hobert (vice president), Edward Prentis, P. C. Turner (cashier), C. Arnold Weaver and J. Newcomb. In fact the bank was a one man concern. Francis B. Loomis owned nearly all the capital stock and directed its affairs from organization to the close of operations. Loomis received government deposits of over $4,000,000 and sold several issues of government bonds—$20,000,000 worth. Returns on the investment of Loomis reached twelve percent most years.

In 1877 Loomis sold the bank to the New London Bank which by then operated as the New London City National Bank. The latter only had $15,000 on deposit and received $90,000 which the Loomis bank held plus $10,000 which William H. Rowe brought in. Rowe became cashier of the New London City National Bank.[32]

Two financial institutions were established in 1867—the Equitable Trust Company and the Mariners Savings Bank. The Equitable Trust Company had $1,000,000 in capital. Jonathan Edwards of New York was president, Henry Bond secretary-treasurer and directors included Charles Barns, Henry Bond, Augustus Brandegee, Robert Coit, Jr., Henry P. Haven, J. N. Harris and John Jacob Astor. Officials operated from the Mariners Savings Bank. The declining fortunes of the port saw a reduced financial activity. In 1881 the Equitable Trust Company went out of business.[33]

The Mariners Savings Bank, founded by merchants connected with whaling, received a state charter in May of 1867 and began operations in July using office space in the National Bank of Commerce. Among merchants organizing the bank were Captain Daniel Latham, first president; Henry Haven, vice-president; Ebenezer Morgan; and Thomas M. Waller. The bank proved to be prosperous and innovative declaring its first dividend in 1868, as well as pioneering in night banking and thrift programs. In 1872 it moved to the Crocker House block and finally into its own building at 224 State Street in 1903.[34]

The Mariners Savings Bank deposits reached $100,000 by 1875 even with the depressed conditions following the Civil War. The bank encouraged individuals to purchase their own homes by providing them with twelve sets of plans for one family houses including the names of seven local builders and contractors who would build them for $3,500.

A deposit box developed by P. LeRoy Harwood, an executive officer of the bank, allowed the institution to begin providing twenty-four hour service in 1926. The bank building itself was a museum and huge murals of whaling and sealing scenes hung on the walls. The banks operations ceased in 1939 due to the actions of several of the executive officers. Harwood, vice president and treasurer committed suicide August 3, 1939 and an investigation by the State Bank Department disclosed shortages in the bank's accounts. The trustees of the Savings Bank of New London after negotiations agreed to merge with the Mariners Savings Bank. No loss was suffered by any depositors as the Bonding Company and Mutual Savings Bank Central Fund covered all accounts. The collection of the whaling industry objects located in the museum were turned over on a loan basis to the Marine Historical Society in Mystic, Connecticut.[35]

A third savings bank began operations in 1873, The Dime Savings Bank. It went out of business in 1882. New London Trust Company was founded in 1874. It accepted no deposits or trust accounts and limited business to loans on western real estate.[36]

Despite the economic difficulties of 1883, 1890 and 1893 during which there were business or economic panics and bank failures, New London banks were able to carry on business as usual. The banks were fortunate in securing clerks possessing fine penmanship and skilled in the use of figures since all records were kept by hand. All correspondence was hand written and adding machines were not used until 1894 in the city banks.

1901 - 1929

The New London Trust and Safe Deposit Company received a state charter in 1904. Incorporators included: A. Brandegee, Robert Coit, Benjamin A. Armstrong, A. H. Chappell, B. F. Mahan, Frederick S. Newcomb, Walter C. Noyes and William J. Brennan. Capitalization was to be $50,000 which would be increased to $150,000. No record of actual business operations exist, although as late as 1921 the incorporators requested an extension of time so that they could finish organizing and open for business.[37]

With the enactment of the Federal Reserve Act which became law December 23, 1913, the three remaining national banks in New London—New London City National Bank, National Bank of Commerce and the National Whaling Bank—were required to join the system.

A financial institution directed towards aiding in the purchasing of homes was organized January 21, 1914. Known as the New London Building and Loan Association it specialized in mortgage lending. The incorporators included Henry R. Bond, Jr., James A. May, Walter A. Smith and Simon L. Ewald. Henry R. Bond served as first president and J. Humphrey as first secretary. A number of different locations served as "home base" from 1914 to 1961 when the building then being used at Bond and Golden Streets was purchased. This had been the home of the New London City National Bank. The name changed in 1964 to the First New London Savings and Loan Association. Assets reached $8,666,000 in 1973.

A group of New London citizens secured a charter from the state in 1921 to organize a new commercial bank. Known as the Winthrop Trust Company, it began business in the Morning Telegraph office, January 10, 1922 with a capital of $100,000. P. LeRoy Harwood served as president, E. E. Rogers as vice president and Harry E. Hastings as secretary-treasurer. The office was located at 302 State Street, the Dewart Building. After fifty years the Winthrop Trust Company merged with the

Union Trust Company of New Haven in 1972 and became the Winthrop office of that bank.[38]

1930 - 1973

Not until 1930 were the banks able to develop a closer harmony among themselves through the creation of a Clearing House Association. At a meeting on May 27, 1930 held at the Union Bank and Trust Company representatives of the seven local banks agreed to create a clearing house and elected Joseph A. Stanners (Union Bank and Trust Company) president, Earle W. Stamm (National Bank of Commerce) vice president, Edward S. Huntley (Winthrop Trust Company) secretary and Alfred D. Forbes (New London City National Bank) treasurer.

The depression brought about new pressures and forced many changes. By 1932 with money tight city officials were forced to request financial aid from the banks. After presenting the city's request for a $300,000 loan on May 9, 1932 at a Clearing House Meeting, the member banks agreed to the request in the following manner:

Savings Bank of New London	$125,000
National Bank of Commerce	50,000
Union Bank and Trust	50,000
Mariners Savings Bank	25,000
National Whaling Bank	25,000
New London City National Bank	25,000
	$300,000

Despite the panic and large scale bank failures throughout the country, New London Banks were able to carry on their normal business until Saturday March 4, 1933. On that date the Governor closed all state banks. March 6 the Federal Government closed all banks—State and National. Ten days later the banks were allowed to reopen. The Winthrop Trust Company alone of the Commercial Banks had restrictions placed upon its transactions until August 31, 1933. When the banking act of 1933 created the Federal Deposit Insurance Corporation's three National Banks and the Winthrop Trust Company joined thus insuring their savings and commercial accounts. Since the Union Bank and Trust Company operated under a state charter it was not required to insure its accounts and decided not to do so. The Reconstruction Finance Corporation strengthened the Winthrop Trust Company through the purchase of $75,000 first preferred stock. For the protection of the savings banks the Mutual Savings Bank's Central Fund was organized.

The New London Federal Savings and Loan Association was organized by several people involved with building activities in order to promote home ownership. Organized on September 5, 1935, its first officers were William W. Miner—president, A. Graham Creighton—vice-president, Henry L. Bailey, Jr.—treasurer, and John Sexton—secretary. It began business in an office on Meridian Street. After several years of growth and prosperity, it moved into new offices on Masonic Street in 1951. A merger with the Mystic Savings and Loan Association provided a branch office there and the Association has established others in Groton, Niantic and Waterford.[39] Successful operations had resulted in assets of $87,000,000 by 1973.

During World War II all banks took part in the sale of war bonds. They made loans to corporations based on their war contracts in order for them to develop the facilities necessary to the manufacturing of war materials. When sugar, coffee, meats and gasoline were rationed the banks handled the ration accounts for those customers engaged in retail trade. The extension of hours with Saturday afternoon openings later replaced by Friday evening openings aided the war workers and servicemen. On December 1, 1943 the New London City National Bank opened a facility at the Electric Boat Company for the convenience of the workers at the plant and the sailors aboard the submarines at the shipyard. It was closed at the end of the war.

No aspect of New London's development better shows the ability and sound business leadership than banking. In war and peace, good times and bad, the financial institutions endured and aided, yes and even led in the town's growth. They showed their strength after the 1929 Crash when not one New London bank went under despite thousands which did so in the country in 1930-31, some Connecticut banks closed, twelve into receivership by 1932 and three more failed in 1933. The innovative banking services indicate the lack of the usual staid conservative banker in the city. It seems safe to say that whatever success New London enjoys today more than a little is owed the banking business 1791-1973.

Insurance

New London supported a number of insurance companies during the nineteenth century. Some flourished for a number of years, but all ended with the demise of whaling. Early insurance companies were organized to handle marine risks. In 1805 the Union Insurance Company of New London received a charter from the state and was one of five in operation

at the time—all dealing with marine insurance. Capital of the Union
Insurance Company was to be $100,000 with an increase to $150,000
authorized if needed. Only ten percent cash was required to be paid in two
installments—the other $90,000 could be in notes secured and unsecured.
One can see how little actual cash was required to begin a business operation during this period. As the shares were $200 each, only fifty had to be
sold.

The petition to incorporate the Union Insurance Company at New
London had been submitted by Jared Starr and others and received
approval in October of 1805.[40] Jared Starr became president and David
Coit secretary. The nine directors included: Jared Starr, Elisha Denison,
Jonathan Hurlbut, Edward Hallam, William Williams, Jacob B. Gurley,
Isaac Thompson and Richard Douglas II. By the late 1820's whaling
merchants such as T. W. Williams and W. W. Billings began to assume
directorships in the company. During the 1830's the company ended
operations.

A second company petitioned for incorporation in 1818, the Thames
Insurance Company (marine insurance), by James Mitchell and others.
Approval came in October of 1818.[41] No record of its operation exists.

The Fire and Marine Insurance Company received approval with
$250,000 capital in 1831. The company ceased business operations in
1842.

Whaling interests organized the New London Marine Insurance Company with $100,000 capital in 1847. Colby Chew served as president and E.
H. Learned secretary. The directors included: Colby Chew, T. W. Williams II, Thomas Fitch II, Benjamin Brown, Henry P. Haven, Elias Perkins and Lyman Allyn. Operations ceased in 1849.

Thus New London's first four insurance companies covering the period
from 1805 to 1849 all concerned themselves with the sea and all failed to
flourish. A number of companies failed to operate after being granted a
charter. In the days of whaling despite the volume of available business
New London companies enjoyed little success and out of town companies
received the policies.

Fire hazards led to the organization of companies to meet this need.
Again New London companies appeared to have little success in develop-
ing prosperous enterprises. The Norwich Fire Insurance Company ap-
peared to have many of the New London businessmen as directors—Jacob
Gurley, Isaac Thompson, John Mitchell and Henry P. Haven. The New
London County Mutual Fire Insurance Company directors included:
Increase Wilson and Joseph Lawrence.

An early attempt at health insurance came in 1852 with the Mechanics and Workingmans Mutual Benefit Association at New London—offices at 25 State Street. Although local companies failed to survive, local agents handled most of the companies which existed and thus offered the various types of protection needed.[42]

7 Business and Industrial New London in War and Peace 1784 - 1973

Since its beginning in 1645, New London lacked major industries other than those connected with the sea. This does not mean that the port town lacked industrial establishments—on the contrary, there has been a rather long and varied history of companies and products. Some of these remained in business for over a hundred years, but none developed into an organization that could in volume of business or employment, rival the maritime industries and activities.

Many who contributed so much to the town's life represented retail businesses, particularly in the 1784-1827 period, when no factory existed in town. Early businesses consisted of stores designed to meet the needs of the town's retail trade. Thus, shops selling dry goods, provisions, shoes, drugs and gold and silver items early dotted the streets of the settlement. Also, as a port with people gathering to deliver or pick-up goods from many vessels, hotels, boarding houses, taverns and places of amusements were common.

By 1774 a shortage of land existed and the available farmland under the agricultural methods of the day would not support a larger population. Increasingly young men had to find other means beside farming to make a living. This meant going to sea, working with a maritime connected industry, clerking in retail business, becoming a craftsman or after 1827 working in a factory or mill.

Chief among those which contributed so much to the growth and economic development of the town are: Wilson Manufacturing Company, Boss Cracker Company, Albertson and Douglas Machine Company, Sheffield Dentifrice Company, New England Collapsible Tube Company,

Brown Cotton Gin, Palmer Brothers Company Mills, New London Steam Woolen Mill, Pequot Chemical Company, Rogers Ice Company, H. A. Brown & Company (Canning Company), Columbia Steam Saw Mill, Brainerd & Armstrong Company, Babcock Printing Company, Hopson & Chapin Manufacturing Company, D. E. Whiton Machine Company, Bingham Paper Box Company and R. T. Palmer Company.

1784 - 1827

Two colonial crafts which remained in demand at New London concerned clockmaking and silversmithing. No fewer than six craftsmen built clocks from 1769 to 1792: James Watson, Samuel Post, Ezra Dodge, Gurdon Tracy, Jonathan Trout and William Cleveland. There were twenty-two individuals and firms engaged in silversmithing after 1784. Their numbers proved far too many for the business and from 1790 to 1820 an acute depression forced many to leave the profession. By 1835 the modern jewelry store with its manufactured articles replaced the craftsman in his small shop.[1]

Three establishments provided quarters for those visiting or passing through. Reopened in 1785, the City Coffee House on Main Street became a meeting place for the leading men of the city. Here one could learn the latest news and stories as well as enjoy "choice Maderna, Lisbon and Port wines". Dr. S. H. P. Lee ran the Steamboat Boarding House and "Promises to keep up reputation of a Genteel Boarding House, both for Fashionable Strangers and City Borders."[2] The Union Coffee House on Bank Street run by Captain Elijah Bingham became more famous as the place where the yellow fever epidemic began in 1798 than as an eating and boarding spot.

No major industry except marine developed prior to the War of 1812. During the war little activity took place in any field of endeavour. Once peace came, the postwar development included beginnings of the factory system. Postwar activity and prosperity failed to match or even approach pre-revolutionary levels by 1826 even though New London's great whaling day lay just ahead. Population had reached an excess of 3,500 including 300 Blacks of whom six were slaves.[3]

1827 - 1860

New London's first manufacturing began in 1827 when Increase Wilson established a factory to produce coffee mills. At first Wilson operated a hardware store where he began to manufacture wood screws and coffee mills of his own invention. Finding he could sell more coffee mills than he could produce while in the hardware business, Wilson sold the store so he could devote full time to the mills. Four buildings on Washington Street housed the plant and in 1832 William Albertson, in charge of the machine shop, introduced steam power.

Workers were paid seventy-five cents to $1.25 if men and twenty to fifty cents if boys per day. Capital at the beginning amounted to $8,000 and sales from $10,000 to $15,000 a year. When the patent for the coffee mill ran out, hardware manufacturing became the major item of business. The firm produced hardware for whaling vessels until 1853. Profits increased rapidly over the years.[4]

One type of hardware Wilson refused to manufacture was shackles for slaves. Politically he believed the Free Soil the only party to support. He kept to himself and constantly worked on methods to improve products and production, thus the townspeople did not have much familiarity with him.

A large number of men who directed businesses began their careers at Wilson's. These included William Albertson, Artemas Douglas, Peter Galleher, John Comstock, Giles and Leonard Dart. Many found it such a good place that they worked from youth to old age at Wilson Manufacturing. Factories paid wages when employees needed them. There were no regular paydays and the Company held part of their pay for months or even years. This provided a safe place when banks would not accept small amounts and besides banks were more likely to fail. Any worker could receive wages due at anytime.[5]

Increase Wilson married Rachel Wright Fox in 1810 and they had five sons and six daughters. In 1817, Wilson joined the First Congregational Church. Only one of the five sons lived to old age. The first born, George Childs Wilson, was a talented outgoing admirable person. Not only did he join the business, but he became active in the Connecticut State Militia and politics. At the age of twenty-one he became a colonel, at twenty-two a brigadier general and at twenty-six a major general. After being a member of the Conecticut House of Representatives and elected mayor at the age of twenty-seven, George C. Wilson, (the youngest to ever hold the office) suddenly sailed on the *Palladium* for a long whaling cruise to the Indian Ocean. The whaler left port on July 17 and Wilson travelling for reasons of health died a few days after sailing. The craft returned with his dead body by the 27th.[6]

Increase Wilson's other business ventures included joining with others to organize the Savings Bank of New London in 1827. He also developed a reservoir from springs on his property and piped water along Golden Street to the wharves of Miner, Lawrence and Company and Frink and Prentis as well as to some stores along Bradley Street.

The Wilson family purchased the Captain Elisha Hinman house and lived in it until 1897 when the family sold it to the United States government for a Post Office site. Colonel Increase Wilson died December 1, 1861, but part of his original plant remained until torn down in 1940. A son, Norman, became an officer of the plant in 1862, but died at the age of twenty-eight, July 26, 1864. Only William, the third son, enjoyed a long life.

January 12, 1855 the business became a stock company with 3,200 shares at $25 or $80,000 capital. Reportedly, Wilson felt it necessary to provide for the future of the company as he was aging. The officers and stock held by each:

Increase Wilson	2,400 = $60,000	President
Nathan Belcher	350 = 8,750	Secretary (son-in-law)
John W. Tibbits	250 = 6,250	Treasurer
William Wilson	200 = 5,000	(son)

Increase Wilson withdrew from the business shortly after 1855 and Nathan Belcher became president. Capitalization increased to $100,000. Nathan Belcher (1813-1891) of Griswold arrived at New London in 1841, after study at Amherst College and Harvard Law School and the practice of law in Clinton. He left law and became active in the Wilson Manufacturing Company. He married Ann Wilson, daughter of Increase. When the company incorporated in 1855, he became secretary and upon the death of his father-in-law became president.[7]

A Democrat, he served in the Connecticut House of Representatives, 1846-1847 and Senate, 1850 as well as in the Congress 1853-1855. He served as director of the Union Bank and as a trustee of the Bulkeley School from its incorporation in 1850 and treasurer from 1876.

Nathan Belcher's son, Judge William Belcher became a prominent lawyer, served as Judge of Probate and had the distinction of being president of two local banks, namely The Savings Bank of New London and the New London City National Bank. William Belcher's son Nathan followed in his father's footsteps, became a lawyer, Judge of Probate and an official of The Savings Bank of New London, serving as Executive vice president and secretary-treasurer of the New London Cemetery Association.

The Wilson Company named William H. Barns president, C. M. Daboll superintendent, Edward T. Brown secretary in 1866. In 1873 the Company had 100 workers employed on 2 acres with a site investment of $200,000 and spent $100,000 yearly on labor and materials which produced $140,000 in sales. In the 1870's a prominent product was the People's Mowing Machine while other products included jack screws, turning lathes, solid box vises, anti-friction bushing, block and tackles, and burglar and tramp stoppers. William Belcher and William Wilson held the offices of president and secretary when the R. T. Palmer Company purchased the business on July 2, 1888.[8]

For eighty years Water Street housed the Boss Company (1831-1911). It started as the New London Bakery of Elizar Goddard in a little wooden building where bread, cakes and crackers for the town and vessels were baked. William Hall, Chris Jeffrey, and William Guy operated the business from 1812 until 1831 successively. At that time the Boss brothers, Charles D. and Philip M. took over as P.M. and C. D. Boss. After Philip Boss quit, a new partnership began of James Jeffrey and C. D. Boss which lasted until C. D. Boss purchased the whole business in 1834. During the time of whaling voyages the major business carried on was the supplying of crackers for the vessels. At the height of whaling 500,000 pounds were produced. The Boss Company was the first to use steam power beginning in 1860.[9]

Charles D. Boss, Jr., became a partner in 1863—C. D. Boss and Son. A fire destroyed their building in 1864, but in three months they were back in business. When the new building reached completion it was one of the best in the country. One of the major items produced was the patented lunch milk biscuit—Boston Soda Crackers. By 1874, they paid twenty employees $20,000 a year in salary on $156,000 in orders. C. D. Boss retired in 1878 and C. D. Boss, Jr. and Robert R. Congdon carried on a partnership as of December 31, 1878. C. D. Boss' only daughter married Robert R. Congdon. By 1885 business had increased to ten times that of 1875.[10]

C. D. Boss and Son put a new baking powder on the market in 1895. The plant had used it for years. The company's long existence came to an end in 1911 when labor problems and competition of the National Biscuit Company proved too much. Boss sold the company's rights to the National Biscuit Company and leased the building to the Mohegan Cotton Mills for $3,000 and later sold the building to the Connecticut Power Company for $60,000.[11]

C. D. Boss, Jr., died in 1921 at the age of eighty-four. He served as

Works of the C.D. Boss & Son, manufacturers of biscuits and crackers.

director of the Bank of Commerce for forty years besides being in the bakery business. The factory was torn down in 1972.

William Albertson, founder of the Albertson and Douglas Machine Company, arrived at New London to work for Colonel Increase Wilson in 1828. As superintendent of the machinist department he remained with Wilson until 1839 when he established a partnership with Henry Clark. Clark and Albertson manufactured cotton gin castings and materials which Clark, living in Alabama, sold there. In 1841 after a fire destroyed their building, Clark retired and Albertson formed a new partnership with J. W. Smith—Albertson and Smith. They erected a building on Main Street for a machine shop with an iron foundery in the rear.[12]

The firm's business consisted of making cotton gins and ship work, mostly for whaling ships. When Smith retired in 1846, William Albertson, Artemas Douglas, Peter C. Turner, Charles W. Strickland and James Strickland formed the Albertson, Douglas and Company. In 1853 it became the Albertson and Douglas Machine Company with William Albertson and Artemas Douglas holding all the stock—$60,000 worth. At one time they manufactured one-half of all the cotton gins produced which sold for $300 apiece.

After business had been poor for several years and in 1863 a fire destroyed the boiler shop, the company was reorganized[13] into a $100,000 stock company. Elias F. Morgan president, James M. Albertson secretary and Artemas Douglas superintendent now built a business quite varied and worldwide manufacturing steam engines for vessels, steam elevators for hotels and businesses, ornamental and plain iron railing, mill work, plantation machinery, cotton presses and circular saw mills.

In 1873 they occupied the site where James Stewart, the British Customs Official prior to the American Revolution, had a home. The plant consisted of two acres east of Main Street, bordering on Winthrop Cove. One hundred and fifty employees received $75,000 to $90,000 in salary and produced $200,000 worth of products.[14]

James M. Albertson and Artemas Douglas appear to have contributed actively to the business world of New London over a long period of time. The former, an especially talented man, held a large number of patents over the years. Elias F. Morgan took over the whole operation in 1868 through stock purchases. Albertson died in November of 1875 and Douglas in 1878.

Hotels were necessary and numerous in the first half of the nineteenth century. The New London Hotel on Bank Street formerly Shepard's Hotel and Stage House, City Hotel, David Frink's Hotel and the Steamboat Boarding House all offered accommodations. The City Hotel and Steamboat Boarding House enjoyed excellent reputations by 1840 when Daniel Webster stayed overnight at the former during bad weather which forced a delay in his trip between New York and Massachusetts. Travellers arrived and many departed by steamboats, sailboats, stages and the ferry. Most freight entered or left by sailboats as steamer rates were high. It took a week for a voyage to or from New York. Many merchants travelled to New York in order to replenish their stock. It cost $2.00 to travel to Norwich by stage, one round trip a day; $6.00 to Hartford or New Haven in the summer, $8.00 in the winter—with three trips a week being made. A number of sloops would carry one to New York for $1.00 plus 12½ cents per meal. The silver currency was mainly foreign. A Mexican dollar was accepted at par, a five franc piece at 95 cents and six shillings equalled a $1.00. United States currency rarely appeared.

Some idea of the domestic help families required as well as duties and salaries can be seen from the following advertisement:

> Wanted first rate Cook, Washer & ironer—satisfaction required or don't apply salary $8.00 a month[15]

Concern for the newly emerging factory workers in Connecticut led to the establishment of a newspaper at the town. The *Connecticut Centinel* (1828-1829) formerly the *Republican Advocate* (1818-1828) published by John Eldridge presented a strongly pro-labor stance. It proposed more opportunities for workers in the area of education, urged unity by joining together in labor organization and attempted to bring about a general improvement in the attitude of society toward the workingman.

In the fall of 1829, a Mechanics Association of Laboring Men was established at the town and received the backing of the *Centinel*. The Assembly election of 1830 found the workers and *Centinel* backing New Londoners Thomas Mussey and Henry Douglas for representatives. They won as did the labor ticket in the New London town election. To celebrate their victory and first year of activity the Mechanic's and Laboring Men's Association held a large parade on December 1, 1830.

Dr. Charles Douglas (1792-1851), a New London doctor, became a very active worker for labor. From 1830 to 1850 he spent so much time in labor's activities that he received the honor of being selected president of the New England Association in 1834 and in 1835 served as president of the Boston Trades Union. He helped establish the first national organization of workers, the National Trades Union.[16]

Conditions in 1846 for the sales people improved somewhat. A number of merchants in the town agreed to close their stores at eight o'clock rather than nine or ten, except Saturdays when they would close at ten, September 1 to April 1. Druggists and confectioners were not a part of the agreement.

As industrial establishments developed in the area it became common to read advertisements seeking families for work such as:

> 2 families wanted, 4-6 children each . . . Good recommendations required[17]

or

> Wanted, . . . one or two families, consisting of several boys and Girls, of suitable age to work in the Factory[18]

Stores tended to be general ones, such as Joseph Sistare's at the corner of John and Main streets where drugs, boots and shoes were for sale or W. P. Benjamin's Long Store which began as a dry goods store in 1833. He engaged in whaling as an agent, 1844 - 1849. The store which he began stayed in business until 1919 when the Cook, Eaton Company of Portland, Maine purchased it. He died at the age of seventy-five in December of 1887. Benjamin served as deacon of the First and Third Baptist churches.

Another important store, J. N. Harris', opened in 1838. Starting with groceries, he added tools and agricultural implements by 1848. Harris was the first to bring in toys for the Christmas Season, 1838. He also operated the Harris Iron Store, the New London Agricultural Warehouse, acted as general agent for Perry Davis' Vegetable Pain Killer and was a Commission merchant.[19]

Merchants had trouble collecting debts even then, but their reminders seem pretty up to date. Debtors were warned that:

> Unless they pay up within three weeks . . . their accounts will be left with the smartest lawyer in the city, for collection (No joke) Those whose addresses are unknown will have their names and sums owed printed in paper.[20]

It was common for a merchant to get endorsements for his products from leading citizens and publish these names along with the virtues of the product.

What a change occurred in the port by the 1840s. The entire harbor bustled with activity and 400 to 600 sailors moved about the streets. All the wharves were busy and money appeared plentiful. With all this prosperity, the town lacked sidewalks, lamp-posts and even policemen to keep order. Some sections near the waterfront developed bad reputations especially places where rum cost three to four cents a glass.

Among the necessary businesses was that of H. Stayner "an experienced Undertaker" who "will attend personaly at Funerals". He carried a complete assortment of "Ready Made Coffins of his own and other manufacturers" conducting business on the Parade over a paint store.[21]

For the ladies an ice cream parlor opened in 1846 over W. W. Kingsley's news office. The entrance was private without any connection with any apartment. No gentlemen could enter unless accompanied by a lady.

For those wishing to clean up, Major Charles French operated a public bath, hot and cold, back of the Whaling Bank. It opened from 5 A.M. to 10 P.M. Also Captain Charles Hobron manufactured a shower bath which consisted of a hard wooden square box, one poured a pail of water in while the person bathing would stand on a platform which pumped the water through. It was recommended as it would take not more than one minute "and ALL who bathe—and they are becoming more numerous every day" should appreciate the saving of time.[22]

Apparently the emphasis today on footware seems to represent no new fad as no self-respecting whaler went to sea without boots or shoes from the shop of Charles Butler.

Gold fever reached New London as elsewhere in the country. It became common to see advertisements in which the merchants offer all their goods for sale with the statement that: he "doesn't care about profit—going to California . . ." With so many ships sailing for the gold fields supplies were in great demand and prices high. C. D. Boss did an excellent business

Washington W. Sheffield. Established the Sheffield Dentifrice Company in 1850.

supplying bread to the ships, especially those in New York port.[23]

New Londoners formed associations in which each individual put up a sum of money ($400 each in some cases) allowing them to charter vessels and stock them with supplies for passage to California. Most firms sent out vessels carrying supplies and passengers although it was dangerous, for vessels were often abandoned by their crews seeking gold. The stores in New London even sold "Regular Gold Miner's Picks".[24]

Thomas Fitch II and H. T. Fitch ran a grocery business which ended in 1849 when the partnership was dissolved only to have F. W. Fitch continue the business alone. Later Thomas Fitch II established a real estate business in 1866 on Water Street which his son Charles P. Fitch joined in 1869.

In the decade before the Civil War despite the growth of local industry which supplied markets across the country and in some cases around the world, basically New London remained a small town lacking in many of the refinements one might have expected. Generally each house had a small yard in front with a larger yard to the rear. The streets were never clean since the livestock and pigs wandered around and there was no sanitation department. The town lacked lights and sidewalks. If one purchased goods, he carried them home or the shopkeeper delivered them in baskets or wheelbarrels.

Dr. Washington Wentworth Sheffield, a dentist, established the Sheffield Dentifrice Company in 1850 to manufacture and sell tooth powder and later paste. He began as a carpenter and then became a dentist. He used German metal tubes and later established the New England Collapsible Tube Company. In 1911 the present plant on Broad Street was built with additions in 1959. In 1971 it was the second largest employer in New London and lacking room for expansion appeared to be considering a move. The plant decided to remain with the understanding that state money would aid in expansion, $456,000 to purchase properties on the Broad, Waller streets and Connecticut Avenue block. It employed 450 people in 1971. A new contract with the union provided for a twenty cent an hour increase, the first year and fifteen cents the second year with improved medical insurance and a new pension program. The Company marketed Dr. Sheffield's Creme Dentifrice, Dr. Sheffield's Tooth Powder and a mouth wash, Dr. Sheffield's Elixir Balm.[25]

Another company of Dr. Sheffield's, the International Tooth Crown Company held patents on tooth crowns and bridge work. Dr. James Low started the work in 1877 for which he received patents. Sheffield bought out Dr. Low's rights and established a school to teach the methods and made a number of improvements. Other dentists paid $25 a year and fifteen percent of the cost of work done following Dr. Sheffield's methods. At one point a law suit became necessary to enforce his patent rights. The court recognized Sheffield's position. When Dr. W. W. Sheffield died in 1897, his son Dr. L. T. Sheffield continued the business. At his death in 1901, his sons, L. T. and W. K. Sheffield, ran the business.[26]

The New London Foundry Machine Company was established in 1852 with directors: Richard Cranston, M. M. Comstock, Henry P. Haven, while others involved included Thomas Fitch II, T. W. Williams, Benjamin Brown, Colonel Increase Wilson, James Albertson and Artemus Douglas. With a capitalization of $45,000 it decided to erect its plant on Water Street. The Company ended its short operations in 1859 and Thomas Fitch purchased the property in order to develop a marine railway along the waterfront.[27]

In the 1850's piano fortes were manufactured by T. M. and J. H. Allyn on Golden Street until a fire temporarily closed their door. T. M. Allyn and F. S. Bidwell carried on the business after reorganizing in 1854.

The Nameaug Manufacturing Company was organized in August of 1856 with $12,000 capital. Directors included: N. S. Perkins, president; Lorenzo Hodsdon, secretary-treasurer; Thomas W. Perkins; Leonard Shaffer and Daniel Shaffer. The Company went bankrupt in August of 1858 but was reorganized and by 1859 had twenty-five employees.

New London became a center of cotton gin manufacturing. Albertson and Douglas produced nearly fifty percent of the total made. Later the Brown Cotton Gin Company became the largest producer. Israel F. Brown, born in New London County, had been raised in the South and developed a cotton gin manufacturing business which received a medal from South Carolina for producing an improved model. Before the Civil War, 1858, Brown moved north and established the Boston Cotton Gin Works in New London which later became known as the Brown Cotton Gin Works.[28]

As business prospered the Naylor Works on Fort Neck were purchased and the Brown Cotton Gin Company developed a complex of buildings which included much special machinery designed by Brown. He used water and steam power machinery and with an investment of $50,000, employed sixty people and produced sales of $75,000 a year. Edward T. Brown, son of Israel, was business manager. In 1873, the plant operated only eight hours, three days a week but by the end of the year, the full labor force had been recalled. Business continued to improve with more help hired and in 1880 the Company on Pequot Avenue increased its facilities by purchasing the Dawson property.[29]

Israel F. Brown continued to work on improvements for the cotton gin. An excellent and respected boss, his workers showed their feelings for him in 1882. He was summoned to the main factory area from his office after being told the men had stopped work and wanted to see him. Hurrying to the area the seventy-one year old boss demanded of the assembled workers the cause of the stoppage—after a period of silence he was presented with a gold headed cane inscribed:

> Presented to Israel F. Brown
> By the Employees of the
> Brown Cotton Gin Co.
> on 71st Birthday
> December 31st, 1881.[30]

Business kept increasing with 1884 being an outstanding year and a new addition became necessary in 1890. In 1897 when many companies were laying off help, more workers—twenty—were hired. Israel F. Brown (President), Edward T. Brown (Secretary-Treasurer), C. H. Osgood, F. T. Osgood and George Colfax acted as directors and officers in 1891. The founder and director of the company, Israel F. Brown, died at the age of eighty-nine, March 24, 1900. His son, Edward T. Brown, carried on as president.

Israel F. Brown, founder of the Brown Cotton Gin Company.

Works of the Brown Cotton Gin Company.

The manufacturing of Cotton Gins still continued to be an excellent business for several years. Brown produced 1,800 a year at $180 to $250 while employing 250 to 300 people. In 1918 the Brown Cotton Gin Plant (Now the Reed-Prentice Plant) was to be sold at public auction.

The New London Horse Nail Company formed in 1859 turned out a large number of nails daily. During the Civil War business reached its peak. In 1878 the Company went out of business. It was located on Canal

Street with the following directors: Isaac C. Tate president, Moses Darrow secretary, W. H. Starr, Horace Durrie and George Rusher.

1861 - 1899

Business conditions began to improve in the spring of 1859 after being very slow. As the Civil War approached, New London Streets were lighted by oil and horse-drawn buses carried people to the outskirts of town and back. The Civil War produced both good and bad effects in New London. The town had its connections with the South. Frances M. Caulkin's nephew, Harvey, served on General Robert E. Lee's staff. Also, Abner Bassett's daughter, Lucretia, was married to Gustavus Smith of Kentucky who became a General in the Confederate Army. Upon learning of her mother's illness, Lucretia Bassett Smith returned home only to be asked to leave town as she was considered a spy. She was watched until her departure by train.[31]

When the news arrived about Fort Sumter, the city flag was raised and flags were shown all over the city. Vessels displayed the flag in the harbor. On the 19th of April, Mayor J. N. Harris received a communication to send a company to Fort Trumbull which had been without a garrison since 1853 when the troops were transferred to California. Harris sent the City Guards to the Fort. At a courthouse meeting that same night a large crowd gathered both inside and outside to listen to a number of leading merchants and businessmen urge support of the Union. The people decided to raise money for the equipping of troops and they raised $10,000 right on the spot with some of the leading merchants giving $500 each.[32]

Judging from the articles and meetings in New London strong anti-union forces existed as well as substantial pro-union forces, especially in 1863. Most merchants backed the Union cause actively and subscribed to each loan needed by the state. In fact New London paid over $46,000 for the support of families and $18,000 in bounties for volunteers and substitutes. Also the town sent clothing and comfort boxes to the soldiers.

Numerous volunteer companies were formed of men including all ages. Recruitment of a naval brigade for coastal defense proceeded rapidly and in a short time a full company of volunteers was ready. The town rather quickly (1861) complained that the United States Engineers were not preparing to develop Fort Trumbull and Fort Griswold into proper defense forts. Fort Trumbull reached a state of readiness by January of 1862 with men and supplies. In the draft announced on January of 1862, New London had to provide 127 men. A recruiting depot at Fort Trumbull in February of 1862 met this quota.[33]

Quite a few men with sea experience received appointments to the navy—captains appointed included John W. Brown, Gurdon Allyn, George Harris, Joseph H. Rogers, J. M. Williams, William R. Brown, John M. Keeney, Robert B. Smith and Alexander Tillinghist. Charles D. Boss was appointed paymaster in the navy. By May of 1862, twenty New Londoners served as volunteer officers and 272 were in the ranks.[34]

Real aspects of the war began to reach New London as men experienced in battle arrived in town. One soldier arrived home in June of 1862 after having been taken prisoner at the first Battle of Bull Run. After the battle of Bull Run men became difficult to obtain and attempts at recruitment increased. The United State Frigate *Sabine* opened a recruiting office on Water Street in the Bishops Building in July of 1862. "Those who wish to be enrolled among the gallant heroes of the American Navy should not let this opportunity pass." The town gave volunteers from New London a $100 bounty beginning in August of 1862.[35]

President Lincoln appointed Edward Prentis collector for the District of New London in 1861 to the dismay of Thomas Fitch and his supporters who felt that his appointment was assured. There was quite a bit of a furor for a few weeks over the development.[36]

The stationing of troops at New London increased the police problem. Things such as the selling of liquor to soldiers at Camp Thomas, soldiers drinking and fighting, and ladies of the night openly soliciting occurred. In September of 1862, a riot occurred on Water Street. A soldier last seen drinking at John Lopez's place was discovered dead on the railroad tracks. When word reached the fort, 100 or more soldiers armed with swords, pistols and axes attacked John Lopez's building reducing it to ruins in thirty minutes with only two casualties. The officer in charge of the fort rushed to the area after learning of the riot and removed the troops. Later that night somebody set the building on fire and it could not be put out until two buildings were destroyed and several others damaged. Although the rioters were not brought to justice, a man named Gleason was arrested for the murder of the soldier. He was released when there was not enough evidence to convict him.[37]

Several New London vessels under lease by the government transported troops and supplies. One of these, the *Comstock,* was seized by the federal government for trying to carry illegal merchandise. Release came by the order of the Secretary of Treasury after the owners paid a fine of $97.17 and gave up the liquor on board.[38]

Business boomed for the few industries New London possessed. The New London Horse Nail Company operated day and night, the Wilson

Manufacturing Company made pikes for the United States Navy, and copper wheels for navy gun carriages. They employed sixty men full time days and worked several hours at night. Albertson and Douglas Machine Works received quite a bit of business outfitting vessels with boilers and machinery.

The shipping of the port suffered while wharves were lined with unemployed vessels—coasters, fishermen, merchantmen and whalers. By February of 1862, 122 vessels lay idle in the harbor. With the end of southern trade—tropical fruits and out of season vegetables ceased to be imported. However, New London shipping interests opened a new West Indian supply route for fruits and vegetables.

A wave of drunkenness, tavern fights, shootings and beatings made some areas unsafe, especially at night. Many citizens felt the type of soldier constituted the main problem. They charged that Fort Trumbull housed an unruly lot and that the fort acted as an avenue for "deserters to crawl out of the army . . . for cripples to crawl in." Numerous street fights between soldiers and civilians took place. Juvenile delinquency increased with fathers away and mothers working, leaving their children free to roam and engage in petty mischief and disturbances. Deserters became common in the state and it seemed that almost as fast as they were taken to Fort Trumbull they escaped. The accounts of arrests and escapes became legend.[39]

Colonel Francis B. Loomis purchased the New London County Machine Works for $13,000 to convert into a woolen mill to meet government contracts which he had secured. He became the largest and most successful woolen mill operator during the war period. He made a fortune in shoddy and genuine woolen cloth. Shoddy was coarse wool or cashmere of the poorest quality, worked up from worn out fabrics and sold at high prices to the military. Usually, it wore out in a week. Loomis had 1,200 workers on day and night shifts. He made so much money that towards the end of the war, with the men scarce, he offered to raise, uniform and supply 1,000 volunteers for 100 days at his own expense. Lincoln did not accept his offer. This would have cost Loomis $1,000,000.[40]

The end of the Civil War saw the organization of the Palmer Brothers Company Mills, established in 1865. Captain Palmer, who operated a packet between New London and New York, after being asked to sell some quilts saw the possibilities of the market. Using the $2,000 back military pay of brother Elisha L. Palmer, who had been in Libbey Prison for eighteen months, Elisha L., Howard A. and Frank T. Palmer set up the business. They became aware of the market for bed comforters in 1872

Bird's-eye view of New London, summer, 1907. Palmer Quilt Mill at center; Allyn Hall, First Baptist Church and Palmer Mill beyond.

and developed the Palmer Quilting Machine by 1884. When the company incorporated in 1899, George Palmer became a part of the firm.

In 1918 the company closed the Washington Street Mill because of war conditions and the need of labor for the war effort. Their property on Water Street was sold in 1942 to become a garage for buses.

The New London Steam Woolen Mill manufactured repellents, ladies cloth and cashmeres. Dr. Elisha W. Sholes, a large shareholder was superintendent from 1867 until his death December 5, 1879, then Alonzo W. Sholes, his son, ran the business. In 1884 the mill built a two story extension and in September of 1895 it closed indefinitely due to a dull season. It remained closed until 1902 when Reuben Palmer and Frederick Mercer reopened it. Much employment had been provided in the past and the townspeople hoped for a return.

In 1869 New London industry included the New London Steam Woolen Mills Company, the New London Horse Nail Company, the W. W. Tobey Shirt Manufacturing Company, Wilson Manufacturing Company and the Albertson and Douglas Company.

New London merchants established the Board of Trade in September of 1870 to encourage new businesses to locate in town and to plan improvement of the city. By 1871 (December) membership totaled 119 with R. H. Chapell as president. The Board of Trade proposed the establishment of a rolling mill for production of railway iron. W. W. Sheffield, Elias

Morgan and William M.Tobey were appointed a committee to pursue the matter in 1871. John Bolles, secretary of the Board of Trade advocated that New London should be the eastern terminus of the Northern Pacific. Their major success came from their suggestion and efforts to provide the town with a waterworks.[41] After it ceased operations, a second Board of Trade began to function in 1886. William H. Barns as leader worked to promote New London and did an excellent job. Very little if anything happened in which the Board did not take a hand as far as concerned the city.

The Pequot Chemical Company, although not organized until 1870, represented a business which had been established in 1786, the Ways Soap and Candle Factory. Cortland Starr purchased both that company and a second business organized by Edward Pratt. In 1869 Ezra C. Whittlesey became Starr's partner after working for him for twenty-five years. At Starr's death Whittlesey continued the business. When kerosene became popular he gave up the making of candles. Starr Family Soap continued as the major product until the business became Pequot Chemical Company in 1870. Dudley B. Chapman, head of Pequot Chemical Company, added National Shampoo and Magic Laundry Soap to the line.[42]

A new company established at this time, Rogers Ice Company, became the largest in Connecticut. P. M. Rogers (president) and George Rogers had been in the confectionery business earlier. The Company delivered a ton of ice for $1.00. They built a storage barn on Mountain Street and drew upon a large area for their ice. After several good years, the winter of 1889-1890 proved too warm for suitable amounts of ice to be acquired. At this time Rogers Ice Company decided (January of 1890) to put in an ice making machine if weather conditions did not improve. Albert W. Rogers, son of P. M. Rogers, sold the Company to the Perry Ice Company organized in 1900. William H. Bentley, oldest of the ice dealers, also sold to Perry after supplying fishing boats for years. Actually, Perry had two companies—Winthrop Spring Hygeia which supplied artificial ice and Perry which sold natural ice. Business was excellent and required additions to the plant from time to time.[43]

Poor business conditions existed in the early 1870's with the boom of the Civil War long past. No less than 40 vessels lay idle in the harbor. The Pequot Glass Works closed November 15, 1873 adding 60 men to the unemployment list. To meet with unemployment problems, James M. King opened an "Intelligence Office" at 10 State Street for "People who want Help [and] Help who want work".

Ice Men on Broad Street about 1912. Lafayette G. Sharp on right.

Andrew J. Coit, son of Captain Elias Coit who had been a pioneer in New London whaling, returned to town after an absence of thirty-five years. He expressed disappointment in the town. There were sixty whaling vessels when he left and business was flourishing. Now, whaling nearly had ended and little commerce existed. Loafers lounged on street corners, especially State and Main and State and Bank streets. Sidewalks were filthy with tobacco juice and the conversation contained language that would offend many. Industry, the *New London Daily Star* reported, did not bring in the profits as whaling had.

According to some, New London became a dull and sleepy town lacking in enterprise.[44] That things were dull also appeared to be the view of *The New London Telegram:*

> A carboy of vitriol exploded in front of a drug store this afternoon. No one was near enough to it to get hurt, or even frightened consequently this is not much of an item, and is put in only because there is nothing else to tell of.[45]

Hotels were considered poor following the Civil War which led to the formation of the New London Hotel Company in December of 1871 with a capitalization of $25,000. Directors A. W. Ramsdale president, Benjamin Stark, Robert Coit, Jr. secretary-treasurer, W. H. Barns, H. P. Haven, A.

Brandegee and M. W. Bacon decided to build a new hotel on property owned by Major Brandegee. A brick building was begun in April of 1872 on the corner of State and Union streets. The directors hired Henry S. Crocker to run the operation which became known as the Crocker House.

Crocker had earlier earned an excellent reputation as the proprietor of the Pequot House, a popular summer hotel at the mouth of the Thames. He also had been manager of the Federal (Street) House (1849-1852) during the ownership of Franklin Smith. The New London Gas and Electric Company wired the hotel for irridescent lights. Unfortunately, New London Hotel Company could not profitably maintain the business and sold it to E. Foster Cooke in 1874. Over the years a number of renovations have taken place—1891, 1925, 1942, 1956 and 1965. It received the title New London's Friendly Hotel.[46]

Little industrial growth occurred during the 1870's. With all its apparent promise of becoming a leading port, naval station and manufacturing center so many capable people moved to other towns that: "Formerly of New London" became a familiar phrase when reading of visits of people or success in other towns. The only industry in New London at this time with the end of whaling were three silk mills, one woolen mill, one cotton gin factory and a few iron works.

Not until 1879 did a new industry move into the town. Prior to that date the new businesses of the 1870's consisted of a department store, canning factory and saw mill-lumber yard. Even these did not begin until 1877. The department store established in 1877, Hislop, Porteous and Mitchell remained under local ownership until 1929. At that time the business, the James Hislop Company as it had become in 1892, sold out to New York interests. After fifty-two years the owners decided they could not compete with the mass buying of chain department store operations.[47]

Everyone in town was aware of the H. A. Brown and Company Canning business. It had an air about it that hardly allowed for indifference. In fact, the *Telegram* on November 11, 1873 referred to it as a "sickening odor". The Hempstead Street firm produced canned goods of all kinds and exported to Russia, England, France and Germany. Starting in 1873 with eighty workers, the force reached 130 in 1877 and later 200. It was the outgrowth of a vinegar and pickle factory established in 1850 on Mountain Avenue by David Bishop. He produced 700 to 1,000 barrels annually mostly for the whaling business. As the whaling business declined the Toby and Brainard Shirt Company took over the plant. Then H. A. Brown bought them out and produced vinegar, pickles and horseradish until 1873, when he established his cannery business on Hempstead Street and sold the Mountain Avenue business. Some 2,000 acres were under cultivation to produce vegetables for canning.[48]

A very extensive business developed at New London under the direction of Andrew Jackson Bentley. He began as a sailor in the coastal trade. When twenty years old, Bentley became a captain and sailed until 1859. He engaged in the shipping business out of New York City until 1879, when he established the Columbia Steam Saw Mill at New London. Bentley took up residence at the port in 1882. With his business on the waterfront, Bentley could bring in timber from his 80,000 acres in Columbia County, Florida, directly to his wharf and unload for his large lumberyard on South Trumbull Street.[49]

Benjamin A. Armstrong worked as a clerk in local stores before going to New York City. There he worked in the office of a silk firm and with a salesman from its firm, James P. Brainard, formed Brainard and Armstrong. They sold other mill's products before establishing their own at New London in 1879. As business increased, the firm put in new machinery (1883) which required the addition of fifty to sixty workers. The following year Brainard and Armstrong purchased property on Church Street to erect a silk mill. Brainard left the firm that same year. The company's new mill began operations in 1885 and eventually added two mills at New London and one at Norwich which employed 1,000 workers. By 1912, the mills did a $3,000,000 business.[50]

When business conditions were bad in 1893, the weavers at Brainard and Armstrong went on strike. They asserted that they could only earn four to six dollars a week at piecework, while the company claimed that the firm had kept the works open at a loss and that the weavers averaged $1.66 a day. The dispute ended in a week and by the following spring the mill employed five hundred. Still more employees were added as business improved unlike the other mills which received few orders. 1902 proved to be another bad year for the company. A union movement led to the laying off of all involved with it.[51]

In 1919 the company introduced a pension plan. A male worker could retire at 65 and a female at 55 after 25 years of service at fifty percent of the average salary for the past five years. Business continued to be excellent and in December of 1919 a seventy percent salary increase was granted the 250 employees. However, by 1920 orders fell off and the plant had to reduce its work week to four days and by September to two days. Benjamin Armstrong bought out the Nonotuck Silk Company of Florence, Massachusetts manufacturer of Corticelli Silk in 1921 and retained that product's company name. The newly enlarged business became the Corticelli

Spinning Department, Brainard & Armstrong Company.

Silk Company. His death in 1929 along with the poor economic conditions brought operations of the concern to an end in 1930.[52]

The Belding-Heminway Company purchased the Brainard and Armstrong Company at a considerable loss to the stockholders. However, the new company was not successful in operating the plant and severed their connection with New London in 1934. A manufacturing building on Union Street of the former Brainard and Armstrong Company was leased and operated by a subsidiary of the Celanese Corporation of America until the early years of World War II.

An improved economic climate could be felt by 1883 and these improved conditions continued until 1892. In 1884 a large amount of construction was going on—a new armory, a silk mill on Church Street, a new building on State Street and a building for the Babcock Printing Company on the site of the Old Brown Cotton Gin Company.

From 1885 to 1888 over 250 houses had been built. The population reached nearly 15,000 in 1887 and land values increased from 50 to 200 percent. With better hotels, sewer systems, improved streets and the conversion of Lawrence Hall into an opera house, New London became an attractive town.

The Babcock Printing Manufacturing Press Company organized in 1882 began production in 1884 with C. B. Maxson as president, Nathan Babcock as secretary-treasurer and C. F. Fenton as superintendent. The plant enjoyed excellent sales—five different styles of presses were sold throughout the country.[53] The difficult economic conditions in the early

1890's affected the company and they exhibited their products at the World's Fair in Chicago as did other New England businesses in an attempt to gain new orders. Nathaniel Babcock, one of the founders of the company died suddenly in 1902. In 1904 the company employed 400 persons and was the second largest employer in the town. Business continued to be good through the First World War period. Under the leadership of James E. Bennett, president, a number of benefits were gained by the employees such as group life insurance in 1920. It continued production through the 1920s and 1930s despite severe economic problems.

During World War II with contracts for the making of shells the company flourished and enjoyed a high employment rate. At the end of the War the cancellation of contracts hurt business as it did many other plants and in 1947 the company purchased a surplus war plant in Canton, Ohio and ended its operations in New London.

The Hobson Chapin Manufacturing Company, originally located at Wethersfield in 1880, moved to New London in 1885. Located on Hamilton Street, the plant manufactured hot water and steam heating equipment including the "Pequot Boiler". A prominent factory producing fine iron and machine work, its employment exceeded 100 men many times.

D. E. Whiton Machine Company incorporated in 1886 took over a business in a newly built factory. Under the direction of D. E. Whiton, president and L. E. Whiton secretary-treasurer, it produced gear cutters, centering machines and drill and lathe chucks. Within ten years orders increased at such a rate that it became necessary to run the Howard Street plant nights. An addition doubled production. The company gave a clubhouse to its employees in 1902. Over the years relations between workers and company officials appeared to have been excellent. A Mutual Aid and Benevolent Association was formed in 1914.

Employment was good during the First World War but by 1921 business declined. Ninety men were laid-off that year as only a skeleton crew was needed to operate the plant. After a difficult period during the 1920s and 1930s with temporary closings by the plant defense orders brought better days and increased employment.

After World War II orders became scarce again and layoffs occurred. Then George A. Highberg president of a new corporation, took over the property and business of the company in 1947 from Lucus E. Whiton president of D. E. Whiton Machine Company. In 1971 the Terry Corporation of Windsor took over the business and sold the property on Howard Street.[54]

D. E. Whiton, manufacturers of gear cutting and centering machines, drills and lathe chucks.

Bingham Paper Box Company began in 1887 on Mountain Avenue. The first products consisted of paper boxes, then in 1890, the printing of books and job printing became services of the company. By 1912 it was producing paper boxes, books, job printing and labels employing sixty workers.

A new business began in 1889 in a shed at 13½ Truman Street; C. W. Tarbox began to manufacture stove polish according to his own formula. Over the years it became a valuable business with several varieties of stove polish, nickel polish and stencil ink being produced. In 1921 the pressure from large companies forced the company out of business.

The R. T. Palmer Company had a flourishing bed comfort business in 1889 with a branch store in New York City. With a large plant on Washington Street it manufactured bed comforters for the steamship lines for the use of immigrants from Europe. Unfortunately, the company accumulated debts of $750,000 and these proved to be too much for the income. Palmer Brothers Company purchased it in 1904.[55]

The Port even had a water closet manufacturing company— Elemendorf. Business was so good that the maker opened branches in Oakland and Chicago in 1892.[56]

Business conditions became poor in 1892. Some improvement came later that year when work at the New London Northern Car Shops increased and some people were recalled to work. However, in general conditions through 1893 continued to be poor. When a man stole a bag of flour the officer sent to arrest him found the man's children so hungry that they were eating the dough before it could be baked. The grocer learning of the situation, refused to press charges.[57]

No less than sixty applied for work in one day when a jewelry store advertised for a worker in November 1893. One hundred and twenty-five unemployed men were listed with Louis Huhns and W. D. Fox, November 1893. It was the time of Coxey's "army" march on Washington. "General" Moore who was to lead Norwich's "army" to Washington arrived in New London May 3, 1894—alone. His entire "army" of thirty-five had deserted.[58]

By the summer of 1893 over 100 workers were idle as depression continued. A "tramp colony" or camp became a part of "Lewis Woods" during the good weather of 1893 but disappeared in the November chill. High hopes for the business activities of New London had been held when the World's Fair began in Chicago—the Babcock Printing Company, Brown Cotton Gin Company, Elemendorf Water Closet Company, Hopson & Chapin Manufacturing Company, Whiton Machine Company, Whiton Letter Book Company and L. T. Sheffield Company all took part.

Instead of an improvement in business conditions the stock market slumped in 1893 and Monroe, Miller & Company, stockbrokers, abandoned their New London office in September which had proved quite unprofitable. When the market slumped, a number of New London people purchased the heavily depressed stocks which promised a large profit when economic conditions improved.

The slump in economic conditions forced the Orlo Atwood & Son's Silk Mills to shut down in 1893. The business began in the Bishop Building at the foot of the Parade in 1873. Business prospered so much that in 1878 the company purchased the New London Horse Nail Company on Canal Street. Now it had to add its workers to the unemployment rolls.

A number of business developments took place in 1893 despite poor economic conditions. New London Real Estate and Improvement Company, R. T. Palmer Company, New London Business College, Oneco Company and the Columbian Construction Company all received approval of incorporation from the Connecticut Assembly. The Harris building annex on Masonic Street was built in 1893. F. H. Chappell and Company built a new building on Bank Street which indicated town growth in the last two decades of the 19th century had been along Bank Street. Of all the new buildings in the past ten years only the Harris and the Crown buildings had not been on Bank Street.

Although tramps were increasing in number—450 per month— in 1894, it was believed that the corner had been turned on economic conditions and things looked better for the new future.[59] The Palmer Mill decided improved conditions warranted an addition on Union Street. A new silk business began in 1894 with seven workers—the New London Wash Silk Company. By 1912 the concern employed 100 with an investment of $100,000 which produced over $300,000 in business.[60] A new concern, the H-K-H Silk Company was formed by the Hammond-Knowlton, the Eureka Silk Manufacturing Company and the New London Wash Silk Company. The H-K-H Silk Company became the Hemenway Silk Company in 1924.[61]

Frank A. Munsey decided in 1895 to publish his magazine in New London. He bought the Bacon property on State Street and had a steel frame building erected. Choosing New London for the Munsey Magazine meant a $100,000 savings in labor costs a year. Unfortunately, labor difficulties in 1897 brought a decision to end operations. It was claimed that Munsey moved to New London to save wages only to run into union labor problems. In 1897, he had the operation shifted to New York City. He started the workers removing presses one morning and had a crew work all night to complete the job. In 1897 Munsey remodeled the building into an eight floor hotel—the best in the area including New York and Boston. He then decided to change the hotel into a department store. Unfortunately New London could not support an operation as large as the Mohican Stores and after several years of unsatisfactory business, he changed the building back to a hotel. The Mohican Hotel came to be owned by Jean G. Venetos, who once was a cook at the hotel and was becoming a very successful businessman from this humble start. He owned a number of other hotels also.[62]

In the last years of the 19th century military affairs dominated rather than business conditions. Some vessels apparently utilized New London harbor as a base during the Cuban War from which to ship arms and men to the area. As it became increasingly clear that the United States and Spain were on a collision course the port became concerned about its possible attack by Spanish navy vessles from the sea and urged the improvement of the harbor defenses.

Fort Trumbull had been manned by a coast artillery unit since the Civil War. During the Spanish American War, the army developed three forts for the protection of the area. There were Fort H. G. Wright on Fishers Island, Fort Michie on Little Gull Island and Fort Terry on Plum Island. Regular army personnel were stationed at these forts and supplied by ferries which were operated by the United States Army.

When war came there was no difficulty in filling ranks. However, some changed their minds a little too late as did four members of Company D Third Regiment New London. They decided they would rather go home and were dishonorably discharged. The regular army troops of the area caused disorder in the town through drunk and disorderly conduct which sometimes involved as many as fifty soldiers. By March of 1899 the volunteers began returning from the war.[63]

1900 - 1970

Following the end of the Spanish American War, the turn of the century found financial conditions poor again. Stock broker, G. C. Raymond and Company in the Harris Building, failed when Sullivan and Sullivan of New York "went under". The following year the brokerage firm, F. A. Rogers in the Neptune Building could not settle with its customers.

The New London Chamber of Commerce was established in 1914. It actually began in 1898 as the New London Business Men's Association. Earlier the business leaders had established similar groups aimed at helping New London realize its commerce potential. Both of these organizations were known as the New London Board of Trade. The second of that name merged with the Chamber of Commerce in 1916. A number of city improvements received the backing of the associations such as sidewalks, Grand Trunk terminal for summer tourists, development of the harbor and the development of a women's college.[64]

Economic conditions remained poor through 1907. However, an improvement developed when a new industry in 1908, the Standard Brass and Copper Tube Company, provided a large number of jobs. During World War I the Bridgeport Brass and Copper Tube Company purchased it. With the postwar slump, the plant was closed in 1920 and 100 jobs ended.

J. N. Lapointe moved the Arnold Electric Tool Company to New London in 1914 and housed it on Trumbull Street. It manufactured portable electric drills. Later, it became the Onondaga Textile Mill. Even with these new plants and an optimistic New London Chamber of Commerce economic conditions once again became depressed by 1914. In October of that year the New Haven Railroad laid off about 50 men as freight and passenger service was light.

Once again war conditions began to stimulate New London economy. New London plants began to receive large orders by December of 1914. With Europe well into World War I the Brown Cotton Gin Company enjoyed full employment, working six days a week. The Babcock Printing Press Company became busy and Brainard and Armstrong were almost working full time by 1915. The new prosperity of orders brought a number of wage increases by 1917 as well as a number of new concerns. Henry Bond, Jr. became one of the officials of the General Ordnance

Company of Connecticut while Louis Lubchansky established the Connecticut Metal Company at 53 Howard Street. The Company purchased three feery boats from the New York and Cuba Steamship Company —*Baltic, Hamilton* and *New York* which were scrapped. Jacob Rosen established the New London Paper and Supply Company on Bank Street. The Old Forbes Plant on Trumbull Street which had been idle for sometime was prepared for government operation in October of 1917. The United States Government also took over the Morgan Iron Works and the Marine Iron Works. The New London Brocading Machine Company with Frank I. LaPointe, president, began manufacturing machines and tools in 1917.[65]

Labor difficulties caused the Reed-Prentiss Company to close for three weeks and D. E. Whiton Company closed for one week.

The local Connecticut National Guard Units received orders to enter service and two units of the Connecticut State Guard replaced them at the town from March of 1917 to 1919. Business was good and during the war population of the town tripled. Sailors lived in private homes, marines were stationed at the Palmer House and Mrs. Henry H. Stoddard gave her home for use of chief petty officers. Servicemen received places to sleep in the Y.M.C.A. each night, the Knights of Columbus gave concerts and showed motion pictures at the Crown Theater and the New London Camp Community Service held dances. The Bulkeley School trustees did their "bit for the war" by eliminating the study of German.[66] For the first time the United States moved to daylight savings time in November of 1918.

During World War I coast artillery units were trained at the army island forts, which had been established during the Spanish American War—part of the 56th Regiment of Coast Artillery and the 68th Field Artillery, were both trained at the Forts before serving in France. The former included members of the first and tenth of the Connecticut State Militia and the latter draftees from Illinois.

The conclusion of World War I meant the readjustment of the economy of the town as so much of it had become dependent upon war contracts and the revenue generated by the large number of service personnel stationed in the area. The army personnel was reduced to the 11th coast artillery stationed at Fort Wright. Fort Terry became a National Guard summer training post and Fort Michie was closed.

New London received the end of the war with a gala celebration. Even with the end of the war prosperity continued for several months and a number of new businesses continued to be formed. The Garfield Block

10th Company CNG Coast Artillery. Capt. David Connor, leading. July 4, 1917.

68th Regiment before leaving, July 1918.

Official Group at Municipal Building.

D.A.R. motor section forming for Liberty Loan parades.

Red Cross workers on parade.

was sold to the Mohican Company in 1918. Century Corrugated and Paper Supply Company was established by Simon Balkansky in 1919. Another new industry, the Lenox Shirt Company, began that year.[67]

While three more were formed the following year, the Connecticut Broach Machine Company was incorporated to deal in machinery, broaches and similar items in 1920. Officers included C. S. Amadon, L. E. Peck and S. Victor Prince. They leased the building of the former H. R. Douglas Company on Bank Street. The Silk Manufacturing Company purchased the Perry and Armstrong building on Sparyard Street July 24, 1920 while the Abram Bloom Company bought a site to build a factory in 1919 on Garfield Avenue and finished it in 1920. Charles Ponzi, Boston financial wizard, arrived in New London and went before the town clerk to establish an office in town in 1920—branch of the Security Exchange Company of Boston.[68]

The city ran a piggery to take care of the town's garbage and also to produce revenue. It cost $2,000 to build but eliminated the garbage problem and brought in a handsome return. The first shipment of pigs to market brought $526 in 1920 and in 1928 the city received $3,500 from the operation.[69]

By the 1920's the population reached 25,000 and enjoyed the facilities of a modern, advanced city: street cars, new schools, paved streets, a park system, hospitals, Ocean Beach, a municipal building, new post office and a State Pier. Still the twenty's were a troubled decade with some factories closed through labor strife which continued until the "great crash".

In the 1920's the town faced an unusual situation. On the one hand there was large scale unemployment, on the other those still employed were receiving higher wages for a shorter working week. The youth of the 1960's and 1970's feel there are too many objections to their hair and dress and believe they are the "first to do their own thing" and look different. However, we find similar problems in the 1920s. A local businessman reportedly would not hire short-haired girls saying "Bobbed hair and roll top stockings may be all right for a circus or on the stage, but by hecky, not in my office."[70]

In 1921 the Salvation Army gave much and helped in the finding of jobs. Companies cooperated by sending word to the Army when openings occurred. By 1922 all welfare agencies began to coordinate efforts offering shelter to men from the ages of fifteen to seventy-two. Some were seeking work while others were avoiding it. They gave shelter to 102 men in just one month. Pawn shops business dropped in 1922 by seventy-five percent. Most were overstocked with goods—especially jewelry.[71]

While other companies had a shortage of orders the R. and J. Waist Company on Bank Street had an excellent business, increasing output from 1,500 to 3,100 or 3,500 children's garments a month. The Sidney Manufacturing Company (Sidney Sulman president) on Shapley Street manufactured beds, springs, mattresses and also renovated mattresses in 1922. Also Edward Bloom built a silk mill on McDonald Street that same year.

There was quite a bit of talk about Henry Ford locating a plant at New London in 1923. The former Mayor, B. L. Armstrong, offered him a fine piece of land—thirty to forty acres—part in New London, part in Waterford and along the Railroad. Ford refused saying a plant at Kearny, New Jersey met their eastern needs.[72]

In 1923 industrial production looked good for the winter of 1923-1924. However, conditions were poor in the summer of 1924, but the feeling appeared to be that the presidential election would create better conditions in the fall. At that time the Mayor reported that the city had not advanced in the last 25 to 50 years due to a lack of industry. Despite difficulties the population grew 25% from 1920 to 1926.

Naturally, economic conditions were poor from 1929 through the decade of the 1930s. A prediction by P. LeRoy Harwood made in January of 1930 that "1930 should be good, business uncertainty over" was wide of the mark. The Board of Relief reported a record 1,602 applicants in February of 1930. For Christmas of that year the charity organizations of the town joined together to provide Christmas dinner for 400 families plus toys and clothes. The organizations sold apples and produced benefit shows to raise the funds needed. Connecticut's Lt. Governor and past president of the Connecticut Chamber of Commerce, Ernest E. Rogers, failed to win control of the state in the gubernatorial election. He was the only Republican on the state ticket to lose. It is believed that heavy unemployment and unsatisfactory business conditions as well as the more forceful personality of Wilbur Cross, led to the New Londoners rejection.

Connecticut's unemployed labor force exceeded the national rate of unemployment and this rate increased alarmingly during most of the 1930s. There was even a hunger march on Hartford urging relief programs. The various federal projects provided relief and work programs. New London's unemployed along with others in Connecticut were aided by several of the federal programs—the Civilian Conservation Corps (1933), the Federal Emergency Relief Act (1933), a State Relief Commission (1933). In the winter of 1933-34 the Civil Works Administration provided work on a number of projects and home owners were aided by the Home Owners Loan Corporation. The Public Works Administration aided the New Haven Railroad. For the youth the National Youth Administration provided aid such as a woodworking shop on Howard Street and the making of hooked rugs in 1939.

On top of all the other difficulties came the hurricane of 1938. When the storm ended the destruction caused by water wind and fire amounted to at least $4,000,000. Some businesses were years getting all their rebuilding completed. A second blow in 1944 brought reminders of the 1938 hurricane as well as considerable damage. A number of important changes took place for the businesses of New London. The Railway Express Agency moved into its new building in 1942 at John and Water Streets. Its first permanent home had been destroyed by the hurricane in September.

Even before the German forces struck Poland in September, 1939, New London's business economy had been recovering from economic ills which dominated most of the 1930's. The interest in national defense meant orders for the many industrial plants in the city as well as increased payrolls for the increased military installations of the area. Once again the army forts were put on an active footing and considerable construction carried out.

Charles B. Gardner of Gardner Storage Company was made head of the local Allied Industry Committee for salvage in 1942. The Stanton School had been leased in 1942 at $6,000 a year by the army for a military police barracks.[73] In 1943 The Bloom Silk Mill on Garfield Avenue was leased to the army by the Savings Bank of New London and the government leased the Municipal Wharf at $200 a month. To aid the servicemen the Huntington Street Club reduced overnight lodging from forty cents to twenty-five cents in 1942.

A whiskey drought developed by 1943 with rye and bourbon depleted, scotch very limited and beer being served at twice the replacement rate. Also the Y.M.C.A. established a Community Youth Center in November of 1943 to help the younger boys and girls. The town's population increased from 30,000 to 50,000 by August of 1943. At one point rooms were so scarce that men slept in jail and in their cars. Still, labor became very scarce. It was necessary to develop a labor stabilization plan over hiring and job transferring by August of 1943.[74]

In March of 1945 the manufacturing firms reported to the War Manpower Commission that by July they would need 132 more employees. By fall over 730 vacancies existed. New London had 3,500 enter the armed services from October of 1940 to 1945, of these 59 died. August 15, 1945 the war ended and once again New London celebrated—this time for two days. Jacob Solomon, a Main Street merchant, had hoarded 2,500 metal horns to be used for V-J Day. The U.S.O. closed after four years on October 16, 1946.[75]

Wartime officially ended on September 30, 1945 but had been in effect since February 9, 1942. By October 21, 1945 the job surplus turned into a labor surplus and 990 unemployment claims were filed—up 39.2 over the previous week. August of 1945 brought peace but it also brought a lay-off of 1,600 workers. Once again New London was in trouble and in need of new industry. The Templeton Radio Company which employed a sizable number of persons through its war contracts had to curtail operations and lay off workers at the end of the war. Unable to weather the economically difficult period from wartime to peacetime operations it eventually went out of business.

The army presence at New London was greatly reduced after the war when it abandoned Fort Terry, Fort Michie and part of Fort Wright.

The State A.F. of L. planned to hold its convention in New London but the lack of housing and hotel accommodations forced it to cancel its plans October of 1945.

By 1971 unemployment reached an all time high. The New London office of the State Employment Security Division reported that New London had the highest rise in the state. At the same time the pay rate was the highest in Connecticut, $171.40 weekly—$4.13 hourly. The unemployment rate was 7.4% while Norwich with a weekly rate of $132.18, hourly rate of $3.28 had unemployment of 8.9 percent.[76]

A new Mall of sixty-eight acres with forty stores was planned as a shopping center to be built on I 95 Waterford. New London was to build a Mall on State Street with $50,000 local money and $400,000 federal money. The Governor Winthrop Parking Garage reported a profit after ten months even though it was expected to lose monies for a year. In August of 1971 it made $300 after expenses and in September $1,000.[77]

8 Some 19th Century Business Figures 1800-1899

The nineteenth century proved to be the period of greatest growth at the port. Whaling, banking, shipbuilding, maritime commerce, industrial and mercantile establishments flourished. It seems only proper to detail the careers of some of those responsible.

ALLYN

Captain Francis Allyn (1791-1862) became a captain in the Atlantic trade. He lost the Swallowtail packet, *George Canning,* when it was beached on the Jersey Shore January 7, 1832. A cherished part of his life involved a close friendship with General Lafayette. He received a signal honor in 1824 when Lafayette rejected a United States Navy vessel ride in order to travel to America with Captain Allyn. When Allyn returned permanently to New London, he purchased several whalers. Active poltically, he became mayor of New London 1838 to 1841. Allyn was one of the organizers and president of the New London Cemetery Association. He died August 27, 1862 at the age of seventy-two.[1]

A Montville native, Lyman Allyn, arrived in New London at twenty-one and shipped out on whalers of Daniel Deshon and N. & W. W. Billings. He became a captain for Billings and prospered enough to send out his own vessels as whaling agent. Success appeared to have come early and lasted throughout his career. Born in 1797, he settled at New London in 1818. His home was that of his former employer, Captain Deshon, built in 1815.

Lyman Allyn served in the State Legislature and actively supported the Democratic Party. He became a member of the Episcopal Church. A

Captain Francis Allyn, 1791-1862.

Acors Barns, 1774-1862.

daughter, Harriet Upson Allyn, left a million dollar fund for the Lyman Allyn Park and Museum in 1926.[2]

Interestingly, a second Lyman Allyn, born in Groton, also moved to New London where he operated a store furnishing ship hardware and parts. In

1827 he moved to New York and owned and invested in whaling vessels. He died in Jersey City in December of 1869 leaving a fortune of two million dollars.[3]

BARNS

Acors Barns, born May 13, 1794 in Westerly, Rhode Island, became one of the leading merchants of New London. Starting as a sailor in the coastal trade, he advanced to captain and then to owner of his own vessel. During the War of 1812, he lost his vessel to the British and became a prisoner. Upon regaining his freedom, Barns took part in raiding expeditions on the British and carried correspondence between Stonington and the British Fleet during the attack upon that town.

Once peace came, he had to start over again, in fact now he had the debt of the lost vessel to pay. Barns became a sailor in the cod fishery and once again advanced to captain, carrying fish to Spain and Portugal as well as dried fruits to New York. A rather long association with the Williams family began when Barns, who operated out of Stonington, went to work for General William Williams. In 1827 he moved to New London and began working for Major T. W. Williams and from 1828 to 1858 Barns devoted most of his time to the Williams and Barns Firm. He retired from the firm in 1858, last of the original members to do so.

Acors Barns remained active in the coastal trade and organized a large fleet of sloops, schooners and later propellers. In 1844 he became one of the organizers and owners of the first propeller line between New London and New York. As an Incorporator and director of the New London, Willimantic and Palmer Railroad, he took an active role and much of the success of the New London Northern Railroad resulted from the direction he gave it. In 1852 he became an incorporator and president of the Bank of Commerce. Acors Barns served as district commissioner for the New London School Society. New London lost an excellent businessman when he died November 18, 1862 at the age of sixty-eight. Barns married Hannah Dickins of Stonington in 1817 and they had three sons, William H., Charles and Thomas.[4] Their son William H. Barns (1821-1886) joined Williams and Barns in 1847. After the whaling business decline, he became president of the Wilson Manufacturing Company. In his last years he became president of the National Bank of Commerce and president of the Mariners Savings Bank. He died in 1886 at the age of sixty-five.[5]

Charles Barns joined the whaling firm in 1856 after being in business in New York. He was director and president of the National Bank of Commerce, a member of the Board of Sewer Commissioners and Connecticut

House of Representatives. He never married and died of Brights disease in 1902 leaving an estate of half a million dollars.[6]

Thomas Barns slipped on a piece of wood at the Mansfield Railroad Station and had his leg crushed by a train. He bound up his own wound. As a result the leg had to be amputated and he died November 10, 1852.[7]

BILLINGS

Coddington Billings (October 25, 1770-February 6, 1845), a merchant of Stonington, married Eunice Williams daughter of General William Williams. Billings later moved to New London and engaged in various businesses. His sons Noyes (1800-1865) and William Williams (1802-1885) were merchants and whaling agents in their own firm N. & W. W. Billings.[8]

Noyes graduated from Yale in 1819 and entered a partnership with his brother in 1823. He married Isabella Steward in 1826. Entering politics, Noyes served as mayor of New London 1835-1837. Also, he became Lieutenant Governor in 1846, the first state office held by New London since Governor Gurdon Saltonstall's term. Travel became Noyes' main occupation during retirement.[9]

William Williams Billings graduated from Yale in 1821 and began his merchant career in a counting house. Later he made voyages to Portugal and France before forming the partnership with his brother. In 1828 he married Louise Trott. He was a member of St. James Episcopal Church. The brothers operated a soap and candle manufacturing business (1822-1851), as well as a very successful whaling business. Operations ended in 1851.

In retirement W. W. Billings travelled on board his steam yacht and raised valuable cattle. By 1887 he had become one of the last whaling merchants still alive. He died in July of 1887 and left an estate in excess of three hundred thousand dollars.[10]

CHAPELL

Richard H. Chapell (1826-1874) attracted the attention of Henry Haven while in the Gilead Sunday School in 1837. So taken was Haven that he took Chapell into his own home to be educated and trained him for a business career. He began his career with Williams and Haven, becoming associate advisor and finally a partner.

Chapell opened several new business ventures for the firm—sea elephant hunting in the Antarctic, the Guano Industry in the McKean Islands and the Seal Industry in Alaska. These business developments

Richard H. Chapell, 1826-1874.

meant a great deal of travel abroad. In 1867, Chapell sailed for San Francisco via the Hawaiian Islands where he became one of five trustees of the Alaska Commercial Company. He went to Scotland in 1871 and purchased the bark *Fame*. In 1872 he travelled to England on business for the Alaska Commercial Company.

An effort to stimulate growth of the town led to the formation of the Board of Trade by leading merchants. Chapell became president in 1874. He served twice in the State Legislature and among other posts served as a member of the first Board of Water Commissioners, a director of the New London City National Bank, an organizor of the Mariner's Savings Bank and prepared the Civil War Stone Fleets.

Chapell remained active in Congregational Church affairs throughout his life. In 1852 he became secretary-treasurer of Cedar Grove Cemetery and served until his death. Cornelia B. Wetmore of Brooklyn became the wife of Chapell on October 4, 1855. He had a new house built on Hempstead Street in 1873. Death ended this outstanding career on August 29, 1874 at the age of forty-eight.[11]

COIT

Leadership of the Coit family continued in the nineteenth century. Joshua Coit's son, Robert (1785-1874) began his career by travelling between New London and the West Indies for the Coit family interests. Later

Robert Coit, 1830-1904.

he became involved in the ship chandlery business and a dealer in lumber and coal. One of the founders of the Savings Bank, he became its president in 1852-1858. A strongly religious man, Robert Coit served as deacon in the Second Congregational Church. Of his seven children, four girls and three boys, three of the daughters married ministers and one of the sons became a minister.

Civic responsibility, an obligation readily accepted by the New London merchants, meant Robert Coit gave much of himself for others. Thus he acted as secretary and treasurer of the Smith Memorial Home and trustee of the J. N. Harris estate. His son Robert and grandson, William, had outstanding business and legal careers.[12]

Robert Coit Jr. (1830-1904) graduated from Yale in 1850 and after three years of law study with William C. Crump and at the Yale Law School, was admitted to the bar. Law led to a judgeship, 1860-1864 (Judge of Probate) and Registrar of Bankruptcy 1864-1867. The business interests of this man were many and varied. His posts included being treasurer of the New London and Northern Railroad Company, director of the Central Vermont Railroad, president of the Union Bank, vice president of the New London Savings Bank, president of the New London Steamboat Company and president of the New London Gas and Electric Company.

Robert Coit was one of the Republican political leaders of New London.

In1879 he became mayor, representative in 1879 to the lower house of the assembly and served four years in the State Senate.[13]

William Coit (1862-1920), only son of Robert Jr., followed a career similar to his father—attendance at Yale, law studies with John C. Crump and admission to the bar in 1887. He became Judge of the City and Police Courts, Clerk of the Court of Common Pleas, Prosecuting Attorney of New London and a member of the State Legislature 1901-1903.

He had extensive business activities. Coit was Vice president of the Union Bank, director of Savings Bank of New London and district manager of the Mutual Life Insurance Company. Civic and social activities included the post of secretary and treasurer of the Smith Memorial Home and memberships in the Winthrop Club, Thames Club and Pequot Casino Association.[14]

Alfred Coit, son of Robert (1836-1879), born at New London, graduated from Yale 1856 and Harvard Law School 1858. He was admitted to the bar and led the usual active life of a Coit. Even though he attended a private institution he worked for the improvement of public schools, served on the State Board of Education in 1865 and became State Senator in 1868. Other posts held included Judge of the Common Pleas Court and first vice president of the Savings Bank of New London.[15]

CRANDALL

Herbert L. Crandall (1844-1927) became one of the last New London merchants to begin his career as an office boy in a whaling firm. When he was seventeen, Henry P. Haven employed him and through hard work he became a bookkeeper and then executive of the Williams and Haven firm. His connection with whaling only ended when C. A. Williams and Company ceased operations with the sale of their last ship in the 1890's. Crandall became an expert in commercial law and laws of navigation.

He had been born in New London and in 1879 married Alice M. Greene, daughter of whaling captain Samuel Greene. His business interests included the secretaryship of the Fisher's Island Brick Company, a directorship of the New London City National Bank as well as vice president and an officer in the whaling firm of Williams and Haven and C. A. Williams, its successor.

In civic areas he held the posts of trustee of the Second Congregational Church, treasurer of the Thomas W. Williams II Fund and member and treasurer of the Board of Education. He served as secretary-treasurer of Cedar Grove Cemetery for forty-five years and kept the records until he resigned on October 29, 1919. His death came January 18, 1927 at the age of eighty-three.[16]

FRINK

David Frink owned Frink's Coffee House on Bank Street and engaged in the West Indian trade of mules and molasses from his own wharf. His sons, E. N. (1776-1836) and A. M. Frink (1793-1867) engaged in the whaling trade and other businesses with brother Adam as a silent partner.[17]

E. M. sold oil and engaged in foreign businesses besides acting as whaling agent. He died at sixty in 1836. His long years of service to the port resulted in the lowering of all colors to half-mast in honor of his ability.[18]

Andrew M. Frink, born at New London June 29, 1793, owned a shipping fleet and engaged in whaling, being a member of several firms. He also operated a fleet of merchant vessels. As one of the directors of the New London, Willimantic and Springfield Railroad, Frink was responsible for much of the success in saving the business. He served as mayor of New London 1843-1845. He died June 19, 1867 at the age of seventy-four.[19]

Adam Frink (1780-1869) and A. M. Frink owned a wharf which they sold to the New Haven, New London and Stonington Railroad for a station site on Bank Street. Adam died March 8, 1869.[20]

HARRIS

A leading merchant of New London, Jonathan Newton Harris (1815-1896), was one of the very powerful leaders of the nineteenth century not directly connected with the whaling industry. While the Harris family arrived in New London about 1690, J. N. Harris' family lived in Salem and he did not move to the port until 1836. The next sixty years were full ones as Harris engaged in business activity, not just in New London but all over the world. His educational, political, religious and social activities were also extensive.

From 1838 to 1865, he operated a New London business, both alone and with partners, which began as a grocery store and expanded over the years to a general operation selling supplies, tools, agricultural implements and patent medicines. Harris closed his general store business as his other interests were far more lucrative and important.

In the patent medicine field, he owned and distributed the Davis Pain Killer and the S. A. Weaver line of medicines. In addition he organized and held the presidency of the J. N. Harris and Company of Cincinnati from 1848 to his death. He was one of the organizers and president of the Fellows Medical Manufacturing Company of Montreal which had

Jonathan Newton Harris, 1815-1896.

branches in London and New York, a director of the Davis and Lawrence Company of Montreal and he operated a coal and lumber business in Pennsylvania.

If these worldwide businesses were not enough to keep him busy, he served as president of both the New London Steamboat Company and New London Gas Company, and as director of the New London Northern Railroad Company. The banking activities of Harris extended over forty years and included posts as a director of the Bank of Commerce and as president of the New London City National Bank from 1876 to 1896. In 1885, when seventy years of age, he built and directed the Harris Building, a spacious structure which housed three large stores, thirty offices and eleven large apartments on State Street in New London.

J. N. Harris devoted much time and money to civic affairs. He donated $10,000 for the erection and maintenance in 1891 of the Memorial Hospital.[21] The Y.M.C.A. proved to be one of Harris' favorite organizations. He helped form the New London Y.M.C.A. in 1852 which was the ninth in North America. When the Harris building opened, he gave the "Y" space and provided $5,000 when the time came to move to larger quarters in 1891.[22] A firm supporter of Christian education and a close friend of Dwight L. Moody, he aided Moody's Northfield Seminary for girls and became a founder of Moody's Mount Hermon School for boys to which he gave enough money to erect two buildings. Harris served as president of the Board of Trustees of Mount Hermon School from 1893 to 1896.

For twenty years he was a leader in the open air meetings held on the streets of New London each summer. During the Civil War he held religious service at Fort Trumbull nearly every Sunday. Harris gave $100,000.00 to Doshisha University of Japan for the Harris School of Science in 1889.[23]

Active in politics, he served as mayor of New London from 1856 to 1862. A fellow Republican and close friend of Governor Buckingham, Harris wholeheartedly supported his administration. He was a representative to the State Assembly in 1855 and a State Senator in 1864.

Married twice, his first wife was the daughter of Benjamin Brown and his second wife the granddaughter of Governor Strong of Massachusetts. The first marriage produced eight children. He built a lavish mansion on Broad Street.

Harris made a pilgrimage to the Holy Land and gave lectures on it to church groups in 1871. Stricken with heart disease, he died October 18, 1896 at the age of eighty-one after an overnight illness. After his death his home became the site of the Williams Memorial Institute and funds were left for scholarships.[24]

His will created a trust fund for certain religious, educational, humanitarian and charitable organizations. Outright bequests from his will included $2,000 to the Bradley Street Mission of New London, $2,000 to the Reverend James W. Bixler, pastor of Harris' church, $2,000 to the International Y.M.C.A., $15,000 to the American Board of Commissioners for Foreign Missions, $15,000 to the Home Missionary Society, $10,000 to Northfield Seminary, 41 shares of the Northfield Hotel to be divided between Northfield Seminary and Mount Hermon School. Mrs. Harris gave the Second Congregational Church a parsonage.[25] The trust money came from rentals and thus was known as the Harris Building Charitable Trust. However, in 1924 the Probate Court gave the trustees permission to sell the building and invest the funds. Since that time the trustees have distributed the income to the seven beneficiaries. The five trustees who control the trust distribute over $40,000 annually at the present time.

HAVEN

Of all the leading merchants in New London's history, none combined "puritan religiosity and Yankee shrewdness as well as Henry Philemon Haven (1815-1876). Religion remained a dominant part of his life to the day he died, a classical example of a God fearing New England Puritan

Henry P. Haven, 1815-1876.

who achieved success through hard work and service. A poor boy, who became self reliant early, Haven's life sounds like an Horatio Alger story. His mother, Fanny Manwaring married Joshua Caulkins in 1792, who died of yellow fever in 1798 at Port au Prince while on a trading voyage to St. Domingo. Left a widow with two daughters, Fanny Manwaring Caulkins married Philemon Haven in 1807 only to be widowed a second time in 1819. Henry had been born February 11, 1815 in Norwich, one of three children of the second marriage.[26]

They were quite poor and he learned early to carry his share of responsibilities. The family moved to New London by 1830 where his half-sister, Francis Manwaring Caulkins, became principal of a female academy. At this time Henry P. Haven approached the whaling firm of Major Thomas W. Williams seeking work. Once hired, the hardworking, shrewd and ambitious boy rose rapidly in the firm.

A very capable businessman, he had a reputation as a very hard man, despotic to employees, witty in speech, and sharp in business deals. Henry Haven had wide interests in banking, sea-elephantry, sealing, railroading and whaling. He directed the affairs of a number of firms for some thirty-eight years, 1838-1876. During this period he found time for Sunday School teaching, church leadership, political office-holding and service to educational and charitable organizations. He gave much to charity and encouraged others to be generous in their giving. Although Haven was always ready to help those less fortunate, he disliked anyone being late. He was always on time himself and would reject job applicants or discharge employees for being late.[27]

Haven became active in the management of financial institutions—the Bank of Commerce, the Equitable Trust Company, Mariners Savings Bank, and the New London City National Bank. He was an organizer and a director of the Bank of Commerce, an organizer, a director and the vice-president of the Mariners Savings Bank, the vice-president of the Equitable Trust Company and the president of the New London City National Bank.[28]

Haven, an investor in the New London, Willimantic and Palmer Railroad Company, was one of the trustees who took over the line when it had financial difficulties in 1859. Under his leadership the company reorganized as the New London Northern Railroad Company with Haven as president.[29]

Sealing proved one of the more profitable enterprises of Haven. In thirty-eight years his company sent sealing expeditions out to the Arctic and Antarctic Circles, St. Paul, St. George, South Georgia and the South Shetland Islands for returns worth three million dollars. In several parts of the world Haven's sealers opened new sealing grounds. To increase the margin of profit he decided to have sealing ships sail with tenders, usually schooners, which remained in the sealing grounds collecting skins and oil while the ships returned as soon as filled with cargoes. A pioneer in the development of the Alaskan fur fishery, Henry P. Haven was a partner in the Alaska Commercial Company which leased the Islands of St. Paul and St. George in the Bering Sea.[30]

He organized the Phoenix Guano Company and established a colony of Kanakas at the Phoenix Islands in Western Pacific to load the guano on vessels. He shipped it to European as well as American ports—70,000 tons to Europe. Although investments did not always go well and some business ventures required considerable investment before any return was realized he kept his faith and many services were performed by Haven.[31] His company possessed the first trustworthy chart of Kergullen's Island which had been made by one of the firms captains. The United States government used it in 1874 to send a scientific party to the island to observe the transit of Venus. His captains had orders to pick up and set down where desired any Arctic explorers they might encounter and to supply them freely.[32]

In his youth Haven attended school irregularly due to the lack of money and time. He valued education and gave much of his time to educational matters. He established evening schools for those unable to attend regular school. Also he served as chairman of the New London Board of Education, a trustee of the Board for the State Normal School (now Central Connecticut State College), and president of the American College and Education Society. Haven became chariman of the New London Board of Visitors and examiner of teachers for the New London schools from 1856 to 1876. He even found time to be active in politics from 1853 to 1856. He held the office of mayor of New London and a seat in the General Assembly. In 1873 he ran for the governor's seat against H. B. Harrison of New Haven and lost. A severe disappointment came to him when he lost as he was accustomed to being successful and working hard for that success, defeat came very hard.[33]

Henry Haven, a very active member of the Second Congregational Church in New London, devoted much of his life to the Sunday School movement in town and the surrounding areas. His interest in the Sunday School came when a young lady, Harriet Lathrop, was refused the use of the church for her school and began to use the porch of the church for classes. After a time she was allowed use of the church and Henry learned a great deal about organizing and running schools from her work. In 1836 he offered to help start a Sunday School in the Gilead section of Waterford, an area with a bad reputation as a relaxing stop for sailors from New London port. It turned out that he was the whole staff but Haven pitched in worked hard and within four years he had the school well organized. He developed a staff and served as superintendent for forty years, appearing each Sunday afternoon, summer and winter. In 1858 he became superintendent of the Sunday School at the Second Congregational Church at New London. He began a number of other Sunday Schools and also organized several churches. Haven preached until ministers could be hired, taught Sunday School where needed and headed such schools as superintendent until he could train someone to take over.

Due to the great demands upon his time Haven was well organized and kept excellent minute records. Every Friday evening he held an institute or normal class for some 200 teachers of the New London Sunday Schools, Saturdays he rode to Waterford and addressed a Sunday School at noon and then preached in the afternoons at a Baptist Seventh Day Church. Saturday nights he met at his home with his Sunday School teachers for the morrow's lessons. On Sunday morning he opened Sunday School at the Second Congregational Church in New London.

The first to arrive would begin to sing and as each came in they joined the singing until all were there. After Sunday School he rode to Waterford and preached in a Baptist Church, directed its Sunday School and in the afternoon directed the Sunday School at the Waterford Congregational Church. After classes ended he held a meeting with his Sunday School staff and then in the evening he returned for services at the New London Second Congregational Church. During the week he met with his teachers for an hour between five A. M. and six A. M.[34]

With all this he still found time to be secretary of the New London County Foreign Missionary Association, a member of the American Board of Commissioners for Foreign Missions, vice president of the American Sunday School Union, vice president of the American Bible Society and director and vice president of the American Tract Society. Henry P. Haven served as president of the Systematic Benefice Society whose members set aside part of their income for benevolent purposes.

He travelled about the world for Sunday School meetings including trips to Indianapolis as a delegate from Connecticut to the Fifth National Sunday School Convention in 1872 and to London as representative from the United States to its Congregational Union of England and Wales held in 1875.

Haven was elected by the State Sunday School Convention of Connecticut to be a delegate to the National Sunday School Convention as well as being chosen president of the State Convention. He was a representative of the New England International Denominational Committee which prepared Union Sabbath School lessons. Amherst College honored him with an honorary M.A. degree in 1873 where his son H. C. Haven studied before attending medical school at Harvard.

In 1869 he became vice president of the Soldiers Orphan Home for New London County. Haven urged the formation of and worked to found the New London County Historical Society which he served as director.[35]

Haven married Elizabeth Lucas Douglas of Waterford on February 23, 1840. He maintained a large household, living at first in his mother's home with his sister Elizabeth and his two half sisters as well as his wife. In 1842 they moved to a new home where the family group was increased by the birth of three children Anna, Henry Cecil, and Thomas Williams. R. H. Chapell, a friend and partner, also lived in the Haven home for eighteen years. A fountain added to the attractiveness of his home surroundings as did his hobby, flower raising. His greenhouse presented an outstanding exhibit of rare flowers including the night blooming cereus.[36]

A series of deaths among the people around him, saddened Henry. His sister Elizabeth died of consumption in 1842, his mother in 1854, his half sister, the well known teacher and author, Frances Manwaring Caulkins to

Sebastian D. Lawrence, 1823-1909.

whom Henry had become quite close, in 1869, his son Thomas in 1870 at the age of twenty-three. 1874 dealt him a double blow with the death of his wife and R. H. Chapell, friend and partner.[37]

In 1876 Henry Haven's busy life came to an end. He died at sixty-one, just three years after having relinquished direction of the firms he had directed for thirty-five years. After feeling ill for a week he died at his home on the corner of Broad and Hempstead Street home April 30, 1876. He carried out his duties as usual to the last and as the church bells called the Sunday School members together he passed away.[38]

Haven left his ample fortune to each of two surviving children and to charity (one-third each). The New London Public Library building was built with the one-third left for charity.[39]

Thomas Williams Haven, son of Henry P. Haven, trained in the counting room of Williams and Haven, became a partner in the Williams, Haven & Company organized in 1869. After a business trip south for the firm he came down with jaundice and died in August of 1870.[40]

LAWRENCE

Probably the richest of the nineteenth century merchants at the port, Joseph Lawrence (1788-1872), engaged in many business activities in addition to whaling from which much of the family wealth originated. The family business interests included coastal and foreign trade, banking, railroading, business properties as well as stocks and bonds.

Lawrence's vessels carried whaling and sundry cargo from New London to various coastal ports and foreign ports. Among the firm's vessels was the huge 700 ton *Atlantic*. Joseph Lawrence was one of the organizers of the Whaling Bank in 1832-1833 and the New London County Savings Bank in 1855. He worked with a group of merchants to obtain a rail connection for the port. After failing to get a rail extension built from Norwich to New London, Lawrence joined a group which received a charter for a railroad, the New London, Willimantic and Palmer in which he became the third largest investor. He built and operated Lawrence Hall, the leading amusement place in New London, the Exchange Building and Union Hall on Golden Street, store property on Bank Street and several dwelling places including his residence, an Italian villa at Federal and Main Streets.[41]

A very energetic businessman, Joseph Lawrence, had no less than five advertisements in the *New London Gazette* of July 30, 1828. These included offering a schooner for sale, seeking cargo for a coastal schooner and general merchandise for sale at his store. He was always kind and polite, he would not waste time in idle talk. Headquarters for his developing business empire became the Lawrence Wharf which Joseph built in 1830 with his office in the basement. An inventory of his estate in 1833 totalled $162,750 attesting to a considerable fortune which gives one an indication of a first rate businessman.

Cash on hand	$102,000
Merchandise	2,000
Farm at New London	2,000
Sloop *Independence*	6,000
Notes	3,000
Gilbert Cooper	5,000
Elias Perkins	3,000
House in New London	8,500
Ship *Tuscarora*	30,000
Misc. (Not accounted for)	1,250
	$162,750[42]

Joseph Lawrence established a regular line of packets between Philadelphia and New London in 1840 with vessels departing every two weeks. He married Nancy Woodward Brown, daughter of Jeremiah Brown, wealthy farmer in 1817.[43]

His three sons, Joseph Jeremiah, Francis Watson, and Sebastian Duffy all attended Bacon Academy in preparation for college, but only one attended college and he did not finish. Joseph J. (1820-1893) went to sea as a boy and became a clipper and packet ship captain by the age of twenty-one. Although his papers indicate close New London ties, the Lawrence Company Papers and information about the rest of the family contain no references at all to Joseph J. Lawrence. He lived most of his life in New York City, except for a short residence in Europe, and sailed between New York and Liverpool.[44]

Usually the vessel he commanded was owned by himself and several New London merchants, with one or two owners from outside New London. For example the *Hindoo* which he captained was owned by J. J. Lawrence, Joseph Lawrence, Sidney Miner and John McCrea of Philadelphia. Lawrence was a capable captain as indicated by an incident entered in the log of the ship *Hindoo* on March 11, 1845. He had boarded the *Hindoo* to replace a Captain Proctor only to find the crew refused to accept the change. Lawrence had the crew called out on deck and read the ships articles to them and only three then agreed to work. Finally he gave them ten minutes to go to work or receive a thrashing. At the end of the ten minutes all went to work. His comment in the log "so ended this squall."[45]

Joseph J. married and had three daughters. He retired at the age of sixty-eight and died suddenly December 7, 1893 at his luxurious home. Although a stone containing his dates of birth and death has been placed in the Lawrence family plot, Cedar Grove Cemetery, his body is interred at Milford.[46]

Francis W. (1821-1895) went to Yale for two years before illness forced him to return home. He then entered the family business. Sebastian D. (1823-1909) joined the family business in 1843 after being educated at local schools and the Bacon Academy, Colchester. The brothers worked as clerks and Sidney Miner was confidential manager until they formed a partnership upon the retirement of the father in 1844.

The firm, Miner, Lawrence and Company, prospered and had a fleet of over one hundred vessels in all types of trade. Miner retired from the firm in 1850 and the brothers operated a business known as Lawrence and Company. In all the years the firm sent out ships, no more than five failed to return and only two lives were lost.

Francis W. Lawrence handled the firm's real estate holdings such as Lawrence Hall, the Exchange Building and Union Hall block, several store properties, several residences in the city and real estate investments in the midwest. Suffering from chronic asthma for thirty years, it finally forced his retirement in 1895, the year he died. Francis never married and his brother received his estate.[47] Sebastian Duffy Lawrence served as president of the National Whaling Bank, which his father had help establish, from 1863-1909 and as director of International Fire Insurance Company of New York. S. D. Lawrence invested heavily in stocks and bonds and kept a large account, as much as forty thousand dollars, with a New York firm, Euyler, Morgan and Company, for investments. Although he invested in several types of stocks and bonds, railroads attracted most of his attention. Altogether he held stock in twenty-seven different railroads over the years. Also records indicate holdings of lands and stocks of the following: National Park Bank, North American Company, New York and Texas Land Company, Amalgamated Copper, Otis Elevator Company and General Electric Company.[48]

S. D. Lawrence kept several large sums in several New York banks. In 1902 he had $52,000 at Colonial Trust Company at three percent and $92,000 at Guaranty Trust Company at three percent. Lawrence requested each pay five percent on deposits over $50,000. Both refused, but the Colonial Trust did raise the rate to three and one-half percent. He often donated to those in need as attested by several documents.[49]

One of the wealthiest merchants of Connecticut, a Democrat and a member of the Episcopal Church, he had the Soldiers and Sailors Monument built at a cost of more than $20,000 in 1896 and in 1897 the Firemen's Monument for $3,500.[50] Sebastian Lawrence, last of the family, left ten million dollars at his death in 1909. His will of 1895 provided for a number of needy items in the town.

$50,000	for an Alms House
5,000	for dinners on Thanksgiving and July 4 for those at the Alms House
15,000	St. James in honor of his father
2,000	Maintenance of pew
1,000	Maintenance of plot—New London Cemetery
20,000	for Protestant Church of Connecticut (the establishment and maintenance in small communities)
10,000	for Aged Clergy and their families
6,000	to St. Marys Star of the Sea (to complete spire)
1,000	New London County Historical Society
1,000	Jibboom Club
500	W. Perkins Post (GAR) plus other numerous gifts to friends.

Also Lawrence asked that the Whaling Bank be closed, while the trustees decided not to do so. The most valuable provision provided for a free public hospital. He left land, Lawrence Hall, a granite building, $100,000 for buildings and a $400,000 endowment fund for such an institution. It remains a fitting monument to the business success of the Lawrence family and the whaling port.[51]

MINER

The Miner family appeared at New London in 1643, where Thomas Miner's son, Manasseh, was the first European male born at the port. The diary of Thomas Miner is a valuable account of colonial days in Southeastern Connecticut. The family settled on the east side of the river. Frederick Miner born September 28, 1768 at Stonington moved to New London in 1795 and engaged in mercantile business. He died July 9, 1849.[52]

His son, Sidney (December 16, 1805-December 20, 1881), began his career as a dry goods store clerk, then went to work for Joseph Lawrence. In 1844 he became a partner with Lawrence and later formed a firm with the Lawrence sons. He retired in 1855. Miner then entered the coastal trade with several vessels.

Politically he favored the Democratic Party and served as alderman, assessor, financial treasurer, on the board of relief and the school committee. Miner resigned in 1873 from the finance committee due to the Mayor's "strongly censuring my management as chairman of the finance committee . . ."[53]

He was a member of the First Congregational Church. He married twice—Mary Ann Ramsdell in 1834 who had three children and Lydia Jewett Belcher in 1844 having two children. He built a mansion house in 1851.[54]

PERKINS

When the Shaw merchant leadership ended with the death of Thomas Shaw in 1795, the Perkins family, based in the Shaw homestead continued on the tradition of marine commerce and civic leadership so splendidly begun by Captain Nathaniel Shaw early in the eighteenth century. Thomas Shaw's niece, Lucretia Shaw Woodbridge married Elias Perkins. The Perkins took an active part in New London affairs in the nineteenth century. The major family members from 1784 to 1905 were Judge Elias Perkins (1767-1845), his son, Dr. Nathaniel Shaw Perkins (1792-1870) and grandsons, Elias Perkins (1819-1883) and Nathaniel Shaw Perkins (1822-1905). With the death of Nathaniel Shaw Perkins the male side of the line ended.[55]

Elias Perkins married Lucretia Shaw Woodbridge, niece of Nathaniel

Shaw and Thomas Shaw and moved into the Shaw Mansion in 1790. A lawyer, he became judge of the Connecticut Supreme Court. Perkins studied law with Oliver Ellsworth (1786-1788).

> Mr. Elias Perkins has Studied Law with me two years—during which his application & I think Proficiency, have been good. He has had the honors Yale College, & is of a fair moral character.[56]

He was admitted to the Bar on the first Tuesday of November 1788. Perkins served as judge for a number of years, being appointed in 1807 to the Superior Court, 1810-1817 to the County Court and in 1821 Chief Judge of the County Court. He was a Federalist who served in the United States Congress 1801-1803, in the lower house of the General Assembly 1795-1800, 1814-1815 and the upper house 1817-1822, holding the Speakers post in 1798 and 1815. Perkins became mayor of New London 1829-1832.[57]

He was a member of a group which established the Hartford and New London Turnpike Company in 1800. A strip of land known as the Connecticut Gore caused trouble between Connecticut and New York when an error in the drawing of the New York-Pennsylvania boundary line led to Connecticut claiming an area two and one-half miles wide and two hundred miles long. Elias Perkins, Nathaniel Smith and John Sturges were appointed commissioners from Connecticut to settle the dispute with New York. To secure clear title to the Western Reserve, Connecticut gave up its claim.[58]

In 1796 he became a member of a bridge company which built a toll bridge across the Niantic River and was appointed as bridge commissioner in 1812. He also served as trustee to the Bacon Academy at Colchester in 1807.

Mary Perkins, the second wife of Elias, also exerted leadership. She petitioned to establish the Lewis Female Cent Society for relief of indigent persons. The Judge died at the Shaw Mansion the 25th of September 1845 at the age of seventy-eight.[59]

Judge Elias Perkins' son, Nathaniel Shaw Perkins (1792-1870), a doctor engaged in various merchant activities. He was a member of the corporation which established the Savings Bank in May of 1828. He also invested in western land, actually midwestern, in Indiana and held $11,050 of stock in the Norwalk, Ohio Bank. The return from the last appeared excellent as records indicate a 102 percent return. He was a member of the First Congregational Church, married Ellen Richards on May 19, 1818 and had fourteen children.[60]

Elias Perkins (1819-1883) son of Dr. N. S. Perkins attended Yale but had to withdraw because of illness. He invested in western land and had the power of attorney for a New London group which had invested in the Norwalk (Ohio) Bank. He acted as secretary of the New London Railroad Company from its founding to 1863 when he resigned to become consul to Hawaii. N. S. Perkins, Jr. and Elias Perkins, brothers, formed Perkins and Smith firm with Captain Franklin Smith. Elias acted as agent in Hawaii for the firm.

Perkins and Smith went into bankruptcy in 1857 and Dr. N. S. Perkins mortgaged part of his property to aid his sons. Later the Fisher's Island Navigation Company took over the wharf property.[61]

Thomas Shaw Perkins (1793-1844) brother of Dr. N. S. Perkins sailed to Hawaii on a whaler for health reasons, then to Valpraisio, Chile where improved in health he decided to return home. Unfortunately he died on the homeward voyage in September of 1844.[62]

His son, Roger Griswold Perkins served in the Confederate Forces. He married and moved south where he was a lawyer in South Carolina. While a sergeant in the confederate army he caught typhoid fever and died at his father-in-laws, Benjamin in Camden, South Carolina, 1862. His cousin, Lt. William Williams Perkins (1841-1862) son of Dr. N. S. Perkins died December 14, 1862, killed in action at Kingston, North Carolina. His brother, Benjamin R. Perkins (1832-1871) enlisted as a private in the Union Army in the Civil War and died February 7, 1871 at Fort Whipple as a major. Their brother, Francis A. Perkins married Anna Haven. N. S. Perkins, son of Dr. N. S. Perkins, was the last male of the line.[63]

STARR

William Holt Starr (1808-1884) had a long and interesting business career. He started as a carpenter, taught school, became a grocer and entered the fruit business. He operated businesses in New York City and Pennsylvania as well as in New London. By the end of the Civil War he had been successful enough to have $100,000 a year income.

He lost his fortune when the Civil War ended and iron and coal prices fell. His coal, gas and iron works were lost. Starr operated a number of businesses in town—New London Nursery, Starr Coal Company, New London Oil and Lumber Company and the *New London Repository*. He was also quite active in politics—1858 in the state senate, alderman and Commissioner of charters. Starr wrote a *Centennial Historical Sketch of New London* (1876) and was secretary of New London County Historical Society 1874-1884. He belonged to the First Congregational Church.[64]

WEAVER

C. Arnold Weaver (1821-1893) son of Wanton A. Weaver merchant, moved to New London in 1828 where he worked for Weaver and Rogers until he left in 1843. When he returned in 1846 he received a partnership with Weaver and Rogers operating a ship chandlery and grocery business as well as whaling. He was a member of the Baptist Church, a Republican, a director of the First National Bank and a member of the County Council. He married S. Augusta Brown in 1846.[65]

WILLIAMS

General William Williams (1765-1838) began in the West Indian trade with operations from Stonington. He expanded to coastal, fishing and foreign trade. Coddington Billings worked with him in the shipping business. General Williams moved to New London and engaged in world wide maritime activity. His sons and grandsons became powerful merchants in New London during the nineteenth century.[66]

William Williams, Jr., and Thomas Wheeler Williams, sons of William Williams learned the business working for their father's firm. William Williams, Jr. (1784-1870), began his career at fifteen with W. S. Robinson of New York 1800-1806. Then he acted as supercargo for his father to Labrador and Europe—1806-1808. At twenty-four he moved to New London and then Norwich involving himself in the manufacturing of flour and cotton. After his cotton mill failed he went into shipping, 1821-1827 and made a number of successful commercial voyages to Europe and South America before becoming a whaling agent.[67]

He lived on Golden Street in New London and attended the Second Congregational Church, but in 1841 he left the business to his son Thomas Williams, II and moved to Norwich. He became a major-general in the state militia, an incorporator of the Merchants Bank of Norwich 1833, serving as its president for twenty-five years and he also was an organizer of the Norwich Academy.[68]

Very civic and religiously minded he held membership in many organizations. Among others he was an incorporator and member of the American Board of Commissioners for Foreign Missions, vice president of the Bible Society, Seaman's Friend Society and Home Missionary Society and active in aiding the Mohegan Indians. In his will he left $500 income to be used for the Mohegan Indians, $1,000 to the Second Congregational Church and $1,000 trust income for New London indigent seaman.[69]

Thomas W. Williams II, son of William Williams and member of Wil-

Charles Augustus Williams, 1829-1899.

liams and Barns, became a well known merchant in New London. He died suddenly September 12, 1855. Williams had overseen the departure of the *North Star* and suffering from a headache went to the barbers for a shampoo. When this gave him no relief, he asked the barber to pour cold water on his head. He complained of being chilled and became unsensible. Williams was carried home where he died about five that evening in his Huntington Street home at only forty years of age.[70]

Harriet Peck Williams (March 17, 1795-October 14, 1880) wife of William Williams, Jr., founded Bela Peck Library of Norwich Free Academy and left money for a high school known as Williams Memorial Institute for girls in New London as a memorial to her son T. W. Williams II.[71]

T. W. Williams (1789-1874) began his career as a supercargo on the schooner *Alexander Mansfield* of New London to Archangel from New York, 1811. After mercantile training in Russia, England and New York, he became a whaling agent. He married Lucretia Woodbridge Perkins. A Whig and Republican in politics, Williams was elected to Congress in 1838 and served two terms. A leading promoter of New London, Wilimantic and Palmer Railroad, he became its first president. A member of the Second Congregational Church, T. W. Williams served many civic and religious groups and became especially active in temperance movements. His full life ended in 1874.[72]

Charles Augustus Williams (1829-1899), son of Major Thomas W. Williams, joined his father's firm. He travelled to a number of ports learning the business. He lived in Hawaii for several years as agent for his father's firm and operated a whaling business there of his own. From 1852-1873 with Alfred Mitchell as a partner, then he established coastal trade between San Francisco and the Puget Sound. Originally he travelled to the Hawaiian Islands for reasons of health. He married Elizabeth C. Hoyt, had a son William and daughter Mary. Their home was at State and Huntington Streets.[73]

He was one of the organizers of the Phoenix Guano Company and of the Alaskan Commercial Company. After the death of Haven, he operated the Williams and Haven firm as C. A. Williams. He was a member of St. James Episcopal Church. Among his other business affairs, Williams held a directorship in the National Bank of Commerce and organized the Oneco Manufacturing Company. In politics he was Republican and served as mayor of New London from 1885 to 1888.[74]

Civic activities included being president of the library, president of Williams Memorial Institute and president of the New London Cemetery Association. He gave funds to establish a Memorial Park and was a member of the Thames Club.[75]

Charles Augustus Williams became well known in New London as a liberal and enlightened public spirited citizen. He worked hard for sewers and a water system. He died on December 31, 1899 at the age of seventy-one.[76]

William Williams, son of C. A. Williams, was in the United States Department of State and served as junior counsel for the United States Government in the Bering Sea Arbitration Case.[77] His daughter, Mary, married Brigadier General Crozier, Chief of Ordnance, United States Army, and upon her death, Connecticut College received a large bequest which made possible the construction of the Crozier-Williams building on its campus.

9 Maritime New London 1784-1973

New London's streets swarmed with sailors during its maritime heyday. Yankees, Portuguese, Hawaiians—men of many races and backgrounds mixed together at the hotels, saloons and on board vessels. Clerks worked in small dingy offices handling the paper work for millions of dollars worth of goods entering and leaving the port. Above all the din of repairs, shipbuilding, loading and unloading filled the air.

Shipbuilding

While the shipbuilding tradition of New London continued during and after the whaling era, it figured less importantly in the overall economic picture than it had in the colonial period. A number of yards built vessels ranging from whale boats to steamships. At one time New London boasted of over forty shipyards while Boston had only twenty.[1] The Beckwith yard in East New London appeared to have been one of the most active from 1850-1871. Vessels from one-hundred to four-hundred tons were built for fishing, freighting in the African and coastal trade, as well as clippers and yachts and even a whaler, *The Acors Barns*.

Beckwith received orders from as far south as Mobile. Jason Beckwith, with his six brothers, began shipbuilding before the Revolutionary War. When Jason died his sons, Elisha and James carried on the business. In the 1850's James and Daniel Beckwith moved to East New London where they employed fifteen to twenty men the year around.[2] Workers earned $1.16 per day working from sunup to sundown. James Beckwith, of Beckwith and Son, directed the yard from 1850 to 1865.[3] Orders received in 1856 required the employment of a large number of workers. Among the vessels contracted for that year were two schooners valued at five thousand dollars each, one valued at six thousand dollars and a one hundred and fifteen ton fishing schooner. By the following March two more fishing schooners were in the stocks. The yard continued to flourish, even when the Panic of 1857 led to a general depression, turning out fine vessels such as the ship *Julia* launched in 1861. James Beckwith's death in 1865 placed the yard under the direction of E. P. Beckwith. He directed the business through the difficult times following the Civil War. In 1866 Beckwith built several fishing vessels of forty, seventy-four and seventy-five tons.[4]

Amasa Miller operated a busy shipbuilding yard from 1810 to 1828, building vessels as large as four-hundred tons.[5] In 1810 he launched one two-hundred ton and two four-hundred ton for the merchant trade. In 1828 no less than thirty ship carpenters worked at Amasa Miller and Company.[6] Master shipbuilder, William Miller—son of Amasa, produced several large wooden vessels. One of the largest was the bark *N. S. Perkins* in 1852, a three-hundred and ten ton vessel costing eighteen thousand dollars.[7] The William Miller yard built all sizes of vessels from 1848 to 1873.

Story's Shipyard built a whaling vessel of three-hundred and fifty tons in 1822.[8] There seemed to be no other mention of this yard. James Davidson built vessels in New London for forty-seven years, the first on Fort Neck. He built fifty vessels from fishing smacks to eight-hundred ton craft for coastal and foreign trade. Davidson began operations during the 1840's and continued into the 1890's with the Crocker and Davidson partnership lasting for twenty years.[9]

MacDonald and Anderson built vessels at Winthrop's Neck (1892-1896). Their largest, a one-thousand ton, three masted schooner begun in 1893, cost about $32,000. Among the several built by the yard was a seven-hundred ton schooner in 1892.[10]

Whale boats were built by several firms but the Rogers Boat Shop became the best known and lasted the longest. The first whaleboat used by a vessel from New London had been built at the shop he bought and operated. Rogers built whale boats at New London for sixty-two years, 1832-1894 and operated his own shop for fifty-seven years on Bank Street. So skilled a craftsman was Rogers that orders often were so large that it took a year to fill them. He retired in 1894 because, he said, the whale boat building business appeared to be at an end. The fact that he was seventy-nine years of age does not seem to have been a factor in his decision. The boat shop was torn down in 1907.[11]

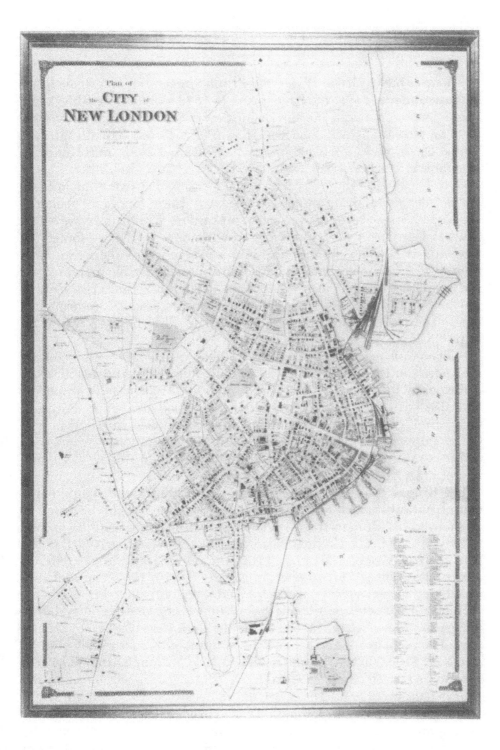

Plan of
the CITY of
NEW LONDON

S. Reeves had a yard at Water and Prison Streets. He built whale boats, sailboats and made oars and handspikes. In 1848 he added on to his yard at Prison Street.[12] Captain William H. Burdick began building whaleboats in 1896 on Howard Street. A busy shop in 1902 included Captain Burdick, Frank Davis and George Shipman.[13] William Bishop and Henry C. Hawthorne began another shop in 1919.[14]

U. N. Gordon, a Water Street boat builder, added an extension in 1838. He had all kinds of boats for sale—whale boats, yawls, fancy race boats and sea boats.[15] Samuel Moxley, Jr., had a shipyard on Winthrop's Cove across from Hallam Street. The railroad—New London Northern—forced the yard out of business so it could build a bridge across the Cove. Sixty workers lost their jobs when Moxley could not find a suitable spot for a new yard and the $12,000 in railroad stock paid for his business became worthless.[16] It should be mentioned that Allan and James Manwaring had one of the largest shipyards in New London. They built several whale ships.[17]

William Coit, a sea captain, became a builder of several vessels including the *Norwich* in 1836.[18] J. H. and H. D. Smith built vessels at Brown's wharf in the period following the Civil War.[19] Fitch and Brainerd built propellers from 1873 to 1877 in East New London. They had great experience and built vessels of fast speed. During 1873 their yard was extremely busy.[20] Other shipyards or builders included John E. Abramson's yard at Winthrop's Cove in 1893.[21] Also located there were John Butler (1890) and Simon Frazer (1888) at the old shipyard.

The Bragaw Shipyard, located on Fort Neck during the 1850's, had a marine railway for repairs and in 1889 Elias Morgan bought the property and moved his Morgan Iron Works there. Morgan enlarged the marine railways in 1894. The Company had become known as The New London Marine Iron Works and after incorporation in 1906, underwent reorganization with T. A. Scott becoming president in 1912. The company had three marine railways and employed seventy-five men.[22]

For a number of years, towards the end of the nineteenth century, hopes of New London centered about having the Bath Iron Works move to the port. The company agreed to move if a number of conditions could be met—e.g. $100,000 for loss on sale of property in Maine; $150,000 worth of bonds to be purchased by New London people; city to sell land along the river (a park area) at cost; donation of the Beckwith property; railroad to donate land above the bridge and fill it in as needed; city to give a low water rate; nominal taxation for term of seven years. If these would be met the company planned to build a four million dollar plant. Although talks went

Eastern Shipbuilding Company. Photo taken immediately before launching of the Minnesota, *April 16, 1903.*

on for a long time, the only major progress in shipyards came on the Groton side of the river.[23]

A most promising venture came when the Eastern Shipbuilding Company leased land for eighteen years or rather three years with five renewals of three years each in April of 1900—possibly at $250 a year. The company planned to build large ships and had a contract to build two steamers for James J. Hill at $5,000,000.

They built the largest vessels in the world as of that date—the *Dakota* and the *Minnesota*—which proved too large for regular trade. Quite a crowd gathered to see the launching of both steamers—the *Minnesota* April 16, 1903 and the *Dakota* February 6, 1904. While these two vessels were being built, a new corporation began to buy up various shipyards and The United States Shipping Corporation took over the Eastern Company in 1902. Although it finished the two vessels unfortunately the corporation went broke shortly thereafter.[24] The *Dakota* went down off the coast of Japan and the *Minnesota* was purchased by T. A. Scott to be scrapped.

A new company, the New London Ship and Engine Company, organized in 1910, took over the site of the Eastern Shipbuilding Company (the United States Shipping Corporation). By July of 1911, three hundred men began the work of manufacturing heavy oil engines.[25] This was the first production of marine diesel engines in the United States.

During World War I the New London Ship and Engine Company supplied engines to power submarines as well as submarine parts and gasoline for sub chasers. The war period resulted in another attempt at shipbuilding when Charles W. Morse established the Groton Iron Company. Several million dollars went into developing the facility which employed 4,000 people at its height with a payroll of $80,000.

The Post War Period saw the Groton Iron Works go bankrupt however, it found New London Ship and Engine Company producing engines for the Electric Boat Company. John Holland, developer of the first submarine for the United States Navy, organized the Electric Boat Company and received orders for other submarines. By 1924 the Electric Boat Company had purchased 92% of the stock of the New London Ship and Engine Company. During the same year the local company received contracts to build two submarines and a number of torpedoes. The first submarines built at the yard were for Peru—four were produced for that government by 1928. Fifteen hundred persons gathered to watch the launching of the first one in 1926. With submarines and torpedoes to build, New Londoners found a steady source of employment just across the river.[26] Since the New London Ship and Engine Company was owned by the Electric Boat Company and produced almost solely for it, the name was changed in 1928 to the Electric Boat Company.

The building of submarines for the United States Navy began with a contract in 1931 for the *Cuttlefish* which was launched November 10, 1933. This submarine began the era of the welded hull. By the time World War II began in Europe, Electric Boat Company had completed seventeen submarines.

The Pearl Harbor attack resulted in a tremendous expansion of the Electric Boat Company. The war demands resulted in new facilities. The South Yard opened in 1941 with eight new shipways. Even the former Groton Iron Works pressed into service through purchase by the United States Navy and a lease arrangement with Electric Boat Company. This renovated yard became known as The Victory Yard and began production in 1942.

The Electric Boat Division built 105 fleet submarines from 1935 to 1946. The last one launched and commissioned for World War II contracts was the *Corsia* on May 3, 1946. Two hulls had been started and were completed but not commissioned.[28] Electric Boat had over 12,000 workers at its peak.[29] A truly remarkable record resulted from the production of the Yard. Submarines built at Electric Boat are believed to have accounted for 39% of all the Japanese shipping destroyed in the Pacific and an even more remarkable statistic concerns the activities of the *Flasher* which is credited with sinking 100,231 tons.

After a period of declining employment in the postwar period condi-

Electric Boat Company, post WW I.

tions began to improve as Charles Pfizer began operations in 1946. The Victory Yard ceased operations once government contracts were cancelled and when it was put up for sale only Charles Pfizer bid on it. In April of 1946 Pfizer took over and established a chemical plant. Victory Yard involved 28 acres and Pfizer purchased another 78.[30]

Over the years the pharmaceuticals produced by the company made it the anti-biotic production center of the world. To increase the applications for Pfizer products, the Pfizer Medical Research Center was established in 1960. The company also entered the synthetic sweetener and the organometallics fields. So well has the Charles Pfizer Firm developed that today it provides substantial employment for the New London area.[30a]

With the work force reduced from over 12,000 to a mere 1200 in 1945 at the shipyard, the New London area saw several years of readjustment before the "age of nuclear power" opened up new work for the people of the area as the navy began to develop a new kind of submarine force. By 1962 the work force had not only reached the level of 1944 employment but surpassed it by nearly 5,000.

The *Nautilus,* the world's first atomic powered submarine joined the fleet in 1955. It opened a new era of construction at Electric Boat Company, now a Division of General Dynamics. No less than thirty-three contracts for nuclear submarines were secured by Electric Boat of the first projected 92. The Company also became involved in a program for the development of submarines for research as well as for deep sea salvage.

Captain Thomas A. Scott, 1830-1907.

Charles Pfizer Company.

A last link with a great shipbuilding past, the Thames Shipyard and Repair Company, remains in New London. This was formerly the Chappell Yard which dates back to the 19th century. John A. Wronowski purchased the business from the family and continued to operate it at the same location although the United States Coast Guard purchased the land for

USS Nautilus *launching, January 21, 1954. World's first atomic submarine.*

future expansion of the Academy. When the Coast Guard needed the land, the shipyard had to be moved and a new location, United States Government property at the foot of John Street became available. Thus shipbuilding and ship repairing continues. That proud industry which began in colonial days continues to exist.[31]

T. A. Scott Company

Thomas Albertson Scott (1830-1907) was born in New Jersey and had the usual background of many mercahnts. He went to sea as a youth, worked his way up to captain and became part owner of a vessel when just twenty-five years of age. He then began operating a store. Here the story changes for instead of developing a flourishing merchant business, he returned to the sea and became a master diver, salvaging lost cargoes and vessels. In 1871 he moved his family to New London while working on the construction of the Race Rock Lighthouse to the west of Fisher's Island.[32]

From 1871 to 1878 one can follow the career of T. A. Scott as he worked on the Lighthouse. It proved to be a very difficult task, believed by some to be impossible, as can be judged by the fact that it was 1874 before the foundation was in and 1878 before the lighthouse was completed. After this difficult task was finished, T. A. Scott remained at New London, entering into the marine salvage and construction business on his own. Reliable companies in the salvage field were few, in fact none existed until 1860. Captain Scott added the special talent of construction.[33]

T. A. Scott's tugs appeared busy most days towing into port disabled vessels or hauling them off islands or the coast where they ran aground. Scott removed the piles from the old railway ferry slip in 1889 and built a bridge across Alewife Cove. Scott used his new stone barge for work on Government Fortifications on Little Gull and Fisher's Islands in 1896.[34]

One New London tug acquired a new whistle which it persisted in sounding long and loud. A number of complaints were made and police promised to arrest the captain if the noise continued. Captain Scott suggested that he might try such a whistle on his tug boat. The *Gazette* of June 13, 1879 then announced that "A Committee to go aboard and burn out Captain Scott will assemble at eleven this evening."

The Company did towing, lighting, dredging and pile driving, wharf, bridge and foundation building as well as submarine work and wrecking. Business remained excellent and grew from the establishment in 1878 to the merger which ended its operations in 1922. The firm was incorporated in 1903 as the T. A. Scott Company, Inc., with Scott's son, also named Thomas Albertson Scott (1877-1961) as president. Business operations greatly expanded under the younger Scott, especially in the construction field.[35]

In 1904, Scott designed and built a plant in Jersey City, New Jersey for the Mutual Chemical Company and in 1907 a plant at Afton, New York for the Ansco Company. In 1911 Scott purchased the Boston Tow Boat Company. Their monument in New London, the Connecticut State Pier, was built in 1914 with a warehouse added in 1915.[36]

World War I created much salvage business. Scott resigned as president of the company to become a naval officer directing all government salvage in American waters and much of it in European waters. From 1918 to 1920 he served as a member of the United States Shipping Board, before returning to the presidency of T. A. Scott. In 1922 Merritt-Chapman Derrick and Wrecking Company, itself the result of a merger of the two leading salvage firms in 1897, merged with Scott to form the Merritt-Chapman and Scott Corporation and ended its New London operation.

T. A. Scott served as president of the company until 1951.[37]

Chappell Marine Activities

The Chappell interests included a shipbuilding yard, barge towing business and a coal yard. The company had a shipyard on Winthrop's Neck under the direction of John Forsythe which built vessels. Tugs, barges and steamers seemed to be primary products of the yard. In 1895 the yard moved from the cove and had T. A. Scott build a wharf for a yard and marine repair work in 1900. Forsythe continued in charge of the Riverside Shipbuilding Yard and Marine Railway. The yard built and repaired wooden and iron vessels.[38]

The Thames Tow Boat Company originated in Norwich in 1865. A re-organization brought it under the control of the F. H. and A. H. Chappell interests who moved it to New London in 1879. It developed into quite a business which required the constant adding of new and larger barges and tugs. In 1896 they moved to new offices on Bank Street. The company towed to all parts of the Atlantic seaboard using barges of three-hundred to four-hundred tons. In 1909 the company had nine ocean going tugs and three river tugs. Employees numbered five hundred. Officers in 1915 were F. H. Chappell, Donald Chappell, Lawrence H. Chappell, Frank H. Chappell, Jr. and Lee S. Denison.[39]

The F. H. and A. H. Chappell company began in 1865 at New London. It handled coal and lumber and was formed by Frank H. and William S. Chappell. In 1898 the company incorporated with Frank H., Alfred H. and Frank V. Chappell as officers. They owned three wharves at New London, one at Newport, Rhode Island and one at New Haven. By 1912 they handled $1,500,000 of business a year. They furnished fuel and supplies to factories, public and private institutions, builders and contractors on the Eastern seaboard. Barges carried their goods.[40]

Maritime Trade

While most maritime activity from the War of 1812 until the Civil War centered about whaling, West Indian, coastal and foreign trade continued to be actively carried out as was fishing.

West Indian commerce, engaged in by vessels from seventy-four to two hundred and thirty nine tons involved cargoes similar to those of colonial days—horses, mules, produce and sundry articles. A number of cargo manifests merely report American "produce." The schooner *Betsey*, 113 tons, with a seven man crew cleared New London April 6, 1836, with

Frank H. Chappell.   Alfred Hebard Chappell.

beans, twenty-six head of cattle, cheese, hay, two horses, ten casks of oil, two hundred and thirteen pounds of potatoes and sperm candles. The bark *Condon*, 239 tons, cleared port October 19, 1839 with country produce, sixteen horses and fifty mules. The bark *Hyder Ali*, 192 tons, cleared port October 20, 1840 with horses, mules and sundry articles of country produce. Customs records for the nineteenth and early twentieth centuries disclose that fifty percent of the vessels were brigs, twenty-five percent sloops, nearly twenty-five percent schooners and include a few barks.[41]

In many ways the West Indian trade remained the same as earlier. Disease, pirates and sea disasters were still a part of the price paid. Horses, mules, country produce and sundry articles made up trade to the West Indies and sugar, rum and molasses were still imported as were candles and cheese. Workers were sent from New London to the West Indies to cut live oak in 1795 and on the other hand we find Benjamin Banell at New London on January 31, 1805 as an agent for J. and D. Hinsdale, West Indian merchants.[42]

New London firms shipped and received cargoes from a large number of coastal ports during this period with Boston and New York continuing as the major areas. Coastal vessels tended to be small as in the case of the *Hero*, a schooner, which carried a crew of five and sailed to Boston and Saint Johns from the port. The largest of the freighters was the Lawrence Company's *Atlantic*, a seven hundred ton vessel, which sailed between New

London and Boston and New London and New York.[43]

The major New London individuals and companies engaged in the coastal trade consisted of Acors Barns, Miner, Lawrence and Company, N. and W. W. Billings and Williams and Haven. Much trade concerned the dispensing of whaling products. New London coastal trade carried American cotton, rice, oil, wood, tobacco and whale products.[44]

The Williams firm sold oil and candles in the United States as well as Europe. They generally sold to companies who retailed the products. Augustus Durand and Company and Welles and company of Paris, J. and H. Rose of Charleston and J. Bradlee and Company of Boston appeared to have been the major customers of Williams. Competition could drive the price down as when the average price per gallon for whale oil was thirty cents and T. W. Williams was informed:

> New Bedford people anxious to sell, few gals. have been disposed here at 26 cents a gal. Whale oil is a dull seller. Yours being in very large casks we shall find them hard to sell at more than 25¢[45]

Among the ports most commonly visited were Elizabeth, New Jersey; Boston; New York; Edenton, North Carolina; Key West; and San Francisco. Although payment was by wages and not lays, the vessels and cargoes usually represented investments of several individuals. The *Joseph Lawrence* in 1857 showed the following investors:

Francis W. Lawrence	4/16	
Sebastian Lawrence	3/16	Partners of the firm
Sidney Minor	8/16	
Captain L. Rogers	1/16	Master of vessel[46]

Masters' pay varied considerably in coastal shipping. In 1853 Stephen Perkins of the *Palutine* received $40.00 a month while in 1854 James Smith of the *Yankee* received $150.00 a month.[47]

New London vessels visited much of the world. Foreign shipping included several types—freighting connected with guano, sealing and whaling, the carrying of whaling products to ports all over the world, general merchandise shipped from or received at the port. Whale products provided many cargoes, especially to Europe. Antwerp, Bordeaux, Bremen, Cadiz, LaRochelle, Lisbon, Liverpool, Marseille and Rotterdam were the chief ports for New London vessels carrying rice, tobacco, whale products and wood. A number of African and South American ports were visited regularly. The *Active, Atlantic, Carrier, Charles Carroll, Flora, General Williams, George, Iris, Mary Ann, Pizarro,* and *Superior* doubled as whalers and

Whaleback barge 110 of Duluth in Winthrop Cove, early 1900's.

cargo vessels.[48]

Examples of whalers used as cargo vessels and cargo carried:

> *Iris,* George Tauile, Master to Bremen 1840 Rice, Oil, Wood, and Tobacco
> *Atlantic,* Lamb, Master to Antwerp 1838 1900 bbls. whale oil, 142 bales of
> cotton[49]

The Hawaiian Islands became a center where sealing and whaling vessels unloaded cargoes, picked up supplies and exchanged crew members. Vessels from New London took supplies and crews to the Islands and returned with cargoes of oil and bone.

Crew's pay and ages of crew were typical of that cited below.

Typical Crew List

Ellen	Schooner	1853 to the Indian Ocean and return	
	Master	Joseph Comstock	$55 per month age 28
	Mate	Alonzo A. Williams	20 per month age 23
	Cook	Walter Caswell	11 per month age 17
	Seaman	Joseph Baker	16 per month age 22
	Seaman	Ezra Setzer	16 per month age 22
Ordinary	Seaman	Archally Dykes	10 per month age 21
	Greenhand	Henry Brown	10 per month age 21

New London Light. William T. Godding, 1882.

George Destin received $100.00 for serving as captain on a trip from New London to the Hawaiian Islands and back. This rate seemed common as William M. Baker, Nathaniel Middleton, Jr., William R. Brown, Alfred Turner, Braddock Chester, John Rice and Isaac Allen all received the same pay for voyages from New London to the Hawaiian Islands during the period 1853 to 1868. In addition, masters often received a percentage of the profits from the sale of the cargoes.[51]

Fishing

New London fishing began to thrive in the eighteenth century. It had large markets in New York and the West Indies for the catch. Fishing continued to be an active industry at the port, although figures are lacking to provide a complete picture. One historian of the port claimed that New London ranked third in the number of tons of black, blue, mackerel, salmon, sea trout, shad, spanish mackerel, striped bass and swordfish caught. New London supplied local markets, New York, and areas as far away as Canada, Michigan, New Orleans and Wisconsin.[52] Offshore and deep sea fishing were carried on. Small vessels comprised most of the fishing fleet, even in the deep sea areas. Cuban waters attracted many New

London fishermen, where four to five man crews operated in thirty-to forty-nine ton vessels.[53]

The Spanish government did not always welcome American fishing trips. A number of vessels were seized and expelled from Cuban waters. In 1858 the New London fishing vessel *Greyhound* was expelled from Cuban waters and refused supplies of food and water. It left the area with only twenty biscuits and five gallons of water, but arrived safely in Charleston, South Carolina after a four-day voyage.[54] Mackerel fishing was quite popular. A large number could be picked up in and near the harbor. The mackerel schooners had fifteen to twenty man crews and fished five to six months a year and then went into halibut or cod fishing.[55]

G. M. Long and Company of Railroad Avenue began in 1869 and became the largest wholesale fishing concern in Connecticut. It operated both oyster and lobster boats. In fact, the *George M. Long* was the largest oyster boat in Narragansett Bay. When Daniel Webster negotiated with the British for a treaty (1842), New London became quite concerned because of its fishing. The industry had a long and valuable history—a true nursery for seamen.[56]

C. H. Cyphers, a temperance advocate, operated a fish market in New London in 1889.[57] Hamilton and Powers Fish Market at the foot of State Street sold fish for eight to nine cents a pound, oysters and clams twenty cents a quart and lobsters ten cents. One could choose a fish, have it cleaned and take it home.[58] Fulton Fish Market, New York City, was owned by the Fishmongers Association. Several New London firms were members—A. L. Rogers and Company, Rogers and Edwards, Wallace and Keeney and John Comstock.[59]

Ferguson wharf overhauled and fitted fishing vessels while the Thames Shipyard repaired and stored fishing vessels for the winter. In 1920 the fishermen were denied use of the old Ferguson dock by the Shore Line Rail Road after they had enjoyed its use for years. Authorities claimed they abused their privileges. They found other space but had to pay a dollar a day while the old area was free.[60]

New London's fishing fleet in 1870 consisted of seventy-five vessels. Of these thirty were cod-fishers; twenty, halibut; ten, sea bass; and fifteen, general fishers.[61] Usually twelve to twenty vessels were outfitted for halibut fishing off St. George's Bank. Fifteen halibut vessels of fifty tons each costing $100,000 employed 160 men. Members of the crew received $30.00 per month, and captain and mates received shares. They were generally out from March to November and fished off St. George Banks, Middlebanks and Cape Brown.[62] In 1874 few halibut fishing vessels remained while most shifted to cod. Usually upwards of twenty vessels formed the halibut fleet but at this time there were only two.[63]

By 1891 many kinds of fish were rare in the Sound and fishermen had to go quite far to find them. Where once seventy to eighty vessels with hundreds of men went out, now only twenty or so vessels left the port. However, smacks were quite numerous.[64] It could still be a valuable occupation for larger vessels. Schooner *Gypsy Girl* came into port in November, 1892 to spend the winter after a $10,000 fishing season.[65] However, in 1893 Captain Richard Forrest and his son of the smack *Ada R. Terry* received $5,000 within a six week period.[66] One large vessel would cost $100,000 to outfit and would require a crew of 160 while the smaller vessel would be less expensive to operate. In 1893 New London had a fishing fleet of thirty-nine vessels requiring 180 fishermen and an investment of $56,640.[67]

In 1896 90 to 100 fishing smacks were in operation.[68] The oyster season did not prosper in 1893 due to pollution from factories up river. So it would seem that the pollution problem is not a new one.[69] By 1923 all of Connecticut's lobster industry was centered in New London.[70]

In the twentieth century the use of large vessels disappeared and mainly boat fishing continued. For many during the 1930s it became the only way to feed a family. The Italian fisherman of New London were deprived of their livelihood when war came until they were declared friendly aliens.

United States Coast Guard

It is quite fitting that a town so long identified with the sea and one which had suffered many losses of life at sea should be the home of the United States Coast Guard Academy. New London had no revenue cutter or life saving station during most of its history until the Revenue Cutter Service transferred its service school to Fort Trumbull. Until that time no vessel was available with a crew trained to handle mishaps at sea or other emergency situations which might arise. A number of individuals had commented upon the lack of precautions taken at the port despite the large number of vessels using its facilities.[71]

The Coast Guard began in 1790 as the Revenue Marine. Later it became the Revenue Cutter Service. A training school for officers of the Revenue Cutter Service was established July 31, 1876 on board the schooner *Dobbin* which had its home base at New Bedford. In 1900 the school was moved to a landsite at Arundel Cove, Maryland. The schools quarters were moved to New London in 1910 being housed at Fort Trumbull. In 1915 the life saving service and revenue cutter service were merged to form the United

Secretary Andrew W. Mellon laying cornerstone of the new Coast Guard Academy, May 15, 1931.

States Coast Guard.[72]

The Coast Guard's main activity during the first World War was the training of an increased number of cadets. Following the War the Cadet classes were once more reduced in size.

Undoubtedly the activity which made the Coast Guard a household word was enforcing prohibition. Rum running has become a favorite topic of books, movies and television. New London was commonly referred to as one of the wettest towns in the state.[77] As many as twenty-two places selling and/or making illegal liquor were raided at a time.[78] Rum running replaced sword and tuna fishing, because it represented much more income for fishermen. In town fish became scarce and higher priced.[79] One fisherman reportedly had difficulty paying wharfage fees before prohibition. However, during it he had a $15,000 sword fishing smack.[80]

The Coast Guard had twenty percent of its force, 1,553 officers and men and forty-two vessels at the port. It reported in 1927 that the service spent $2,500,000 at New London.[81] Captured rum running vessels, tied up in large numbers, became a common sight at the Customs House. Large quantities of illegal alcohol filled the Customs House. American, British,

Canadian and French vessels were captured by the Coast Guard. Up to 1923 not many had been seized—then pressure began as 1924 brought sixty-five vessels, 1925—sixty-three vessels and 1930 fifty-three vessels. Cargoes in 1925 totaled $1,500,000 but in 1930 reached $2,500,000.[82]

Fishing vessels, tugs, freighters, pleasure boats and row boats were all used. Cargoes of $300,000 on a single ship were seized and as many as six vessels at once were caught.[83] By 1929 killings became common as vessels caught began to try and "shoot" their way out. Also brave New London youths in groups of four or more would attack the Coast Guard personnel if only one was present.[84]

The 1933 ending of prohibition relieved the Coast Guard from a difficult, unpleasant task. They were free now to return to their life saving duties—not that they had neglected them in the past. Vessels had continued to recruit crews from New London for ice patrol in the North Atlantic.[85]

By the 1920s the quarters at Fort Trumbull proved to be insufficient. The city provided the present site on Mohegan Avenue at a cost of $100,000 while the United States government spent $1,750,000 to develop the area into an academy.[73] In 1931, the year ground was broken for the new academy, the first four year class began its training. The Service School moved to its present site in 1932.

The lighthouse service became a part of the Coast Guard in 1939. Plans were developed that same year for the establishment of facilities at the former Morton F. Plant Estate in Groton on Avery Point. The installation began operations in 1941. Reservists, Spars and Regular Coast Guard Enlisted Personnel received training there as did a number of future officers.[86] The Coast Guard also established an operations base at Fort Trumbull.[88] World War II saw the enlargement of classes at the Coast Guard Academy to meet the demands of the war.[74]

The Academy has attempted to keep up with the rapidly changing world by constantly providing the educational training necessary for officers in the modern world. As a result of the pressure of increased numbers of students and the expansion of educational horizons new facilities have been necessary. Most recently a $3,800,000 science and lecture building and a nearly $3,000,000 library have been built.[75]

Throughout its history the Coast Guard has remained a small force with the academy at New London providing most of the officers. In 1972 we find this tradition continuing. Yet, while it is small compared to other services, it has grown. In 1939 the Academy had 300 cadets. This had

USS Sabine *at anchor, New London Harbor, late summer, 1862.*

increased to 1,000 in 1972 to meet the Coast Guard's increased responsibilities. There were 800 officers in 1939 and there are 4,000 at this time.[76]

Naval

The struggle to locate a naval yard on the Thames lasted for many years and when it finally happened—Groton not New London became the site. While it was 1868 before the yard existed, as early as 1799 articles began to appear in the town's newspapers suggesting the excellent port area for a naval yard.[89] Naval vessels frequently came into the port. In September of 1818 several officers examined the harbor for several days seeking a suitable site for a Naval Depot. Lack of ice blocking the harbor in winter was an important factor in the possibility of using it as a site for a naval yard. Again in 1819 its advantages are stressed while in 1826 the *Hartford Times* proposed New London as a site for the United States Naval Academy instead of Annapolis. A meeting held in Allen's Hotel, February 23, 1826, discussed having the Academy at the port.[90]

A number of people appeared to have actively worked to have New London become the site of a naval yard, such as Commodore Stephen Decatur "I wish there might be a Navy Yard at New London, for I know of no harbor in the United States possessing so many advantages."[91] The city itself held meetings to decide how best to go about getting a naval yard. Local newspapers presented many editorials in favor of the project. A number of Committees inspected the harbor. Their reports showed the advantage offered by New London. Still no success. Gideon Welles, a native of Connecticut, became Secretary of the Navy and it was hoped that he would back New London. He did not.[92]

A French fleet found New London an excellent spot in 1866. It was pointed out that the mixture of salt and fresh water would preserve the ship timbers and little or no dredging would be needed. John R. Bolles, father of the naval yard on the Thames, worked for thirty years to have the United States establish a base at New London. Finally, a Commission picked a site on the east side of the river, three miles above New London. One mile of river frontage was reserved in 1867. Congress appropriated $50,000 for the naval yard so New London could guard New York "as the natural key and strategic protection . . . [to the] eastern approach to [the city]." Connecticut gave a deed (gift) March 20, 1867 to the United States of 100 acres with a wharf 1,600 feet long. Grounds were graded and a large building erected, but for several years its only use was a depot for laying up old naval vessels.[93]

A wharf was built in 1871 and when finished, it was suggested that the Brooklyn Naval Yard would probably close down. A new wharf built in 1874 by F. N. and W. J. Chappell for $19,890, brought activity and hope for a very active yard as several vessels arrived, but by the end of the year the Senate reportedly hoped to abolish the yard.[94] Although it did not happen, the same fear developed in 1881. It became a coaling station for early torpedo boats for some time. The Board of Trade, mayor and some leading citizens worked for the establishment of a Naval Engineering School at the base in 1895.[95]

The government decided to establish a U.S. Marine Corps training school in 1909 there which seemed fitting since the first commission granted to an officer of the Corps was to Samuel Nichols of New London, November 28, 1775.[96] The Spanish American War led to the transferring of the Marines out of the yard. In 1915 the first submarine arrived. With the coming of World War I, the Navy decided to develop the yard as a Submarine Base.

Naturally, it became quite active during World War I and had its facilities greatly expanded. Submarines were outfitted, serviced, based and prepared for overseas service. More than 10,000 officers were trained for the submarine service. Ocean liner captains were trained on methods of

Submarine Base shortly after WW I.

dealing with U-boats.[97] The Navy established an experimental station for the testing of torpedoes along side Fort Trumbull.

An unusual event occurred during World War I when the German commercial submarine, *Deutschland,* arrived in port. As can be imagined its appearance created quite a sensation and several officials of the town were allowed on board. While leaving the harbor it collided with another vessel and had to return. After the Germans had posted a bond, the Americans allowed it to leave port. The *Deutschland* made two voyages to the United States in 1916 bringing valuable dyes to the port of Baltimore and New London and departing with rubber, tin and nickel.

From 1919 to 1939 things were quite calm at the base. It became the Atlantic base for the United States Naval Submarines. A number of submarine disasters occurred which led to the considerable experience in naval salvage and rescue methods. The Momsen Lung was developed as a submarine escape device. To meet the demands created by this activity several schools and training facilities were added to the base.

As World War II drew close, naval vessels were sent to operate out of New London in 1939. The Navy Department wanted to prepare mines for the harbor in case of war in 1940. A $2,073,000 water front construction program for the submarine base development was approved by President Franklin D. Roosevelt in 1940.[98]

Fort Trumbull housed three major activities. The largest was the

Escape Training Tank, Submarine Base.

Maritime Officers School begun in 1939. By the time it closed in April of 1946, 15,000 persons had graduated. The Maritime Service took over the school in 1942.[87]

Columbia University established an Underwater Program at the Fort in 1941 which is still in operation today. In March of 1945 all such groups around the country became a single unit—The Navy Underwater Sound Laboratory. It developed anti-submarine devices and means to aid in air—sea rescue.

Although the activity of the submarines out of Pearl Harbor may have received more notice in the movies and press, New London served as the harbor for the Atlantic submarine fleet which worked so hard to do its share in winning the war. The United States Navy Submarine Base in 1941 consisted of 112 acres and 86 buildings. By the end of World War II the base included some 775 acres and 275 buildings.[99] Unlike World War I,

USS Philadelphia *(SSN 690). Launching, October 19, 1974.*

the postwar period of World War II increased rather than lessened the importance of the base as a new age developed. The *Nautilus,* the world's first atomic powered submarine, was launched at Groton in 1954 and a whole new concept and job developed for the base.[100]

The Groton base is the largest sub-base in the United States. It supports the boats of Submarine Flotilla two which includes the Holy Loch based Polaris submarines. The school teaches 40,000 students annually. It is the largest fleet school in the Navy and the only school providing basic submarine instruction to officers and enlisted men. In 1968 the school became a separate command.

State Pier and the Port

Even though the Port had diminished in importance over the years, still a considerable amount of shipping operated out of New London as the twentieth century began—45 steamers, sixty schooners, fifty sloops and thirteen yachts.[101]

A major boost for the town came with the State Pier. Mayor B. F. Mahan worked hard in the State Legislature to obtain $1,000,000 for it. It took several years for the planning and building to reach completion. The General Assembly set up a Commission in 1909, which examined the area

Lighthouse, New London. Photo taken October, 1906.

1909-1910 and developed a report. A Commission set up by Connecticut to develop the New London harbor began its meetings in 1911. Connecticut acquired from New London 4,500 feet along the west bank of the Thames River. The Pier was built during the time of the first World War and when finished it operated under a private corporation for a fee. The town spent $32,000 to develop the municipal wharf at this time.[102] The Navy took over the Pier during the war and trained thousands of reservists.[103]

Direct trade connections with the Pacific Coast continued after the War. Lumber, flour, sugar, syrup and molasses were the main cargoes brought in.

New London became a popular yacht center between the wars. The New York Club in particular visited the port each summer with many well

known businessmen and entertainment people as well as those socially
prominent. Often their yachts were placed in the harbor over the winter
season. Twelve or more often entered together with two score or more
anchored during any one time. The income could be quite large from the
pleasure boats. In one three week period, three yachts spent $875 for
groceries at one store.[104]

With World War II drawing to a close in 1944, a Development Commission in Hartford discussed the possibility of a trans-Atlantic port at New
London. New London harbor still has coastal and foreign trade. Also it still
has dreams of returning to the busy days of an earlier period. A research
committee of the General Assembly considered the city for a seaport
complex in 1971. The Committee suggested that the New London site was
the best location for it as it would have the least impact on marine environment.[106]

The Army Corps of Engineers developed a plan in 1972 to dredge the
river up to the State Pier and also create a thirty-three foot channel from
Long Island Sound to Allyns Point. Some hope exists also that the State will
develop a harbor at New London for Southeastern Connecticut. The
attempts to revive the railroads should provide freight and markets and
restore to New London the hinterland it had lost by 1819.[106]

New London still has strong maritime ties. The New London Laboratory of the Naval Underwater Systems Center is the largest employer in
the town. The Coast Guard maintains a Buoy Depot at the port and a
Coast Guard Cutter Mooring at Fort Trumbull. The training Barque
Eagle bridges the past and present by providing Coast Guard cadets
with sailing experience on the former Nazi Naval Cadet Training Vessel.

10 Transportation 1784-1973

As a result of its port activity New London developed a network of roads over the years. Its geographic location between New York and Boston via Providence assured New London of inclusion in the post road system.[1] The lower Post Road ran one hundred and fifty-six miles from New York to New London and from New London via Providence one hundred and ten miles to Boston—a through stage and mail route.[2] When the turnpike era began, New London built the second turnpike established in the United States. Officially known as the Mohegan Road, it connected New London and Norwich.[3] It received authorization from the General Assembly in May of 1792 and served as a toll road until that body abolished the fees in 1852. No company ever was incorporated and a public committee oversaw the operation of the road.[4] Once the toll road opened, travel time was reduced from two days to two hours and stage coaches made two daily trips between the towns. Cattle drives became one of the most important uses of the road. When the Stage Company claimed low returns for their service they were granted a reduction in tolls. The New London, Willimantic and Palmer Railroad paralleled the Mohegan Road in 1849 and its influence apparently led to the ending of tolls in 1852.[5]

Another toll road connected New London and Hartford and a committee appointed in 1796 laid out the route. In 1800 it received a charter as the Hartford and New London Turnpike Company.[6] A third turnpike authorized for New London began with plans for a New Haven to Rhode Island toll road. In 1796 plans were drawn up but only a section opened and a part of this which connected New London and the Connecticut River was operated by the New London and Lyme Turnpike Company, incorporated in 1807. In order to aid the company, five hundred dollars and materials for a bridge across Bream Cove were given by the port.[7] A fourth toll road gave the port direct land connection with Rhode Island and beyond via the Stonington Turnpike which ran from the Thames River to Providence. A ferry completed the New London connection.[8]

Just six years after Winthrop's arrival a ferry began operations across the Thames River. From 1651 to 1929 various individuals and companies, as well as the town itself, operated the ferry. Such an important convenience had a careful watch kept over it. Originally, all had to pay fares except Post Riders, until 1729 when magistrates and deputies on official business were allowed free passage. Public officers, physicians and midwives had special status on crossings and were allowed to board first. The ferryman was an important person who could refuse passage to individuals, and after 1729 was licensed to keep a tavern and received a grant of land. On the other hand, the ferryman had to provide a proper boat and equipment, not overload, and not overcharge or else he could be fined. From 1702 to 1785 the ferry income was reserved for a New London grammar school fund.[9]

The importance of the ferry seemed obvious and New London along with Saybrook charged the highest rates of any ferry crossings in the colony and state. Rates were further increased each winter during the months of December, January and February.[10]

Goodman Edward Messenger, reportedly an Indian, received a grant in 1651 to operate a ferry on the river for twenty-one years. A canoe appeared to have been the first ferry-boat. He left the area in 1654 but Cary Latham took over on a fifty year lease and built a house on the east side of the river. Despite such long grants, the early operators lasted only a short time. Hugh Hubbard had charge of the ferry in the late 1670's and John Williams in the 1680's. Williams lived in the first ferry house built on the river and used a small scow which could hold four or five horses and several passengers. In later years he used a sailboat.[11]

The lease in the eighteenth century generally ran five to ten years for five to ten pounds each year. In 1724 the operator of the ferry was licensed to keep a house of public entertainment on the east side of the river. A wharf was built in 1767 at the New London ferry landing north off Water Street at a point where Winthrop's Neck provided protection for the sailing ferries. The ferry wharf at the foot of the Parade was built in 1794 by contributions of $500 from townspeople and accepted by the town fathers as the only one. Rebuilding took place several times beginning in 1815.[12]

Ferryboat Mohegan *in the New London slip, 1862. Capt. Avery Perkins in pilot house with Engineer Chas. Fenner standing nearby. Capt. William Beckwith is on main deck.*

On November 25, 1820 Dr. S. H. P. Lee, Isaac Thompson, Abraham Shephard and Youngs Morgan leased the ferry. They moved the Groton landing to an area owned by Morgan's family which increased the distance. Up to this time sails or oars were used. The ferry became a horse team ferry in 1821 and better connections were enjoyed. This appeared to have been the period when Peter Williams ran the ferry. For forty years he had charge and seemed to have been most noted for "two sets of natural teeth and the throwing of kids overboard if they became too rough." Unfortunately, while such behavior and unusual physical features were attractions, they failed to help the service.[13]

Service became so poor by 1833 that complaints were heard constantly. An attempt at steampower in 1835 failed and a return to horsepower occurred. Poor service continued and town meetings took up the question from 1839 until a council form of government took over. Then the Mayor and Council, later city manager and Council heard the complaints until 1929 when the ferry ended.[14]

It became "Our miserable Ferry" with complaints about the small fee the city realized and the inadequate service. Despite numerous meetings, the conditions continued pretty much the same until 1849, although another attempt to provide steampower was tried in 1845. A town meeting called in March of 1849 decided upon a steamboat ferry and the town granted the lease to M. M. Comstock in August for ten years, provided he used steam. Comstock had the *Mohegan* built ar Mathers Wharf on the upper end of Main Street in Winthrop's Cove. Still the complaints continued during his ten year lease—the breakdowns and waiting irritated most, especially as it seemed to breakdown most often in the rain. Small boats were used while repairs were carried out.[15]

In February of 1859 Thomas Fitch II bought the lease for ten years for $670. A partnership with Christopher Brown resulted and they bought the $3,000 *Mohegan* from Comstock. Service did not improve much and delays and breakdowns were frequent. When Fitch's lease expired in February of 1869, the city tried to operate it with John Bishop as operator. When this did not prove successful, M. M. Comstock received a new ten year lease in October. He used a new steamer, the *Uncas*. Still this proved unsatisfactory. He paid $5.00 a year for the lease and charged four cents to cross—eight cents after 9 P.M. In answer to the request to provide more service he claimed he would have to give it up because anything more would lose money. Claims were made that he used large sums of money to hire a lobbyist in the legislature to prevent any changes in service.[16]

Whatever the case, in 1874 the legislature passed a bill requiring service

6 A.M. to 10 P.M. and set a rate of $1.00 per month for foot passengers or thirty-two cents one way and fifty cents round trip. Comstock had said he would give up the lease and the town must buy his equipment if it passed. After legal steps were taken it was decided in October of 1874 that Comstock had $18,079 coming and the legal costs were $375 which were to be paid one-half each by Comstock and the town.[17]

The town again ran the ferry until 1875 when Captain E. A. Delanoy leased it for one year at $1,400 and paid $15,000 for the ferry boat— actually a company had been organized, with Frank H. Chappell president and Frederic H. Harris treasurer, The Thames Ferry Company. With Delanoy managing the ferry from 1875 until 1885 the city realized $10,000 profit. In 1887 another company was established with B. A. Armstrong president, Walter R. Denison secretary-treasurer and manager. Still another new company was added December 1, 1899 by F. H. and A. H. Chappell which paid $18,000 for the *Ledyard*. The *Governor Winthrop* was added in 1905. Rates were reduced by the legislature in 1885 to three cents which they remained until 1920.[18]

During the building of the Eastern Shipbuilding Yard, the workers from New London found the ride to the Groton ferry slip left them a long way to walk from their work, so they organized a ferry service of their own in 1901. The regular ferry's company objected and obtained an injunction prohibiting the company's operation. The Eastern Shipbuilding Company backed its workers and the injunction was removed and a new lease arranged. Under the old lease the city received $2,700 plus a share of the profits, about $3,000 total. A new lease gave the city $4,000 plus one percent of the gross take. Also it provided for a ferry directly to the shipyard.

In December of 1917 the city assumed the responsibility of the ferry and purchased the *Ledyard* and the *Governor Winthrop*. Lights were installed for those arriving or leaving after dark. The city had many of the same disruptions of service due to breakdowns and even a collision with a submarine tender in 1919.[19]

There had been other ferry boat companies including the Railroad Ferry from 1858-1889 at the town. In 1942 The Fisher's Island Navigation Company, which had operated steamer services between New London and the island since 1902, lost out when the New York legislature established a Fishers Island Ferry District and took over control of the service. Block Island still has service from New London. A large three-decker ferry makes two four-hour round trips.[20]

The highway bridge of 1919 cut into the ferry traffic, but many wanted to keep it going. When losses became heavy the city decided to end the

City of Worcester *leaving with excursion. Highway ferry* Uncas *at center. RR ferry* Groton *at right. 1881.*

Ferryboat Governor Winthrop *at right. SS* Orient, *left. 1905.*

ferry service in 1923. Groton objected strongly and after negotiations it was decided to continue the service and Groton agreed to underwrite one-fourth of the cost. It was almost ended in 1926, then finally did end March 10, 1929, when too few used it. Crandall and Sheehan had paid $6,000 to operate it in the final years. The town assumed responsibility for upkeep and repairs of over $1,000. The ferry boat was sold to Jamestown, Rhode Island, August of 1929.[21]

Steamboats

Long Island Sound provided a travel route which saved the traveller from a long, uncomfortable stagetrip between New York and Boston. However, until steamboats appeared on the Sound that route suited only those passengers who were not in a hurry. They could take a packet sloop to New London and a stage from there to Boston. With the development of steamers, New London became the terminus for New York to Boston service via the Sound in 1816. This advantage to New London lasted only until 1822 when as a result of the fight against the Fulton-Livingston monopoly, Connecticut passed a law prohibiting New York owned steamboats from entering her ports until the monopoly ended. By the time it did, 1824, Providence had become the terminus—still events prevailed upon a return to the New London area of steamboats between New York and Boston. Railroad construction caused the change. Providence lost to Stonington when New York businessmen made it (Stonington) a rail terminus from Boston. The excellent steamers operating between Stonington and New York picked up and discharged passengers at New London. Railroads developed additional steamer activity at New London when the Norwich and Worcester extended its line to Allyn's Point and thus established connection with New London via steamers. Even when rail connections between Boston and New York were completed, many chose to travel by night steamer to or from the New London area and then use the rail connection between there and Boston.[22]

New London and its seamen had an early and long history of steamboat activity. The port's regular steamboat service began in 1816 when the Sound Steamboat Line effected a direct connection between New London and New York. Two vessels were in operation, the *Connecticut* which made two trips weekly between New London and New Haven, and the *Fulton* which made two trips weekly between New Haven and New York. In 1817, service was extended to Norwich from New London and three round trips weekly were made between Norwich and New York via New London and New Haven.[23]

The Connecticut Steamboat Company began regular service between Hartford and New London in 1823 making two trips weekly.[26] More freight than passengers appeared to have been carried in the early days. Steamers were built at New London as early as 1817 when Gilbert Brewster built the *John Hancock* for service between New London and Norwich. He also built the *Eagle* for service between the same towns.[27]

A number of merchants operated steamers to handle their shipping needs. Steven Rogers and his brother-in-law, Gilbert Rogers, used the *Galena* and the *Frederick* to carry freight and passengers between their brick and lumber yards in New London and Hartford.[29] Several companies were organized to operate steamers between the port and other Sound and river towns. Passengers and freight connections were established at New London between steamers and toll roads, stagelines and after 1849, railroads. As the port became a convenient center of various land modes of travel, a large number of steam transportation lines made connections between New London and other ports. Some of the finest Sound steamers used New London as a home port. So distinguished did certain captains become that many people would travel only with their favorites.[30]

As a writer in the *People's Advocate* put it, steamers give good service and deserve all the patronage one can give them.[31] Captain Williams of the *Worcester* was known for his prudence, skill, courage and politeness. Called first among the captains by many, Captain Van Pelt of the *Cleopatra* had an excellent reputation as a sailor although some complained he lacked courtesy on some occasions.[32] Captain White of the *Alice* was very popular as he treated all passengers with equal courtesy and maintained a record of punctuality.[33]

From the deck of his majestic vessel the steamer captain often felt master of all he surveyed. Sometimes such pompousness received a severe blow delivered by less lofty users of the river. George W. Rogers, the boatbuilder, and Zeb Rogers had been fishing and were selling their catch at the wharf when a steamboat began to move towards their boat. Its captain, wearing a lot of gold braid, ordered them out of the way or he would run them down. They told the captain that it would be only a few minutes and he could have the spot. He gave them five minutes and began to move again even though the Rogers had not finished. Zeb Rogers grabbed an axe and chopped off part of the gold wreath around the name of the steamer as it backed in. The captain ordered the steamer pulled away and threatened the Rogers but he waited and never crowded the fishermen again.[34]

The New London and Providence Steamboat Line linked the two towns by water in 1824. Two new lines added competition in 1832—the Boston and New York Line's *General Jackson* plied between New London and New York and the New London and Norwich Steamboat Association. In 1826 the *Fanny* and *Long Branch* of the Union Line began to provide connections between stages and steamboats.[35]

When the Norwich and Worcester Railroad began operations, a steamboat line was organized to link New London and other Sound ports with the terminus at Norwich—the Norwich and New London Steamboat Company. Operations began with two steamboats, the *Worcester* and the *Connecticut* in 1848. In 1855 the *Commonwealth* was added. The line also operated four freight propellers—the *Charles Osgood, Shetucket, Decatur,* and *Quinnebaug.* Operations ceased in 1860 upon the dissolution of the company.[36]

Among the several steamer lines servicing New London port was the Norwich and New York Line which began business in 1821 and had twelve steamers between Norwich and New York during the twenty-two years of service.

Long Branch	*Norwich*
Henry Eckford	*Huntress*
New London	*Worcester*
Fanny	*Charter Oak*
Experiment	*Cleopatra*
General Jackson	*New Haven* [37]

The New London Steam Transportation Company was established in 1854 with William Albertson president and J. N. Harris secretary-treasurer. It had a capitalization of $21,600.[38] A line connecting Norwich, New London, Mystic and Westerly began service in 1855 using the steamers *Tiger Lily* and *Water Lily.*[39] The *Osceola* and *Charles Osgood* began service in 1858 for the New London and Norwich Propeller Company. Several new companies began operations in 1860. The Norwich and New York Transportation Company became another link between the Norwich and Worcester Railroad and the Sound ports. Beginning operations with its *Commodore C. Vanderbilt* and *Connecticut* in 1860, the Company added *City of Boston,* 1861, the *City of New York* and the *City of Norwich* in 1862, *The City of New London* in 1863, the *City of Lawrence* 1867.[40] Two steamers, *Plymouth Rock* and *Commonwealth* were owned by the New York and Stonington Line. Others of the year 1860 were the Independent Line (New London to New York) and the Norwich and New York Steam Navigation Company

City of New York, *right, with sister ship* City of Boston, *far left. Long Dock of the Central Vermont railroad in the foreground. About 1876.*

City of Worcester *beached near west shore of Thames. 1898.*

which purchased all the vessels of the Norwich and New London Steamboat Company except the *Commonwealth*. The Norwich and New York Propeller Company established in 1890 operated a number of steamers in and out of New London including: *Delaware, Chelsea, J. N. Harris, Hanna, Thames, Cape Cod, Postmaster General, John M. Worth, Major L'Enfant*.[41]

George W. Bentley, Augustus Brandegee, Benjamin Stark and others petitioned the General Assembly for right to establish two steamboat companies—the Ocean Harbor and River Excursion Company and the New London Steamboat Company in 1882. Among the other companies organized were the Pequot Ocean Transit Company 1880, Long Island and New London Steamboat Company 1891, City of Richmond Steamboat Company 1893 and the Montauk Steamboat Company 1901. The very length of the account of steamboat companies from 1816 to 1946 indicated how lucrative the business once was and the important role New London played in the network of freight and passenger routes.[42]

Among the leading captains of steamers were John H. Woods, Edward Smith, Edward Green, Nathan Keeney, William B. Abbeley, T. Harvey MacDonald, Henry Nickerson, Horace C. (Pop) Lamphere, S. Cleveland Geer, William D. Ward, Stiles E. Shirley and Jerome W. Williams. Many of the steamer captains had formerly served aboard whalers.[43]

Several terrible disasters occurred on the Sound involving steamers plying between the New London area and New York. The *Lexington* of the Stonington Line left New York for Stonington and caught fire off Bridgeport. All boats were lost in the panic which followed. Only one passenger, the pilot and one fireman escaped out of seventy-eight passengers and thirty-four officers and crew.[44] The Norwich and Worcester Railroad had a steamer, the *Atlantic*, built in 1846, the first to be lighted with gas. Unfortunately, the steamer's career proved short. On the eighteenth of August 1846, service began and a little over three months later it ran aground on Fisher's Island—November 27, 1846 with the loss of fifty passengers. The town was reminded of the accident by a bell of the *Atlantic* which began to toll after the wreck with the motion of water against the hull. It tolled a number of times which acted as a sober reminder of the tragedy.[45]

On August 15, 1857 the Steamer *Metropolis* ran into the Steamer *J. N. Harris* cutting it in half. Fourteen were lost including three children of the captain. The *Charles Osgood* went down in 1858 after a collision with a schooner. Seventeen lives were lost when the *City of New London* burned in the Thames River off Montville in 1871. Captain Horace C. Lamphere, the three hundred pound master of the *City of New York* earned fame when he saved 214 people after the *Narragansett* and *Stonington* crash of 1880. The *City of Lawrence,* one of the first iron-hulled, was wrecked at Eastern Point opposite the Harbor of New London in July 2, 1907.

On the other hand some steamers, despite more than one mishap endured for long periods of time with little or no loss of life. An excellent example of this was the *City of Worcester* which began its Sound service in 1881 and was not scrapped until 1914 in spite of having gone aground on Bartletts Reef in 1890, aground again in 1893 on Eastern Point and sank at New London in 1898.[46]

Major steamboat accidents of the area include:

STEAMBOAT	DATE	CASUALTIES	LOSSES
New England	10/9/33	17	$ 50,000[14]
Lexington (Burned)	1/13/40	120	80,000[14]
Atlantic (Stranded)	11/26/46	40	80,000[14]
Commonwealth (Burned)	12/29/65	1	800,000[14]
City of Norwich (Burned)	4/18/66	11	150,000[14]
City of Boston (Disabled)	7/2/68	?	15,000[14]
City of New London (Burned)	11/22/71	17	150,000[14]
Metis (Sunk)	8/30/73	30	150,000[14]
Massachusetts (Disabled)	10/4/77	?	350,000[14]
E. H. Northam (Burned)	11/27/77	3	700,000[14]
Narragansett (Sunk)	6/11/80	80	350,000[14]
Rhode Island (Disabled)	11/6/80	?	150,000[14]
TOTAL		319	$3,025,000[47]

Acors Barns developed a plan to make steamboats safe. A water gate in the vessel's bottom was to fill the boat in approximately fifteen minutes and put out the fire while copper cylinders on cans would buoy up machinery and keep the vessel floating. The cost would be from two to five thousand dollars in 1840.[48] Other undesirable results of the steamboats were pickpockets, mishaps in loading or unloading freight, suicides and ease of travel for criminal elements. As steam became the popular means of power for vessels, a number of excursion steamers operated out of New London. *The Golden Gate, L. B. Camp, Gypsy, Osprey, Cygnet, Cecile, Niantic* and *Nelseco* became the most popular.[49] In 1881 the *City of Worcester* began service to New London from New York—it was only the second of the Sound steamers to use electricity for lighting.[50]

Steam propellers began to operate on the Sound in 1844. In 1850 New London had 5,008 tons of steam shipping which employed 112 men. They carried 73,083 passengers for an average distance of 155 miles.[52] Deck

City of New York *at mouth of Thames River. 1896.*

hands of *City of Worcester* went on strike in 1893. They wished to have the right to halt work during the loading of freight at midnight in order to eat supper.

Fares fluctuated according to the competition. In 1824 it cost $5.00 between New London and New York; 1832 still $5.00, but in 1845 it dropped to $1.00 even if travelling from Norwich and stopping at New London—still $1.00 and berths were free. Depending upon the vessel, 1850 found the charge $1.00 to $2.00 including free berth; in 1853 New London to New York cost $1.50 per cabin, $1.25 per cabin and $1.00 on deck. In 1846 one could take a boat to Long Island and then the Long Island Railroad to New York City—for $2.00. New London to Boston was $3.25. Steamer trips between New London and New York on the New England Navigation Company cost $1.50 one way in 1917.[52a] Sag Harbor was a popular port and steamer connections were available.

Norwich and New York Transportation Company employed four hundred in 1879—two hundred and ten as officers, freight hands, stewards and waiters. Captain Lamphere, *City of New York* set a record of six hours and twenty-five minutes—from New London to New York in 1874.[52b]

The New York Transportation Company's boat landing received a lot of unfavorable comment and finally in 1895 they built a new shed to replace the former eyesore. The Connecticut Assembly passed a bill appropriating $150,000 for the steamship terminals. It would allow the state to buy the wharves, build a road, put in a sprinkler system and a lighting system.[52c]

The Providence and Stonington Line ended operations in 1896, the

Stonington Line was moved to New Bedford in 1904. Most lines were taken over by the railroads and later shut down as the depression crept in. The New Haven took over the Fall River Line, 1894 and the New England Steamship Company (old Norwich and New York Transportation Company on Norwich Line). Travel on the Vermont Central steamers continued into the 1930's after it took over and operated the New London Steamboat Company in 1901. It continued freighter service to New York until 1946 when a labor dispute shut down the service and the company decided to end it.[52d]

During the heyday of the steam excursions, as many as a thousand people would be walking about the streets of New London during their layover. The days of the steamers were numbered as the 1890's began to draw to a close. Railroad competition, automobiles, war and the depression of the 1930's left only a few. Then the Second World War and rising labor cost plus increased safety requirements meant that only a very few could remain as ferry and excursion boats into the 1970's.[52e]

STEAMSHIPS

While New London was becoming part of a steamboat network connecting all major ports on the Sound, it was also developing steamship connections with the chief seaports on the Atlantic, Gulf and Pacific coasts of the United States. The port's role in steamship history began early and came to the attention of much of the world when two New Londoners directed the first crossing of the Atlantic Ocean by a steamship. Moses Rogers served as master and Stevens Rogers as sailing master. The Rogers were brothers-in-law and shared a love for the sea. Moses learned about steamers on the Hudson River. Stevens early dreamed of going to sea and left school in Plainfield to sail out of New London.[24]

They took the *Savannah*, a fully rigged ship of three hundred and fifty tons with an engine of eighty to ninety horsepower across the Atlantic. It steamed part of fourteen days of the twenty-two it took to reach England in 1819. Although reportedly enjoying the trip, Stevens Rogers returned to sailing vessels after the voyage.[25]

The area's other outstanding event of steamship history occurred in 1903-04 when the *Minnesota* and the *Dakota* were built at the Eastern Shipbuilding Company (Groton) for James J. Hill and the Great Northern Railroad. At that time they were the largest in the world.[28]

Steam navigation between New London and the Pacific became important when Hawaii and San Francisco became centers of the whaling

Steamship Savannah, *first steamship to cross the Atlantic. 1819.*

Captain Moses Rogers, commander of the Savannah.

industry. Commonly, steamers took out supplies from New London as well as crews while they returned with whale oil products. A direct link with the Pacific lasted until February 1922 when the North Atlantic and Western Steamship Company discontinued service from New London to Pacific ports.[51]

One of several New London whaling captains who entered steamship service, John M. Cavarly, has had his life set down for all to read in *Annie's Captain* by Kathryn Hulme. He moved to San Francisco and became a master for the Pacific Mail Company steaming from San Francisco for China, Central America and South America.

RAILROADS

Connecticut's rail age began in 1832 with the granting of two charters for railroads. These were for the New York and Stonington Railroad and the Boston, Norwich and New London Railroad. In spite of the names, neither road had a rail connection with New London. Steamboats provided that link for passengers and freight from Stonington and Norwich to New London. The former line, first to operate in Connecticut, connected Stonington with Providence which had a direct link with Boston. From Stonington steamers made the connection with New York. The latter road connected Worcester, which had a direct connection with Boston, to Norwich where steamers made the New York link.[53]

New London was the last port town on the Sound to have a rail connection. Although the first railroad to operate on Connecticut soil began service in 1837, New London did not receive a charter for a railroad until 1847 and service did not begin until 1849. Very early in the railroad age New Londoners contemplated a trans-continental railroad which would link together the two best natural harbors of the United States—San Francisco and New London. However, merchant initiative for a rail system failed to develop until the late 1840's when the peak of whaling had passed.[54]

Rivalry with Norwich kept New London from a rail link north into the hinterland for several years. The Norwich and Worcester Railroad which provided such a link for Norwich ended thirteen miles above the port. New Londoners established a committee on February 25, 1841 consisting of Noyes Billings, Acors Barns, Jonathan Coit, Francis Allyn, Charles Lewis and John Brandegee. These attempts by merchants to have an extension of the line to New London failed even though they were willing to offer almost any terms. The Norwich and Worcester Railroad extended its line on the east side of the Thames River across from New London—

and then only as far as Allyns Point leaving the port seven miles short of a rail connection.[55]

Such developments, although annoying, did not cause much concern to New London merchants until the whaling industry began its decline in 1846. As the merchants found themselves with idle capital, unused docks, unneeded vessels, empty warehouses and little indication that the whaling industry would have an upsurge, their attention turned to possible ways of stimulating business. With the great emphasis on whaling little other industry had developed except that connected with the whaling industry. Since most people in the port and adjacent areas depended upon the industry for a livelihood, its decline meant serious unemployment and business failures.

New London merchants decided that economic recovery would be possible only if a rail connection could be made between the port and its hinterland. Since most whaling agents also operated general shipping businesses, visions of a great world port developed, using the facilities and vessels already available. The merchants, deciding to make a joint effort to develop a rail line, marshalled the port's resources. Thomas W. Williams, Joseph Lawrence, A. M. Frink and Acors Barns led the movement. They renewed the attempt at an extension of the Norwich and Worcester Railroad from Allyns Point to the Parade in New London. They offered to loan the Norwich and Worcester Railroad the money to build an extension, or would build the continuation themselves and either lease or sell it to the line.[56]

Norwich opposed the extension of the railroad to New London. In a rather unpleasant editorial, the Norwich newspaper took recognition of New London's desire to have a rail connection. The people of the port, according to the author, were wiping the cobwebs from their eyes and finally realizing it takes a "little exertion" to keep up with times. It seems that the merchants of New London had refused to buy stock in support of the Norwich and Worcester Railroad. These merchants, it was claimed, expected that the road would have to be extended to the port anyway so they would not need to invest when others would pay. Norwich developed a strong lobby to fight against a bridge across the Thames, which was needed to complete the link. New Londoners claimed the railroad's business was so poor that only an extension would save it. None of this, not even the pointing out to Norwich of how important the extension would be for the town, succeeded.[57]

Unable to gain the assent of the Norwich and Worcester Railroad the merchants decided to create a rail system which would tap the Springfield area. An editorial in the *People's Advocate* in 1845 at the height of whaling suggested that development of a railroad would be wise should whaling falter in the future. The writer believed a connection with Springfield would be wise as it would avoid direct confrontation with Boston and New York. Only Hartford and New Haven would be direct competitors to New London. To build such a line the several whaling agents applied for and received charters from Connecticut and Massachusetts.

In 1847 the merchants under the leadership of Thomas W. Williams received a Connecticut charter for the New London, Willimantic and Springfield Railroad and in 1848 received a Massachusetts charter for the New London, Willimantic and Palmer Railroad. The Connecticut charter authorized a capital stock of $500,000 which could be increased to $1,500,000. Backing quickly came from the whole town which subscribed to the idea that the port had little future without a rail link. Unemployment and empty shops left little doubt as to the seriousness of the economic situation of the town. With a rail link to the hinterland where a growing textile industry and an expanding market for industrial products existed, the prospect of New London becoming a major port appeared excellent.[58]

NEW LONDON, WILLMANTIC AND PALMER RAILROAD

Whaling merchant involvement in the development of the New London, Willimantic and Palmer Railroad can be seen by their holding of offices and private investments. When two corporations merged in 1849 under the name New London, Willimantic and Palmer Railroad Company, the following whaling merchants served as directors:

> Thomas W. Williams, W. A. Weaver, E. V. Stoddard, Joseph Lawrence, Acors Barns, W. W. Billings, Lyman Allyn, Elias Perkins, Thomas Fitch II, N. S. Perkins, Henry P. Haven.

Officers included Thomas W. Williams, president; Thomas Fitch II, vice president; and Richard Chapell, secretary. Thomas W. Williams served as president from 1847 until 1860 save for one short period, also as a director and was the largest stockholder.[59]

The Corporation issued 4,607 shares to 924 investors for an average holding of 4.99 shares per person. Of these investors, 692 were New London individuals who held 3,955 shares representing 85.85 percent of the total number. Non New Londoner's for an average had only holding of 2.81 or a mere 14.15 percent of the total. Within New London the greatest support came from the whaling industry. Twenty individuals connected with the industry held 1,190 shares, almost one-third of the total held by

New Londoners for an average holding of 59.5. This amounted to nearly twelve times the average holdings at the port. New London whaling merchant control is obvious.[60]

Backing from the town was strong and included some rather unusual poetry:

> See the Fifty Thousand Dollars!
>   Mr. A. now writes his name.
> He has done the thing so boldly,
>   Mr. B. will do the same:
> Mr. C. reclines contented
>   With his feet upon the chairs—
> Thinks the serious matter over—
>   "Put me down for fifty shares."
>   So we have an operation
> In the little mill to grind,
> While the road to Willimanic
>   Agitates the Public Mind.
>   Sure't we'll benefit the city,
> Bring the Fact'ry Girls to town—
> Make us look as tho' we really
> Meant to do the thing up brown.
>   There's no use in being quiet
> When we now can reap a harvest
> If we will, ere its too late.[61]

The newspapers enthusiastically backed the proposal—"We want it done now ... (and) see action in our City again".[62] It was belatedly recognized that whaling would not enable the city to prosper. In fact some claimed that only the officers, crews and agents made money out of the industry. Of course this was nonsense, for if the whaling flourished it would provide work for all. The real problem was not lack of prosperity from the industry, but the decline of whaling and the port's unhealthy dependence upon that one enterprise. On a more logical level much was made of the reduced cost of transporting commodities in and out of the area if rail traffic was possible.

Stock sales were pushed in every way possible. There is no doubt that the merchants as well as most of the town's people had finally realized the necessity of developing hinterland control. Port activity increased as some of the materials for the building of the railroad came by ship. November 15, 1849 at 9:30 A.M. the road opened its first section of track—a link between New London and Willimantic, where a connection was made with the Hartford and Providence Railroad.

The first cars over the completed line started from the Palmer depot on Saturday, August 31, 1850. Regular service began November 6—New

The T. W. Williams Locomotive, built in 1849 by the Taunton Locomotive Works. Photo about 1885.

London to Palmer—three hours and twenty minutes for the sixty-six miles. At the northern terminus a connection with the Western Railroad provided direct service with Boston to the east and Albany to the West. After years of efforts a rail link between New London and the hinterland became a reality. Steamer connections provided for the carrying of freight and passengers between New London and other Sound ports.[63]

A number of Massachusetts towns desiring a rail link with New London received encouragement from individuals connected with the railroad. Several of these towns received such a connection with the organization and building of the Amherst and Belchertown Railroad of which W. W. Billings, William H. Barns and Alfred Coit served as directors. In 1853 after the investment of considerable New London money, this line was completed and leased to the New London, Willimantic and Palmer Railroad Company. The New London, Willimantic and Palmer was linked to the New York markets by the New Haven and New London Railroad. New Haven served as the terminus for the New York and New Haven and the Hartford and New Haven Railroads.[64]

Accidents became common as the railroad began operations. One of the usual occurrences came from crewmen being knocked off the top of cars or injured while heads or arms were placed outside the cars when passing under a bridge. A less common accident occurred when John H. Crocker fell and broke his knee when attempting to re-enter a train after having been put off. It seems from the court case when Crocker sued for damages that he had tried to purchase a ticket at the station, but could not find anyone to sell him one. Crocker then boarded the train but refused to pay the higher fare required if paid to the conductor. As a result the conductor put him off the train with the resulting injury. The jury fixed the amount due as $8,275 which the judge claimed was too high and he sent the jury back, they returned with a judgement of $7,500 and were sent back again. Finally the judge awarded Crocker $6,500 which he felt was still too high, however, a jury could only be sent back twice and he had to let it stand.[65]

The New London, Willimantic and Palmer Railroad never became a success. Unfortunately, the line competed in an area with a number of other more direct lines for the transporting of goods. Not only were there several other railroads in the area—the Western Railroad, the Hartford, Providence and Fishkill Railroad, the Norwich and Worcester Railroad, The New Haven, New London and Stonington Railroad, and the New York, Providence and Boston Railroad—but most provided more direct shipping with fewer changes than the New London link could provide. Personal management lacked the professional skill required to put the firm on a sound financial basis. Too little capital was set aside for maintenance of the roadbed and the rolling equipment. Under such conditions, equipment broke down, schedules could not be kept and competition with other lines proved impossible. Short term notes were resorted to and a number of merchants increased their support of the venture by putting additional funds into it.[66]

There is little question about the town's cooperation. Land owners along Water Street and along the wharves gave property to the railroad and the town gave use of property in the center of town for a nominal fee. Additional pleas for the purchasing of stock always brought more money, but it never proved to be enough. No dividends were ever paid. Later a number of people recalled those days of railroad stock selling as high pressured salesmanship days. Meetings were held daily in factories and businesses where people felt obligated to buy. Promoters promised high dividends and pledged to re-purchase stock should anyone want to sell later. However, the charges came only after the line failed, none seemed to air these while the prospect of profit remained.[67]

The railroad officials in 1850 asked the city to invest $100,000 in the road. After rejecting the proposal several times the city voted to loan the money in April of 1852—$75,000 immediately and $25,000 when needed. In 1853 the line had to cancel its lease of the Amherst and Belchertown Railroad Company when it added little business to the New London Company. By 1856 the road's financial difficulties became perilous when payments could not be made on short term notes and in the hard times of 1857-1859 more capital could not be attracted. On January 5, 1859 the road could no longer operate and trustees took over the line. In 1860 under the leadership of Henry P. Haven the line was reorganized as the New London Northern Railroad Company.[68]

Henry P. Haven served as president from 1860 to 1866, when he refused to continue as president despite re-election several times from 1866 until his death. He did continue to serve as director while A. N. Ramsdell became president. As the railroad began to revive under the trustees, it was decided to put a wharf and depot on the lower part of Water Street at a cost of $80,000. The reorganized road extended its control to other lines. In 1862 it purchased the Amherst, Belchertown and Palmer Railroad Company. The Stafford and Springfield Railroad Company had the same officers as New London Northern.[69] In 1880 the New London Northern leased the Brattleboro and Whitehall Narrow Guage Railroad Company.

Vermont Central

Under its new name and administration the road was able to provide service and increase revenue, however, it failed to achieve the strong position needed to maintain an independent existence.[70] In 1871 an arrangement with the Vermont Central provided for a twenty year lease (to December 1, 1891) and gave ten percent of the New London Northern capital stock to the Vermont Central. The New London Northern received $150,000 a year with the town to benefit from having a carshop established at the port.

1874 brought the advantages hoped for by the lease. A large round-house, repair and workshop buildings were begun. The wharf underwent rebuilding to prepare it as a major shipping point for the Vermont Central. By this time the New London Northern had twenty-one engines, fifteen passenger cars, 113 freight cars, eight baggage cars and 537 employees. Certainly a rather valuable business for New London.[71]

By 1877 the New London Northern had spent $175,000 building a stone wharf which it hoped would stimulate shipping business at the port. It was a T shaped wharf—1,100 feet long and 150 feet wide except at the end where it became 250 feet wide. Railroad track extended along the length and large vessels began to use it very quickly, especially colliers. In 1878 a fire destroyed the car house of the New London Railroad which had been built in 1875—a loss of cars valued at $18,300 and building valued at $35,000.[72]

By 1893 only the Central Vermont, as represented by the lease of the New London Northern, remained outside the control of the New Haven Railroad. The government took over the line during World War I and the

The Robert Coit Locomotive, at Roundhouse, East New London about 1878.

Road made a profit. Then during the 1920s various difficulties, especially flood damage, forced the Central Vermont into receivership. Defense preparedness brought better days in the late 1930s. A long term lease continued the Central Vermont's lease of the New London Northern in 1940.[73]

The Second World War meant all the business they could handle. However, the end of the war found the road having trouble maintaining the service. Passenger trains ended in 1946 but not passenger service since freight trains had a passenger car attached. The Central Vermont Transportation Company operated freighters between New London and New York until 1946. The former New London Northern continues as part of the Central Vermont Railroad System linking Long Island Sound and Canada.

New Haven and New London Company

The New Haven and New London Company had been incorporated in 1849 and made several appeals to New London for support. Elias Perkins, Nathaniel Shaw Perkins, Jr., and Andrew M. Frink were chief among the New London merchants backing the project. Norwich hoped to divert the road to itself rather than New London, but lost out. Thousands of workers were put to work, a large number were lodged at the City Hotel while working on the New London end of the line. In 1852, the second rail connection for the port opened as the New Haven and New London reached Lawrence's Wharf. On July 22, regular rail service between New Haven and New London began.[75]

The city gave a right of way on Water Street which allowed for a connection between the new line and the New London, Willimantic and Palmer Railroad. A new railroad station which opened on October 18, 1852 provided joint facilities for the two lines. The New London, Willimantic and Palmer Railroad line ran in front of the station while the New Haven and New London Railroad tracks passed behind the station and connected with the ferry.[79]

New London and Stonington—New Haven, New London and Stonington Railroad Company

Whaling merchant leadership developed a third line linking New London eastward to Providence and Boston. In 1852 Asa Fish, Thomas Fitch, F. W. Lawrence, Charles Mallory, N. S. Perkins, Charles P. Williams (all whaling merchants) and others petitioned the General Assembly for permission to organize the New London and Stonington Railroad Company. They received a charter authorizing the issuance of $150,000 in stock which was later increased to $600,000. Before completion, a merger was made with the New Haven, New London and Stonington Railroad Company.[76] Although no bridge was constructed across the Thames River between New London and Groton until 1889, a ferry completed the rail link in 1858.[77]

New Haven Railroad

The New York, New Haven and Hartford Railroad Company took over the New Haven, New London and Stonington in 1870 and operated it as the Shore Line Division. It took over the Old Colony Line (Providence to Boston) and the New York, Providence and Boston (New London to Providence). Sometimes the whole New Haven system went by the name Consolidated Line for the large number of roads then taken over.[78]

Other Railroad Developments

Over the years a number of complaints concerning the jointly used Railroad Depot were voiced. Finally, the New Haven decided to improve their facilities if they could get a long term lease for land which would include the waterfront. The area was surveyed for a place to build a new depot. The Shore Line purchased a section of land from S. D. and F. W. Lawrence in 1881 along the waterfront for $7,500 with the agreement to keep open the way to the Lawrence Wharf. Also if a long train blocked the

Public landing, foot of State Street about 1890. Dispatch boat Lily *ran to the Navy Yard (now Submarine Base).*

Union Depot, early 1890's.

way for more than five minutes, it would have to be separated.[80]

Not until the station burned in 1885 did the railroads agree to establish a new station. The state government wanted it on the Parade and the city council agreed to that in 1884. The railroads and city agreed in March of 1886 that the land on which the station would stand would go to the railroads for $15,000, they would make no claim to the waterfront and would move the ferry to the south side of the city wharf. In May of 1886, the New York, Providence and Boston Railroad joined in the depot agreement.[81]

Use began in July of 1887 of the new facility, Union Station, which was staffed by all three railroads using it. A clause provided that if the station should ever be removed, the land would revert back to the city.[82]

The idea of a railroad bridge over the Thames was considered for many years before one was finally built. Much backing developed for the bridge which would create an all rail route from New York to Boston through New London. However, many feared the span would cut off water traffic above New London and used their influence on members of the legislature to block approval for quite some time. Likewise Norwich interests did what they could to block legislative approval. Even when all legal blocks were removed on the state level, a number of cases had to be settled at New London, e.g. Thomas Fitch pursued a case based on rights—he claimed it came from John Winthrop's rights which had never been relinquished. Finally, the way became clear and at a cost of $1,400,000 the bridge was built thus ending railway ferry service.[83]

On September 15, 1889 the 11:10 train from Providence became the first to cross the new bridge even though it was not officially open until 10/9. Now the Shore Line could keep its schedule. It was the longest double tracked drawbridge in the world, 502 feet. Unfortunately, by 1903 it proved to be unsatisfactory because of the heavy locomotives and cars being used. The bridge carried twice the weight it was designed to carry and a new one had to be built. By 1918, the new bridge was in use.[84]

The Norwich and Worcester Railroad again talked of extending their line from Allyn's Point to Groton in 1883. It would cost $300,000 and end the $40,000 a year rental charged to run over New London Northern tracks. Not until 1897 was the Norwich and Worcester, now the New England Railroad, prepared to build a rail link from Allyn's Point to New London. In 1899 the connection was made at last, fifty-eight years after New London first tried to obtain such a connection.[85] By 1891 sixty-eight trains a day passed through the town carrying scores of people.

Some anger developed towards the railroads when the Vermont Central closed the carshops and moved the work elsewhere and the Shore Line began to buy up the waterfront. It began to take over land by 1895 and by 1898 the Shore Line hired Captain T. A. Scott to construct a new long dock with a large shed—375 feet by 80 feet.[86]

Even with a railroad network, New London found it could not obtain the status of a major port. Captains preferred to unload goods for New London and its hinterland at New York or Boston where a return cargo was more assured. Although the rail lines helped the economy of the town,

Picking up Locomotive No. 92 after running through derail at Shaw's Cove drawbridge. September 29, 1893. Shaw Mansion at rear, right.

New London lines could not operate independently and eventually all were taken over by the New Haven System except for the New London Northern Railroad which continued operations under lease to the Central Vermont Railroad.

The golden age of railroad passenger service ended with World War II as a gradual decline in passengers began. The floods of the 1920s, the depression of the 1930s, the hurricanes of 1938 and 1944 could not accomplish this but the personal wealth allowing possession of individual automobiles and the rapidly expanding highway system almost ended railroad passenger service. As noted previously, the Vermont Central ceased running passenger trains in 1946 and the New Haven began sharp curtailment of operating passenger trains over its system. Even the Penn-Central which took over in 1968 had to continue curtailing service due to continued losses. Service which had almost become an institution such as the Clam Digger train had to stop. During the depression people rode it (Clam Digger) to Stony Creek clam beds between Guilford and Branford.[89]

The future of rail traffic for New London depends upon the Amtrak System and the Central Vermont proposal to make New London the key link in its line to St. Albans, Vermont where its major service center is located. The Central Vermont is now a subsidiary of the Canadian National Railways and thus a direct link from Canada to New London exists.

In 1971 the urban renewal program for New London proposed the removal of Union Station.[87] It had been designed by Henry Hobson Richardson, 1885 and proved to be one of his last works and only large railroad station. Quite a disagreement developed as a number of individuals wished to save the building. Those who considered it a work of America's greatest architect launched a campaign to preserve it.[88] Perhaps it will follow into oblivion as another landmark did—the railroad foot bridge built in 1912 by order of the Public Utilities Commission and torn down in the 1950s.

Streetcars

No regular public transportation system existed in the city until streetcars were running. However, hackmen provided inexpensive transportation in 1846—only charging twelve and one-half cents to any part of the city. Several other modes of transportation are worthy of mention. An Omnibus Line attempted to provide service in 1852, especially soliciting the "favor of ladies". Joseph A. Burr furnished transportation between the Union Station and the Pequot House in 1887. Earlier he had the first route in New London between the City Hotel and the resort.[90]

After several years of discussion concerning the need for a reliable inexpensive transportation system, a company requested incorporation from the State Legislature for a horse railroad in 1886. A company organized at Philadelphia ran into the opposition of the power structure at the port which refused to allow the charter to receive approval until they were included in the company. These included:

C. A. Williams	Robert Coit
Augustus Brandegee	Alfred H. Chappell
John Tibbits	George F. Tinker
George Williams	William S. Chappell
Frank H. Chappell	Ralph Wheeler
J. N. Harris	B. F. Mahan
Charles D. Harris[91]	

As a matter of fact, the company never went into operation. Instead, the New London Street Railway Company was organized in 1891 and used the charter previously granted to the New London Horse Railroad

Car #35 on Montauk Avenue, 1904. Motorman, Wm. Stanton, Conductor, Lafayette Rudd.

Company. Many expressed the belief that New London was too small to support an electric railway. However, despite this idea, 1892 saw the laying of track for an electric line along the streets of the town. The Connecticut Tramway Company, organized and owned by Tracy Waller, Charles A. Gallup and Dwight Townsend (New York), constructed the line. Main, Bank, Williams, Blackhall, Broad, Boulevard, Montauk Avenue and Washington Streets had track laid between August and September. The crews worked very rapidly. They could lay a mile of track in a week, with poles placed and finally the wires strung very quickly.[92]

C. A. William's Oneco Company increased its plant to provide the power for streetcar use. The first trolley car in Eastern Connecticut arrived in New London, November 1892 and began service the twenty-second of that month. Martin B. Waller, son of former Governor T. M. Waller, became superintendent of the Line. An excellent business resulted with three cars in service by December, a fourth arrived for use as a spare and the Washington Street Loop was in use. 1893 saw the extension of the Line to the beaches. A ride cost five cents.[93]

Despite the good start, the New London Horse Railroad Company sold the electric line to the owners of the Norwich Company in 1893. In 1896 the company began to build their own power house to adequately supply the system. Gradually the port received street rail links with the nearby towns. The Montville Street Railway, owned by the operators of the New London line, connected the town with Norwich in 1900. No

Baptist Church picnic group going to Golden Spur about 1908.

advance notice was given as to when the first car was to make the first trip—it was greeted by seven small boys and a yellow dog.[94]

The East Lyme Street Railway Company connected the port with East Lyme and Niantic in 1905. A welcome development came in 1921 when Groton and New London each put up $1,500 for a connection over the bridge between the Groton and Stonington Railroad Company and the Shoreline Electric Railroad Company.[95] Four trolley lines provided service to the town. The Consolidated Railway Company of New Haven purchased the stock and in 1904 took over the trolley service in the town. Later the Connecticut Company assumed control and leased operations to the Shore Line Electric Railroad Company until the depressed period of the post-World War I when the Connecticut Company again assumed control (1920).[96]

A problem developed when automatic hand registers for fares were introduced on the Shore Line Electric Railway Company in July of 1918. Conductors threatened to walk off their jobs unless the registers were taken away. They considered their honesty in question. However, both remained.[97]

The terminal for the four trolley routes was at the Parade and even with the introduction of buses in the 1920s streetcars continued to run until 1932. While the Connecticut Company owned all the trolley routes and ran buses in town, they had six competitors covering bus routes to other areas. As in other communities the best days for the companies ended with

Ocean Beach car at State Street, 1914.

World War II when increasing ownership of automobiles, higher wages and operating costs gradually brought an end to the bus service.[98]

Automobiles

Streets in the town remained dirty and dusty in summer, muddy in spring and fall and frozen ruts in winter—until 1880 when blocks were laid on State and Bank Streets and growned oyster shells spread on Pequot Avenue. In 1891 macadam became common on the streets, then brick pavements on State, Main, Bank and Washington Streets 1903-1909. Concrete began on Broad Street in 1919.[99]

As the automobile age came, New London suffered as did other towns with streets that were too narrow for safe two-way traffic and parking. The "devil" came to town when Henry F. Macomber bought a steam locomobile in 1900 for $1,300. Colonel E. T. Kirkland had the second auto which was also a steamer. The first gas powered automobile was owned by the druggist Rogers. C. H. Klinck owned the first automobile-truck, an Atlas, ten cylinder delivery truck, 1904. Although the first two cylinder automobile could obtain a speed of twenty-five miles per hour, State law restricted speed in the city to twelve miles an hour and twenty in the country. Prices were high and few purchased cars in the first years. Bordal and Company, 76 State Street, was the first to sell autos in town.[100]

In the early days salesmen frequently travelled to other areas to drive back cars sold in New London. Merchants did not wholeheartedly or quickly end their love affiar with the horse. Cars were a sideline with them for the first years. William H. Starr had a livery stable and he took in cars along with horses—the past and future side by side.[101]

Manufacturing of automobiles also took place at New London. The Brown Cotton Gin Company designed an automobile for themselves. In 1908 they had an order to build 100 six cylinder cars, gas engines and air cooled. The first complete auto built in the town was constructed by Manuel D'Avillar for Edward T. Brown of the Brown Cotton Gin Company in 1915.[102]

Enough cars were being operated in New London by August of 1920 that the merchants requested a section be set aside near the shopping areas for parking. The last hackdriver, Terence Cook, spent forty-eight years driving his hack before giving up in 1920 and purchasing an automobile. With large numbers travelling by car, the port considered the wisdom of an auto camp in 1921 to increase the number of tourists. After fifty years, the oldest livery stable in Connecticut, G. G. Avery and Son, ended business in 1925.[103]

Thames River drawbridge, early 1900's.

Some idea of what problems faced the town in dealing with the automobile can be seen by the fact that traffic lights were not installed until the end of 1928 and stop streets were ruled legal at that time. Parking meters were installed and during the period from 1941 through 1946, the city realized over $45,000 profit.[104]

In the age of the automobile the highways were paved but New London lacked a network of modern highways until after World War II. When the railroad built a new trestle the American Bridge Company received a contract in 1918 to convert the old New Haven Railway drawbridge into a steel highway bridge across the Thames River at a cost of $290,000. It opened as a modern highway bridge in 1919. Work on The Gold Star Memorial Bridge, a mile long structure, started before World War II began. The last gap on the bridge was closed September of 1942 and work was ordered stopped by the War Production Board, Washington, D. C., November 29, 1942. Finally permission to finish came in 1943.[105]

The old State Highway bridge opened in 1919 was taken down in 1943-1944 and the last traces went in 1945-1946. In 1971 a much needed second bridge was started over the Thames for Route 95 traffic. Our Lady of Perpetual Help which had lost its rectory when the Gold Star Memorial Bridge was built in 1939-1943 now lost all—Church and grounds.[106]

In 1947 the Chamber of Commerce campaigned for a new highway to connect New London with the Massachusetts line and the Hartford area. Interstate 95 has provided a rapid route to New Haven, Providence and Boston but no direct tie-in with Hartford exists. The vast building program to provide for easy entrance in and out of the city, the new Winthrop Parking Garage, the interchange to connect the route to Hartford with the bridges and the new roads into town should finally prepare the city to live much more comfortably with the automobile.[107]

11 Health and Charities 1798-1973

New London appeared to have had more than its share of excellent doctors, dentists and charitable organizations. Still there are several indications that the gullible had many temptations in the form of advertisements to lead them to rely upon patent medicines and assorted healers. Little policing of medical or dental practices or self restraint by the newspapers appeared evident until late in the nineteenth century. This is not to say that concern about the level and honesty of treatment did not exist. Indeed, the first medical organization began in 1774 and the major impetus came from those concerned about "quacks and charlatans". The New London County Medical Society held regular meetings following the American Revolution.[1]

The first medical school began in 1765 at Philadelphia and several New London doctors received their training there. A few studied under doctors with an excellent reputation and then began their practice. Most, after earning enough money, went to medical school. That may seem unusual, however, many doctors received their only training from working with other doctors.

Dr. Elisha North studied under Dr. Lemuel Hopkins, Hartford and entered practice before attending medical school at Philadelphia. He arrived at New London in 1812 and practiced until 1843. New London gained fame in the early nineteenth century as a result of Dr. North's skill as an eye surgeon. So successful did his treatment prove that it attracted much attention abroad as well as in the United States. A number of individuals who had been blind for years regained their sight after treatment by Dr. North.[2]

Dr. Davis T. Frances began his career in the same manner as North. He kept himself up-to-date by studying in London and Paris. He amassed a large fortune and died at the age of sixty in 1883. Dr. Isaac G. Porter served as principal of the Young Ladies High School before becoming a doctor while Henry Potter worked at mechanical pursuits until 1861 and at 36 or 37 went to Yale Medical School. He practiced at New London from 1864 to 1880, serving as city physician for a time. Dr. Oliver H. Jewell, in practice at the town from 1849 to 1895, graduated from a Botanic College and was a Botanical Thomsonian practitioner.[3]

If none of the doctors in residence met one's need, a number of doctors travelled from city to city taking care of those who wished to consult them. Dr. C. C. Bennett, Director of the Misrecordra Institute of Physical Science appeared in town May 7, 1867, to lecture and "heal the Sick in New London After the Ancient Apostolic fashion."[4]

Early dentists advertised and made some hard to believe claims. Most insisted that they performed their work "without pain." J. Washington Clowes advertised that he "Has knock down prices for operating on the natural teeth so low that all who love themselves and value their 'biters' will be able to 'drag out' the where with requisite for repairs." His price for extracting seemed reasonable—twenty-five cents.[5]

Of course if you did not wish to consult a doctor or dentist the family druggist could supply: ointment for piles; laxative pills; nipple salve; toothache drops; pills for blood; various lotions, pills or powders for baldness, cancer growths or other such problems. Testimonials were listed by the sellers of the cures to prove their value. Druggist, E. V. Stoddard, promised an "infallible remedy for ringworms, tellers, scald head, barbers or Jackson itch, perfect Cure, no cure—no pay". Just buy A. B. and C. Sands, $1.00 per box. Long standing obstinate cases would be cured by special agreement. Dr. Gay's Medical Depot on Coit Street used electricity to cure illness in 1851. He claimed it was the best machine in the area. If your hair was thinning, falling out, greying or going rusty you could buy from William Anderson on Bank Street a restorer and preservative which would grow new hair, increase the growth of your hair, remove scurf and dandruff and restore color. A large size cost just fifty cents.[6]

Successful marketing of a product could result in an imitation being similarly packaged and marked. Dr. S. H. P. Lee had a patent on a pill which he sold all over the country and an S. Lee in a nearby town marketed a similar one. Many charges and counter-charges were made, but both pills continued to be sold.[7]

One advertiser wound up in jail—Oliver P. Brown—a printer who had worked for the *New London Gazette*, posed as a retired physician, Dr. H. James, who had a cure for consumption, would send it for one shilling and three cents plus return postage. An item in common use which may seem shocking to present day society was opium. J. C. Sistare reported in 1828 that he had opium for sale—150 pounds. In an advertisement in 1839 another doctor told of the virtues of opium and reported using 100 ounces with good results. He listed the names of the doctors who had it.[8]

The port suffered so many times from epidemics as a result of disease brought in on ships, that the Board of Health of New London established a quarantine ground for the port—lying between a line due east of Hurlburt House on White Beach and a line due east from New London lighthouse. Vessels from any foreign port or south of the capes of the Delaware had to anchor in this area first.[9]

The worst outbreak of disease at New London was a yellow fever epidemic in 1798. The first death came August 26, 1798 and the last on October 25. The death of Captain Elijah Bingham, of the Union Coffee House, began the series of deaths. Most of those infected lived or worked in the northern part of Bank Street. In that area a large quantity of dried fish had been spread over the docks and streets to dry and together with an overflowing privy created a very offensive odor. Lack of proper sewage disposal and food inspection meant unsanitary conditions, especially when the weather turned hot and dry.[10]

It was from this area that most people fled the town. Two hundred and thirty-one of the three hundred and fifty who became ill had been in that part of the city before being stricken. Only Dr. Samuel Holden Parsons Lee and Dr. James Lee, a relative remained in town to treat the people.[11]

Vessels entering from west of the Byram River were quarantined.[12] A Committee of Health was established and on the eleventh of September it reported that the fever was dying out as only three new cases had occurred during the past twenty-four hours. At that point the town had forty-six ill, four seriously, with twenty-five on way to recovery. Unfortunately, the end was not at hand. By the 19th of September another five died of yellow fever. Reports arrived of a yellow fever outbreak at New York on the 29th of September. Those who left were warned not to return. Deaths remained high until the week of October 17th-24th when no new deaths resulted. Dr. S. H. P. Lee became ill but fortunately he recovered and enjoyed a deserved reputation as the hero of the epidemic. This can be seen in its proper perspective if one realizes that only 111 died at New London during all of 1798—21 from yellow fever.[13]

Smallpox was another feared disease at New London. For many years smallpox inocculation paid for by the town took place at the Fort Trumbull Hospital. In 1810 the town hired Sylvanus Fransher, M.D. to vaccinate those who had not had smallpox or been vaccinated. People were urged to take advantage of the service as "only Sloth and stupidity will keep people away". Even in 1840 the port town still vaccinated at its expense. In the 1870-1882 period there were outbreaks of smallpox, diptheria and yellow fever. Large numbers died, larger numbers became ill and much of the activity of the people had to be curtailed in order to try and reduce the spread of the disease.[14]

New London lacked a regular hospital until nearly the twentieth century. Complaints were frequently voiced concerning this lack and local leaders often urged the establishment of one. A number of private places were set up from time to time to meet the need such as a small hospital in 1781 on the west side of Harbor's Mouth Road. The Cottage Hospital existed in 1848—the top story of a private home on Blackhall Street. Several of the wives of leading men organized and ran the hospital with a Mrs. Crocker as the manager. Reports indicate that it was kept very clean and could handle twenty to thirty patients. Charges were made only for those who could afford it. Another private hospital in 1883 was located at "Hell Hollow" in Mrs. Blodgett's house. Since the "hospital" seemed to cater mostly to sick females of childbearing age, it was rumored to be a place of illegal abortion. In 1887 only one place was in operation—the Bacon House kept by a Mrs. Gavitt. It remained until the Memorial Hospital began.[15]

The United States Marine Hospital Service needed a facility at the port for many years. Treatment of sick and disabled seamen had to be at local boarding houses and units set up temporarily as hospitals. These places received fifty cents a day for such patients. The Bacon House was used as a marine hospital.[16]

So many children died from disease over the years that the town decided it needed a Pest House to isolate the ill so disease would not spread. George F. Tinker, Alderman, had one built on city land at a cost of $620.63. He promised to pay for the cost himself if the city refused. After much delay, the town agreed to accept it. First use came when Mrs. Neilan and six children moved in after one child became ill with smallpox. The Health Committee had a doctor and a nurse available for the Pest House.[17] It was renamed Detention House in 1900. A new law led to the appointment of a medical examiner in 1883—Dr. A. W. Wilson. He was to pay fifty cents to each person reporting or finding a dead person and if the cause of death were unknown, to take charge of the body.[18]

Memorial Hospital, opened August 1, 1893.

Finally, J. N. Harris gave $10,000 to start a fund for a hospital. He wanted a two story administration building connected to cottages or wards by corridors. Harris felt it should be called "Memorial Hospital". The first meeting of trustees took place March 31, 1892—Robert Coit, J. N. Harris, George F. Tinker, H. R. Bond and William Belcher—and they formally organized to erect the building. They acquired four acres from the town for $1.00 in April and received incorporation from the legislature in 1893. It opened August 1, 1893 under matron Mrs. Wallace on Garfield Avenue. When funds fell short for furnishing the upper floor of the hospital, J. N. Harris agreed to pay the bill.[19]

It proved to be a very popular addition to the life of the city and required constant aid to meet the drain upon its resources. In 1894 a new ward had to be planned and was called the George F. Tinker Ward for the funds given. The number kept increasing and in addition the Marine Hospital's patients were transferred there. People unable to pay were given the care needed.[20]

Always seeking new means of treating their patients the hospital acquired an x-ray machine—run off a battery in 1897. The report of the superintendent in 1899 indicated that the building had been wired for electricity and connections made to water and sewers. The hospital had a contract with the government to take care of the marine patients.[21]

Earliest reference to nurses is in 1858 when Mrs. Mary A. Demar established herself in New London to nurse the sick. Three nursing schools have existed at the town, one each at Memorial, Lawrence and Home hospitals. Facilities were provided at Memorial Hospital to help the nursing school develop. A nurses home opened in 1902, completed at a cost of $5,000. It contained a sitting and waiting room, library and kitchen as well as dorm rooms in the three story colonial style building. Five nurses graduated in 1903. A number of people helped develop the hospital with donations of funds. Mr. and Mrs. Alfred Mitchell gave $2,000 for a maternity ward in 1902 and $16,500 in 1903. Churches took up special collections for the hospital.[22]

Despite support from many in the town and the constant attempts of the Board to keep the institution up to date, by World War I the institution needed another site where a more modern facility could be built. By March of 1918 the Memorial Hospital Association sought a new site. On April 1, the government officially took it over for the Navy. In August the trustees of the Memorial and Lawrence Hospitals decided to consolidate.[23]

In 1918 the town was hit by the Spanish influenza and all public meeting doors were closed. Cases increased rapidly, 67 new cases in one 24 hour period. By September 28, 1918, several hundred were ill in town and a number of emergency hospitals were set up to care for them. The armory became an isolation hospital for the 100 ill soldiers. All this of course put a strain upon the town's ability to handle the problem. Lawrence and Memorial Hospitals expanded, the Home Memorial Hospital was organized and Dr. Hugh F. Lena began his private hospital on Broad Street. Mental problems received the attention of two doctors in 1918 who established a Mental Clinic in the Associated Charities building. Dr. Birdsall and Dr. Franklin S. Wilcox could be consulted three days a week.[24]

A second hospital at New London had its origin in the will of S. D. Lawrence. Upon his death in 1909, Lawrence's will provided land, Lawrence Hall, a granite building and $100,000 for the establishment of a free public hospital. A $400,000 endowment was also part of the bequest. Following his request it was named for his father and the Joseph Lawrence Free Public Hospital opened April 1, 1912. When the Memorial Hospital merged with the Lawrence in 1918, it became the Lawrence and Memorial Associated Hospitals. There are separate boards for each as well as an additional one for several institutions making up the hospital complex of today and a joint board to oversee the affairs of the total facility. The Mitchell Isolation Hospital is part of the Memorial Hospital and has been in operation since 1920—authorized July 1, 1920 by the Joint Board of Managers for the city of New London. Another hospital of the group is the Manwaring hospital for Children built in 1929. The trustees of the Wolcott

B. Manwaring Fund borrowed $85,000 in 1916 and built the Manwaring Building. By 1929 they had paid back the money and had $25,000 a year income from the building. Another institutional area is the Frank Loomis Palmer Building. It was not built until after World War II. Virginia S. Palmer left $200,000 for special use and a building fund of $200,000. The facility was for a tumor and cancer clinic with quarters for a cafeteria, dining room and x-ray department.[25]

Free treatment for those unable to pay has always been a part of the hospital's service. This has meant that deficits have also been incurred and the struggle for funds is continuous. In 1921 it was decided to build an administration building. A class "A" standard was received from the American College of Surgeons in 1922, one of eleven in Connecticut. New wings and wards have been built constantly to meet the needs of New London and as funds are available. A new maternity ward opened in February of 1923. During World War II a seventy-two bed maternity ward was added to Lawrence Memorial Hospital. Built by the federal government and leased to the hospital, the five story building had the ground broken September of 1942 and was opened March 8, 1944.[26]

Mitchell Isolation Hospital was closed for a time in 1943 when no patients were there. A fire destroyed the Home Memorial Hospital and its patients were moved to Lawrence and Memorial Hospitals in 1944. A last direct link with the hospital's origin ended February 17, 1945, with the death of Charles H. Pond, last surviving member of the original board of incorporators of the hospital and executor of the S. D. Lawrence will.[27]

In 1971 a mental health clinic was established at the Lawrence Memorial Hospital. During 1972, a new six million dollar north wing was dedicated. The rising costs of hospital care can be seen by the fact that at Lawrence Hospital in 1917 a private room cost $20.00 per week while maternity care patients paid $25; in 1942 the rates were averaging $39.69 a week; while in 1971 semi-private rooms were $455.00 a week and private rooms were $483 to $560 a week. Some 100,000 people live in the area and are serviced by the hospital. It now has its latest addition of over 400 beds and 48 bassinets, a coronary care unit, improved laboratory and x-ray facilities.[28]

The Joseph Lawrence School of Nursing began in 1913. The first class graduated June 8, 1916. In 1918 the hospital purchased three lots at the corner of Faire Harbour Place and Ocean Avenue in order to build a nurse's dormitory. Funds were solicited and a $200,000 new nurse's residence was ready in 1928. The classes were small, although two classes a year began until the second World War. In 1942 ten graduated from a class which began with thirty-one, the largest to that date. Then in 1943

Lawrence and Memorial Hospitals.

the class reached forty of whom thirty-nine were in the Cadet Nurse Corps, and in 1944 reached fifty-five. A course in public health was added in 1942, the first such offered in the state of Connecticut.[29]

Until the Second War, area nursing schools provided enough nurses to meet local needs. In 1945 several floors had to be closed at the hospital due to a nursing shortage. The Joseph Lawrence School of Nursing in its 58th year (1971) had a class of sixty, the largest to that date. Included were ten men and thirteen "Never too late" (older individuals).[30]

Unfortunately, in December of 1972 the hospital president, John F. Mirabito, announced that the nursing school would end in 1976 after 63 years. The freshman class of September 1973 would be the last entering class. Costs and the lack of degree granting powers were cited as major reasons for this decision. Hopefully the hospital will be able to offer clinical training for a degree program at an institution of higher learning. A new program being planned for nurses at the Mohegan Community College, the first new nursing program at the port since the Home Memorial Hospital ended theirs in 1929, may fill the void which the closing of the Joseph Lawrence School of Nursing will create.[31]

A third public hospital, the Home Memorial, was organized in 1920, to provide a homelike atmosphere and to be open to the public whether or not they could pay. Captain T. A. Scott became president and Malcomb M. Scott, treasurer. The institution had a nursing school from 1923 to 1929. In 1929 they decided to offer a course for attendant nurses. There would be six weeks of classes in Boston at the Household Nursing Association of Boston and 10½ months at the hospital. A fire ended the hospital's service October 1, 1944.[32]

By 1971 New London had been blessed with an excellent hospital complex provided over the years by gifts of money and time and above all by the willingness of the townspeople to accept their responsibility.

Charities

Over the years, various individuals and groups tried to meet the needs of the less fortunate in New London. In particular needy sailors and their families most often were the recipients of the concern felt by townspeople.

An Almshouse began in 1761 and the town used such a facility until well into the twentieth century. Much controversy developed at different times over cost, improvements needed or type of aid given. William H. Moosbroker and wife served as superintendent, cook and matron for thirty-eight years with thirty-six hours off for a vacation in all that time.[33]

In 1877 the town opened a soup kitchen which fed as many as seventy people a day. The Charity Department with a commissioner of charities to run the town farm and almshome and dispense aid became the official town aid center. A city physician took care of those needing medical care. The Hillside Home (Almshouse) in 1922 was called a fire trap—especially for the bedridden on the third floor. There was a great deal of criticism received in 1927 and 1928.[34]

An early Society, the Lewis Female Cent Society was founded in 1810 and incorporated in May of 1819 to aid the poor and indigent people in New London. A number of individuals assigned part of their estates to the Society. Mrs. Harriet Lewis left $500, Matilda Wright $500, Ezra Chappell $7,000 and Jonathan Coit $3,000.[35]

One of the most active aid organizations, the Seaman's Friend Society, began April 15, 1845. It still remained active in the 1920's aiding families of old whalers. Most of the leading ladies of New London took part. Frances M. Caulkins, who served as secretary, and seventy-five other ladies who belonged the first year began the practice of holding a two day fair in the spring to raise money. They also worked to establish a hospital and boarding house for sailors. During the first year they acquired enough money to aid several families.

It cost fifty cents a year or fifteen dollars for a life membership. Incorporation of the Society took place in 1847. Mrs. T. W. Williams, Mrs. W. A.

Weaver, Mrs. John McGinley, Mrs. W. H. Barns, Henry P. Haven, R. H. Chapell, Mrs. John Rice, Mrs. Albert McCellan and Mrs. A. M. Frink among many others were active in the Society. Jonathan Coit left $2,500 in his will.[36]

From one Mission School an aid society developed which became a valuable part of the charitable scene. The Central Mission Sunday School of the Second Congregational Church began in 1859 on Bradley Street, at that time the heart of the poor section. On April 28, 1861 it was moved to the third floor of Dart's Hall and that Christmas Eve began distributing clothes which became a regular annual November event. In 1862 it moved to Bishop's Building on Water Street where a daily lunch program was begun. In 1864 R. H. Chapell served as superintendent. It became the Bradley Street Mission in 1890 with Thomas W. Gardiner as superintendent. By 1899 the mission was able to operate in the "black".

During the economic crisis of 1893 several local citizens donated money for a soup kitchen to be run by the Bradley Street Mission. By 1916 the Bradley Street Mission—now known as the Billings P. Learned Mission fed and lodged those needing aid. B. P. Mission in 1916 extended aid to families as well as caring for individual boys and men needing clothing, food and lodging. Richard W. Mansfield spent thirty-five years working with the Mission and served a long term as superintendent besides being town probation officer.

A soup kitchen was opened during the post World War I period as well as in the 1930s. In 1924 the Mission sold its property on Bank Street and moved to the Lawrence property on Main and Federal streets.[37]

Among several other attempts to aid the needy at the port one finds that the Frank Loomis Palmer fund was created from profits of the Palmer Brothers Company for the support of New London, religious and welfare charities. The family also made gifts to the city and Connecticut College.

In 1855 Jonathan Coit left $10,000 of invested funds of which the interest was to be distributed among the poor. The Thomas W. Williams II Fund set up by his widow, Mrs. Amanda G. Williams, in 1858 was to be spent on needy sailors and others when the income reached $1,000. The Smith Memorial Home for aged women opened in the 1880s. New London Benevolent Society held fairs to raise money to help the needy. Ezra Chappell gave the Society $10,000 in invested funds in 1866.[38]

The Salvation Army helped at the port from as early as 1884. However, despite their efforts to help they received orders not to play their instruments in the street in 1920. In its early days it sent men to the Bradley

Street Mission for food and lodging. The Salvation Army purchased the three story Neptune Building in 1920 with sleeping space for forty-five. A low level was reached in 1925 when the Captain and his family fed themselves on bread and onions while using all funds available to help the needy. In 1930 a soup kitchen was set up. In 1972 a new building was opened at 318 State Street for servicemen and also a teen center on Governor Winthrop Boulevard.[39]

It took several years for a single organization to head all the efforts for the needy. The United Workers was founded in 1892 by women to systemize charity. Then in the early 1920's the New London Associated Charities brought many of the groups together. The various charities joined together in 1928 to provide aid—it became the Family Services of the Community Chest of Greater New London.[40]

The Jews organized a number of societies, but the first official charity organization was the New London Hebrew Ladies Aid and Educational Society in 1901. It received a charter in 1903. A Jewish Community Center began on Blackhall Street in 1925. This Society became the Hebrew Ladies Aid and Educational Society in 1926. The United Jewish Appeal was organized March 17, 1938.

New London Jews supported the Hebrew Home for the Aged in Hartford until 1954 when they shifted to the New Haven Home. The New London Jewish Association for the Aged formed in 1849 supported the New Haven facility. When it disbanded in 1954 the Hebrew Ladies Aid and Educational Society took over the connection with New Haven.[41]

Charitable facilities which remain today include: Hillside Home, Bacon-Hinkley Home, Smith Memorial Home and Learned House. The only public facility of the area in 1971 was the Hillside Home. It had a fifty-five capacity with thirty-three patients there then—fifteen were confined to bed. The state paid ninety percent and the city ten percent of their costs. The wills of Morris Bacon and Samuel Hinkley provided funds for homes for the aged. The Bacon Memorial Home Corporation and the Hinkley Home Corporation united in 1941 and established the Bacon-Hinkley Home for aged, indigent respectable men of New London, sixty-five and over who had been residents of the city. The former Frank L. Palmer residence became the site. Smith Memorial Home, long a fixture in New London and often the recipient of funds by leading citizens remains in operation. The Learned House replaced the B. P. Learned Mission. It aids men and offers religious programs the year around. It has been focusing on the Youth of the Community.[42]

12 Religion 1645-1973

Puritans moved to the New World to establish their "city on a hill". New settlements usually were established by congregations from other areas or at least a minister accompanied the founders. The minister occupied a very important place in the community—religious leader, teacher of the young and advisor to the political leaders. Much of each settlement's life centered about the church. Religious services occupied much of the people's time with two services on Sunday and one or two meetings during the week.

The first minister at New London, Reverend Thomas Peters, had been in Holland with Thomas Hooker, served at Saybrook and then joined with John Winthrop, Jr. to establish New London in 1645. Peters was an uncle of Mrs. Winthrop's and brother of the Puritan leader Hugh Peters. He did not remain long at the settlement. Like many Puritan leaders, Peters returned to England during the Cromwellian period.[1]

The town lacked a religious leader from 1646 to 1650, when the Reverend Richard Blinman of Gloucester was called to New London. A large number of his congregation followed him to New London so that the history of the town church for many begins in 1642 at Gloucester and continues on in 1650 at New London. Blinman received a house, five acres and sixty pounds a year. A minister usually farmed in addition to preaching.[2]

A barn on Meeting House Hill—the south corner of Hempstead and Granite Streets—served as the First Church. The Blinman Meeting House was built on the hill in 1655. There was no bell until 1675 and the people were called to worship by a drum. Since most of the people of the town belonged to the church, town meetings (during colonial days) handled church affairs. These would involve assignment of pews, salary and any disputes which developed.[3]

The town appointed sextons who dug graves, kept the youth orderly at services, cleaned the Meeting House and chased away the dogs. Members were required to sponsor prospective members. Marriages remained a civil function until 1684 when religious ceremonies began. After several years of success, Blinman angered a number of church members by opposing the separation of Mystic and Pawcatuck from New London. The dispute began in 1653 with Captain George Denison and Thomas Miner leading the opposition. After years of controversy, Blinman gave notice on January 20, 1658 and left shortly afterward for New Haven.[4]

John Tinker preached often after Blinman left. Interestingly, he was also a licensed distiller and retailer of liquors, a most unusual combination for a Puritan church. Even more startling, he died at Hartford awaiting trial for treason.[5]

A new minister was not secured until 1661, when the Reverend Gerson Bulkeley of Concord accepted the post at eighty pounds a year plus a payment of eighty pounds. The town also agreed to furnish a house and a barn. When the town could not provide suitable housing—he agreed to find his own. Once again the harmony of the first few years failed to continue. The minister developed a colony-wide reputation and served on several committees for the General Court and even preached the annual election sermon one year. However, there seems to be a suggestion that his religious views angered some who considered he was leaning more towards Presbyterianism than Congregationalism. By June of 1665, he decided to leave and ended connection with the town which demanded and received repayment of the eighty pounds.[6]

A new minister, Simon Bradstreet, arrived in May of 1666 and was accepted by the town in June. Not until October of 1670 was his ordination carried out. Church records were not kept until October 5, 1670 when Reverend Simon Bradstreet began them. He started at eighty pounds and later received one hundred pounds, the top fee paid in New England at that time. When he became ill in 1680, the town raised his salary to one hundred and twenty pounds. A home built by the town with a lot was made available for his use. It remained in possession of the church until it was sold in 1697.

With a growing population, a new meeting house was needed and in 1678 it was decided to build one alongside the Blinman Meeting House. The Bradstreet Meeting House was finally finished in late 1682. Another event of note during Bradstreet's ministry was the Rogerene movement. By 1680 Bradstreet's health began to fail and he wished to resign in 1681, but the town refused and raised his salary. He died in 1683.[7]

From November of 1683 to May 1688 the town sought a new minister. Edward Oakes received the post in June of 1684 at one hundred pounds but by September of 1685 he left town. Thomas Barnet arrived in September and in November received the post. He left sometime during 1686. No reason for either man's departure is known.[8]

The New London church finally secured a minister when Gurdon Saltonstall, after preaching the winter of 1687-88, accepted the town's offer in May. He proved to be a strong religious leader and was a good friend of the Winthrops. During his ministry a bell finally replaced the drum call to worship. While he did not find his path any less filled with thorns or obstacles than his predecessors, Saltonstall proved to be of firm resolution. Despite his strict moral position, the strong Rogerene movement and the effect of the Half-Way Covenant, church membership rose from thirty-three (twelve males and twenty-one females) to 141 names during the 1688-1708 ministry.[9]

The New London Church did not follow the Half-Way Covenant until Saltonstall's ministry. The official policy of Congregational Churches was to admit only the visible saints into membership until 1662. Their children received baptism, but many upon reaching adulthood could not make a confession of faith and provide evidence of a religious experience to entitle them to enter church. Their children could not be baptised and thus could never become church members. Still they led virtuous lives and some churches began to allow them to become a part of the church while some refused. To meet this, the Synod of 1662 allowed baptism of children of those who led excellent lives, but who had not joined the church. The children as adults could then join the church. Saltonstall became the first New London clergyman to accept the Half-Way Covenant. He also began to perform marriages.[10]

Loss of the Bradstreet Meeting House in 1694 by fire necessitated building a new one—the Saltonstall Meeting House which was ready for use in 1698. It was the third and last built on Meeting House Hill. Many believed that the Rogerenes had set the fire but no evidence existed. Two outstanding developments during these years were the Rogerenes and the Liveen legacy. The latter has been discussed elsewhere, so the former is all that need interest us here.

James Rogers became the baker for the area in May of 1661 in a house next to the Town Mill. He became a wealthy man of large holdings as his business grew. Rogers produced biscuits for seamen, Colonial troops as well as for the local area. The family joined the Seventh Day Church in Newport beginning with his third son, John and wife Elizabeth Griswold, and his son James in 1674, his son Jonathan in 1675, then the father and mother with their daughter Bathsheba in 1676. Rogers left that church in 1677 and began to develop a group of his own, known as the Rogerenes—sometimes referred to as Quakers or Baptists since their beliefs were similar to those of both groups. While their religious views were basically orthodox and they were obedient to the civil laws, the Rogerenes got into difficulty by demanding freedom of conscience and religion. They objected to being taxed for minister's and teacher's salaries and for support of the religious institutions. They opposed oaths, public and private prayers unless they were moved by the spirit of God. They rejected the black garb of clergy, churches, medicines and civil or religious rites for marriage. After worship they went to work on the Sabbath. While few today would see anything very terrible in these views, to people of that day the Rogerenes were terrible people seeking persecution.[11]

A favorite story of this period, but one without proof holds that the Reverend Saltonstall outwitted Rogers when the latter without a regular ceremony, took a wife. They publicly declared their marriage in the county court before the judges and spectators. Saltonstall supposedly met them one day shortly afterward and cleverly led them through a marriage service and declared them legally married. This account gives little credit to Rogers for intelligence.[12]

For their views, the Rogerenes received severe punishment—fines, confinement in the stocks and whipping. Instead of stopping their independent ways they began to interrupt church services thus became as guilty as their oppressors. While wanting freedom to worship their own way they denied others that same freedom. They shouted in services, denounced ministers, interrupted sermons with noise and disorder. The death of John Rogers, October 17, 1721, brought the disorders to an end save for one other short period.[13]

The Liveen estate which Saltonstall helped the town secure, provided £1,900 which the town invested and the interest paid the ministers' salary for many years. In some way the fund disappeared and no one appears to know what happened to it.[14]

Saltonstall enforced strict ecclesiastical rules and all who strayed from the established order were dealt with in a severe and summary way. Saltonstall used excommunication, suspension of church membership and refusal of baptism to those children whose parents were not living the orderly life required by the church. When five leading members presented a list of complaints against Reverend Saltonstall to the General Court they were censured and suspended from the church. Another group of church members signed a protest of this action and were in turn suspended. Only by openly acknowledging their errors in opposing the minister were any allowed to return to church membership.

A separate church was organized in Groton in 1704 after a vote of approval in 1702 and with the joint aid of those on both sides of the river. Reverend Ephraim Woodbridge became pastor. Reverend Gurdon Saltonstall left the ministry January 1, 1708 for the governorship.[15]

Reverend Eliphalet Adams came to town at the request of Deacon William Douglas and John Plumbe who were sent to Boston to seek a minister. They received land lots as payments for their journey. Adams was given £ 188 and £ 90 yearly salary. Ordination took place February 9, 1709, the last time the town ordained a minister. His was a very successful ministry and added many new members. One of the new members was Catherine Garrett—convicted murderess. She took communion twice before execution. Reverend Adams preached (lectured?) among the Indians and established Indian Schools at Lyme and Groton. A number of Indians joined the church under Mr. Adams including Benjamin Uncas, and his son Benjamin, Jr., both sachems of the Mohegan Indians. The major event which took place during Adam's ministry was the Great Awakening.[16]

A slackening of religious fervor took place after 1660 which led to several revivals, especially in 1719, 1721 and the 1740's. A General Association met in New London on June 15, 1742 with Mr. Adams as moderator and took a strong stand against revivals. On November 29, 1742 John Curtis, Christopher and John Chrstophers, Peter and John Harris withdrew from the church. James Davenport, separatist leader, grandson of Reverend John Davenport, caused quite a commotion at New London July 18, 1741 with his preaching but the high point appeared to have been March 6, 1743 when the official forming of the Separate Society took place. On this occasion he preached that a pure church required the destroying and burning of every idol—whether books, wigs, sermons, or other objects. The people rushed home and seized their valuables and at the head of present Hallam Street started a large fire—in which they burned books, clothing and other valuable objects.[17]

About one hundred withdrew from Adam's church to form a Separated Society. They held very emotional, almost daily meetings at first. The county court granted them the right to hold meetings and worship together. Timothy Allen, a suspended minister of New Haven, arrived and presided in a house of Samuel Harris called "The Shepard's Tent" at the corner of Blinman and Truman Streets. It served as a place of worship and a theological seminary. Women freely took part and members were expected to relate their religious experiences. Timothy Allen had been ousted for stating that "The reading of Holy Scripture without the concerning influence and operation of the Holy Spirit will no more convert a sinner, than the reading of an old almanac." After a short time he left New London and later returned to good standing in the church.[18]

When Allen left no new preacher came and by 1748 the Separatist Church ended. It lasted as long as it did because several ministers of the Separatist persuasion preached at New London. In 1745 George Whitefield passed through town and preached at the church apparently with the approval of Adams, although the General Association of Connecticut advised against it. He was hoping to prevent a further split in the church. The last major separatist effort came with Gilbert Tennent preaching three sermons on March 30 and four on the 31st to large crowds in 1746.[19] New London Congregationalist church membership was reduced not only by the separatist, but by the creation of new churches. As the population of sections grew they disliked travelling to Meeting House Hill for services. In 1722 the Congregationalists in Montville and in 1724 East Lyme had their own churches.[20]

A further development was the establishment of other churches than Congregational at the port. A Baptist development in New London began in the section which is now Waterford. Baptisms were carried out as early as 1674 and meetings held as early as 1704. A Baptist Church was organized in 1710, the second in Connecticut. The first pastor was Stephen Gorton, ordained November 28, 1726. They built their church upon Fort Hill in 1730 known as Pepper Box—due to its unusual shape. It remained until taken down in 1847. During the late 1740's the church had difficulties when their minister was charged and tried before a Baptist convention in Rhode Island. While the charges were not proven, they advised his removal. Gorton refused to resign and the church split. A majority stayed and supported him but by 1774 the church ended. A group which left in 1748 established a new church at West Farms where Nathan Howard became the first pastor in 1752. When Waterford was separated from New London in 1801 it became the First Baptist Church of Waterford. Another Baptist group met in New London under Noah Hamond for a short time before joining with Howard's group.[21]

An Episcopal Church was organized in 1725 with a building ready in

1727. While no Church of England people appeared to have been among the early settlers, two Church of England ministers visited the town during Saltonstall's ministry and preached sermons, 1702. In 1723 and 1724 a number of baptisms were carried out at the town. The first took place at Thomas Mumford's an uncle by marriage of Reverend James McSparran from Rhode Island who became the first minister of the Episcopal Church. The founders of St. James appeared to have been English businessmen who had established themselves at the port and opposed the Puritan faith.[22]

Early members met at John Shackmaple's home. He was collector of the port, surveyor and searcher. His son John, later collector at port, married merchant Richard Christophers' daughter, Elizabeth. Several of the leading merchants of New London belonged to the Episcopal Church including Thomas Mumford whose daughter married Reverend Samuel Seabury. Edward Palmes, merchant and husband of Lucy Winthrop, was a member of the Episcopal Church.[23]

In 1724 a building fund was begun, but not until September 27, 1725 did an effective organization begin. The first house of worship stood on the Parade, facing west, built by John Hough. Its completion did not come until the fall of 1732, but it was enclosed and contained an underfloor, desk and pulpit by November 28, 1727. Samuel Seabury became missionary of the Society for the Propagation of the Gospel to New London in 1733. A former Congregational minister, he renounced it in 1731 and went to England where he was ordained by the Bishop of London and returned to America.[24]

Reverend Samuel Seabury served as minister from 1733 to 1744. During his tenure, a bell steeple was built, a bell recast and enlarged, and a clock was added. Funds for the bell came from many outside New London and included two names which are marked as Jewish. John Still Winthrop was the largest donor. The Church was not called St. James until 1741. Earlier it was called Episcopal Church of New London. When Reverend Seabury left, the church had no minister until Reverend Matthew Graves arrived in 1747. The Winthrops had a pew there about this date and were members from then on. Graves reportedly was the only non-native minister in Connecticut and kept himself aloof from the congregation.[25]

With new churches being organized a number of changes took place in the Congregational Church. In 1726 the church dropped the requirement of relating a personal religious experience. The Half-Way Covenant had been followed for some time, but the church had not officially accepted it.

As people of other religious groups settled in the town, it became impossible to levy a church tax on the town, so the First Ecclesiastical Society was formed January 23, 1727. This marked the end of town meetings choosing a minister, setting a church tax and assigning pews. Each church still exercised control over each member for his everyday life and admonished him and even excommunicated him for offenses such as excessive drinking and immoral behavior, or even jailed for causing a disturbance.[26]

The Reverend Adams developed a colony wide reputation and in 1724 was called to the presidency of Yale, but refused it. The ministry of Adams had an unfortunate event on August 31, 1735 when the church was struck by lightning as Mr. Adams began a prayer, killing one, striking down about forty and damaging the meeting house so badly it was decided to build a new one. However, quarrels over a site and the Colonial Wars caused them to repair the church and use it until 1785. Adams faced some disorder by the Rogerenes but it did not amount to very much. Reverend Adams married Lydia Pygan on December 15, 1709 and they had six children. A son, Pygan Adams, became a leading merchant in New London. Reverend Adams' long ministry ended October 4, 1753 when he was seventy-six.[27]

No successor to Adams was hired until 1757 when Mather Byles, Jr. received the acceptance of the congregation. An attempt to employ Reverend William Adams, son of the late pastor failed by a vote of 45 to 42. Byles received one hundred pounds plus a gratuity of two hundred and forty pounds to be paid in four years, he was twenty-three at the time. Before his coming the church voted not to accept the Saybrook Platform as a rule of discipline. This opposed the 1743 action of the Connecticut Legislature which made the Saybrook Platform the established Order in Connecticut and obligatory upon churches.[28]

Reverend Byles, while an excellent preacher, had a quick temper and became irritated easily. Unfortunately he was just the type to encourage the Rogerenes activity which began again, led this time by Jack Rogers, grandson of the founder. While the disorders lasted only from June 1764 to December 1766, as many as thirty-two were arrested at a time and on a few occasions some of the Rogerene's men and women, were tarred, whipped and thrown into the river in winter by the church members. They could anger Byles by attending church with their hats on or just by sitting on the steps of his home or the meeting house. He would not walk from his home to the church if they made an appearance or continue his sermon or prayer if they were present with hats on. Thus they used all these to anger him. Also Byles would not speak or answer any questions they asked. He shocked the congregation when he announced April 1, 1768 that he had received an offer from North Church, Boston to become their pastor if as they understood "he was disposed to think favorably of the communion of the English Church !" They offered £ 208 a year, house, expense of moving to Boston and cost of travel to England to be ordained in the Church of England. A rather warm discussion followed, but no amount of urging him to consider their needs and his duty to "walk with them and watch over them" could change his mind. Some accused him of giving old sermons while studying for the Church of England and neglecting pastoral duties. Byles made it clear that he was determined to leave and offered to repay the £ 240 if immediate consent would be given. The town agreed on April 12, 1768.[29]

Ephraim Woodbridge, a Yale graduate, became minister in 1769. He was the son of Captain Paul Woodbridge, seaman and late tanner in Mystic. After ordination in the church at New London, October 11, 1769, Woodbridge married Mary Shaw, sister of merchant Nathaniel, Jr., October 25 and received a house on Main Street opposite the head of Hallam Street. Woodbridge ran into opposition from church members due to his strong views, especially over the Half-Way Covenant, but he stood his ground. Attacks on his views by committees of church members, and even a vote by the church members to adhere to the Half-Way Covenant did not sway him. A number of prominent New London people became angry over his refusal to baptize their children and being forced to pay for his salary while not being members—still he would not bend.

In spite of their opposition to his views, the members accepted him as pastor. His wife died June 10, 1775 of consumption at the age of twenty-six and he died September 6, 1776 also of consumption. No new minister was chosen until May of 1787. A number of ministers filled the void during this time. Thus during most of the American Revolution the church had no regular leader.[30]

With the coming of the revolution the Episcopal Church faced difficulties. Reverend Graves received much disfavor as he continued his prayers for the royal family and anger grew until a parish meeting of November 14, 1778 declared that no pastor would enter the church unless he openly praised the Congress of the United States. He refused to agree and the following Sunday gave the usual prayers for the King only to have David and Thomas Mumford each seize an arm and lift him out of the pulpit carrying him out of the church. Thus services ended at the church for the duration of the war. Graves went to New York in 1779. The church was burned during Arnold's Raid in 1781. While most members were strong whigs—such as John Deshon, Thomas Allen, and the Mumfords, several were suspected of being Tory—James Tilley, Roswell Saltonstall, Matthew Stewart and the Winthrops.[31]

With the end of the war, religious affairs needed considerable attention. The Baptist Church ceased to meet in 1774, the Congregational Church had not had a regular minister since 1776 and needed a new meeting house and the Episcopal Church had not had a meeting since 1778 and needed both a minister and a church. As late as 1806 only St. James and the First Congregational Churches held regular Sunday services. The Methodist and Baptist Churches irregularly held services. In 1804 the First Baptist Church was formed by fifty members of the church in Waterford who lived in New London. They wanted to put up a building at Pearl and Union streets but James Tilley, who owned the land refused to sell it as he disliked Baptists. A non-Baptist purchased it from them, telling Tilley it would be good for a hog pen—Tilley always referred to the church afterwards as the "hog pen". They began building in 1805 and finally finished in 1815.[32]

A leader for several years, Reverend N. Dodge, was expelled in 1823 for having Universalist views. He then became a tavern keeper. Disputes led to two splits in the membership. In 1840 the minister, Reverend C. C. Williams and several members left and established the Second Baptist Church which built a house of worship on Union Street in 1840.[33]

First Baptist Church called the Reverend Jabez Swan to be their pastor in 1843. He was earnest, blunt, eccentric and extremely prejudiced. Much of his time was spent in revival work. He hated drinking, the Masonic Order, Universalists and slavery. Swan particularly disliked Reverend Dodge for becoming a Universalist and after noticing him at one of the revival meetings in New London, he prayed that the Lord would "seal his lips and take him out of the way." Reverend Dodge was stricken with paralysis and taken home, where he died shortly. Swan liked Deacon Isaac Harris and would often ask him to back up a point he made while preaching—"Uncle Isaac, isn't that so?" The deacon would reply "Yes, Elder, that is so." On one occasion while preaching on Abraham, he called out, "Uncle, if God called on you to sacrifice your little Becky, could you do so?" Uncle Isaac replied, "Elder, I want a little time to think that over."[34]

The Third or Huntington Street Baptist Church originated when one hundred and eighty-seven members of the First Baptist Church broke away, purchased the Universalist building on Huntington Street and asked Reverend Jabez Swan to be their pastor. He left the First Baptist Church in 1848 for the High Street Church in Albany, but heeded their call to return to New London in 1849. It meant the fulfillment of a boast he had made in 1843 when the Universalists were building their house of

Huntington Street Baptist Church.

worship. Seeing some present at a public meeting he said "now plan and build a good house . . . Show your religion and your taste, if you have any . . . I have prayed the Lord . . . The Baptists shall yet possess the house, and I expect to stand in its pulpit and preach. . . ."[35]

The First Baptist Church decided to build a new church at State and Washington streets in 1855. Reverend William A. Sunday (Billy) spoke at the Church April 16, 1895. Reverend Swan became pastor of the Second Baptist Church in 1858 and remained there until 1860. This meant he had served all three Baptist Churches in New London. The Second Baptist Church moved to Montauk Avenue where the church burned in 1914. They rebuilt it in 1917[36], and it became known as the Montauk Avenue Baptist Church.

The Episcopal Society needed both a building and a minister after the American Revolution. They rebuilt their church on a new site, 1785-87. It was ready in 1787. Samuel Seabury (1729-1796) Bishop of Connecticut in 1784, took over at St. James—his father's parish and became bishop of Rhode Island when it became part of his area in 1790. He died in 1796 and was buried at New London. A third member of the family became minister (1796-1814) Charles Seabury.[37]

A new church structure for St. James was decided upon in 1846. The architect who had drawn the plans for Trinity Church in New York City was engaged to plan a new church at Huntington and Federal Streets.

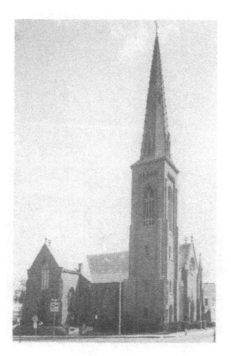

St. James Episcopal Church.

Architect Richard Upjohn estimated a cost of $25,000 for the structure. However, the builders wanted $42,352. The church found a foreign builder who agreed to do it for $27,000. Actually it cost $42,352 and the work stopped twice before enough money was raised to complete the building. At that the church owed $7,000 and lacked the funds to place the bell in the tower until later. Bishop Seabury was re-interred in the Chancel of the new church.[38]

The first problem the Congregationalists dealt with after the Revolution was their church. As the meeting house had been in very poor condition for some time it was decided to build a new one in 1784 on the same spot. However, in 1785 Stephen Bolles agreed to sell land on Bolles Hill, Union Street and to lay out a new street, Masonic. The subscription list began with Thomas Shaw leading it. The same families which had contributed leadership to the town since 1645—Shaw, Law, Learned, Richards, Deshon, Saltonstall, Green, Coit, Colfax, Belden and Mumford gave money but more often labor and materials. The last service in the Saltonstall meeting house took place August 23, 1786 and use of the new meeting house began by 1787.[39]

January 25, 1787 the church invited Henry Channing to become the minister. Channing, originally from Newport, Rhode Island and a Yale graduate in 1781, preached the sermon for Hannah Occuish who was executed December 20, 1786 for murder. One of the church's first concerns was money to finish the new meeting house. The Society applied and received permission to hold a lottery to raise the needed funds before Channing became officially accepted May 17. Instead of a lottery another subscription list began with Thomas Shaw again leading the list and the house was completed November 8, 1789. Shaw also donated a house on Main Street to the church for a parsonage. During Channing's ministry the annual meeting changed in 1792 from January to April. Also a new cemetery was opened in 1793—the Second Burial Ground.[40]

The bell of the Saltonstall meeting house was moved to the new meeting house but cracked in 1794 and a new bell procured from Benjamin Hanks of Mansfield for eighty pounds was used until 1831. Church membership appeared simple enough under Channing. If one wished to be a member and no good reason existed to reject him, he could join and take part. No rebirth or religious experience had to be related. However, Channing's views angered many and his pastorate was marked by disputes and inadequate pay. His views appeared to have become unitarian to many. As early as 1789 those most orthodox in viewpoint saw in his statement of profession and convenant evidence of this change since Jesus is not referred to as the Son of God nor is there any reference to the Trinity.[41]

The matter of the salary became a problem as Reverend Channing's proved too small, but no increase was granted although the members voted extra amounts from time to time. He requested an increase in a letter of January 21, 1797 but nothing was done except to pay an extra amount of sixty pounds that year and fifty pounds the following year. Then too, since Reverend Channing's views seemed to anger several they were more concerned with this than his salary needs. Complaints increased over the years from 1799 to 1806. March 27, 1806 he proposed to resign and approval was given unanimously on April 26, 1806. At a church council meeting May 20th that year the ministry officially ended.[42] Due to the neglect of his financial needs, nearly a year after his dismissal from the church he received $325.

Reverend Abel McEwen, selected July 14, 1806, served until 1860. The land on the hill occupied since 1650 by the church was traded for land behind the new church lot on State and Union streets and a house for the sexton was purchased in 1809 on Church Street. The First Society received a new "Statement of Doctrine" which was proposed in 1807 and accepted in 1810 by 139 members. McEwen's preaching was strong, revivalist and attracted many new members. On the other hand a number of members were excommunicated for absence from services and/or conduct.[43] Among the changes that took place during McEwen's service was the appropriation of funds from the state legislature. The state received federal funds to repay money spent for defense during the War of 1812. One-fifth of this sum was given by legislative action to the Presbyterian or Congregational Churches of Connecticut. Besides this, Mrs. Harriet Lewis left $1,000 to the Society in 1819. The same year a Session House was built for weekly meetings of conference and prayer on Church Street. In 1821 the women of the church established a missionary society. An organ was paid for by subscriptions in 1825 and choirmasters received their pews free.[44]

The question of a new building was brought up in 1832 and not acted upon until 1847, meanwhile a split occurred and nineteen members left the First Church and established a New Society—the Second Ecclesiastical Congregational Society, later known as the Second Congregational Church. T. W. Williams gave land at Jay and Huntington streets and the Society built a church which was finished in August of 1834 and dedicated April of 1835. Despite the split, relations did not appear strained between the churches and in fact the First Society used the Second Society Meeting House while repairing its own.[45] Finally, in 1847 First Society took action to acquire a new meeting house. $18,000 was subscribed between September 6, 1847 and February 1, 1848 and the building committee consisted of Andrew M. Frink, Sidney Miner and Nathaniel Shaw Perkins, Jr. The Society sold the Main Street property and purchased the house and lot of Carly Leeds which stood between the Channing Meeting House and State Street. All was ready by August of 1849 for the new building and cost was to be $21,500. The last religious service held in the old home occurred September 30, 1849. An exchange with school property behind church property provided a straight property line. The granite building was ready in August of 1851 and pews were sold August 4th. In October the architect recommended that the walls of the central tower be taken down and rebuilt due to defective masonry. Instead the walls were bolted and filled with cement.[46]

A clock was provided for the tower by the city. The Society agreed to give six months notice if it wanted the city to remove the clock and it would pay the city for fitting a room in the tower if the clock were removed before ten years had passed—as it was used for public purposes as well as church. A new clock had been installed in 1912 and was made electric in 1955. In 1971 the city decided that it no longer wanted to maintain the church clock after having done so since 1852.

A new organ ($6,000) was acquired in 1870 and the following year the minister's salary was increased to $2,500. The Sabbath school support

First Church of Christ, Congregational. Built in 1850.

came with a revival meeting in 1872. A new bell was required as the old one cracked in 1876.[47] The First Church decided to build a $10,000 chapel on the site of the conference house on Union Street in 1880.

Asa Otis, First Church member, died at the age of 93 in 1879. He began as a clerk in a store in New London and then went to New York City where he entered the wholesale auction and commission business. By the age of fifty in 1835 he had become wealthy and retired with $60,000 a year

Second Congregational Church.

income. Returning to New London he engaged in no business, but belonged to the First Church and gave much to it each year. His estate was well over one and ½ million dollars. Otis left $106,000 to public institutions and $91,300 to individuals and the rest to the Church Board of Foreign Missions which amounted to over one and one-half million dollars.[48]

From First Congregational Church came the Stonington Church (1674), the Groton Church (1704), the Montville Church (1722) and Second Church, New London (1835). In 1868 the Second Church burned and a new one was built in 1870 at Broad and Hempstead Streets. While a new building was in progress, First Church offered the use of its home. Henry P. Haven made his first confession of faith at the church's first communion service. He served as Superintendent of the Sunday School. When the church reached its fiftieth anniversary only one of the original nineteen who broke from First Church remained alive—Mrs. Charles Butler. Of the 107 members of the first year, eight still were alive. A church school existed from the beginning of the Society and the church operated as many as five mission schools at the same time.[49]

Moody and Sankey, world renowned revivalists made a visit to New London in 1885 and while they planned to speak at Second Church, the crowds were so large that they spoke in the new Armory building instead.[50]

A Universalist Society was formed at New London in 1835. Much opposition existed among the townspeople and only after much difficulty was a lot purchased. Only Dr. Ulysses Dow, teacher, would sell them a lot. He received much criticism for the act. Feelings against Universalists were so strong that at a Union Church Service no one would stand beside the Universalists leader except a dentist and later the dentist had to leave the city.[51]

A church began in 1843 with a home built and dedicated March 20, 1844. They sold it to the Huntington Street Baptist Society in 1849 to pay off their debts and bought the old Episcopal Church. They built a new church on Starr Street in 1882 to replace their building at Church and Main Streets. The Society lasted until 1894 when it disbanded and sold the church in 1896.

The Unitarians began meeting in the Cronin Building in 1895—later, 1898 the Lyceum Theater and the Bethel Chapel in 1905. The Unitarians and Universalists merged in 1907 and established All Souls Church. They moved into a new building on Huntington Street in 1910.[52]

Methodism entered New London's religious life about 1789 when Jesse Lee preached at the Court House on September 2nd. He preached again in 1790 and Bishop Francis Asbury did so in 1791. Richard Douglas and his wife were among the first converts. Meetings in the Douglas home grew until in 1793 a church society was organized. They built a church on what is now Methodist Street, 1798-1800. A new building was dedicated in 1817. Trouble developed within the church by 1827, and by 1840 the congregation split over slavery. When the Independent Methodists left the Conference and established their own society they organized a church in 1842 and kept the building on Methodist Street. They became known as the Wesley Methodist Church, while those who remained in the Conference represented the Methodist Episcopal Church. They met in the Court House in 1842 before their building was opened that year on Washington Street. In 1855 they moved to Federal Street. The Methodist Episcopal Church occupied a new home on Broad Street in 1921. Two places of worship were operated by the Wesleyan Methodists—The Seaman's Bethel, formerly the Union School, at the corner of Huntington and Jay Streets and the former First Baptist home on Pearl Street.[53]

Reverend Ezra Withey preached to those who followed the sea—at the Seaman's Bethel corner of Hunting and Jay Streets as well as at the regular church services on Pearl Street. A quiet and reserved man once when asked to speak to a boy who loved to practice the violin and was disturbing everyone around him, Reverend Withey said: "William, for my sake, and your mother's sake and for God's sake stop that fiddle." Both Seamen's Bethel and the Wesleyan Methodist Church which had become

The Methodist Church, Federal Street.

the People's Christian Church closed in 1903. The members decided to sell the properties and divide the assets among themselves.[54]

Congregationalists began a system of sunday schools and mission schools for religious and secular instruction of the poor of all backgrounds. Sabbath school work in New London began July 28, 1816. Matilda Wright established the first Sunday School in her home on Main Street. She already had a small private school. Five ladies, two of them Episcopalian, were the teachers with sessions before morning services and after the afternoon session. Hymns and Bible passages were learned by heart and the teachers covered planned lessons.[55]

Thirty dirty unkept "kids" appeared the first Sunday, forty the second and the number kept increasing each Sunday. Fanny Coit upon becoming superintendent, made sure that children were taught to read, write, spell and memorize. They received one meal ticket for each ten verses learned. They went to church services in a group after Sunday school. The women teachers found the boys very unruly. Robert Coit, Lyman Allyn and Erastus Smith took over and in 1817 began a school for boys at the Old Female Academy on Greene Street. When girl's groups became quite large, they asked for the use of the Court House and when it was refused, they moved in anyway. The two schools became one in 1819 with sessions held in the Conference House of the First Church. At first, the minister feared the school would take away from family unity on the Sabbath and would violate the holy day as secular as well as religious instruction would be given.[56]

The schools received several fine Bibles in 1819 from the Connecticut Bible Society and in 1821 Miss Wright decided that a library must be developed. A five dollar donation from Ezra Chappell began it. In 1821, a male Sabbath School was formed with Ezra Chappell as superintendent. After 1830 the pressure was taken off the First Congregational Church when other churches began Sunday and mission schools.

Special classes were formed to teach English and job skills to Blacks, Germans and Chinese. Many of the district schools served also as Sunday Schools. The Sixth District School was also the Ocean Avenue Chapel on Town Hill Road which served the area for over fifty years. While a Baptist group directed the Sabbath School, others than Baptists attended. Deacon Charles Butler often visited the school and took part. One Sunday he asked a boy the wages of sin—"Eight dollars a month", replied the young man. It seemed that his wages on a farm amounted to that sum.[57]

The Eighth School District building was used by Henry Haven for a Sunday School. It became known as Gilead on its twentieth anniversary in 1856. An evil reputation existed around the area where drink, girls and music attracted sailors from the whale ships. A chapel was built with whaling profits in 1876 across from the school. In 1860 Joshua Learned began Sunday School Concerts every second Sunday. In 1863 the Union Concerts were begun by First and Second Congregational Churches.[58]

Roman Catholics, few in number in the early days, did not have a formal church organization until 1843—St. John's on Jay Street. However, the first mass was said in 1650 by the Jesuit Father Druilette while visiting John Winthrop. Roman Catholics from Acadia and San Domingo kept the townspeople from being unaware of this branch of Christianity. Father Roux died while visiting the town during the 1770's and was buried in the North Church Yard. About the same period Father Maltgnon preached in New London. Bishop Carroll visited one Sunday in 1789. Construction at Ford Trumbull brought a number of Roman Catholics to town—three families and five unmarried members of that faith by 1831. Worshipers used an upstairs room on the Long Bridge in 1842.[59]

The real organized movement came with Reverend James Fitton who conducted Roman Catholic religious affairs irregularly from 1843 to 1848.

St. Mary's Church. Built in 1875.

Father Brady helped out. Reverend James Gibson became the first resi-
dent priest in 1848 and was followed by:

Reverend Peter Blenkinsop	1850
Peter Duffy	1851
Thomas Stokes	1851
Thomas Ryan	1852

By Father Ryan's time the faithful had increased to 500 from two dozen
of 1843. St. John's bought land on Truman Street in 1855. The name of
the church became St. Patricks and became St. Mary's Star of the Sea in
1866. A new church cornerstone was laid in 1870. The new Catholic
Chapel was dedicated Sunday, September 28, 1873 and St. Mary's new
Roman Catholic Church was blessed Sunday, May 7, 1876. The Old
Roman Church became a tenement in 1873.[60]

Our Lady of Perpetual Help Church was incorporated in 1907. A
building was dedicated in 1915 on Huntington Street. The State bought
the area in 1972 and the church is planning to move to Quaker Hill. In
1910 St. Joseph's Roman Catholic Church was created. The Polish Inde-

pendents decided to establish a church after Our Lady of Perpetual Help removed a priest for being too much of a Polish Nationalist. They established S. S. Peter and Paul Polish National Catholic Church November 20, 1921. A Syrian Roman Catholic Church began in 1929 and dedicated a building, St. Anne's, in 1930 at the corner of Connecticut and West Coit.[61]

Not until 1843 were Jewish citizens of Connecticut legally allowed to form religious societies. Thus, although merchants carried out business transactions at the port and Jews began to settle there during the Civil War, a sufficient number to create a religious society did not exist until 1878. Achin Sholom Congregation began that year, but the first service was not held until 1892 when a "miryam" or quorum of ten was present at a second floor apartment on Bradley Street. A plot of land was purchased in Cedar Grove Cemetery in 1878 for a Jewish Cemetery by Joseph Michael, Samuel A. Goldsmith and others.[62]

The first Cantor and Shoket in New London was Solomon Protas in 1890 of the Ahavath Chesed Congregation. Congregation Ahavath Chesed used Allyn Hall for their religious services and later the New London Opera House on Bank Street. It organized a sick benefit society, Haavas Kesed in 1892 which purchased land in Waterford for burial purposes and collected dues to pay benefits for needy, aid the sick and bury members.[63]

In 1895 the Sick Benefit Society of Rodeph Sholom bought a burial ground in Waterford, next to the Haavas Kesed ground. They joined together in 1905. Religious instruction began 1898 in the Ahavath Chesed rooms on Douglas and Bradley Streets. Another burial society, Chevia Kadisha was organized in 1899 to prepare the dead for Hebrew burial. Ahavath Chesed purchased land on Shapley Street for a synagogue, December 2, 1902 and had their dream of many years fulfilled July 2, 1905. The pews were from the former Second Baptist Church on Union Street. Abraham Nathan Schwartz became the first Rabbi in 1906 and Jacob Mendelsohn the first Cantor.[64]

January 13, 1919 the Temple burned and others offered their buildings. The former Methodist Church on Federal Street was purchased and converted into a synagogue. High Holy Day services were held stretching a canvas roof and side wall. They burned their mortgage June 22, 1952.[65]

The Ohave Sholom Sick Benefit Society purchased a burial ground near the Ahavath Chesed in 1911 and laid the cornerstone of their building on Blinman Street in 1919.[66]

A third synagogue, Temple Israel, received a charter September 12, 1924 and opened July 12, 1925 on Park Street, Ocean Beach. It provided

Temple Beth El.

services not only for people of the area but summer resort people as well. These three congregations were orthodox and in October 1932 a Conservative Congregation was formed—Beth El. Their first services were held November 4, 1932. They rented a Community House on Blackhall Street first, then rented a hall on Union Street. March 1933 a cemetery association formed by members, purchased land in Groton. They organized a choir and a library in 1935. A building fund began in 1943 and property was purchased on Ocean Avenue in 1948. May 4, 1955 the dedication was held.[67]

New London's long and varied religious history has included different churches and religious groups. Not all can be described in detail but a number of those which have added so much to the life of the town must at least be mentioned: Bethel Methodist (1867), Union Baptist Church (1889), Shiloh Baptist Church (1894), Calvary Pentecostal Church, A.M.E. Zion (1911), Zion Evangelical Lutheran (1916), Mount Morial Fire-Baptized Holiness Church of God, Christian Science, Swedish Congregational Church, Seventh Day Adventists Church, Church of God and Saints, St. Sophia, The Glad Tidings Assembly (Reorganized Church of Jesus Christ of the Latter Day Saints), Church of Jesus Christ of the Latter Day Saints, the Spiritualist Temple and the Salvation Army.[68]

13 Education 1650-1973

The modern school board so familiar to most of us today, has operated for so long, that it may be difficult to understand that it has not always existed. Indeed, the different governing bodies of public schools in New London did not join together as one until 1856. By then the town had had several educational institutions—the town elementary school originated in 1650, the town grammar school started in 1678, the Union School established in 1750, the Female Academy organized in 1799, a Charity School began in 1774, a Black School commenced in 1837 and a number of private schools opened.

Puritans placed great value upon education and a literate people since "It being one chiefe project of that old deluder Sathan, to keepe men from the knowledge of the Scriptures . . . ."[1] Every town with fifty householders was required to keep a grammar school and one with a hundred house-holders had to provide a Latin school which would prepare for entrance to a college.[2] New London does not seem to have applied as much vigor to its educational needs as might be expected. As a result, many in the second generation could not write their own names.[3] A local school began in 1660 under the direction of a "Master Brigadon" at a time when the first children born in the town were thirteen.[4] However, the first schoolmaster appeared to have been the Reverend Blinman, thus instruction for the young was available during the 1650's.

A boost to education came when Robert Bartlett willed his property to the town to provide a free school for poor children. He died in 1673 at about the age of seventy-eight without relatives, leaving a homestead on

Close Cove, a farm of 250 acres north of town and a few other parcels of land.[5] New London had difficulty in keeping a school going, with teachers difficult to obtain and more difficult to keep.

These difficulties led to New London being fined in the county court 1682, for not having a grammar school as well as a fine for not having an English school for reading and writing. In 1700, the Grand Jury returned a complaint about New London not keeping a grammar school.[6] A regular grammar school had to wait until May of 1701 when the town decided to use the town's school funds and the Bartlett income, one thousand pounds, for such an institution.[7] A three man committee had been set up to handle the Bartlett estate in 1698.[8] The teacher situation improved after Yale was established in 1702. Still teacher tenure remained short—George Dennison 1708-1711, Nathaniel Baronham 1711-1713, John Gardiner 1713, and Jeremiah Miller 1714-1731. Six more served from 1731-1747. No record exists from 1747 to 1756 when John Owen took over the next thirty-nine years.[9]

In 1713 most of the Barlett land was sold and a fund established for education. The first schoolhouse, a brick building, was built in 1713 and called the New London Grammar School. A number of private schools were established in the town for those who wished to prepare for college. Quite early private schools for the young women who wanted to learn to read and do needlework were taught by a succession of school "marms". While these were for those who could pay tuition there were charity schools for the poor.[10]

Females were allowed to be taught at the town grammar school either before or after regular hours.[11] Six hundred acres granted to the town for education were sold in 1725 for £120. One-half went for a grammar school in the North Parish and one-half for the New London Grammar School. In 1738, a new brick schoolhouse was built for the town replacing the one built in 1713 and it was replaced in 1774 by another new one.[12]

In the post-revolutionary period, John Owen continued as teacher of the town grammar school until 1795 and then Dr. Ulysses Dow took charge. His long tenure, which lasted until 1844, became noted by strong feelings of support or criticism as a result of his methods. His school room, near the court house, represented the domain of the "iron schoolmaster" who used corporal punishment frequently. A large man, he used his strength to discipline the boys. If they were deserving of correction, he would seize them and lift them from their desks. He crippled one boy this way as the lad had his leg around the leg of the desk and it caught when Dow "jerked up" the boy.[13]

Nathan Hale Grammar School, early 1900's.

Although many parents disliked him, more apparently like him or he would not have been kept so long. His gift of land to the Universalists, when no one else would sell them land for a meeting place, caused much displeasure for him. Finally, when the Whigs had control of the school board in 1838, he was fired only to be rehired when the Democrats returned in 1840.[14]

His long career came to an end in 1844 when a former scholar of his who had boasted that he would have Dow ousted, had the pleasure of informing him that a Whig would replace him. Dow died a few months after his removal, December, 1844, at the age of seventy-eight. Most of the leaders during the nineteenth century were taught by Dow or were the sons of those who had been.[15]

The building of 1774 was replaced by a school on land given by Major Thomas W. Williams in 1834. From this date to 1873, the school, now under the New London School Society, became known as the Bartlett School and developed into Bartlett High School under E. B. Jennings, 1850-1873. E. B. Jennings arrived in 1850 to take charge of the town grammar school after being principal and professor at Tuskegee Institute. When the school closed in 1873 he became city surveyor.[16]

A rival of the town's grammar school began in 1750—the privately owned Union School. Quite a rivalry developed between the public and private schools which reached its height during Dow's long tenure. It would appear that the teachers of the institutions did little to discourage the strong feelings.

Richard Law, Jeremiah Miller, Thomas Mumford and Duncan Steward help put up a school house located at Huntington and Jay Streets to give a thorough English education and a classical preparation. From 1750 to 1833, its enrollment was confined to sons of those who owned shares. Nathan Hale became principal of the school after its incorporation by the General Assembly in 1774. He instructed twenty young ladies from five to seven A.M. and thirty-two boys during the day.[17]

Several teachers served until the school ended in 1850. Some of them were Mr. Bull, Joseph Hurlbut, Mr. Smith, James McClane and Erastus C. Jones. The Union School proprietors were allowed by the October session of the 1810 Assembly to levy a tax upon shares of the proprietors to run the school. In 1826 the shares became personal property by authority of the Assembly. In 1833 the corporation ended and the New London Union School was incorporated in 1834 to replace the old exclusive school, accepting all who would pay tuition. John Brandegee, Archibald Mercer and others were the incorporators. It lasted only sixteen years as enrollment declined when more and more boys began to attend the town grammar school.[18]

The New London School Society, formed in 1834, received tax money and added in 1837 the revenue of the town deposit fund. It was due to the Society's successful efforts to improve the town schools that the public enrollment grew. Declining numbers forced the Union School to close in

Winthrop School.

Robert Bartlett School.

1850 and with only the town grammar school available for academic training the officials decided to remove the tuition charges in 1852. A grammar school committee had charge of the (Latin) Grammar School from 1678 to 1856 when the Board of School Visitors took charge of it.[19]

It is obvious that many parents wanted education for their female children over and beyond what was available from the town elementary school or the special classes at the grammar school before or after the boys classes. To meet this need many "Female Schools" operated during the eighteenth and nineteenth centuries. Some of the subjects offered were not academic—fine needlework, drawing, painting and knitting—but often they taught the same subjects the boys were able to receive instruction in—English, Latin, grammar, geography and history.[20]

In 1799 the New London Female Academy filled the same function for young ladies as the Union School did for the boys. They could study reading, writing, chemistry, natural philosophy, arithmetic, geography and English grammar. It was established on Green Street between Pearl and Golden Streets with William Green as the first teacher, a graduate of Dartmouth. Isaac Thompson, Peter Richards and Samuel H. P. Lee among others, incorporated the school as the Female Academy in the Town of New London in 1819. The school continued until 1834 when the corporation was disolved and the property disposed of as a new academy incorporated as the New London Female Academy by Joseph Hurlbut, William P. Cleveland, Thomas W. Williams, Lucretia M. Mitchell, and twenty-six others took its place. Only two served as teachers—Reverend Daniel Huntington 1834-1841 and H. W. Farnsworth 1841-1855.[21] A Young Ladies High School replaced it in 1855 as a part of the public school system, finally giving the girls a publically supported institution comparable to the Bartlett High School.[22]

The town's present school board had its start as the Board of School Visitors which directed the New London School Society, organized in 1834. Six independent school districts made up the School Society of the town. A separate committee in each handled the levying of school taxes and the hiring of teachers. These handled the elementary training of the town's children, replacing the town elementary school setup in 1650. The Board of School Visitors decided in 1854 to establish the Young Ladies High School which opened in 1855. It offered an excellent course of study. The Board extended its control to the Bartlett High School (town grammar school) in 1856 and its board came to an end after directing the school since 1678. From 1834 when the Huntington Street building on the Williams' property replaced the 1774 building, the school became known as Bartlett School and after 1850 as the Bartlett High School.[23]

Under the new system in accordance with state law, the town provided free education for children between four and sixteen. The younger children in Primary or Kindergarten classes attended in mixed groups of boys and girls. Above these groups the children were separated and taught by different teachers. Each district school building had a separate room for each sex. These schools from 1834 to 1839 consisted of rented buildings, but beginning with 1839 buildings for school use were planned and erected.[24]

Mixed classes of boys and girls in all grades began in 1853 at the Huntington Street District (Number 4) and despite opposition from many, gradually became common throughout the town. The system of autonomous school districts received a great deal of criticism which increased until in 1868 a Union School District replaced the New London School Society. All tuition charges ended for residents at this time for the public schools. Very young children were sent to schools called primary until 1850 when kindergartens replaced them. Neighborhood or elementary schools took care of most children in the nineteenth and early twentieth centuries. Some twenty percent went on to the grammar schools, where ninety-five percent finished.[25]

A school day at the Bartlett School was a full one—nine to five with a fifteen minute break at 10:30 and 3:30 and a lunch period from twelve to two. Wednesday sessions only lasted until 3:30 and Saturdays until twelve.[26] The last Bartlett School building was erected on Brown Street.

In 1873 Bulkeley School for Boys replaced the Bartlett High School. Leonard H. Bulkeley, merchant, left $25,000 for a boys free high school in 1849. The trustees—John P. C. Mather, William C. Crump, Nathan Belcher, Henry P. Haven and N. S. Perkins, Jr.—invested the money and by 1871 had $70,000. At a cost of $40,000 a building was erected at Huntington and Bulkeley Place which opened in September of 1873.[27]

It began with two teachers and two classrooms and a fund of $47,000 which brought in $3,000 annually. As needs increased the city began to pay part of the cost of the school. Starting with $1,000 in 1893 Bulkeley's fund was increased by donations of Asa Otis $10,000, Henry P. Haven $5,000 and George F. Tinker nearly $11,000. F. W. Mercer gave the school land for an athletic field, Mercer Field in 1927 plus additional land that same year.[28] Over the years many gave generously for materials, equipment and improvements at the school.

Five men led the school from its start in 1873 until its merger with Chapman High School in 1951. The first two men served short terms, E. B.

Walter A. Towne, Principal Bulkeley School, 1888-1921.

Hollister 1870-1873 and E. R. Hall 1880-1888. Walter A. Towne directed Bulkeley School affairs from 1888 to 1921 by which time the school had earned an excellent reputation and many of its graduates attended the leading colleges and universities. Towne's successor, Homer K. Underwood, continued the growth of the institution. As headmaster he encouraged student activities, established a modern assembly hall in the annex, began a school music program, improved the business course and increased the school library. A combined Williams Memorial Institute and Bulkeley School orchestra and choir was organized. After serving from 1921-1944, Underwood retired and Herbert A. Archibald became headmaster 1944-1948. He was succeeded by the last headmaster Arthur L. Hjertland 1948-1950, who became principal of the Bulkeley Junior High School in 1951.

Chapman High School grew out of the need for industrial training which had been recognized as early as 1896. Not until October of 1906 was a Manual High School for boys and girls opened. In 1903 after obtaining a charter from the state the new school received $100,000 from William Henry Chapman. Chapman gifts supplemented the original grant so that not only William Henry Chapman but also his wife, Ellen and their daughter, Mary, were generous donors. Starting as the New London Vocational School it became the Chapman Technical High School.[29]

Only two men directed the school from its founding to its merger with Bulkeley (High) School in 1951 to form the New London High School. Frederick S. Hitchcock served as principal from 1906 until 1937 when Horace G. Wescott became headmaster. Wescott served until the merger and then became principal of the newly formed school until 1952. The Chapman foundation uses the money still held by them to provide scholarship loans.

Another high school, the New London High School of Commerce began as a course of business study at one of the other schools in September of 1915. Proving popular the Coit Street School facilities were used for business courses in 1920. When the Jennings School opened, the New London High School of Commerce used the upstairs. Unfortunately, the Board had not authorized the school and the City Council in 1930, angry over school costs, insisted it be ended. The Board had no choice and transferred the funds to other areas.[30]

The Williams Memorial Institute replaced the Girls High School in 1891. Mrs. Harriet Peck Williams left a trust fund to establish a free girls school as a memorial to her son, merchant Thomas W. Williams II, who died in 1855. Trustees Henry P. Haven, William C. Crump, Robert McElwen, Henry R. Bond, C. A. Williams, Augustus Brandegee, Charles Barns and Benjamin Stark were empowered by the trust to build a school when $150,000 had accrued. In 1881 they announced that $60,000 would be spent, but when the school opened in 1891, it had cost $85,000. City supervision received strong opposition from C. A. Williams as president of the Institute.

Creation of New London High School in 1951 brought about changes in the school's missions. It became a six year preparatory school—grades 7-12 with a limit of 150 students when it was moved to the Connecticut College campus in 1954. The trustees decided to call the school the Williams School in 1963 and changed the title of principal to headmistress. Boys were admitted for the first time in 1971.[32]

Until 1951, the town relied upon the private high schools and no public high school existed. The private high schools were paid tuition as well as given city funds. A single high school replacing the private ones was considered for many years before the New London High School was formed by a merger of Bulkeley and Chapman High Schools.[31]

Teachers organized the New London Teachers League in 1919. This did not include the high school teachers who had their own organization, The New London High School Teachers League. They remained separate until 1947 when they joined to form the New London Teachers Association.[33]

Since 1834 a large number of individuals served long and dedicated years as members of the Board of School Visitors or the School Board. They have been far too numerous to mention but three in particular stand

Bulkeley School. Opened 1873.

out—Henry P. Haven served in many different posts during his long tenure including the presidency, Dr. John G. Stanton served twenty-five years before retiring as chairman of the School Board in 1917 and Frederick W. Edgerton, who began his long years of service before World War I, continued until after World War II.[34]

Black children, of whom there were only a few during the nineteenth century, were not mixed into the general school population without some

Williams Memorial Institute about 1897. Opened 1891.

Chapman Technical School. Opened 1906.

Williams School on Connecticut College campus. Moved here 1954.

New London High School. Opened 1970.

irritation. To relieve the pressure on these children and provide an opportunity for basic studies, Ichabod Pease, a former slave—well respected by the citizens of New London, established a school for black children. The town contributed $50.00 in 1837 and 1838 to the school. No records exists beyond these years. Pease died in 1842 at the age of eighty-six.[35]

Henry P. Haven, as head of the School Visitors, announced the establishment of a free night school at the Bartlett School in 1867. The board made $500 available. Some ninety "scholars" began to study under Newton Fuller that November with Charles B. Jennings and John Duman as assistants. By 1869 the town had two evening schools in operation—one for males and one for females. The elderly were urged to attend to learn to read and write. Also to come as they were—work clothes and all. E. B. Jennings was principal of the boy's division and Marian R. Stayner of the girl's. Graduations were memorable affairs with a number of prizes given to those who achieved excellence and the mayor or other leading citizens would speak. When in 1893 a Connecticut law encouraged people to learn to read and write by requiring evening schools at least twenty evenings a school year, New London had over twenty-five years of such programs.[36]

Local school examiners certified those desiring to become teachers before state certification began. Bulkeley School hired only male teachers until a shortage during World War I forced a change. However, in 1921 it was decided to dismiss the three women and return to an all male staff which continued until World War II. When the depression caused a shortage of jobs, the New London Board of Education ruled in 1933, that women teachers had to resign when they married. In 1943 the rule was changed to exclude elementary school teachers and the following year was extended to all teachers.[37]

New London was the first in Connecticut to open its public schools for the education of the foreign born. The town made extensive use of night schools for this purpose during the 1920's with John C. Ellis as director. One of the valuable areas given attention concerned instruction in voting methods.[38]

New London has been a leader over the years in various programs—especially school clinics, gymnastics and night courses. Opportunity School began in 1919 for those requiring special classes, another first in the state. Veterans Night School at the end of World War II at Jennings School was under the direction of adult education supervision.[39]

Charles B. Jennings served the local system for fifty-two years and as head of the schools for fifty years. He introduced vocal music into the public schools in 1872.[40] The Board of Education was so pleased that they hired a music teacher, Fernando Morgan, who organized a Boy's Band. Jenning's father arrived in New London to run the Town Grammar School. His services were so well regarded that the Coit Street School was renamed Jennings School in his honor. His son, Charles B. Jennings, became the first superintendent of schools in 1908 after being at the Nathan Hale Grammar School from the time it was built. Jennings, as principal of the Hale School, became School Visitor in 1890 and supervised the school system. He was organist at the First Church and organized one of the first boy choirs in the state. The principal of Nathan Hale Grammar School, Warren A. Hanson, succeeded C. B. Jennings as New London School superintendent in 1918.[41]

The subject of salaries has been a difficult one in New London as anywhere else. People want the best but at the lowest prices and resent increased taxes to pay the added costs. That this problem is not new, one can see from looking at the earlier years. The loss of teachers to systems which pay more has also long been a problem. Under the Union School District's Board of Education cost increased from $12,002.55 in 1869 to $27,080.54 in 1878, a little over 125%. During the period 1879-1882 salaries were the lowest in the state, from a low of $200 to a high of $1,200. Yet, in 1893 New London was fifth in the state in annual expenditures for education.[42]

Problem of truancy led Superintendent Warren A. Hanson to request the police to take charge of all children on the streets during school hours in 1920. It was not a new problem as we find in the Report of Acting School

Colin S. Buell, Principal Williams Memorial Institute, 1891-1938.

Horace G. Wescott, Headmaster Chapman Technical School, 1937-1951. Principal New London High School, 1951-1952.

Homer K. Underwood, Headmaster Bulkeley School, 1921-1944.

Visitor in 1892 "I regret to say that truancy is not decreasing. We have had the services of a member of the police force for part of this time each week, but that is not sufficient; . . ."[43] Attendance at the schools ranged from a high of eighty percent at Nathan Hale Grammar School to a low of sixty-three percent at the three other schools.[44]

The town's pioneering efforts in evening schools, adult education, classes for the foreign born shows its strong committment to providing an excellent system. Still the costs have risen so that the City Council in 1972 supported a graduated state income tax to be used for all local costs of education.[45]

Over the years a number of private schools offered training in many areas at the port. Nathan Daboll had a Mathematical School and Jona Dodge operated a Literary, Mathematical and Naval Academy, both needed and rather fitting for a shipping port. Music attracted quite a number of schools between 1823-1857. William Harris taught vocal and instrumental music, Miss N. Hammond gave instructions in music, T. W. Ruddock taught piano, organ and voice, Miss E. Hazzard gave lessons on piano and Mrs. J. T. Magennis had the Magennis Musical Institute. Dancing lessons were available from the schools of Mr. Frazar and Mr. Chesebrough while Mr. Fuller taught young ladies and gentlemen in manners and dancing.[46]

French lessons were quite popular. M. D. Lessone opened a school teaching French and would even go into homes for lessons. Madam Francisco taught French and English on Green Street and many individuals taught reading, writing, English grammar and arithmetic. Widow Leites' was one of the early and well known schools of the 1770's while Mrs. Truman' and Miss M. A. Babcock's schools were also well regarded. Penmanship was also in demand. The O. Green School charged $2.00 for fifteen lessons and the J. N. Spencer Writing Academy charged the same price for twelve lessons. The YMCA held educational classes in 1886 for bookkeeping, penmanship, stenography, shorthand and vocal music classes. Ladies were permitted to attend only the vocal music classes.[47]

Early private schools seemed to have most often been located on Main Street where the Charity School kept by Miss Caroline Richards was housed in the old Coit house. Two out of town private schools became popular places to send the young men of the port—Bacon Academy of Colchester and the Plainfield Academy. Business development at the port led to the establishment of a number of schools to meet the needs of firms. Mercantile training received the special endorsement of whaling firms. Among the business schools were Mr. Winchester's Writing and Book-

keeping Academy in 1841 and the Commercial Academy of R. N. Brown
in the Lawrence Building in 1850.

The earliest evening schools were business ones such as John Griffin's
school for "Youth to be instructed in Reading, writing and arithimetic"
and in 1841 J. C. Woodworth's evening school for young men at Main and
John Streets over Darrow's Store. The fee was $2.00-$3.00 for forty-eight
evenings of instruction. The New London Business College began in
1887.[48]

Religious or church schools had their start with the mission schools of
the town in 1859. Citizens became concerned about the number of poor
and foreign born youth who were not in school. English and citizenship
among other subjects were taught. They proved to be quite popular with
large numbers attending. As the Roman Catholic population increased a
natural development was the parochial school. St. Mary's and St. Joseph's
were established as grade schools and St. Bernard's as a High School for
girls.[49]

A Hebrew School opened in 1914 with eighty-five children under principal Herman Beck. Another opened in 1921 under Dr. L. Papelovitch,
principal, Talmad Torah at Ohav Sholem Synagogue on Blinman Street.
The New London Institute of Jewish Studies of the Congregation Beth-El
opened in 1935. The Board of Education of Ahvath Talmad Torah
planned for entirely new courses in 1943 at the Hebrew School. Dr. Morris
Sulman was president of the board. Rabbi Bernard Gelbart was appointed
principal to conduct an elementary course in Mishnah, basis of all Hebrew
law, and a special course in Rashi, commentary on the bible.[50]

The special and higher educational needs of most young people as well
as older ones could be met in the immediate area. A New London University Association Center was organized in 1899 to present information by
trained specialists from different colleges.[51]

The first academic institution of higher learning to be established in
New London resulted from women finding few opportunities to attend
college. It became especially difficult for Connecticut females when Wes-
leyan University decided to admit males only. At a meeting in Hartford,
March of 1910 a group decided to try to obtain support for the establishment of a new women's college in Connecticut. Three women—Elizabeth
C. Wright, E. V. Mitchell, Mary M. Partridge—spearheaded the drive.[52]
Percy Coe Eggleston made a bid for the establishment of the college at New
London whose citizens gave full support to the project. New London was
accepted for the site January 4, 1911, the town gave $50,000, New London
citizens $135,000, Harry W. Allyn 50 acres and Morton F. Plant

Connecticut College. Opened 1915.

$1,000,000.[53] A charter was granted April 4, 1911 to Thames College but in July the name changed to Connecticut College for Women. Plant and the citizens of New London also built and furnished several dormitories—September 27, 1915 the doors opened.[54]

One of the original faculty in relating her arrival at the unfinished school told of the lack of lighting and facilities. She had to travel some distance away to find a place to eat and upon returning, the streetcar conductor did not know where the school was located and in the dark she was taken past and had to retrace her path. The campus did not remain primitive long. Much building was done between 1917 and 1924 when $850,000 was given and the campus expanded to 341¼ acres.[55] Dr. Frederick Sykes became the first president in 1913 and after launching the school he resigned in June of 1916 and died the following September.[56] Benjamin T. Marshall, professor of Biblical Literature at Dartmouth became president in 1917. He directed the college until 1928. During his tenure the college grew to 569 students and 61 faculty from 265 and 34 respectively. An excellent physical plant took shape. However, difficulty developed between the head of the English Department and Marshall which grew until some members of the Board of Trustees became involved. After months of discussion the president resigned and received a year's salary.[57] A new president, Dr. Katherine Blunt took over in September, 1929. She became the first woman president and directed the college until 1943 when Dr. Dorothy Schaffter took over. Rosemary Park became president in 1947 and remained until 1962 when Dr. Charles E. Shain replaced her.[58] Dr. Oakes Ames assumed the presidency in 1974.

An excellent part of the college is the arboretum which began as a 70 acre gift given by Dr. Charles B. Graves in 1929. It has been added to over the years until today its 370 acres include almost all the specimens of plant life in Connecticut.

Connecticut College has been a welcome addition to the educational and cultural life of New London. Mr. and Mrs. George S. Palmer of New London gave several valuable gifts. The Palmer Auditorium has been a center of cultural gatherings since 1939. Palmer Library, which opened in 1923 and was enlarged in 1941, will be twice as large when a seven million dollar addition is completed. Rather ironically, it is now a co-educational institution.[59]

A preparatory school for the United States Naval Academy at Annapolis was established in 1936 on Pequot Avenue. The Admiral Billard Academy with the schooner *Yankee* as a training ship had excellent results through World War II. It failed to survive the postwar period in New London.[60]

A doctoral thesis led to the establishment of the New London Junior College. Richard Saunders of New York University made a study of the possibilities of such an institution at New London and this led to the Junior College Association of New London in 1937. It acquired the Mitchell property, 46 acres on Pequot and Montauk Avenues, donated June 19, 1938. An advising committee laid the groundwork for the college and in September of 1938 a college corporation took over and December 1, 1939 the college took shape with Dr. Saunders as president. It was decided that the school would offer a business course as well as the usual general course with emphasis on the importance of dependability, courtesy, tact and a good office appearance. Salaries were to be liberal to attract excellent teachers.

World War II forced the closing of the college in February of 1943. It reopened after the war and has developed into an excellent school. In 1956 it became Mitchell Junior College (now Mitchell College) a co-educational institution with its own private beach. The students commute or live on campus.[61]

At the end of World War II, Governor Raymond E. Baldwin applied to the War Shipping Administration for the use of the local Maritime Service Officer's School as a branch of the University of Connecticut. It was estimated that 1,000 to 2,000 returning war veterans would enroll. A branch was opened in September, 1946, despite the objections of Univer-

Mitchell College. Opened 1939.

sity of Connecticut's president, Albert N. Jorgensen, at Fort Trumbull with 1,300 male students in dorms and 100 commuters—all male freshmen and sophomores—no girls.[62] The program ended in 1950.

The other schools are of a more recent date. The Southeastern Branch of the University of Connecticut, which offers the first two years of college, is located at Avery Point in Groton. It opened in 1967 and covers 73 acres right along Long Island Sound.[63]

Thames Valley Technical Institute at Norwich offers a two year program leading to an associate degree of applied science. An addition to higher education in the area—Mohegan Community College—opened in 1970 for the Norwich and New London area. Classes opened in the former Bartlett School in New London with a program at Lawrence Hill School in Norwich.[64]

New London's colleges offer many cultural activities and opportunities. Connecticut College has an American Dance Festival each summer and the Music Vale Opera Company presents a series of operas at Mitchell College. Naturally, each offers lectures, concerts, films and panels as well as sports programs.

14 Politics, The Arts and Leisure 1784-1973

Colonial and State affairs have often borne the imprint of New London. No fewer than four New Londoners have to date, held the office of governor. During the 135 years of Colonial Connecticut three New Londoners held the office—John Winthrop, Jr., his son Fitz-John Winthrop and family friend, Gurdon Saltonstall. Thomas M. Waller has been the only port town citizen since 1725 to hold the post. Four New Londoners have served as Lieutenant Governor of whom only one became Governor—Noyes Billings, Francis B. Loomis, Ernest E. Rogers, and John Winthrop.[1]

Five town's people served as the Secretary of the State—John P. C. Mather, Thomas M. Waller, Theodore Bodenwein, C. John Satti and Chase G. Woodhouse.* Ernest E. Rogers served four years as State Treasurer, while two consecutive holders of the office of comptroller came from New London—Alexander Merrell (1855-1856) and Edward Prentis (1856-1857).[2] Noyes Billings, Augustus and Frank B. Brandegee, John A. Tibbits and Thomas M. Waller all served as Speaker of the Connecticut House of Representatives.[3]

New London citizens were active on the national level as well. Richard Law served in both the Second Continental Congress and the Congress of the Confederation before retiring to New London and serving as mayor in 1784. William Hillhouse also served in the Confederation Congress, in fact Law and Hillhouse served several months at the same time. This was possible because Connecticut elected all her congressmen at large until 1837. Twelve men have served from New London in the House of Rep-

Brown house, Jefferson Avenue. Built end of 18th century.

resentatives since 1789—three Federalists, one Whig, three Democrats and four Republicans. By a large margin the Republicans held office the longest—thirty-five years, the Democrats held it for eight years.[4]

Some unusual political developments took place. In 1836, 1837 and 1845 New London failed to have representation in the legislature as no candidate received a majority of the votes cast.

Abraham Lincoln arrived in New London March 8, 1860 and Julius W. Eggleston, Chairman of the Republican Town Committee, took him to City Hotel. When asked if he desired a drink, Lincoln replied "No, I scarcely take anything of the sort." While Lincoln had dinner, Eggleston tried to find prominent Republicans to meet him. Many refused, as they did not seem to know who he was and did not have time.[26]

As the nineteenth amendment was ratified, Mrs. William L. White became the first New London woman to be made a full fledged voter. She was sworn in by her husband, selectman William L. White, on October 19, 1920. There was a rush to register women voters in 1920. Mary Reese Mitchell became the first woman presidential elector chosen by a major political party in Connecticut (1920) while Miss Mary Belden as city treasurer became the first woman to head a department.[27]

Frank B. Brandegee was elected to fill a vacancy in Congress when Charles A. Russell died in office in 1902. After winning the election to the

Richard Law, member of Continental Congress; first Mayor of New London, 1784-1806.

58 and 59 congresses, he resigned to take the senate seat vacated by the death of Orville H. (Me too) Platt, April 21, 1905. He became the only United States Senator from New London to date. After serving until 1924, Brandegee died in office October 14. His death resulted in an unusual development on the state level as H. Bingham elected Governor November 6, 1924, was elected United States Senator on December 16 to fill Brandegee's term. He was inaugurated as Governor in January and resigned to accept the senate post. He was Connecticut's Governor for only one day.[5]

A number of New Londoners served in posts abroad. Among them were the Perkins brothers, sons of Dr. N. S. Perkins. Elias served as United States Consul at Jamaica and the Hawaiian Islands during the Civil War and Francis as commercial agent at Tahiti. President Grover Cleveland appointed Thomas M. Waller, Consul to England in 1885 and when Benjamin Harrison became president, John A. Tibbits was appointed consul at Bradford, England, 1889 replacing Waller. Tibbits, a collector of customs at New London had been removed by President Cleveland in 1885 and replaced by Democrat Benjamin R. Tate. John R. Meade was named United States Consul at Santo Domingo in 1893 when Cleveland returned to office.[6]

The General Assembly in 1784 accepted the incorporation of New London and four other cities—New Haven, Hartford, Middletown and Norwich. New London's charter, as approved by the Assembly, provided that all city and town officials would hold office for one year terms except mayors and treasurers who held office at the pleasure of the General Assembly. Understandably then the first town officials served lengthy terms. The first two mayors served a total of forty-five years—Richard Law 1784 to 1806 and Jeremiah G. Brainerd from 1806 to 1829.[7] After that date the General Assembly accepted a change in the city charter limiting the term of a mayor to three years after each election. Until 1969 the legislature had to pass a special act for any charter changes. A revised charter was offered to the town in 1873 and voted down overwhelmingly. In June of 1874 a new charter was accepted. The Common Council could make bylaws, regulate houses of intoxicating liquor sellers, put in side walks.[8]

Even though the town and city occupied the same area, each had a separate system of representation. Aldermen were elected by the town and members of the council by the city. A Common Council made up of both boards governed the area.

From 1784 to 1889 the Common Council members, nine selectmen and fifteen aldermen, had been elected at large for the town and city. A ward system from 1889 to 1921 created five wards in the city which elected three from each and the town elected three selectmen at large. The mayor continued to run at large. After 137 years of mayor-council form of government (1784-1921) a council-manager form of government went into effect. People voted 5-3 in favor as 62.9% of the registered voters turned out. The new form of government began June 6, 1921. Seven councilmen elected at large, with one of their members elected as mayor worked with a city manager hired by the Council. New London became the first Connecticut city to have such a system. Lucius E. Whiton became the first mayor and James E. Barlow was the first city manager.[9]

Some people found it hard to adjust to the new Council-Manager system and during the first years attempts to end it developed, but failed. By 1927 almost all seemed to believe that only good had come with the excellent progress of the town under the manager—street improvements, extensions of sewers and the improvement of the city beaches. Still all did not always go smoothly. In 1928 William H. Holt, city manager, resigned because the City Council kept overruling his recommendations. However, all worked out and he continued in his post.

A county court was established at New London in May of 1666. The town had a rivalry with Norwich (each wanted sole possession of the courts). In 1735 the Assembly ordered the Superior and County Courts to be held alternately at the towns. When all the areas had been separated from New London by 1801, it had become one of the smallest of cities— 2,200 acres—3½ square miles. New London wanted to annex the Waterford area to the town. The fight was led by Augustus Brandegee. Finally New London asked the Legislature for 4½ square miles and after a struggle, received 2.7 square miles. It was a small, lightly populated area of Waterford. The merger went through in 1899 and New London increased from 3.5 square miles to 6.2 square miles.[10]

Amasa Learned (1750-1825) a businessman at New London and married into the wealthy Hallam family, took a leading part in the political life of New London. He graduated from Yale in 1772 and taught at Union School before taking part in the Revolution. Returning to New London in 1780, Learned served as a member of the convention which ratified the United States Constitution—he voted for it. In 1791-1795 he served in Congress.[11]

John P. C. Mather, Yale graduate of 1837, began his law practice in 1839 in the office of Lyman Law. His was a very active political life: Mayor of New London 1845-1850, Secretary of State 1850-1853, House of Representatives 1849, Connecticut State Senator 1873, 1879, Collector of Custom 1858, Commission of United States Circuit Court 1861-1886, Judge of Police and City Court 1866, 1867, 1868, 1870, 1873, Judge of Probate Court 1871 and Judge of Court of Common Pleas 1879-1886.[12]

Andrew C. Lippitt figured in two interesting political situations. In 1850, he became mayor over John Mather when out of 60 votes cast, Lippitt received 37. Another unusual political situation developed in the 1862-1863 mayoral race. Andrew C. Lippitt (Democrat) proved unpopular with many because he had allowed the New London, Willimantic and Palmer Railroad to lay its track through Water Street without paying. The Republicans' choice was Courtland Starr but he refused to run and Hiram Willey became their candidate. A number of Young Democrats put up the Dolly Varden ticket and ran Pitts S. Wheeler, planning on votes from both parties. While many felt Wheeler won, Hiram E. Willey received the office.[13]

Thomas Waller became an important political leader while beginning with few advantages. His parents died when he was nine and Robert K. Waller adopted the young Armstrong boy. He became a lawyer and gained political power first in New London and later in the state. Waller, as Democratic mayor, served two terms 1873-1879. When the first provisions

Custom House, Bank Street.

for pay came in October of 1873, he refused to accept it until voters approved. Waller represented the town in the General Assembly, became Secretary of State 1870-1871 and Speaker of the House of Representatives in 1876, before becoming Governor in 1883-1885. In 1888 he received an appointment as Consul General in England with his son Tracey as Vice-Consul. When over eighty years of age Thomas Waller became vice president of the Mariners Savings Bank.[14]

Thomas M. Waller (D) and John A. Tibbits (R) had a law partnership which broke up. Tibbits became Collector of Customs, a founder and editor of the *New London Day.* He became one of the most outspoken opponents of Waller. John A. Tibbits lost his collectorship in 1885 and interestingly, Waller and Tibbits reestablished a law firm with Waller's son, Tracey. Tibbits served as speaker of the house of representatives in 1886 and held the post of city attorney before being appointed consul to England in 1889 by Harrison to succeed Waller. Tibbits also was Judge of the Police Court and served on the Board of Education.[15]

John Brandegee (1799-1857) moved to New London in 1818 and married Mary Deshon. He became involved in the whaling industry and was one of the founders of the Whaling Bank. Earlier he had been a New Orleans cotton broker and had taken part in the battle of New Orleans. Brandegee was an incorporator of Bartlett School and the New London, Wilimantic and Palmer Railroad. He died in 1857. Of his three sons, John was an Episcopal Priest, Frank, a doctor and Augustus, a lawyer.[16]

Augustus Brandegee was born in New London July 12, 1828. He graduated from Yale in 1849 and attended Yale Law School in 1850. Brandegee entered the office of Andrew C. Lippitt and they formed the firm of Lippitt and Brandegee. He served in the Connecticut House of

Augustus Brandegee, 1828-1904.

Representatives 1854, 1858, 1859 and 1861 and Congress 1863-1865. Brandegree was a Republican, before the Civil War he had been a Whig anti-slave leader and backer of Fremont. He also served as judge and member of the City Council and as Speaker of the House in 1871. When mayor of New London in 1873, he resigned claiming the office lacked power and urged a new charter be adopted.[17]

Henry P. Haven sought the governor's post in 1873 and received Brandegee's support. At the Republican State Convention that year every mention of Haven's name resulted in howls from the Republicans there. When Augustus Brandegee spoke for Haven and was hissed, he called them snakes, "copper headed snakes." Haven was not liked by the men of New London, his strong convictions, powerful political connections and religious convictions, put many off. No one would quarrel about his excellent business ability but he had little mass appeal and lost the election by 6,000 votes. Augustus Brandegee died November 10, 1904, at his Pleasant Street home, but his son and law partner had already become political figures.[18]

Frank Brandegee (1864-1924) graduated from Yale in 1885 and was admitted to the Bar in 1888. Very active politically, he served in the General Assembly, House of Representatives in 1888 and 1889 as well as being speaker in the latter term. In 1892 the law firm was Brandegee,

Noyes and Brandegee. Brandegee served as a City Council member for ten years, was in Congress from 1902-1924: the House of Representatives 1902-1905 and the Senate 1905 until his death.

He never married and after having heavy financial losses, committed suicide. His estate, carefully handled by associates, proved more than enough to satisfy all debts by 1927.[19]

A man who brought much progress to the town, Bryan F. Mahan, did so in the face of bitter opposition. He began as a poor boy, but through drive overcame many obstacles and while defeated many times, he always came back. Mahan's programs sometimes split the Democratic party of New London and at one meeting the opposition called for a party caucas. All left the hall with the doors locked behind them but when the opposition returned, unlocked the doors and turned on the lights, Mahan and his group were sitting there. Bryan F. Mahan held the office of mayor three terms 1903-06 and 1909-15. His administrations were responsible for obtaining a municipal building, a State Pier, three miles of sidewalks, Connecticut College, Bates Woods and the Columbus Statue area for the town. He also worked for street improvements, set up a police signal system and double tracked the trolley lines.

The Municipal Building dated back to 1774 and strong pressure existed to keep it. The only way the town would allow money to be used for the building was to improve and enlarge the then existing one. So Mahan had a new building built around the old one and upon completion removed the old building. He served on the School Board (secretary), the Water Board as well as twice being elected to the lower house of the General Assembly, State Senate and United States Congress. Mahan failed to reach the Secretary of the State post when a majority of votes cast did not fall his way. He did act as a member of the Democratic State Central Committee.

He was a lawyer and builder in addition to being a politician. He owned a large number of buildings and houses, but never kept books or track of the holdings. When he left public office the people collected a purse and gave him $5,000. Some politicians may have disliked him but the people loved him. His career ended in November of 1923[20] at his death.

Ernest E. Rogers worked for Brainerd and Armstrong in the accounting department for twenty years before entering the grain and feed business. After several successful years he expanded the business and sold business properties. Finally he sold out and had enough money to devote his life to politics. He became mayor of the town 1915 and as a member of the State Legislature, he pushed for the charter change which created the city

Ernest Rogers, 1866-1945.

council manager plan in 1921. In the Republican victory of 1924 he reached the office of State Treasurer. In this post he refused to accept a raise from $2,500 to $7,500. When selected in 1925 as president of the Chamber of Commerce, his efficient financial management allowed the organization to pay-off its debts. In 1928 he won the post of Lieutenant Governor. Political success, so long his, ended in 1930 when while a candidate for Governor he became the only Republican on the State ticket to lose—Wilbur Cross won.[21]

James May, long in politics, served as councilman for eight terms from 1925 to 1959 and served as mayor 1927, 1929 and 1946. He had been the youngest mayor the town had ever had as he was only twenty-six. Known to all as Jimmy, he was elected mayor in 1946 by a flip of the coin after 14 ballots had been cast. He held the office during New London's Tercentenary Year. May held three city jobs during the past ten years—interim coordinator, Model City Agency, Clerk of the Works for the Nathan Hale School project and administrative assistant with the Redevelopment Agency. As a result of "rocking the boat" he claimed he lost his job in 1971. He won an election after the Republicans refused him a party nomination even though he had been endorsed by the Town Committee. He finally shifted to the Democratic Party.[22]

Dr. John Satti, Democrat, a political power for years in New London was a backer of Senator Thomas J. Dodd. If one wished to see Dodd, Satti was the man to talk with.[23]

Thomas J. Griffin, Mr. Democrat, ended his City Council career after 23 years. He had reached 79 years of age and had been hospitalized four times in 1971. He had been the mayor of New London three times and Democratic Town Chairman three times. A testimonial dinner was held at Ocean Beach Park with 475 people attending. A man of strong views, it was not easy to change his mind. Dr. John Satti backed him.[24]

Emma E. Lincoln, a long time Republican Town Chairman (since 1966), reportedly planned to give up her post for the State Central Committee. Her vice-chairman, Gaspare J. Cavasino, had her support as successor. Some urged Lincoln to change her mind and run for chairman again which she did. However, Cavasino wanted the job and refused to support her even when she asked backing only for the vice-chairman's job. Harold Weiner, her rival, became the new chairman when she threw her support to him (20-16) in 1972.[25]

WEATHER

Weather often creates difficulties as at any port where the town's exposed position along the coast makes it vulnerable. Year after year the port suffered losses of vessels while heavy snow, ice, and gales destroyed wharfs, warehouses, houses, businesses and churches. Snow storms have been common but that of 1888 stands as the worst, when the town remained isolated for twenty-four hours. In 1779-1780 and 1836 Long Island Sound had such an ice cover that people crossed between New London and Long Island, New York. When even the harbor was frozen over (1779-1780, 1821, 1836, 1852, 1856, 1893 and 1918), the town's people made a gala occasion of walking on the ice, crossing with vehicles, skating and sledding. Tents would be put up and refreshments sold right on the river.[28]

The snow provided many hours of pleasure for the whole family in the days before radio, T.V., and movies. With so many hills, sledding became a popular pastime well into the twentieth century. Not for just children but grownups as well, who took advantage of the snow to make a family outing. Often the streets were lined with burning barrels for light, food stands were set up and families would slide well into the evening.[29]

On at least one occasion sledding caused a mishap. A very dignified gentleman while walking one morning down State Street had his feet

The Nellie *on the tracks, Hurricane September 21, 1938.*

Torpedo Shop, US Submarine Base. Subs R-13 and R-4 riding high above Pier "C".

knocked out from under him by a young boy on a sled. "He didn't get mad though. He just smashed the sled without a frown and continued his walk as if nothing had happened."[30]

While earthquakes have been felt several times in the town, little damage has resulted. Winds and the resulting fire and flooding have been the most damaging to New London. Among those which caused the most extensive destruction are—three occasions in the nineteenth century: 1815 which damaged stores along Water Street and flooded the area; 1846 when the Baptist Church lost its tower and the Roman Catholic Church its cross; 1856 which took off the roof of the Railroad Depot and the steeple of the Roman Catholic Church and damaged the steeple of the Second Baptist Church.[31] The worst blow came in September of 1938 when Ocean Beach was completely destroyed, a number of business blocks on Bank Street were leveled and the fire, wind and water caused $4,000,000 worth of damage. The State Pier did not have all its repairs made until 1940. A hurricane of 1944 also caused considerable damage.[32]

New London County Historical Society

A number of leading citizens became concerned about the lack of an agency to collect and preserve objects and records of historical value. Henry P. Haven, Charles J. McCurdy, John W. Steinman, Richard A. Wheeler, Learned Hubbard, John T. Wait, John P. C. Mather, Ashbel Woodward, Nathan Belcher, William H. Potter, S. G. Willard, Thomas A. Clark and Isaac Johnson decided the best method of doing this would be to organize an historical society. It must be made clear that the major force which ultimately resulted in the successful creation of the Society came primarily from four men—Henry P. Haven, Jonathan N. Harris, Charles A. Williams and LaFayette S. Foster.

Official formation of the New London County Historical Society came with approval of the act of incorporation July 6, 1870. The bylaws were accepted and officers chosen at a meeting in November, the first annual meeting of the Society. LaFayette S. Foster became the first president, Charles J. McCurdy, Dr. A. Woodward and Francis B. Loomis vice presidents, John P. Mather secretary and William R. Rowe treasurer.[33]

A major problem from the beginning concerned the lack of a permanent place to house the materials of historical interest collected by the Society. Although it was to have several homes over the years, not for thirty-six years, until the purchase of the Shaw Mansion in 1907, did the organization so devoted to preserving the past find itself a permanent home with the proper historical setting.[34]

The Pequot Hotel where many have had the gayest times of their lives. Built in 1850, destroyed by fire May 7, 1908.

A number of services have been performed by the Society over the years: the marking of the site of Pequot Hill battle with a bronze statue 1889; a statue dedicated to New London founder John Winthrop 1905; helping to preserve the County Court House; purchasing and maintaining the Shaw Mansion as a fitting historical site; and taking over the responsibility for the Old Town Mill in 1922.[35]

A very valuable service of the Society concerns the many excellent papers presented at the annual meetings. A number of these have been printed in the *Records and Papers* published from 1889 to 1912. Other publications of the Society have been equally significant: *The Diary of Joshua Hempstead* (1901; reprinted 1971); N. W. Taylor's *Life on a Whaler* (1929) and E. E. Rogers, *Connecticut's Naval Office at New London* (1933).

The Jibboom Club #1 founded about 1870 by officers on whaling vessels, formally organized January 29, 1891. Membership included deep water sailors and others which they chose to invite. The Club had quarters at Bank and Golden Streets where a museum of sorts developed. Tools and implements were contributed over the years. While regular meetings were not held a "voyage" took place twice a month. The traditional plum duff was prepared each December. A parade through the town, followed by a dinner and dance each Washington's Birthday marked the high point of each year.

In 1894 the Club took steps to incorporate. In the later nineteenth century it had 280 members but the decline of shipping at the port meant a similar decline of members in the twentieth century. During World War I, the forty members voted to offer their collection of spy glasses to the Navy. Further reductions in membership came after World War II causing the Club to end its activities.[36]

ENTERTAINMENT

New London Puritans did not lead the "joyless" life indicated by most accounts of our early settlers. Dancing, cardplaying, sword play, horse racing, drinking and the theater all were viewed with displeasure by the religious leaders but the people engaged in them. In fact their pleasures most often involved picnics, fairs, husking bees, house raisings, hayrides, quilting parties, visits to Newgate Prison and shooting matches. Quilting parties for the older people often ended with a dance. Weddings were considered great entertainment and those who attended received gifts. Thanksgiving time, the great annual festival, meant feasting, drinking, shooting matches and horse racing.[37]

Those selected for military or civil office had to stand treat for cakes and cider or rum. On training days a contest of shooting at a mark would be held with cash awards of several shillings. Hempstead notes October 26, 1736 "Our company shot at mark, closest to center to get 10 s. Corp. Silas Whiple won." An important event, such as a marriage in the royal family, an important victory, or a peace treaty, would be cause for a great celebration with music, wine and sky rockets.

Funerals occurred often and became an important event in colonial life. Hempstead in telling of the many which he attended described the gifts, food and sermons.[39]

Social leaders gave parties for each other such as an elegant ball given by Nathaniel Shaw at his mansion house for 92 leading citizens of New London. They danced 92 jigs, 52 country dances, 45 minuets and 17 horn pipes.[40]

Travelling shows using a tent or tents might be set up and music or other amusements provided. Animals attracted attention early. In 1729 a lion was shown at New London for several days. After the American Revolution animals continued to be excellent attractions. Captain John Prentis' Hall was the scene of the animal acts up to 1824. A group of twenty-five animals were exhibited and later that year a lion arrived from London. Allen's City Hotel played host in a circus in 1825 which included a clown. It spent three days in town.[41]

A large menagerie and Aviary arrived in town in 1835 from the Zoological Institute of New York. It included 49 wagons, 120 grey horses and 60 men. A very popular attraction was the Van Ambarger's Collection of

Lyceum Theatre.

trained animals. They were often at New London. Raymond and Waring's Menagerie appeared in 1847 and "The Traditional Parade" was held. A high point was the driving of an African lion in harness by Mr. Pierce. Barnum's Museum and Travelling Menagerie came in 1851 with Bailey's Show following in 1858.[42]

In the early nineteenth century entertainment continued to be mainly travelling shows which appeared at Isaac Roger's Hall, Captain John Prentis' Hall, Allen's City Hotel and the Steamboat Hotel. Later special halls were built to handle travelling companies of players. The city had several Halls—Aborn, Lawrence, Ledyard, Washington and Odd Fellow's. During the era of the opera house the New London Opera House and Lawrence Opera House were opened. Then the age of theaters began. The Gaiety House, Lyceum, Crown, Rialto and Capitol theaters handled vaudeville and later films. With movies came special theaters such as the Capitol in 1921 on Bank Street, the Garde in 1926 on State Street.[43]

Films were popular although certain precautions had to be taken. When "The Sheik" was shown at the Crown Theater with Agnes Ayres and

New London Public Library.

Lyman Allyn Museum. Charles Platt, Architect, 1932.

Rudolph Valentino, the manager announced that no incense would be burned because a serious fire had occurred at a New Haven theater (1921).

An increase in film going came with the depression. They offered excellent escapism for the adults from economic conditions while the Saturday Matinees provided the children with heroes. The event of the double feature added to the enjoyment. World War II only continued the increased popularity especially with so many servicemen and defense workers in the area.

Since the end of World War II, television and the outdoor theaters have seen the demise of most of New London's town theaters and the present offerings are mainly what are referred to as x-rated films.

A public library did not open until 1891, but this was not due to a lack of effort to establish one much earlier. In 1784 a New London Library Company held a meeting. Apparently the Library Company did not last into the nineteenth century. A New London Young Men's Reading Association existed in 1838 and the New London Young Men's Library

Association began in 1840. It had a new reading room in 1848 which adults paid $3.00 and children $1.00 to use the service. The parents of Thomas W. Williams II gave the Young Men's Library Association their son's 400 volume library and the father added some of his own volumes.[45]

With donations of books, an encyclopedia set, an entire set of the *Niles Register,* among others, the collection had grown to several thousand volumes by 1848. They were housed in Joseph Lawrence's building and destroyed when it burned that year. An insurance policy provided $1,000 to begin a new library.

The YMCA developed a library of its own, which by 1887 had grown to 2,500 volumes. At that time it was donated to the city and the organization urged the city to start a library.[46]

A reading room established in New London received little attention although several people believed there was a need for it. As the *New London Gazette* put it in 1881 "It seems surprising that in a city of 11,000 inhabitants an opportunity to read ... should not be more generally embraced."[47]

Individuals could pay $1.00 for a year's membership and use the materials—in 1881 the fee was raised to $1.50. Still the organization fell short of expenses and one or more businessmen generally contributed enough to keep it going.[48]

Henry P. Haven's will in 1876 left property to be kept in trust until 1890, when the principal could be used for charitable and benevolent purposes. The trustees decided to use the funds for a public library. The successor to architect, Henry Robeson Richardson, Sheplay, planned and supervised the library building. It is located on the corner of Huntington and State Streets across the street from the Court House. The second floor comprises a single large room originally planned for the home of the New London County Historical Society, which later became the librarian's office and now contains a microfilm room, files of articles and pictures, research space, and Connecticut materials. A delightful and congenial spot in which to research, read or browse.[49]

The Lyman Allyn Museum is a memorial to an old whaling captain and was established at the bequest of his daughter, Harriet Upson Allyn, in 1926. She left a bequest of over one million dollars to erect the museum and create a park. It opened on March 5, 1932. The original building was added to with the Palmer Galleries in 1939 to house the bequest of Miss Virginia Palmer; the Alice Bishop Studio Wing in 1959 for art classes; and, finally, a major renovation and the addition of a third story for storage in 1973. The collections encompass world civilizations for some 5,000 years and include paintings, drawings, sculpture, and the decorative arts. The

Museum has had three directors, Winslow Ames (1932-1942), William Douglas (1942-1950) and Edgar deN. Mayhew (1950 to date).

AUTHORS

John G. C. Brainerd of New London was the first poet of Connecticut to be recognized by English critics. He became the first American to use local happenings and traditions as subjects for verse. In 1825 he published *Occasional Pieces of Poetry*. Brainerd was a Yale graduate, lawyer and editor of *The Connecticut Mirror*, Hartford. He returned to New London in 1827 and died of consumption in 1828 at the age of thirty-two.

Other poets include a number of residents: John G. Bolles, Frances M. Caulkins, Anna Hempstead Branch, Walter Learned, George Parsons Lathrop, Rose Hawthorne Lathrop, Bargess Johnson, Mary Bolles Branch and David Merritt Carlyle. Literature concerning the area has been written by Frances M. Caulkins, Richard B. Wall, Mary E. Perkins, Reverend S. LeRoy Blake, Henry C. Bunner and P. LeRoy Harwood.

Frances Manwaring Caulkins (April 26, 1795 to February 3, 1869) became principal in 1829 of the Young Ladies Academy of New London. Later, 1832-1834, she taught in Norwich. From 1834 to 1842 she spent in New York writing. From 1842 to her death in 1869 she lives and wrote in New London. Her publications began in 1816 and continued until her death. The most well known publications were *History of the Town of Norwich* (1845-1866) and *The History of New London* (1852-1866).

The *Weekly Chronicle* of 1853 praised the New London study as an interesting and valuable addition to local, state and natural history. Her numerous religious pamphlets received wide distribution.[51]

Charles Burr Todd wrote a series of articles on New London for Lippincott's Magazine in 1880. His book *In Olde Connecticut* includes an article on New London—'An Old Time Seaport.' Frank Vincent, Jr., grandson of Acors Barns, travelled and wrote the book—*Land of the White Elephant* (1874) for which he received a medal from the king of Siam (1883).[52]

Eugene O'Neill is probably the most famous author of the town. As a boy he lived in New London on Vauxhall Street and later at a summer home, 325 Pequot Avenue, which was dedicated a national landmark in 1971 as "The Monte Cristo Cottage" in memory of his actor father. Eugene O'Neill was unhappy with the home because it was not more elaborate. James O'Neill appeared frequently in plays in New London and the reviews are always excellent. Eugene published a volume of one act plays in 1914. He

James O'Neill house, 1959. House front was used in Eugene O'Neill play "Long Day's Journey into Night".

Eugene O'Neill at seven on the grounds in front of Monte Cristo Cottage overlooking the Thames.

was a friend of Arthur McGinley and they worked together on the *Morning Telegraph* although McGinley suggested that Eugene did little real reporting. A fire or accident would lead him to write "An Ode to Death" in place of the facts about the event. O'Neill organized a club—The Second Story Club—a drinking, general hell raising group—whose activities were not well accepted in New London.

Arthur McGinley was also an author. He became a reporter on the *Day* then on the *Morning Telegraph*. Arthur was a member of the Second Story Club of Eugene O'Neill. He served in World War I before his long career on the *Hartford Times* of fifty years and he still produced six columns a week and covered baseball spring training at the age of eighty-three.[53]

New York Yacht Club Race, 1886 at Station No. 10 foot of Tayler Lane.

RECREATION

An excellent way for New Londoners to relax is to stroll through the Connecticut Arboretum, maintained by Connecticut College. It has a Washington Memorial entrance, gift of the Daughters of the American Revolution. There is a small lake and an outdoor theater. The Bolleswood hemlock forest has been untouched since Indian days. Some of the trees are 450 years old, and three hundred varieties of Connecticut plants are growing there.[54]

New London has 134 acres of parkland put aside for the rest, relaxation and play of its citizens. Several are only small greens and usually contain a statue such as Garibaldi Park with a statue of Columbus, Williams Park where the Nathan Hale statue rests, and Williams Memorial Park. Some are sports fields, such as Caulkins, Mercer Memorial, Morgan and the Veterans Memorial. Still others have several activities to offer. Riverside has the Firemen's Statue, a ball park and a beach. Green's Harbor Park overlooks Green's Harbor Beach. Two are wooded areas—Bates Woods and Mitchell Woods Park.[55]

For a more commercial type of amusement, Ocean Beach is available. Ocean Beach contains various amusement features and replaces the earlier Osprey Beach Amusement Area. That beach area operated from 1881 to 1885 when the residents who disliked the area purchased it and had it torn down. The town purchased White Beach in 1888 and re-named it Ocean Beach, the present facility.[56]

One event which attracted large groups of people to the Thames River was the colorful Yale-Harvard boat races. Beginning in 1852, the schools rowed at various locations until 1878 when the Thames was chosen and the first four-mile race was held. Freshman races began in 1899. As its popularity grew, grandstands were built along the shores of the river where the crowds gathered and an observation train followed the race on the Central Vermont west shore tracks.

The event survived several interruptions—1896-1897 (a football dispute led to a break in athletic contest between the colleges); 1917-1918 (WW I) and 1942-1946 (WW II)—before a change in Yale's academic calendar forced ending the races at New London. On June 16, 1973 Harvard won the last race on the Thames. It was Harvard's eleventh victory in a row and their sixty-first win to Yale's forty-seventh.

THE SIGNALS

——FOR THE——

YALE-HARVARD RACE!

ARE:

Two large balls, in color blue for Yale, red for Harvard, displayed from a mast placed on the north end of the centre pier of the bridge. The code is as follows:

First and second crews, respectively, as they go for the starting point, balls will be hauled to half mast.

Crews in position---Balls to masthead.

Crews off---Balls will be dropped instantly.

As each crew crosses the half mile lines the ball representing that crew, red for Harvard, blue for Yale, will be hoisted and remain at masthead for the space of one minute and then drop.

Postponement of the race will be made known by raising and dropping the balls rapidly six times in succession, but the hour to which the race may be postponed cannot be made known by the balls.

If the weather should prove thick or misty only the mile stations will be taken and displayed from the bridge.

The Day Job Print, 270 Bank Street, New London, Conn.

The Signals. Yale-Harvard Race, 1890.

Yale-Harvard Boat Race on the Thames, June 27, 1907.

Osprey Beach—Ockford & Jerome's Shore Dinner Resort, 1881-1885

Shore Dinner Resort interior.

"Old" Ocean beach.

During the latter half of the 19th century, many homes were built in New London as industry and business flourished. Examples could be found of all styles and tastes from simple, country farm houses to grand, impressive mansions. Most of these homes have long disappeared, but the photos give evidence of the eclectic taste of the century.

Whale Oil Row, early 1900's. Classic houses were built in the 1830's.

Gordon Norrie residence, about 1895. Building still standing on Pequot Avenue.

The Thames Club, about 1890 was located at corner of State and Washington Streets.

James Newcomb residence, Granite Street, built about 1850.

Increase Wilson house, State Street. Telephone Company building now on site.

Crocker house, built about 1874. It was one of the finest in the city, standing well back from State Street.

Frederic S. Newcomb residence, built about 1896 on Vauxhall Street.

Augustus Brandegree residence. A Federal built about 1840 on Pleasant Street.

Williams Mansion after extensive alterations in 1881. House was bounded by State and Meridian Streets; Broad and Huntington Streets. Stone wall went around the four streets.

PEQUOT COLONY. *The south end of New London was referred to as Pequot Colony and was the center of much social activity the latter part of the 19th century to about 1915. The heart of this activity centered on the Pequot House and cottages and the Casino. Large estates were built and a world comparable to Newport at the end of the century occurred in New London.*

The Casino, built about 1895.

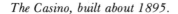

15 Town Services 1645-1973

The town had much law breaking during the Colonial Period which increased during the second generation of settlement. Drunkenness was prevalent as was selling liquor to Indians, swearing, coarseness, assaults and sexual activity before marriage. However, little robbery or theft occurred except for horse stealing.[1]

Colonial justice was quick and to the point. Those convicted faced whipping, branding and cropping of the ears. Hempstead reported September 25, 1713 that "I was in Town ye forenoon to See a man Branded on ye forehead for breaking open a house in Lebanon & Stealing Sandreys & c."[2] Begging also could be dangerous for "a Sturdy Begger was Whipt 15 Stripes" July 11, 1733.[3] The value of a barn could be seen when Katherine Adam, 17, went on trial for her life for setting a barn on fire. While found not guilty, Hempstead stated she was "Guilty Enough."[4]

Ministers tried to keep their flocks on the right path. They openly talked about the weaknesses of members. Thus we find "Ebe Dartt was openly admonished for Excessive Drinking & Scandelous behaviour, it is ye 2d time."[5] Sexual intimacy, especially before marriage, was not uncommon. The records indicate that sexual activity which was illegal had taken place a number of times. Unwed mothers made public confessions naming the fathers of their children, married couples made public confessions of having children too soon. In many cases prominent names such as Caulkins, Harris, Allen, Button, Whipple were named. The guilt feelings of these persons must have been tremendous.[6]

In the first quarter of the eighteenth century Indians were allowed to carry out their own justice. Hempstead reported that on the 15 of

November 1722, he travelled from New London with several others to see the execution of a Mohegan Indian. The Indian had been in prison at New London for several months for scalding the sister of "old" Ben Uncas. Young Ben Uncas received the prisoner and shot him.[7]

Only one non-Indian was executed at New London, Sarah Bramble, for the murder of her illegitimate child. Sentence was carried out November 21, 1753. Hempstead estimated the crowd to be 10,000.[8] There were three other public executions 1738-1807, besides Sarah Bramble. Katherine (Indian Kate) Garrett, a twenty-seven year old Pequot was executed in 1738 for the killing of her child.[9] December 20, 1786, twelve year old Hannah Occuish, a Pequot, was hanged for the murder of Eunice Bolles, a six year old.[10] The last public execution was that of Harry Niles. The newspapers refer to him as a black however he was a Naragansett Indian who lived on the North Stonington Reservation. He killed his wife while drunk. On November 4, 1807 after Reverand McEwen preached an excellent sermon, Niles was executed.[11]

Not all who killed were executed. Sarah Frazier killed a squaw with an axe in 1723 and was found not guilty by reason of distraction.[12] Lucretia Smith jailed on a charge of murdering her bastard child was found not guilty, but returned to jail because she could not pay the costs of her jailing and trial.[13]

While reports persisted that the town suffered from much disorder in the colonial period, no special facility existed until 1667, when the Bulkeley Place Jail was built.[14] Until then petty criminals were placed in private houses while more dangerous ones were sent to Hartford. The Bulkeley Place Jail was under Constable William Morton's care.

A committee of Noyes Billings, T. W. Williams, and J. B. Lyman directed the building of a jail and house in 1845.[15] A report in 1873 referred to it as one of the strongest in the country, sixteen cells, clean with excellent ventilation, food ample—toilet facilities excellent and linen changed weekly. The Constable had no beat and no one to report to. He reported only when called. No regular police force existed until after the Civil War.[16]

Certain parts of town such as Water Street and its saloons, had many fights and disorders. By the early 1850's the situation became quite unpleasant as laborers, sailors and travellers swelled the ranks of men seeking diversion. Steamboats and trains brought more people and not always the best to town. The Common Council received some pressure from citizens to establish a night watch, but the business community did not want to pay the cost. With the coming of the Civil War, the town could no longer delay dealing with the problems of keeping order. Troops became numerous and many soldiers drank and got into fights. Deserters also became common. Atlantic and Water Streets had many drinking places and much of the disorder occurred there.[17] Mayor J. N. Harris hired more constables to help keep order, but they could only serve twenty days at a time. He kept re-appointing the same men for twenty day periods.[18]

When Hiram Willey became mayor in 1862, he worked for a city watch system which finally was approved in September of 1864. Eight men were to be appointed. They were given clubs, belts, sockets and badges. The Council created a police committee of W. H. Barns, T. P. Badel and N. D. Smith with power to appoint. The men hired often lacked devotion to the work. With pay low, if a temporary job paying more came along, they had someone fill in for them and they worked elsewhere.[19]

In December of 1864 the police began to operate out of an apartment in the rear of the Police Court, later—February of 1865 they used the Selectmen's Rooms. They met each evening for instructions and then went on beats. Each received $2.00 a day while the superintendent received $1.00. One watchman on day duty watched trains 4 A. M. to 9 P. M. and passed on information of anything suspicious to the night men.[20]

Many townspeople disliked the expense of a police force and wanted a constable, whose salary came from fines. So much opposition developed that in December of 1865, a petition with 201 names was presented to end the force. Even with T. W. Williams leading the fight for retention of the city watch, it ended in June of 1866.[21]

Complaints by town's people and the newspapers led to an appeal for protection in 1867. Conditions became so bad that a movement was begun for a regular police force to protect the town. The modern force had its beginning in 1868 when a night watch received authorization. A station was built, a small brick structure on the east side of Potter Street, and served from 1868 to 1898. Three men were hired for the watch in December of 1871. George P. Hinckley became Captain in 1872 and Hezekiah B. Smith (day policeman) was hired in February of 1872. The force was on its way at last.[22]

The road to the professional force of today had a long rocky road ahead of it. The early policemen had charge of the streetlights and had to carry five gallon cans plus a stepladder in order to keep each light burning. No uniforms were worn until 1885 and the familiar blue uniform did not appear until 1912. Police wore heavy helmets in summer and caps with earflaps in winter. Salaries appeared to always have been political, so pay was subjected to ups and downs to match the popular feelings.[23]

The New London *Day* appeared to have backed the force. In reporting on new hats worn by the police in 1880, the paper remarked "generous New London kindly permitted the police to buy and pay" for a new head-gear out of reward money.[24] In 1888 an editorial praised the force, but deplored its low pay.[25]

A new station was built after the city purchased a lot on Bradley Street in 1897 and it was ready in 1898. Offices, cells, a courtroom, a records room, rest rooms, detention and consultation rooms were now available. In 1893 the police received two weeks vacation with pay and went on civil service in 1897. The humane club was introduced that same year (wooden covered with rubber).[26] A bicycle brigade was called for in 1899 as it could cover the town better than an officer on foot.[27] A signal system installed in 1903, Gilette-Vibber, would turn on a red light on the beat and the patrolman there knew he should call in the station. The force received its first patrol wagon in 1907.[28]

In 1917 new hats were furnished the traffic policemen. Blue rims with white tops, reportedly very comfortable and apparently somewhat sporty as one stranger seemed to take a policeman wearing the new cap for a yachtsman and asked him various marine questions.[29]

Growth continued in the 1920's. The first woman, with regular status was hired in December of 1923. Earlier, women were called protective officers.[30] A detective bureau began in late October, 1927 with two detective sergeants and a motorcycle policeman.[31] The Department was comprised of 46 men in 1922 for a population of 25,000 or one per 566, while New Haven had one per 500 and Norwich one per 800. A three platoon system developed, but in 1923 was abolished. After much discussion and several years, it was restored March 1, 1929 with eight beats—12 on foot and 6 motor.[32] The Common Council passed a new act in April of 1929 providing for one captain, one lieutenant, eight sergeants, 40 patrolmen and one police woman.

Prohibition caused much work for the police and disorder in the town. It became common to have the police raid several places for bootlegging on a single night. Considered one of the wettest towns in the area, the harbor contained thousands of dollars worth of vessels of the rum fleet at any given time. Sometimes accidents revealed the illegal activities. An attic fire uncovered two stills of Guiseppe Viola, a "dandy" who always carried a cane and was known as the "Count."[34] The biggest round up of alleged violators of the Volstead Act came in December of 1920. Police seized $5,000 worth of liquor with one casualty, a proprietor of a hotel resisted and "fell" down a flight of stairs, but was not seriously injured.[35]

City Hall about 1896.

Trouble came to a head in 1924 over promotions. The City Manager first wanted examinations—then reorganization before promotions would be made.[36] After years of discussion, an investigation began in 1925 into the police situation. City Manager, William A. Holt, became angered over a leak of details in the probe. Holt decided to bring in New York policemen to reorganize the local force which he felt was the only way to straighten it out.[37] Two New York City Police Lieutenants were brought to New London and they recommended: reorganization of the force; keeping the same executive officers; development of a police manual and the organization of a training school. The whole report with all details and names never was made public, but its recommendations were carried out and promotions were made in 1925.[38]

The force had a restriction of 40 patrolmen by directive for the period from 1927 until 1946.[39] The merit system instituted in 1930 included an examination for promotion—testing ones knowledge, judgement, conditions of beat, courtesy, reliability, initiative, discipline and appearance.[40] The depression meant cut backs and in 1933 pay was reduced ten percent while the detective bureau was eliminated. Traffic proved to be the biggest police problem during the 1930s. In 1935 the detective bureau was restored and a fingerprinting procedure was established.[41]

During the War, the age limit was raised to age 35 from age 30 in order to secure enough police. A police auxiliary was organized and used the old

Boss Cracker factory on Water Street until disbanded March 31, 1946.[42] A
three way police radio began in 1943.

A number of difficulties faced the police department in post war years.
A captain and director of the program planning shared a hallway for their
office while the Chief's office was used as a public corridor. The police felt
they lacked the respect and cooperation of the public while the public felt it
lacked protection deserved for taxes paid. Some of the city streets are not
safe at night. New men want faster advancement and higher pay.[43]

On the other hand newspaper reports of 19 policemen making over
$11,000 from police work does not help the police image, especially when
one salary made was $20,183 and the next five were $15,456, $14,365,
$14,332, $14,365 and $14,432.[44] The department needs—new headquar-
ters, modern equipment, new police cars and ways to respond to the needs
of minority groups—must be met if the high standard of New London
police is to continue. To meet the changing needs of the town, City
Manager Driscoll, ordered a 25% increase in blacks on the police force in
1971 and the police operated New London Police Community Relations
Center.[45]

FIRE PROTECTION

FIRE! That wonderful servant which if not handled properly becomes a
fearful enemy, constituted one of the chief dangers to settlements. This
was particularly so when methods to protect people and their possessions
were first developing. Fire engines arrived in Boston from England in
1675.[46] Philadelphia and New York had them by 1730. Not until 1767 did
New London have its first fire engine, gift of Nathaniel Shaw, Jr., purchased from Philadelphia.[47] The first regular fire company began in 1786
with Ebenezer Douglas as captain and twelve men in the company. For
their service the town paid the members' highway tax. The company took
charge of the "Shaw" fire engine which had just returned from being
repaired in New York. Captain Michael Melally and Nathaniel Richards
received the responsibility to construct a building for the engine and
company, at a town meeting in 1786.[48]

By 1802 the city became more concerned about meeting its responsibility for fire protection. A meeting of the mayor, Common Council and
aldermen decided that six fire wardens would be appointed by the court of
Common Council and all would be subject to orders of these officials. The
town now had three fire engines and the fire wardens possessed the power
to appoint three officers for each engine to keep same in good order.
Funds from the city treasury were authorized to take care of parts and

New London's first fire engine.

Nameaug Engine Company. Organized 1850. From left: William E. Cane, 2nd Assistant; Samuel T. Adams, Secretary; Isaac W. Thompson, Foreman; Eldred P. Prentis, Treasurer; Charles L. Ockford, 1st Assistant.

supplies.[49]

These first fire wardens, Jared Starr, Robert Allyn, Marvin Wait, Samuel Green, Winthrop Saltonstall and Samuel Wheat—appointed the following officers for the three companies: North Engine—Charles Kimball, Nathaniel Richards and Simeon Smith; Middle Engine—Thomas H. Rawson, Jonathan Sizer and Isaac Triby; South Engine—Richard Fosdick, Ebenezer Holt and Jonathan Holt.[50]

A general feeling developed that "our fire engines . . . [are] deficient of experienced men." A number of leading citizens signed a petition asking for similar conditions as existed in other Connecticut towns. The town fathers agreed. A city fire department dated from 1805 when the Connecticut Legislature made New London the fourth city so empowered. Three companies of 18 men each were organized around the engines mentioned above. As equipment and training of men improved there seemed to be a corresponding let down by individuals in the furnishing of fire buckets and their conditions.[51]

A fourth company—New London Fire Hook and Ladder Company—was organized with F. W. Treadway, clerk and in operation in 1838.[52] The head of the city fire department held the title "Chief Engineer." Whaling influence can be seen in the fact that in 1841, Acors Barns was the chief engineer and holding four of the six fire warden posts were Charles Hobron, W. W. Billings, E. V. Stoddard and Thomas Fitch II—all five were whaling merchants. In 1848 two of the companies received new engines.

A fifth company was organized November 18, 1850. It was strictly a volunteer outfit but under city control. They purchased their own engine for $1,200.[53] The Reliance Engine Company (Engine Company #5) was housed on Church Street before becoming the Independent Blues on Main Street.

By 1850 the companies had taken names or were reorganized under names. South Engine Company organized in 1802, became the Washington Engine Company after the city fire department began in 1805. Later it became the Niagara but just when or why the name changed is not clear. Sometime between 1840 and 1848 the new name became official. The name either came from the first fire company, Washington, which was founded on the Fort Niagara site in New London or from its new engine in 1848 called Niagara.[54]

An independent company developed when Reliance Company #5 could not obtain a proper building from the town. They changed their name to the Independent Blues and purchased their own house and equipment and offered free service to the town. When they received all the new hose, the other companies became angry and the city companies disbanded in the spring of 1850. However, men continued to gather at the engine houses and in the fall of 1850, Frank S. Fitch became the Engineer and the Niagara Company re-formed.[55]

In 1853 they formed a military company, the Niagara Guard, which used flint lock muskets. As a social center the Engine House even offered a library, set up in 1856. When the Civil War came seventy men, fifty-five from Niagara, formed an army company. They lost only three men in the war. As city water made the Engine Company obsolete, it became a hose company and with steamers in 1884, it once again became an engine company. Socially, the annual concert and ball held November 25 represented a high point of the season. The company moved about a great deal from its first building on the Parade to State Street and then to Bank Street. The Niagara had one of the first auto-engines in the country in 1903. Fifty-one of its members served in World War I and still patriotic, forty-one served during the World War II period. They only lost one man during World War I and none during World War II.[56]

Nameaug Engine Company located on Main Street, organized April 18, 1850 it became the main rival of the Niagara Company. They were the two largest companies and rivalries were so strong that buildings were reportedly lost because the firemen were too busy fighting each other to tend to the fires. The name of the company came from a vessel owned by Williams and Barns. It had been the first three masted schooner at New London. Earlier the company had been the Independent Blues.

In 1854 the company moved to Masonic Street after the city bought the Lyman Law property bordering State, Union and Masonic streets. By 1856 the large Nameaug Engine Company on Masonic Street housed the most powerful engine in New England, had the most excellent equipment and held the best dance in the community. The elite of the town gathered at its functions. It received a new steam engine May 4, 1867. The foreman until 1864, when he became chief engineer, was F. L. Allyn.[57]

The Protector Company (Engine Company #2) was organized May 19, 1854 and located on Huntington Street. By 1869 Engine Company #3 (the Relief Engine Company was organized in 1854) was located on Richards Street. It became the Thomas Hose Company in 1879.[58] The F. L. Allyn Hook and Ladder Company began in 1866 after the city bought its first ladder truck.[59]

Firemen's parades, big events in many Connecticut towns today, were begun in 1873 at New London. The day of the parade in September of

1873, was called the biggest day in the history of the department. All of the New London Companies marched—

> F. L. Allen Hook and Ladder Company No. 1
> Niagara Steam Engine Company No. 1
> Nameaug Steam Engine Company No. 2
> Relief Hand Engine Company No. 3
> Konomoc Hose Company No. 4

and several out of town fire departments were in the parade.[60]

That was the Konomoc Hose Company's first year having been organized in April of 1873. It was a small company, but active. However, by December 1874 too few remained to carry on its duties. It was reorganized in 1876 and later became a ladder company.[61]

A new hose company, Ockford Hose #5, began its existence in January of 1895. A truck company was organized in the upper end of the town in 1895. Another hose company Pequot #6 started in 1905 but failed to gain support of the city until 1923. It became affiliated with the New London Fire Department in 1912. The city furnished a house in 1907 at the corner of the fourth and fifth wards for Pequot, the only company to own its own equipment. In 1923 the city paid $50 a month for the apparatus and provided day and night drivers. Quarterly allowances of $75 were given. It received more than any other company.[62] By 1926 Pequot had become an engine company. The Northwest Hose Company #7 originated in 1907 with over 100 charter members. In 1920 it moved to its new home on Brainerd Street.[63]

The social side of the volunteer fire department cannot be overstressed. Each company gave an annual ball which provided the social highlight of its members' get-together each year. For young men, the fire houses provided the only place outside of saloons to meet with others. The parades were gala affairs with the men showing the equipment and dressing in fine uniforms. Politically the companies became quite active and very important in lining up votes.[64] When one joined a volunteer outfit he paid $10.00 and $2.00 a year dues.

In the beginning, the department used leather hose and hand operated engines. The pump engines were horse drawn while hose companies pulled their own for many years before using horses. Men would line up on each side and pump the water from a well or the river. If they could not reach water, each householder would line up with his two buckets and form a line to fill the tubs for the engine to pump the water. To practice the engines would have "washes." They would line up along State Street with the end engine having its hose in the river and the rest hooked together by hoses. Each would try to flood the engine ahead (wash it) while it tried to pump the water out faster than it came in.[65]

When steamers came in, one man could do the work of forty. The Niagara Company purchased, at its own expense, a 1902 steam propelled apparatus the Auto Maud in 1903—the first in New London. It cost $5,000 and they received $5.00 for each fire they attended. Then in 1904 the driver began to receive $3.00 for each fire. The city had grown so by 1883 that a division of the city into fire districts was deemed necessary. With the division of the city into these districts, an alarm system telling which area had the fire was established. A telegraph system with box numbers was put into effect—districts 2, 3, 4, 5 and 6. Water hydrants were installed in 1873 and when a fire alarm was given, the first member of a company on the scene reserved the nearest hydrant for his company. It sometimes required a wrench to help reserve it and keep others from using it.[66]

The question of a paid department came up many times over the years. The earliest reference was in 1894 when the mayor claimed it would work better. After many discussions a paid force began in May of 1927. The City Manager ended twenty-four hours tours of duty. They now work a ten hour day or fourteen hour night.[67]

The city purchased an American-LaFrance Triple Combination truck for $9,000 in 1912 and gave it to Niagara for Maud. The Company bought her (Maud) back for $75.00 and used her until 1922.[68]

Fire Chiefs (chief engineers) over the years have been men well experienced in various phases of fire fighting and equipment. Quite commonly these men devoted half a century or more to the department. John Stanners retired with over fifty years of service and Charles Rose retired after 54.[69]

Trouble within the departments was unusual but in 1881 two were ousted for the use of language unbecoming firemen and for the good of the department. The City Common Council backed the action of Chief Engineer William B. Thomas.[70]

A fire police company was organized to aid the firemen. In 1884 it had 17 members. Companies then included F. L. Allen Hook and Ladder #1, Niagara Engine Company #1, Nameaug Engine Company #2, William B. Thomas Hose Company #3, Konomoc Hose Company #3.[71]

Firemen fought a fire during frigid weather in 1848 at the Exchange Building on Bank Street. This was the first major fire since an 1837 blaze on State Street.[72] They drank rum to keep warm, became drunk and threw food at each other while continuing to drink and fight the fire. The losses included Lawrence's building erected at a cost of $12,000 only three years earlier and covered by only $5,000 worth of insurance. There were two stores on the first floor, two rear stores, New London Telegraph Company and Tory Men's Library Association, third floor housed the Odd Fellows Club. Four months later the Ocham Factory (Charles Briggs factory) burned in the North End of town and it carried no insurance. It had burned earlier in 1838.[73]

One of the largest fires took place January 26, 1849. Originally it appeared to have started in cooper shops on the Lawrence Wharf, but later investigations indicated that it had been set in several places. It destroyed two cooper shops on the Lawrence Wharf, Adam Frink's office and Frink, Chew and Company offices on Bank Street, Anson Chase's new building and C. C. Comstock's store. Lawrence's new building, Phoenix, was almost lost. From the attempts to burn Lawrence property over the years it would seem that one or more individuals who considered themselves wronged by the company had employed arson as a means of revenge.[74]

A fire broke out at the corner of Union and Methodist Streets on November 18, 1853. Although owned by the Methodist Society building no longer served as a church, but instead housed T. M. and S. H. Allyn who manufactured pianos. Losses included $5,000 worth of goods with $1,000 insurance coverage. The Sons of Temperance rented room in the building and several houses adjoining. Almost everything was covered by some insurance.[75]

A fire began in the Union House, November 9, 1854. The building could not be saved—lost were a book store, hat store, and two other businesses. Thayer's Book Store had let their insurance policy elapse and lost $2,500 in goods. The building was insured for $13,000 and was valued at $25,000. As a rule it appeared that businesses were under insured, usually about fifty to seventy-five percent of the value of the property. Either they had great faith in the fire department or belief that it would not happen to them.[76]

Holt's Block caught fire on January 20, 1857. The fire began in the cellar. In the cold weather and deep snow, only two companies reached the area—Nameaug and Protector. Bacon's hotel burned November of 1866 with a loss of $5,000 to $6,000 and it was not insured. A house and livery stable were lost. There was extensive damage along Bank, Main, State and Golden Streets. Edgecomb's Store, corner of Huntington and Hill Streets burned October 1871. Kerosene and waste had been used to start it. This was the second fire at James L. Edgecomb's store in a short period and he was arrested for arson.[77]

When Boston had a large fire in 1872, both the Niagara and Nameaug Companies wanted to go and Niagara felt they should have the honor. However, they both missed the Boston train at Norwich and had to return. A large fire broke out in Goddard's Block on State Street in November of 1874. Rial Chaney's building on the same street was also damaged. Altogether there was about $9,000 worth of damage done.[78]

A new fire alarm system with boxes throughout the town was tested November 30, 1888. It could be operated only with a key. All police had keys and when a fire started a citizen had to locate a fireman or go to the nearest location where a spare key was kept. All boxes had notices telling where keys could be found.[79]

The system left a lot to be desired and in July of 1897 the Old Bacon House, a landmark, burned to the ground. The fire started early in the morning in the kitchen of the Imperial Cafe and the fire alarms would not work. They had to use the church bells instead. The building had been a hotel and was at the head of steamboat wharf on the waterfront. Bacon Brothers ran it for Norwich Steamers as a Stage Coach Center.[80]

C. D. Boss and Son Cracker Factory had a fire September 19, 1901 which the department was able to keep to a small area. Boss was so pleased that he gave the fire department $300. A much worse fire developed in December of 1901 and five stores caught fire in five minutes. Men were ice covered but only one was injured. Damage was estimated at $100,000.[81]

A storage building located on the Bank of Winthrop's Cove burned all night in January of 1923. The Salvation Army served coffee and six carloads of food. According to the *New London Day* losses by fire in 1923 were $156,000, 1924 dropped to $80,000, 1925 increased to $235,543 and 1926 the loss of the Second Congregational Church alone amounted to $183,000, 1927 there were only three major fires with losses of $97,646 and 1928 losses were estimated at $103,400.[82]

In more recent years several catastrophes of note have taken place. The ones which will most commonly be remembered were the fires caused by the 1938 hurricane and the Home Memorial Hospital fire in 1944.

Eight volunteer companies operated in 1946 with 1,500 men, part were paid and part volunteer. New London appeared to be the only community which used both. Companies were The Ockford Hose Company #5, Konomoc Hose Company #4, Niagara Engine Company #1, Thomas Hose Company #3, Nameaug Engine Company #2, Pequot Engine Company #6, Northwest Engine Company #7, F. L. Allen Hook and Ladder

Company #1.

By 1971 five units remained: F. L. Allen Hook and Ladder Company #1, Niagara Engine Company #1, Ockford Hose Company #5, Pequot Engine Company #6 and Northwest Engine Company #7.[83]

WATER

An adequate water supply long eluded the city. An early attempt to organize a system lasted about twenty-five years. In May of 1800, George Hallam, Benjamin Butler, Robert Allyn, David Frink and Isaac Tribey received a charter for the New London Aqueduct Company. It tapped the springs north of the town and used logs and pipes below the principal Streets. Unfortunately not enough business came in to substain the company.[84]

The fire department suffered a lack of water in fighting fires. Those who looked over the situation felt that $100,000 would construct a system to supply the town from the lakes and ponds to the north.[85] A plan for piping in water from Lake's Pond became public in June of 1871. The New London Water Company was authorized by the General Assembly in 1871. A Board of Water Commissioners was set up in September with William H. Barns (President), R. H. Chapell, G. T. Shepard, Charles M. Daboll and J. C. Learned (Secretary). The town voted for the waterworks—664 to 247—and raised $250,000. Lake Konomoc and 90 acres around it were purchased and a dam built to raise the water ten feet creating a lake of 200 acres. The contract for the construction of the system went to George H. Norman of Newport, Rhode Island, who bid $165,000. At a cost of $260,000 the system was built and water piped from Lake Konomoc to New London.[86] In 1873, the system began to deliver water to the homes and fire pumpers went out as the hydrants supplied the water. Many leaks and breaks plagued the system until cast iron pipe replaced the clay ones in 1898. In 1873 East New London had pipe installed.

While maintenance costs were high at first, still they were exceeded by the income.[87] By 1885 total income reached $317,512.99 while total maintenance costs were $165,392.45. Low pressure developed at times and caused many complaints until the water main was increased in size at a cost of $100,327. Of 1,501 homes served only 26 were metered. However, in 1900 other meters were installed at a cost of $45,000. Barns remained president of the Water Board until his death.[88]

The city added to its water sources several times: 1894—Dam Bean Brook, 1895 Briggs Brook Reservoir, 1901 Barns Reservoir, 1920 Bogue Brook Reservoir which provided ¼ billion gallons of water. A $447,921 development in 1944 by the P. W. A. improved the water and sewage system.[89]

Sewers were authorized in 1885 by the City Council but ran into much difficulty. Inspite of illness, odor and unpleasantness, many objected to paying for the sewers. Finally, in 1888 the town voted to finish them after much discussion and opposition. People even went to court to fight paying for them. Next, the problem of treatment of sewage came up. As the town grew, dumping sewage into the harbor could not continue. In 1905 the water and sewage departments were joined together and decided to put in a sewage disposal plant. It opened in 1929. New sewers to connect different parts of the city continued to be built for many years.[90]

TELEGRAPH

The first telegraph Company, established in 1847, connected New London and Norwich. By 1848 full time operators of the company put New London in communication with Norwich, Worcester and Boston. The Norwich and New London Telegraph Company ran a line to Norwich and connected with the Franklin Company. The officers included R. H. Chapell (president) and Henry R. Bond (Treasurer).[91]

The New London, Norwich and Worcester Magnetic Telegraph Company stockholders considered the offer of the New York and Boston Telegraph Association to purchase the line and connect the two towns with the New York and Boston line in May of 1849. The Union Telegraph Company in 1859 ran a line between New London and New Haven. United Lines Telegraph Company office was located on Bank Street in 1887.[92]

Eventually the Union Lines, Atlantic and Pacific, Franklin Postal Telegraph and Western Union Telegraph Companies replaced the New London companies and of course Western Union only survived. It has closed its office at New London and operates out of New Haven.[93]

TELEPHONE

Telephones were installed first in 1880 and mainly for businesses. The New London Northern used telephones to connect their offices in Palmer and New London.[94] A New London Telephone Company began operations after being organized by A. H. Chappell, J. Ivers Louis, Mason Young and others. Western Union bought out the firm and in turn sold out in 1881 to The Connecticut Telephone Company. It operated the service until 1882, when the Southern New England Telephone Company, organized that year, purchased the total capital of the company.

There were 120 telephones at the time.[95] When the new railroad station was completed the telephone company moved its offices there in 1887.

The Eureka Telephone Company established an office on State Street in 1888. It did not last long.[96] A New London Telephone Company in 1899-1900 failed to gain permission to offer service.[97] Snetco established nine telephones from boxes for the switchboard at Police headquarters in 1914. Interestingly, the phone company had one book for the whole state until 1920, when five different ones were issued for five sections of the state.[98]

By 1917 business increased so that the top floor of the Marsh Building was leased to Snetco and the headquarters was shifted from Norwich. The New London Exchange grew to 6,600 subscribers by 1921 when 5,000 directories were mailed out. Dial phones were installed from the fall of 1925 to the beginning of 1928. A statewide dial system began January 7 at midnight. Connecticut became the first state to have it.[99] Telephones were hard to obtain during World War II and by the end of 1945 the company could meet one request out of every four. Civilian phone manufacturing increased rapidly to meet the demand. Gradually phone requests were met and those desiring phones were able to have them installed. Not only do families have the one phone today but a number of extensions as well as separate phones for children have been installed. There has been a gradual reduction in New London local operators as not only a statewide dial system exists but a national dialing system prevails.

GAS AND ELECTRICITY

New London began lighting the streets in 1853. A company—the New London Gas Light Company furnished the service. The officials were A. C. Lippitt (president), J. N. Harris (treasurer and clerk), Rial Chaney, E. V. Stoddard, A. Menell, S. S. Button, and M. M. Comstock.[100] Another gas company formed in 1881 furnished gas for stores. It had little development. C. A. Williams established the Oneco Company in 1885 and furnished electricity for the city.[101]

The Connecticut Railway and Lighting Company purchased both the gas and the electric companies in 1897 and they were merged as one with a new charter, the New London Gas and Electric Company under the direction of Robert Coit as president.[102]

Another company, The Marine Power Company, was established in 1899. The major force behind the company seems to have been a large construction company of Boston—Stone and Webster. In 1913 it created a large utility company by merging the New London Gas and Electric Company and the Marine Power Company, known since 1905 as the Connecticut Power Company. By 1920 the Connecticut Power Company had purchased six other Connecticut Utility companies and leased one giving it control of the entire gas, electric and power business of New London plus all the power and light business in ten other Connecticut communities.

One of the leaders Viggo E. Bird of the Connecticut Power Company, formerly an executive with Stone and Webster, became vice-president of the new utility company. He was also director of two New London Banks and treasurer of the New London Northern Railway Company. In 1920 the Hartford Electric Light Company took control of the Connecticut Power Company through the purchase of Stone and Websters common stock. Bird's leadership qualities were recognized by the president of Hartford Electric Light Company, Samuel Ferguson.[103] He backed Bird for the position of executive vice president in 1929 after checking a rumor that Bird had mis-used church funds. Finding no evidence, Ferguson had him named to the post and A. D. Colvin replaced Bird at the Conn. Power Co.

The depression meant difficulties for the companies due to the reduced consumption of power, however, wages and employment remained at the same level. A rather vocal group in Connecticut demanded public ownership of the utility company. Among the public debates held concerning that issue was one at Bulkeley School Auditorium in New London on April 6, 1934. The company seems to have at least established its position equally as well as the opponents. With continued success Viggo E. Bird moved into the presidency of Helco in 1935.

Bird's success story came to an abrupt end in 1939. He had used New London Northern securities as collateral in covering some poor invest-sentenced from two to five years at Wethersfield Prison. Once more, Samuel Ferguson became president.

The power company responded well to the hurricane disasters which struck New London in 1938 and 1944. Under the leadership of Ferguson and A. D. Colvin, The Connecticut Power Company was able to provide the power facilities needed for the expansion of the U.S. Coast Guard Academy and the early beginnings of the Underwater Sound Laboratory and defense activities as World War II approached. The company continued its expansion during World War II and during the post war period which followed. In 1958 the Connecticut Power Company was merged with Helco.

Today New London is part of a vast power operation, Northeast Utilities, which was formed in 1965. Helco and originally two other and later three utility companies formed Northeast Utilities, one of the largest public utility operations in the country. The area had advanced into the nuclear age with the development of the Millstone Atomic Energy Plant in Waterford.

NEWSPAPERS

The printing press came to Connecticut in 1709 when Thomas Short arrived at New London. He studied under Bartholomew Green and became the first official printer of the colony. Thus New London became the site of the first printed work in Connecticut—"The Saybrook Platform." After Short's death in 1714, Timothy S. Green, Sr. of Cambridge became the Connecticut printer. The printing business of Green continued long after his death in 1757. His son Samuel worked with the father until his death in 1752.[104]

The second newspaper in Connecticut began at New London in 1758, founded by Timothy Green, Jr., brother of Samuel. *The New London Summary* or the *Weekly Advertiser* was published from August 8, 1758 to September 23, 1763. Timothy, Jr. died August 3, 1758 and the paper continued under his nephew Timothy III for a few weeks. By October Timothy III decided to end publication and instead began on November 3 the *New London Gazette,* essentially the same paper of 1758 under a new name. The paper became a fixture in New London from 1758 to 1844.

The *Gazette* took a strong anti-Stamp Act stand and generally anti-British restrictions on American trade. Just before Lexington and Concord, April 12, 1775, it became the *Connecticut Gazette*. Printing of the paper was done in the attic of Timothy Green's house on State Street. The British set fire to the house September 6, 1781, however, it was put out before extensive damage could be done. The house can be seen today, raised with a store underneath it on State Street. Strong federal support, especially of President Washington, was offered by the *Gazette* after the Revolution. In 1789, Samuel Green became a partner in the business now known as Green and Son and in 1794, he became sole operator of the printing plant. Ebenezer P. Cady and Nathaniel Eells took over the paper in 1805 when Samuel Green decided to retire. After three years, Green again took charge. An anti-Democratic Party paper, it became the *New London Gazette* in 1823.

Samuel Green sold the paper in 1838 to John Jay Hyde. Hyde took over with the January 3, 1838 issue, but apparently found it not too successful or to his liking and as early as June of 1839 tried to sell it. Finally in 1840, Samuel H. Green, son of Samuel, purchased the paper and published it until January of 1841 when A. G. Seaman took over as the final publisher. It ceased to appear in 1844. An excellent and often witty section of the *Gazette* was the "Marine List" begun by Thomas Allen, later continued by others—unfortunately, lacking much of his wit.

The *Weekly Oracle* was a short lived paper (1795-1800) published by James Springer. A much more colorful, although equally short lived was the *New London Bee,* an organ of the Democratic Party, June 14, 1797 to June 30, 1802. Charles Holt, editor and publisher, proved to be quite outspoken in his opposition to Federal policies during the administration of John Adams. Holt's most severe attacks were for Alexander Hamilton and the provisional army planned during the Quasi War with France. The editor was indicted September 17, 1799 for violation of the Sedition Act. On September 21, he was arrested and taken before the Circuit Court at Hartford where he pleaded not guilty and trial was set for April of 1800. While waiting for trial, Holt increased his attacks. He was found guilty of publishing a libel and received a fine of $200 and a sentence of three months in jail. Although he resumed publishing of the *Bee* after his release, Holt moved it to Hudson, New York and June 30, 1802 was the last issue in New London.

The *Republican Advocate* proved to be another very outspoken newspaper. Established February of 1818 by Joshua B. Clapp and Simeon Francis, it backed the Democratic Party. It referred to Federalists as "speakers of lies" and similar comments. Francis left the firm in 1822-1823 and Clapp carried on alone until 1828 when John Eldridge purchased the paper. Eldridge changed the name to *Connecticut Centinel* (1828-1830). The paper took an anti-Masonic stand and proved very sympathetic towards labor. It campaigned for greater attention to the educational needs of mechanics, improved common schools and opposition to concentration of wealth.

Another pro-labor paper was *The Workingman's Advocate,* a very radical Democratic newspaper 1830-1831. Editors were Dr. Charles Douglas and J. George Harris.

The *People's Advocate and New London County Republican* began August 26, 1840 to promote the election of William Henry Harrison. It remained Whig Party backed. Benjamin F. Bissell published the newspaper until his death September 3, 1842. J. G. Dolbear and W. D. Manning took over in 1843 and the following year Dolbear ran the paper alone. He established the first daily newspaper the *Morning News* in 1844. Both papers were sold by Dolbear in 1848 to C. F. Daniels and F. H. Bacon.

The new owners changed the names of both to "Chronicle"—the *Daily Crhonicle* and the *Weekly Chronicle*. In 1851 Daniels became sole publisher and editor of both newspapers until his death in 1858. William O. Irish took over from 1858 to 1862 with Charles W. Butler as editor on January 21. Upon Irish's death in 1862 Samuel Fox became the final owner and issued the paper August 28, 1862 until 1868 when publication ended.

March 22, 1845 J. M. Scofield and S. D. MacDonald began to publish the *New London Democrat,* a weekly, but MacDonald left in 1846 and Scofield directed operations until 1849. He began a daily, *The Morning Star* in 1848 before selling both papers to D. S. Ruddock the following year. A partner joined later that year, Jackson and later John A. Tibbits who left in 1871. By 1872, Ruddock was alone in the operation of the two papers. Illness forced him to cease publishing. The papers originally supported the Democrat Party in views but changed to Republican during the Civil War. They became quite unpopular at the port by 1873.

John Tibbits established the *Evening Telegram* to replace the *Daily Star,* May 10, 1873 and the weekly *Connecticut Gazette* May 24, 1873 to replace the *New London Democrat.* Both were published by the New London Printing Company. Its plant on Green Street was located in a new building with a steam engine to run the presses. The two papers were published until 1909 reflecting views of independent Republican persuasion. During the period 1845-1871 several papers were started and perished. An obituary carried by the *People's Advocate,* October 15, 1845 stated: "a Locofoco paper died at N. L. some time ago for want of support after a feeble & lingering existance of about 6 months."[105]

The *Weekly Chronicle* ran an obituary January 26, 1865 "Starved to death in this city 24th inst. the N. L. Morning Star, age 6 days . . . Feeble and puny it came into the world, and out of it went a horrid looking skeleton. Everybody rejoiced when kicked its last kick."[106]

The *New London Repository,* published by William Holt Starr, 1858 to 1862, contained many historical accounts of early New London as well as the day to day news. The *New London Press,* an evening paper, of Gilbert Fox, Isaac C. Sistare, Robert Hayes and Daniel Lake, lasted only from January of 1868 to August. E. Rice published the *New London Daily Times,* an independent paper, from July of 1871 to September of the same year.

The *New London Morning Telegraph* began July 15, 1885 with Theodore Bodenwein as one of the founders. Earlier he had been an apprentice on the *New London Day* upon arrival from Prussia. Bodenwein sold his share of

Ye Antientest Burial Place.

the *Morning Telegraph* in 1890 and purchased the *Day* in 1891.

The *Day* began July 2, 1881 when John A. Tibbets, John C. Turner and John McGinley established it. It began as a morning paper first purely by accident and later switched to the evening. Bodenwein bought the *Morning Telegraph* in 1901 and published it as well as the *Day* until 1907. He lost $22,100 before giving it to his managing editor, Frank J. Brunner, free of charge. It still did not make money and Brunner sold it to B. L. Armstrong. It went through many hands before ceasing operations in 1920. Its claim to fame may be that one of its reporters was Eugene O'Neill. The *Day* had several homes before settling on Main Street in 1907. An addition which doubled its space, was built in 1929. It remains the only daily in town.[107]

CEMETERIES

While logically most of this study has concerned activities of the living, the honored dead also deserve a word, or at least their final resting places do. There have been four major cemeteries in the town and a few special places of interment. During the first half of the eighteenth century victims of smallpox had to be buried secretly on Powder Island as people objected to their burial in the regular burying grounds. No records exist of those so treated. A number of bodies were interred under the Episcopal Church when it stood on the Parade, between 1735 and 1781.[108]

The old burial ground or first cemetery, known as Ye Antientest Burial Place, on Richards Street between Hempstead and Huntington served the town from 1652 to 1793. Those families owning tombs continued to use them at least until 1845. Here one finds the graves of most of the settlers and important men of the town's history through the Revolutionary War. It is the oldest cemetery east of the Connecticut River and bears several historical points of interests. Among the grave markers, stand several tombs: the Winthrop Tomb, built by Frances Bayard Winthrop 1789, the Saltonstall Tomb built in 1710, the Jonathan Brooks Tomb built in 1786.[109]

A second burial ground at Broad and Hempstead Streets began with the purchase of four acres from Captain Michael Melally in 1793. The cemetery became filled by 1835. Among the leading people buried here were Captain Charles Bulkeley, General Jedediah Huntington, General Thomas H. Cushing, and Captain Michael Melally.[110] A particularly sad burial concerns a wife of a whaling captain. Captain William (Billy) Hobbs, vessel, *Eliza Jane,* which arrived in port after a successful short voyage of eight months with a cargo worth $80,000. The captain dressed in his best suit, stood on deck searching the crowd for Mary, his wife. One of the owners boarded the vessel and taking the captain to a cabin informed him that Mary had died two weeks before and lay in the Second Burial Ground. Hobbs left the vessel, never collected his share of the voyage and became a familiar waterfront character.[111] A schoolhouse was built on the ground after the bodies were moved, many to Cedar Grove by 1886 with much of the expense borne by C. A. Williams.[112]

A Third Burial Ground was purchased in 1835. It also consisted of four acres—on Lincoln Avenue, Williams and Waller Streets. Among the most tragic reminders of New London's sea connection with the monument to an English family, the Waltons, lost with the steamship *Atlantic* in 1846. The monument is now located at Cedar Grove. In 1890, the bodies remaining were removed as the city prepared to build a schoolhouse on the site.[113]

The New London Cemetery Association was organized in 1850 with a capitalization of $15,000. In January of 1851 the first officers were chosen—Francis Allyn, Henry P. Haven, Enoch V. Stoddard, Nathaniel Shaw Perkins, Jr., and William Albertson. A meeting in March chose the Cedars from some five sites offered and paid $2,000 for 39 acres. Stockholders named it Cedar Grove Cemetery. The city authorized a sum of $5,000, but when a large outcry of protest came, they withdrew the action. An editorial lauded the town's actions: "Citizens of New London are not to be gullied or cajoled into any measure, praiseworthy or otherwise." The consecration of the grounds took place October 8, 1851 and Frances Manwaring Caulkins sang a hymn at the time. Charles Augustus Williams contributed $10,000 to improve the cemetery in 1899.[114]

After thirty years in the Harris Building, the office of the cemetery moved to the Beckwith Memorial Chapel in 1925, located at the cemetery entrance. There are 127 veterans of the War of 1812 buried in Cedar Grove Cemetery, the largest number in the state as well as being the interment place for a large number of Civil War veterans. Dividends were paid only from 1851 to 1865 which repaid the original investment and interest.[115]

State Street from the Depot. From Ballou's Pictorial Drawing Companion, 1855.

CONCLUSION

What lies ahead for New London after nearly 340 years of history? Twice in its existence the town has become a leading port and in each of the major conflicts, from the American Revolution through World War II, has played an important role. Yet, it has never succeeded in building an industrial base sufficient to replace the declining maritime interests. Actually, the port continued to do well enough economically until the 1950's. Since the end of the Korean War, New London, traditionally a city of middle class people, has undergone about eighteen years of change including the breakup of traditional neighborhoods, loss of population, dwindling tax base, large increase in minority groups and increasing city government costs.

An additional problem facing New London is posed by the high percentage of older people. While New London has twice the population of Waterford or Montville its school population is approximately the same and only Hartford, New Haven and Boston have a greater minority student population.[1]

Redevelopment has eliminated several streets and public housing or apartments have displaced neighborhoods. Blacks and Spanish speaking newcomers have also cut into traditional ethnic areas. Redevelopment displaced the Polish Section of East New London while Blacks and Spanish speaking people have moved into the Italian Section of the Shaw Street Area.[2]

Many businesses have moved to the suburbs or closed: W. T. Grants, Sears, Montgomery Wards, G. M. Williams and Genungs moved out.[3] Of

Dedication of Soldiers' and Sailors' Monument at foot of State Street, May 6, 1896.

more than sixty independent grocery stores and markets of the 1950's only twenty-three remain. Of eighteen taverns (beer only) where men gathered after a days work for talk and relaxation only two are in existence.[4]

The budget of 1956-1957 of $4,197,544 increased in 1971-1972 to $13,456,622. The city has lost over $5,000,000 in taxable property to colleges, the Coast Guard, highway expansion and social service agencies.[5]

New building, redevelopment, fires and storms have removed many of the town's historical landmarks. However, a number still stand in New London. The Old Town Mill built by John Winthrop, located at Main and Mill Street, dates back to 1650, although it was rebuilt in 1712 and has been repaired several times since then. The Hempstead House, oldest frame house in the state was built in 1645 by Robert Hempstead and enlarged by Joshua, his son. The family lived in it until 1939. It was opened to the public in 1943 on Hempstead Street. The Huguenot House was built for Nathaniel Hempstead, grandson of Joshua, in the period 1751-1759. A tea room operated in the house from the 1920's to 1937. The New London County Historical Society's home, the Shaw Mansion, Bank and Blinman Streets dates from 1756 when built by Acadian workers. The County

Looking down State Street from the Court House.

Court House built in 1784 on Huntington Street, has been a meeting house, recruiting center, yellow fever hospital, place for "lying in state" and the site of a Peace Ball in 1815. The Nathan Hale School House of 1774 was moved to the Ancient Burial Ground in 1901 and cared for by the Daughters of the American Revolution. The school was the third incorporated secondary school in Connecticut. Later it was moved to Mill Street. The Greek Revival Houses of Whale Oil Row built in 1830 are particularly fine architectural examples of the period.

The link with the sea continues as the Oceanographic Research Center will be located in the Coast Guard Grounds where the Thames Shipyard and Repair Company is now located. Fortunately, a new site has been secured for the company within the city.

The present City Manager, C. Francis Driscoll, has been working for a reorganization of the city government. There has been no overall reorganization since 1921 and the Manager feels New London too often is run by custom and ordinances which do not any longer meet the times. A proposed new charter was defeated by a vote of 2,925 to 1,834 in November of 1971.[6] However, the City Council has authorized the City Manager, Driscoll, to reorganize the City Government with regard to the Department of Real Estate, Office of Management, Public Works Department, Department of Building Inspection, adoption of State Building Code as well as to eliminate the Assessor, Comptroller and Administration Assistant jobs.[7]

New London may well have "turned the corner" as it entered the decade of the 1970's. The Grand List of 1971 showed an increase for the first time in three years. A new spirit of confidence appeared as redevelopment of the town began to reshape and prepare the area to meet and cope with the problems and needs of an American urban area too long reluctant to "shake" free of its New England Conservatism. The old port may well be on its way to a new and prosperous era. Despite present indications and citizens's confidence only time will tell. The sails of the full rigged vessel on the seal of the city may yet fill with wind and launch a bright new period.

Gold Star Memorial Bridge.

Soldiers' and Sailors' Monument.

APPENDIX I

NEW LONDON SHIPBUILDING: COLONIAL PERIOD

Name	Rig	Date	Owner	Tonnage	Cost	Trade	Builder
New London			Wm. Brenton				
Tryall	Unkn.	1661	Daniel Lane	Unkn.	200	Unkn.	
Tryall	Brig	1683	Unknown	18	20	Unkn.	John Leeds
Swallow	Sloop	1683	Unknown	Unkn.	Unkn.	Unkn.	John Leeds
Endeavor	Bark	1690	Unknown	52	Unkn.	Unkn.	James Bennet
Unknown	Sloop	1713	Arnold	Unkn.	Unkn.	Unkn.	Joshua Hempstead
Unknown	Snow	1714	Unknown	Unkn.	Unkn.	W.I.	John Hutton
Unknown	Brig	1715	Unknown	Unkn.	Unkn.	Unkn.	Samuel Edgecomb
Unknown	Sloop	1716	Unknown	Unkn.	Unkn.	Unkn.	Joshua Hempstead
Unknown	Ship	1716	Unknown	Unkn.	Unkn.	W.I.	John Hutton
Unknown	Unkn.	1718	Mason	Unkn.	Unkn.	W.I.	Unknown
Unknown	Sloop	1718	Unknown	Unkn.	Unkn.	W.I.	Samuel Edgecomb
Unknown	Sloop	1724	Unknown	Unkn.	Unkn.	W.I.	Unknown
Unknown	Sloop	1725	Buttolph	Unkn.	Unkn.	W.I.	Ralph Stodders
Unknown	Unkn.	1726	Unknown	Unkn.	Unkn.	W.I.	Ralph Stodders

Sources: Robert Owen Decker, "The New London Merchants: 1645-1909: The Rise and Decline of a Connecticut Port" (Unpublished Ph.D. Thesis, University of Connecticut, 1970.), p. 251.

APPENDIX II

NEW LONDON SHIPBUILDING: COLONIAL PERIOD
COIT BUILT VESSELS

Name	Rig	Date	Built For	Tonnage	Value	Trade
Speedwell	Bark	1660	Thomas Beebe	14	50-82	Unkn.
Hopewell	Bark	1660-64	William Keeny	12-23	50-82	Unkn.
The Endeavor	Bark	1660	Matthew Beckwith	20	50-82	W.I.
New London	Ship	1666	Christopher Christophers	70	50-82	Unkn.
Regard	Bark	1668	Chris. Christophers & Chas. Hill	Unkn.	Unkn.	Unkn.
Charles	Sloop	1672	Chris. Christophers & Chas. Hill	20	Unkn.	Unkn.
Success	Ketch	1677	John Liveen	54	114	C. & W.I.
John and Hester	Ship	1678	John Prentis, Jr.	100	445	Unkn.
Liveen	Ship	Unkn.	John Liveen	Unkn.	600	Unkn.
The Queen	Unkn.	1680	Unknown	Unkn.	Unkn.	Unkn.
The Recovery	Unkn.	1680	Unknown	Unkn.	Unkn.	Unkn.
Edward & Margaret	Sloop	1681	Edward Stallion	30	Unkn.	Unkn.
New London	Brig	1704	Alford Vryland	Unkn.	Unkn.	Unkn.
Love and Ann	Unkn.	1704	Alford Vryland	Unkn.	Unkn.	Unkn.
Grace & Hannah	Unkn.	1705	Alford Vryland	Unkn.	Unkn.	Unkn.
Unknown	Unkn.	1708	Alford Vryland	30	Unkn.	Unkn.
Unknown	Ship	1711	Alford Vryland	Unkn.	Unkn.	Unkn.

APPENDIX II

NEW LONDON SHIPBUILDING: COLONIAL PERIOD
COIT BUILT VESSELS

Name	Rig	Date	Built For	Tonnage	Value	Trade
Unknown	Unkn.	1714	Alford Vryland	Unkn.	Unkn.	Unkn.
Unknown	Unkn.	1714	Alford Vryland	Unkn.	Unkn.	Unkn.
Unknown	Brig	1719	Alford Vryland	Unkn.	Unkn.	Unkn.
Unknown	Brig	1719	Joseph Gardiner	Unkn.	Unkn.	Unkn.
Unknown	Brig	1726	Joseph Gardiner	Unkn.	Unkn.	Unkn.
Unknown	Brig	1731	Unknown	Unkn.	Unkn.	Unkn.
Unknown	Snow	1735	Ben & Isaac Ledyard	Unkn.	Unkn.	Unkn.

Source: Decker, "The New London Merchants," p. 249.

APPENDIX III

LIST OF CONNECTICUT AND NEW LONDON VESSELS
DURING THE COLONIAL PERIOD
BY TONNAGE

Year	No. of Connecticut Vessels	No. of New London Vessels	Connecticut Tonnage	Ave.	New London Tonnage	Ave.
1680	27	7	1,046-1,090	(39.7)	340	(48.5)
1730	42	5	1,305		192	
1731	44	9	1,414		317	
1756	74		3,202			
1761	114		3,527			
1762	114		3,527			
1773	180		10,317			
1774	200	72	10,317	(57)*	3,247	(45)

*is based on 180 vessels—does not include 20 fishing vessels

Source: Decker, "The New London Merchants," p. 256A.

APPENDIX IV

NEW LONDON SHIPPING
ENTRANCES AND CLEARANCES
1758-1767

		Entrances	*Clearances*	*Total*
Coastal		411	573	984
West Indian		295	413	708
Foreign		8	24	32
	Total	714	1010	1724

Source: Decker, "The New London Merchants," p. 256.

APPENDIX V

NEW LONDON SHIPPING ACTIVITY
1758-1767
COASTAL

Port	*Entrances*	*Clearances*	*Total*
Newfoundland	1	2	3
Quebec	0	3	3
Louisburg	2	0	2
Halifax	22	35	57
Falmouth	21	24	45
Piscataqua	4	3	7
Salem	4	5	9
Boston	128	157	285
Plymouth	2	3	5
Nantucket	5	7	12
Newport	37	31	68
New Haven	0	5	5
New York	169	269	438
New Jersey	1	3	4
Philadelphia	4	7	11
Annapolis	5	8	13
Virginia	3	3	6
North Carolina	1	4	5
South Carolina	2	3	5
Georgia	0	1	1
Total	411	573	984

Source: Decker, "The New London Merchants," p. 253.

APPENDIX VI

NEW LONDON SHIPPING ACTIVITY
1758-1767
FOREIGN

Port	Entrances	Clearances	Total
Africa	1	9	10
Belfast	0	1	1
Canary Islands	0	1	1
Essequebo	1	0	1
Fayal	2	0	2
Gibraltar	0	2	2
Honduras	1	1	2
Leghorn	0	1	1
Liverpool	1	2	3
London	1	1	2
Madeira	1	2	3
Surinam	0	4	4
Total	8	24	32

Source: Decker, "The New London Merchants," p. 254.

APPENDIX VII

NEW LONDON SHIPPING ACTIVITY
1758-1767
WEST INDIAN

Port	Entrances	Clearances	Total
Anguilla	4	1	5
Antigua	31	46	77
Barbados	47	122	169
Cape Francois	0	1	1
Dominica	4	18	22
Grande-Terre	5	1	6
Grenada	8	25	33
Guadeloupe	6	24	30
Jamaica	19	52	71
Leeward Islands (Ports Unknown)	0	19	19
Marie Galante	1	0	1
Martinique	5	12	17
Monti Christi	4	0	4
Montserrat	9	5	14
Nevis	6	3	9
New Providence	5	5	10
Turks Island	42	1	43
St. Croix	6	2	8
St. Eustatins	3	1	4
St. Kitts	25	64	89

APPENDIX VII

NEW LONDON SHIPPING ACTIVITY
1758-1767
WEST INDIAN

Port	Entrances	Clearances	Total
St. Martin	39	2	41
Saltortuda	21	0	21
Tortola	5	9	14
Total	295	413	708

Source: Decker, "The New London Merchants," p. 255.

APPENDIX VIII

TYPES OF VESSELS IN NEW LONDON TRADE 1758-1767

Entrances at New London

	Schooners	Sloops	Brigs	Snows	Ships	Total
Coastal	42	177	12	0	0	231
West Indian	26	114	41	2	0	183
Other	1	1	0	0	1	3
Total	69	292	53	2	1	417

Clearances at New London

	Schooners	Sloops	Brigs	Snows	Ships	Total
Coastal	55	249	7	0	2	313
West Indian	33	258	54	1	0	346
Other	3	6	3	0	1	13
Total	91	513	64	1	3	672
Grand Total	160	805	127	3	4	1089

Source: Decker, "The New London Merchants," p. 252.

APPENDIX IX

CONNECTICUT NAVY—AMERICAN REVOLUTION

Vessel	Rig	Date	
Minervia	Brig	1775	Decommissioned (sold and was privateer)
Old Defence	Brig	1775-1776	Decommissioned (Capt. as a state privateer 1778)
Spy	Schooner	1775-1778	Captured
Crane	Galley	1776	Captured
Oliver Cromwell	Ship	1776-1779	Captured
Defence	Brig	1776-1779	Lost on reef

APPENDIX IX

CONNECTICUT NAVY—AMERICAN REVOLUTION

Vessel	Rig	Date	
New Defence	Galley	1776-1780	Captured
Shark	Galley	1776-1777	Captured
Whiting	Galley	1776	Captured
America	Brig	1777	No Record
Schuyler	Sloop	1777	Captured
Mifflin	Schooner	1777-1778	Sold
Guilford	Sloop	1779	Captured

Source: Decker, "The New London Merchants," p. 268.

APPENDIX X

LIST OF MAJOR MERCHANT OWNERS OF PRIVATEERS

Owner	Vessel	Rig	Prizes
Nathaniel Shaw, Jr.	American Revenue	Sloop	
	American Revenue	Sloop	15
	American Revenue	Sloop	1
	Black Sloven	Schooner	1
	Favorite	Brig	
	General Putnam	Schooner	14
	Lady Spencer		
	Le Despencer	Brig	3
	Le Despencer	Brig	2
	Nancy	Brig	1
	Revenge	Sloop	19
	Rochambeau	Snow	1
Total	12		57
Thomas Mumford	Deane	Ship	2
	Dolphin	Schooner	
	Gamecock	Schooner	
	Hancock	Sloop	15
	Hancock	Sloop	1
	Hancock	Brig	2
	Jay	Brig	3
	Lively	Sloop	3
	Marquis deLafayette	Brig	3
	Minerva	Brig	2
	Two Brothers	Sloop	
	Venus	Brig	2
Total	12		33

APPENDIX X

LIST OF MAJOR MERCHANT OWNERS OF PRIVATEERS

Owner	Vessel	Rig	Prizes
John Deshon	Black Sloven	Schooner	1
	Dandy	Brig	
	Enterprise	Schooner	
	Fair American	Brig	1
	Gamecock	Schooner	
	Hermione	Sloop	2
	John	Galley	3
	Patty	Sloop	1
	Spider	Galley	
Total	9		8

Total Recorded Privateers of New London	59
Total of Three Major Merchants	33
Total of Prizes Taken by New London Privateers	157
Total of Prizes Taken by the Three Major Merchants	98

Source: Decker, "The New London Merchants," p. 258.

APPENDIX XI

NUMBER OF SEAMEN REGISTERED AT NEW LONDON AND SELECTED PORTS FOR COMPARISON

		Total No. of Seamen				Foreign Born only			
Year	Month	New London	New Haven	New York	Boston	New London	New Haven	New York	Boston
1796	Sept.	187	24			6			
	Dec.	246	66		522	7	1		230
1797	March	75	44		189	1	2		54
	June	119	61	72	245	2		2	58
	Sept.	98		553				17	
	Dec.	106	59	701		2		31	
1798	March	39	26	330		3	1	17	
	June	106	37	502	878	6		6	2
	Sept.	28	19	225		1		9	
	Dec.	101	27	358	382	1		6	1
1799	March	106	22	556	335	3		14	1
	June	63	34	513	357			2	
	Sept.	31	47	166	316			9 ·	1
	Dec.		123	362	314			1	
1800	March	57	10	363	215			3	
	June	93	63	474	236		1	5	
	Sept.	106	54	377	204	1		3	1
	Dec.	160	82	408	221	1		1	

APPENDIX XI

NUMBER OF SEAMEN REGISTERED AT NEW LONDON AND
SELECTED PORTS FOR COMPARISON

| | | Total No. of Seamen | | | | Foreign Born only | | | |
Year	Month	New London	New Haven	New York	Boston	New London	New Haven	New York	Boston
1801	March	74	34	476	207	2			
	June	86			266				
	Sept.	56		298				1	
	Dec.	73	99		121	1			
1802	March	10		59				1	
	June		74						
	Sept.	6		10					
	Dec.								
1806	March	52			181				
	June	220		407	413				
	Sept.	92		379	211				
	Dec.	97		308	196				
1807	March				155				
	June	242		398	390				
	Sept.			355	134				
	Dec.	85		365					

Source: Decker, "The New London Merchants," p. 269.

APPENDIX XII

WHALING FIRMS

Firm	Years of Service	Number of Vessels
Allen, Lyman	1834-1853	5
Bassett, Abner	1832-1850	2
Beck, William	1841-1842	1
N. & W. W. Billings	1824-1851	12
Brown, Benjamin	1830-1849	9
Benjamin Brown's Sons	1850-1861	7
Chapman, S.	1863-1866	3
Chapell, Richard H.	1855-1870	16
Chew, Coleby	1834-1836	1
Darrow, Mose	1864-1867	1
Deshon, Daniel	1819-1824	2
Fitch, Daniel	1841-1842	1
Fitch, Harris T.	1855	1
Fitch, Thomas	1859-1863	6
Fitch, Thomas 2nd	1843-1858	9
Fitch & Leonard	1841-1842	1
Frink, A. M.	1829	1
Frink, A. M. & E. M.	1832-1833	2
Frink, E. M.	1827-1829	1

APPENDIX XII

WHALING FIRMS

Firm	*Years of Service*	*Number of Vessels*
E. M. Frink & Co.	1831-1836	6
Frink, Chew & Co.	1837-1851	8
Frink & Prentis	1852-1863	5
Green, James	1850-1854	1
Harris, James R.	1908-1909	1
Haven, Henry P.	1864-1865	1
Havens & Smith	1834-1846	22
Havens, Williams & Co.	1875-1880	13
S. Hobron & Son	1864-1866	1
Huntley, George	1855-1862	4
Lawrence, Joseph	1833-1845	12
Lawrence & Co.	1856-1892	14
Learned, E. H.	1843-1844	1
Learned & Stoddard	1844-1848	5
Lee	1821-1823	2
Lee, Dr. Samuel	1804-1809	3
Lord, Samuel Phillips	1797-1798	1
Miner, C. A.	1881-1882	1
Miner, E. P.	1880-1882	1
Miner, Sanford E.	1879-1880	1
Miner, Lawrence & Co.	1846-1857	10
Morgan, Ebenezer	1867-1870	1
Morgan, R. A.	1871	1
Palmer, Robert W.	1899-1900	1
Reed, W. A. (or Chas. Barns)	1856-1857	1
Perkins & Smith	1842-1861	20
Stoddard, E. V.	1849-1863	11
Tate, William	1840-1847	4
Weaver & Rogers	1845-1851	2
Weaver, C. A.	1844-1849	1
Weaver, Rogers & Co.	1850-1859	2
Williams, C. A.	1856-1892	13
Williams, Thomas W.	1819-1841	10
Williams, Gen. William	1798-1823	2
Williams, William, Jr. & Acors Barns	1827-1835	2
Williams & Barns	1836-1875	10
Williams & Haven	1847-1875	22
Williams, Haven & Co.	1868-1878	13
X (Name Unknown & Co.)	1799-1802	4

Source: Robert Owen Decker, *The New London Whaling Industry* (York, Pennsylvania: Shumway, 1973), Appendix II.

APPENDIX XIII

MAIN PORTS INVOLVED IN AMERICAN WHALING 1718-1928

Main Ports	No. of Vessels	No. of Voyages
New Bedford	806	4303
Nantucket	364	1402
New London	260	1000
Provincetown	161	902
San Francisco	164	866

Source: Decker, *New London Whaling Industry,* Appendix V.

APPENDIX XIV

NEW LONDON WHALING INTEREST AND THEIR STOCK
IN THE NEW LONDON, WILLIMANTIC AND PALMER RAILROAD

WHALING AGENTS AND SHARES HELD

Thomas W. Williams	200	Sidney Miner	40
W. W. Billings	150	Lyman Allyn	50
Joseph Lawrence	100	Thomas Fitch	50
Acors Barns	70	A. M. Frink	65
Henry Haven	20	Ezra Chappell	20
Perkins and Smith	70		

WHALING INVESTORS AND SHARES HELD

Robert Coit	10	W. W. Coit	25
N. S. Perkins	90	Joseph Smith	40
Jonathan Coit	50	John Brandegee	85

OTHERS CONNECTED WITH WHALING AND THEIR SHARES

Francis Allyn	35	Andrew Lippitt	20
Charles Lewis	50		

Source: Decker, "The New London Merchants," p. 336.

APPENDIX XV

NEW LONDON, WILLIMANTIC AND PALMER STOCK

Area	No. of Shares Holders	No. of Shares Held	Average Holding	Percent of Total Holders	Percent of Total Shares
All Areas	924	4,607	4.99	100	100
New London	692	3,955	5.27	74.89	85.85

APPENDIX XV

NEW LONDON, WILLIMANTIC AND PALMER STOCK

Area	No. of Shares Holders	No. of Shares Held	Average Holding	Percent of Total Holders	Percent of Total Shares
Other Towns on Routes	223	616	2.76	24.13	13.37
New York	9	36	4.00	.98	.78
All Non-New London Areas	232	652	2.81	25.11	14.15

Source: Decker, "The New London Merchants," p. 337.

APPENDIX XVI

NEW LONDON, WILLIMANTIC AND PALMER RAILROAD COMPANY

Year	Gross Earnings	Expenditures	Taxes & Interest		Net Earnings	Dividends
1850	66,460	28,000	35,000	3,460		
1851	102,055	58,200	31,541	12,314		
1852	114,410	62,509	60,759	8,858	Loss	
1853	129,715	73,820	62,611	6,716	Loss	
1854	137,060	65,356	67,986	3,718		
1855	124,043	57,712	66,111	220		
1856	120,571	69,027	25,350	26,194	Retained but interest only partially paid	
1857	115,803	69,441	41,176	5,186		
1858	104,464	57,235	23,065	24,161		
1859	Into Receivership					
1860	Reorganized as New London Northern Railroad Company					
1861	93,835.82	76,664.60	3,000.23	14,170.15		
1862	151,730.73	101,077.44	11,887.13	38,766.16		30,206.60
1863	195,055.20	121,966.43	16,405.69	56,683.88		43,148.99

Source: Decker, "The New London Merchants," p. 338.

APPENDIX XVII

NEW LONDON NORTHERN RAILROAD

(April to Dec.)	1861	1862	1863
Earnings	93,835.82	151,730.73	195,055.20
Expenditures	76,664.60	101,077.44	108,177.83
Taxes and Interest	3,000.23	11,887.13	16,405.69

APPENDIX XVII

NEW LONDON NORTHERN RAILROAD

(April to Dec.)	1861	1862	1863
Improvements			13,788.60
Net Earnings	14,170.15	38,766.11	56,683.88
Dividends		12,043.04	21,075.32
		18,163.56	21,073.67
Cash on Hand		8,659.56	
Cash from Year Earlier		2,131.23	
Total Cash		10,791.79	14,534.89
Miles travelled		93,269	155,916
Passengers carried		109,169	176,732

Source: Decker, "The New London Merchants," p. 339.

APPENDIX XVIII

FINANCIAL INSTITUTIONS OF
NEW LONDON

Names	Date Established	Date Closed	National Bank
*Union Bank	1792	1963	1865-1882
**New London Bank (N.L. City Nat. Bank)	1807	1953	1865
Savings Bank of New London	1827		
Whaling Bank	1833	1943	1865
Pequot Bank	1851	no record of operations	
**Bank of Commerce (Nat'l Bk., Commerce)	1852	1953	1864
New London County Savings Bank	1855	1858	
Mechanics and Farmers Assoc. and Bank	1855	1858	
First National Bank	1864	1877	1864-1877
Equitable Trust Company	1867	1881	
Mariners Savings Bank	1867	1939	
Dime Savings Bank	1873	1882	
New London Trust	1874	Unk.	
N.L. Trust & Safe Deposit Co.	1904	no record of operations	
N.L. Building & Loan Assoc. (First N.L. Savings and Loan)	1914		
***Winthrop Trust Company	1922	1972	
New London Federal Savings & Loan Association	1935		

Source: *A Century of Banking in New London* (New London: The Savings Bank of New London, 1927),
William F. Hasse, Jr., *A History of Money and Banking in Connecticut* (New Haven: Privately
Printed, 1957) and Francis Parsons, *The History of Banking in Connecticut* (New Haven: Yale
University Press, 1934).

*Merged with Conn. Bank. & Trust Co., 1963.
**Merged with Hartford National Bank & Trust Co., 1953
***Merged with Union Trust Co., 1972.

APPENDIX XIX

MAYORS OF NEW LONDON

Name	Dates	No. Years	
Richard Law	1784-1806	22 Years	
Jeremiah E. Brainerd	1806-1829	23 Years	
Elias Perkins	1829-1832	3 Years	(3 Year Terms)
Coddington Billings	1832-1835	3 Years	
Noyes Billings	1835-1837	2 Years	
Jirah Isham	1837-1838	1 Year	
Francis Allyn	1838-1841	3 Years	
George Wilson	1841	1 Year	
Caleb J. Allen	1841-1843	2 Years	
Andrew M. Frink	1843-1845	2 Years	
John P. C. Mather	1845-1850	4 Years	
Andrew Lippitt	1850-1853	3 Years	
Henry P. Haven	1853-1856	3 Years	
Jonathan N. Harris	1856-1862	6 Years	
Hiram Wiley	1862-1865	3 Years	
Frederick L. Allen	1865-1871	6 Years	
Augustus Brandegee	1871-1873	2 Years	
Thomas W. Waller	1873-1879	6 Years	
Robert Coit	1879-1882	3 Years	
George Starr	1882-1885	3 Years	
C. A. Williams	1885-1888	3 Years	
George E. Tinker	1888-1891	3 Years	
George Williams	1891	1 Year	
Philip C. Dunford	1891	1 Year	(Acting)
Ralph Wheeler	1891-1893	2 Years	
A. J. Bentley	1893-1894	1 Year	
James P. Johnston	1894-1897	3 Years	
Cyrus G. Beckwith	1897-1900	3 Years	
M. Wilson Dart	1900-1903	3 Years	
Bryan F. Mahan	1903-1906	3 Years	
Alton T. Miner	1905	5 Months	(Acting)
Benjamin Armstrong	1906-1909	3 Years	
Bryan F. Mahan	1909-1915	6 Years	
Ernest E. Rogers	1915-1918	3 Years	
E. Frank Morgan	1918-1921	3 Years	
Lucius E. Whiton	1921-1922	1 Year	(1 Year Terms)
John F. Murray	1922-1923	1 Year	
Malcolm M. Scott	1923-1924	1 Year	
Waldo E. Clarke	1924-1925	1 Year	
William C. Fox	1925-1927	2 Years	
James A. May	1927-1928	1 Year	
Malcolm M. Scott	1928-1929	1 Year	
Cornelius D. Twomey	1929-1930	1 Year	
E. Frank Morgan	1930-1931	1 Year	
James A. May	1931-1932	1 Year	
Malcolm M. Scott	1932-1933	1 Year	
Alton T. Miner	1933-1934	1 Year	

APPENDIX XIX

MAYORS OF NEW LONDON

Name	Dates	No. Years
Cornelius D. Twomey	1934-1935	1 Year
Edwin Cruise	1935-1937	2 Years
Leo B. Reagan	1937	
Joseph A. St. Germain	1937-1938	1 Year
Alton T. Miner	1938-1939	1 Year
Leo B. Reagan	1939-1940	1 Year
Robert B. Chappell	1940-1941	1 Year
Lewis B. Doane	1941-1942	1 Year
Theodore N. Hansen	1942-1943	1 Year
Lewis B. Doane	1943-1944	1 Year
Frank N. Kelly	1944-1945	1 Year
James A. May	1945-1946	1 Year
Richard R. Morgan	1946-1947	1 Year
Richard R. Morgan	1947-1948	1 Year
Samuel J. Selleck	1948-1949	1 Year
Fred Benvenuti	1949-1950	1 Year
Frank N. Kelly	1950-1951	1 Year
Moses A. Savin	1951-1952	1 Year
Fred Benvenuti	1952-1953	1 Year
Thomas J. Griffin	1953-1954	1 Year
Thomas G. Martin	1954-1955	1 Year
Thomas G. Martin	1955-1956	1 Year
Moses A. Savin	1956-1957	1 Year
John P. Janovic	1957-1958	1 Year
Anthony J. Impellitteri	1958-1959	1 Year
Wilfred A. Park	1959-1960	1 Year
Moses Savin	1960-1961	1 Year
Harvey Mallove	1961-1962	1 Year
Richard R. Martin	1962-1963	1 Year
Joseph E. Regan	1963-1964	1 Year
Thomas J. Griffin	1964-1965	1 Year
Francis T. Londregan	1965-1966	1 Year
Harvey N. Mallove	1966-1967	1 Year
Richard R. Martin	1967-1968	1 Year
Joseph F. Regan	1968-1969	1 Year
Thomas J. Griffin	1969-1970	1 Year
Richard R. Martin	1970-1971	1 Year
Hubert A. Neilan	1971-1972	1 Year
Daniel D. Schwartz	1972-1973	1 Year
William Nahas	1973-1974	1 Year
Thomas L. Harrington	1974-	

Source: Connecticut *Register and Manual* (Hartford: Printed by State, 1784-1975).

APPENDIX XX

PRESIDENTS OF
NEW LONDON COUNTY HISTORICAL SOCIETY

Name	*Term of Office*
LaFayette S. Foster	1871-1880
David A. Wells	1880-1882
Charles Augustus Williams	1882-1900
Ernest E. Rogers	1900-1916
George S. Palmer	1916-1921
Ernest E. Rogers	1921-1931
Mrs. George Maynard Miner	1931-1940
Elmer H. Spaulding	1940-1950
Frank Valentine Chappell	1950-1952
Dwight C. Lyman	1952-1964
Carlton F. Small	1964-1969
John Winthrop	1969-1974
Harold Cone	1974-

Source: Connecticut *Register and Manual* (Hartford: Printed by State, 1872-1975).

APPENDIX XXI

DEFENDERS OF FORT TRUMBULL

New Londoners Who Fell at Fort Griswold*

William Bolton
Lieutenant Richard Chapman
John Clark
Elias Coit
Lieutenant James Comstock
William Comstock
Captain Peter Richards
John Whittlesey
Captain Adam Shapley
John Holt, Jr.
Benoni Kenson
Barney Kinney
Stephen Whittlesey

Names of the Wounded

Sergeant Stephen Hempstead
Samuel Booth Hempstead
Elijah Richards
Jonathon Whaley

APPENDIX XXI

DEFENDERS OF FORT TRUMBULL

New Londoners Who Fell at Fort Griswold*

Prisoners Carried Off

Elias Dart
Levi Dart
Lieutenant Jabex Stow
Corporal Josiah Smith

*Others, Both Unhurt and Wounded, Not Taken Prisoners

Japheth Mason
John Prentis

Total 23

---

* Most casualties took place on the Groton side of the river as Fort Trumbull's defenders retreated because of British military superiority and attempted to reach Fort Griswold in three boats of which one was captured by the British.

Source: Rufus Avery and Statement of Avery Downer, M.D., Battle of Groton Heights: A Story of the Storming effort Griswold and the Burning of New London on the Sixth of September, 1781 (E. E. Darrow, New London, Connecticut) 1931.

APPENDIX XXII

ELEMENTARY AND HIGH SCHOOL CHART

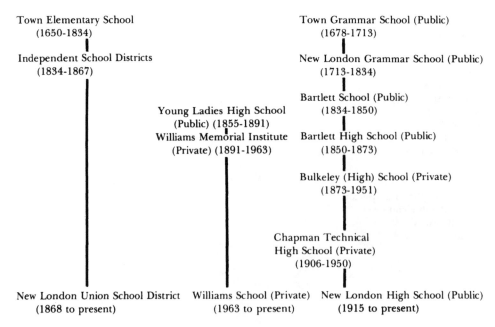

Town Elementary School (1650-1834)

Independent School Districts (1834-1867)

Young Ladies High School (Public) (1855-1891)
Williams Memorial Institute (Private) (1891-1963)

Town Grammar School (Public) (1678-1713)

New London Grammar School (Public) (1713-1834)

Bartlett School (Public) (1834-1850)

Bartlett High School (Public) (1850-1873)

Bulkeley (High) School (Private) (1873-1951)

Chapman Technical High School (Private) (1906-1950)

New London Union School District (1868 to present)

Williams School (Private) (1963 to present)

New London High School (Public) (1915 to present)

APPENDIX XXIII

NEW LONDON SCHOOL SUPERINTENDENTS

1886-1890	Joseph P. Brown
1890-1891	Samuel T. Adams
1891-1907	Charles B. Jennings (Acting School Visitor)
1908-1918	Charles B. Jennings (Supt. of Schools)
1918-1945	Warren A. Hanson
1945-1948	George R. Champlin
1948-1955	John C. Albohm
1955-1961	John F. Murphy
1961-1965	Laurence N. Scanlon
1965-	Joseph E. Medeiros

Source: Board of Education Records.

APPENDIX XXIV

PRINCIPALS OF WILLIAMS MEMORIAL INSTITUTE

1891-1938	Colin S. Buell
1938-1939	Madeleine Freeman (Acting)
1939-1946	Jerome Burtt
1946-1947	Mary T. Talcott (Acting)
1947-1956	Gertrude P. Moon
1956-1960	Evelyn Page
1960-1963	Catherine Oakes
1963-	Marion H. Hamilton (title changed to Headmistress)

APPENDIX XXV

PRINCIPALS OF CHAPMAN TECHNICAL HIGH SCHOOL

1906-1937	Frederick J. Hitchcock
1937-1950	Horace G. Wescott

APPENDIX XXVI

PRINCIPALS OF BULKELEY SCHOOL

1873-1880	E. B. Hollister
1880-1888	E. R. Hall

APPENDIX XXVI

PRINCIPALS OF BULKELEY SCHOOL

1888-1921	Walter A. Towne
1921-1944	Homer K. Underwood
1944-1948	Herbert A. Archibald
1948-1951	Arthur L. Hjortland

APPENDIX XXVII

PRESIDENTS OF CONNECTICUT COLLEGE

1915-1917	Dr. Frederick H. Sykes
1917-1928	Dr. Benjamin T. Marshall
1929-1943 and 1945-1946	Dr. Katharine Blunt
1943-1945	Dr. Dorothy Schaffter
1947-1962	Dr. Rosemary Park
1962-1974	Dr. Charles E. Shain
1974-	Dr. Oakes Ames

GUIDE TO ABBREVIATIONS
USED IN CITATIONS

C.A.	Connecticut Archives.
C.H.C.	Connecticut Historical Society Collections.
C.H.S.	Connecticut Historical Society.
C.R.	*Public Records of the Colony of Connecticut.*
C.S.L.	Connecticut State Library.
C.S.M.	Colonial Society of Massachusetts.
D.A.B.	*Dictionary of American Biography.*
G.B.R.	*Genealogical and Biographical Record of New London County, Connecticut.*
M.H.C.	*Massachusetts Historical Society Collection.*
M.H.S.	Massachusetts Historical Society.
R & M	*Register and Manual,* State of Connecticut.
R & P	*Records and Papers,* New London County Historical Society.
S.M.	Shaw Mansion Collection.
S.R.	*Public Records of the State of Connecticut.*

References

(Footnotes)

Introduction

1. Richard Foster Flint identifies Connecticut's four physiographic sections as the Connecticut Valley Lowlands, the Eastern and Western New England Uplands and the Taconic Section in *The Glacial Geology of Connecticut,* p. 28; William North Rice and Herbert Ernest Gregory divide Connecticut into three major physiographic parts in *Manual of Geology,* p. 17.
2. R. R. Hinman, *Letters from the English Kings and Queens . . . to the Governors of the Colony of Connecticut, . . . From 1635 to 1749,* pp. 138-139.
3. John Bartlet Brebner, *The Explorers of North America, 1492-1806,* pp. 91, 224-225; Howard I. Chapelle, *The History of American Sailing Ships,* p. 6.
4. *Towns of New England and Old England,* II, p. 139, New London *Day,* May 12, 1904.
5. Robert C. Black, III, *The Younger John Winthrop,* pp. 124, 141; Richard S. Dunn, *Puritans and Yankees: The Winthrop Dynasty of New England, 1630-1717,* p. 70.
6. Black, pp. 15, 22, 68-69, 124, 218.
7. Dunn, pp. 59-61, 64.
8. Bernard Bailyn, *The Colonial Merchants in the Seventeenth Century,* pp. 27, 64-70, 72-83, 86, 105-114, 143, 167-168, 193, 201, 209.
9. C. R., III, 297, 299, 301; IV, 374-375, 397; Roland Mather Hooker, *The Colonial Trade of Connecticut,* pp. 12-14; George Clark, *A History of Connecticut, Its People and Institutions,* p. 189; C. A., Trade and Maritime Affairs 1668-1789, I, 43.
10. Dunn, pp. 74-75; Alden T. Vaughan, *New England Frontier, Puritans and Indians 1620-1675,* pp. 122-154; letter from Roger Williams to John Winthrop, Jr., June 2, 1637, *Winthrop Papers,* M.H.S., III, 426-428.
11. Frances M. Caulkins, *History of New London,* pp. 52-54, 126-127; C. R., II, 512.
12. Douglas Edward Leach, *Flintlock and Tomahawk: New England in King Philip's War,* pp. 44-45, 58, 92, 106-107, 113, 122-123, 125, 139, 146.
13. Black, p. 141; Dorothy Deming, *The Settlement of the Connecticut Towns,* pp. 17-18; Dunn, p. 73; Richard A. Wheeler, "The First Organized Church in New London County", R. & P., II, pt. III, 11.
14. C. R., I, 224, 310; II, 557-558; IV, 510-511; S. R., VI, 268-270; X, 349-351.
15. Dunn, p. 74; C. R., I, 310.

Chapter I   Colonial New London: Its Leaders

1. R. & M.
2. Lila Parrish Lyman, *The New London Homestead (1754-1892) of the Winthrop Family,* pp. 3-8; Dunn, pp. 191-194.
3. Dunn, pp. 202-203.
4. *Ibid.*
5. The Will of John Winthrop, M.S. Winthrop Papers, S.M.
6. Dunn, pp. 194-201, 204, 209-210, 234, 241-243.

7. Caulkins, pp. 226-227.

8. Dunn, pp. 295-296.

9. C. R., VII, 136, 571-579; *Diary of Joshua Hempstead, 1711-1758,* p. 490; Charles M. Andrews, *The Connecticut Intestacy Law,* pp. 12-28.

10. *Hempstead Diary.*

11. A number of documents dealing with the Saltonstall-Winthrop dispute can be found in the Winthrop Papers, a document referring to the dispute dated October, 1733; a Deed of partition into five parts of the Winthrop lands, 1750; a deed from John S. Winthrop to Gurdon Saltonstall for land in Massachusetts, 1772; a decree of Norwich Superior Court allowing Saltonstall 450 pounds (30 pounds a year for 15 years), March 4, 1788.

12. S. Leroy Blake, "Gurdon Saltonstall, Scholar, Preacher, Statesman", R. & P., II pt. V, 3-28.

13. *Ibid.*

14. *Ibid.*

15. *Ibid.*

16. Richard Bushman, *Puritan to Yankee,* p. 57.

17. Caulkins, pp. 235, 238, 285-286, 307-308; Frederick Chapman, *Coit Family,* pp. 16-17.

18. *Ibid.*

19. *The New London Repository,* January 10, 1861; Caulkins p. 506n; George Munson Curtis, *Eearly Silver of Connecticut and Its Makers,* pp. 45-46.

20. Elizabeth Gorton, "A Backward Glance", R. & P., III, pt. II, 169-170; Ernest E. Rogers, *Connecticut's Naval Office at New London,* p. 69; *The Latest View of New London.*

21. Rogers, pp. 68, 77, 79, Caulkins, pp. 242, 512; Hempstead, pp. 253, 339.

22. Rogers, pp. 6, 77; Caulkins, p. 512n.

23. D.A.B., XVII, 45; Rogers, pp. 6, 9, 79, 133.

24. Rogers, pp. 6, 9.

25. Many letters of these families can be found in Shaw's Mercantile Letter Book, MS, Yale.

26. Rogers, pp. 77-78.

27. Carl Cutler, Queens of the Western Ocean, p. 14.

28. Appendix VIII.

29. Caulkins, p. 242.

30. Chapman, pp. 16, 29-30; Caulkins, pp. 34, 230-238; G.B.R., p. 13; Charles Burr Todd, *In Olde Connecticut,* pp. 71-73.

31. Chapman, pp. 16-17; Appendix II; Mehetabel Chandler Coit, *Her Book,* pp. 6-8; Hempstead, pp. 1, 32, 92, 166, 241, 294-295.

32. Caulkins, p. 231.

33. Hempstead recorded that Captain Jeffrey launched his "pink sterned ship" December 1, 1729, *Diary,* p. 215. He mentions a new ship at New London harbor, November 28, 1736, built by Jeffrey, p. 312. Caulkins, pp. 237-242; Todd, p. 75, Clark, p. 190.

34. Hempstead, pp. 20, 38, 57, 169.

Chapter II   Colonial New London: Its Commerce

1. C. R., III, 291-300; VII, 580-585; IX, 593-596; X, 619-626; XIV, 494-501.

2. Caulkins, p. 501.

3. Appendix III.

4. Appendix IV.

5. Appendix VII; unfortunately three factors make it difficult to form a complete picture of New London shipping—no complete collection of all issues of newspapers exists; all papers did not carry a marine list; those papers which did include a marine list did not always identify the rig of each vessel.

6. Appendix VI.

7. Appendix VIII.

8. Roger Williams McAdam, *Salts of the Sound*, p. 96; Clark, p. 189; Todd, pp. 71-72; John Stoughton, *A Corner Stone of Colonial Commerce*, pp. 14-15; C. R., I, 380.

9. Hempstead, p. 373; Hooker, *Colonial Trade*, pp. 8-9.

10. Margaret E. Martin, *Merchants and Trade in the Connecticut River Valley, 1750-1820*, pp. 24, 26, 45-46; Appendix V.

11. A. P. Brigham, *Geographical Influences in American History,* p. 57.

12. Todd, pp. 72-73.

13. Clark, p. 190; Caulkins, pp. 232, 241, 483; Todd, p. 74; Hempstead, p. 144.

14. Oscar Zeichner, *Connecticut's Years of Controversy, 1750-1776*, p. 41; Timothy Dwight, *Travels in New England and New York*, I, 22, 236.

15. Caulkins, p. 241.

16. Hempstead, p. 475.

17. Robert Greenhalgh Ablion and Jennie Barnes Pope, *Sea Lanes in Wartime*, pp. 31, 63.

18. John, Joseph and William Shaw were lost in the West Indian trade, Rogers, pp. 7, 80; "Joseph Coit Personal History" MS, C.H.S.

19. Hempstead, p. 61.

20. Hempstead, pp. 61, 66; Caulkins, p. 241; registration form for vessels provided for listing of guns carried, Record Group 45, New London Customs Records, Federal Records Center, Waltham, Massachusetts.

21. "Markets are very dull in all the Islands," New London Gazette, March 4, 1768; letter from Nathaniel Shaw, Jr., to Peter Vandervoort & Co., New York, October 14, 1774, "unless the times alter we had better do nothing than Import molasses", Mercantile Letter Book.

22. Caulkins, pp. 238-242; Hempstead, p. 264.

23. *Pitkin Papers: Correspondence and Documents of William Pitkin's Governorship of the Colony of Connecticut, 1766-69*, C.H.C., XIX, 99-103; Samuel A. Peters, *A General History of Connecticut from its First Settlement*, pp. 271-275.

24. N. Shaw Perkins, "New London Society for Trade and Commerce", R. & P., II, pt. II, 147; Caulkins believed the Society was organized in 1730, pp. 242-243; Andrew McFarland Davis criticized Caulkins for making several errors in her presentation. He claimed 1732 as the date for the organization of the Society, but admitted it might have been earlier. Davis takes no notice of the Perkins article, "A Connecticut Land Bank," C.S.M., V, 98-99; Hooker agrees

with the 1730 date of the organization of the Society, p. 29; C.A., Trade and Maritime Affairs 1668-1780, I, 161-163.

25. C. R., VII, 390-392; Perkins, 146-149; Davis, pp. 97-98; Caulkins, p. 243; Timothy Green, public printer for Connecticut, arranged for the paper and engraving of the notes issued by the Society, Davis, p. 100; a facsimile of one of the notes is reproduced in the C.R., VII, 410; Hempstead, pp. 27, 266, 284; Clark, p. 190.

26. Caulkins, p. 243; Perkins, 146; Clark, p. 190; Hempstead, pp. 27, 284; C.A., Trade and Maritime Affairs 1668-1789, I, 186, 200, 203.

27. C.R., VII, 420-423; *The Talcott Papers: Correspondence and Documents (Chiefly Official) During Joseph Talcott's Governorship of the Colony of Connecticut, 1724-1741,* C.H.C., IV, 268-271; Caulkins, p. 243; Davis, 101, 103, 104; C.A., Finance and Currency 1677-1789, II, 361, 364; Hempstead, pp. 255-257; Perkins, 145-148.

28. C.A., Trade and Maritime, Series 1, I, pt. 1, 101, 167-170, 214-233; II, pt. 1, 92, 94, 95; Series 2, III, 93-95; Finance and Currency, 2nd Series, II, 1738-1753, 140, 141, 142; C.R. VII, 309, 438, 445, 449-456, 490, 491, 492, 508, 560; VIII, 234-235; Davis, 104; Perkins, 150; Hempstead, p. 288.

29. Letter from Nathaniel Shaw, Jr., to Peter Vandervoort, January 29, 1773; letter from Nathaniel Shaw, Jr., to Lane & Fraser, December 22, 1774, MSS, Yale.

30. Caulkins, p. 483n.

31. Bailyn, pp. 80, 90; Caulkins, pp. 234-235; Rogers, p. 7; Dwight, *Travels,* I, 222, 236.

32. *Early Connecticut Probate Records,* I, 101.

33. Robert Owen Decker, "New London: Its Maritime Story" *Stamford Genealogical Society Bulletin,* XV, Nos. 1, 2, 3, (September, November, January, 1972-1973).

34. Letter from Samuel Welch to Ebenezer Grant, February 11, 1766, MS, C.H.S.; letter from William Packwood to Shaw, March 27, 1769, Shaw Papers, S.M.

35. Letter from J. Gaignard to Shaw, October, 12, 1772, Shaw Papers, S.M.

36. New London *Gazette,* September 20 and 27, 1791; *The Groundfish Industries of New England and Canada,* Circular 121 United States Department of Interior, Fish and Wild Life Division (Washington Government Printing Office, 1961).

37. Hooker, Colonial Trade, pp. 11-13, 17-18; Bailyn, pp. 149-150; C.A., Trade and Maritime Affairs, 1668-1789, I, 53, 62, 76, 516, 576.

38. C.R., V, 149.

39. C.R., V, 149, 513; VI, 95; Hooker, *Colonial Trade,* pp. 19, 24-26; C.A., I, 61, 72, 75, 98.

40. *New London Summary,* December 8, 1758, March 21, 1760, September 26, 1760, April 10, 1761; New London *Day,* April 7, 1926.

41. Rogers, pp. 4, 68-69; Hempstead, pp. 367, 445, 451, 662; Caulkins, pp. 469-470.

42. Caulkins, p. 474; C.A., Insolvent Debtors, I, 1762-1782, 2, 39-42, 100-102.

43. Letter of Gerard G. Beekman to David Lewis, February 5, 1753: Philip White (ed.), *The Beekman Mercantile Papers 1747-1799,* I, 171-172.

44. Letters from Gerard G. Beekman to Joseph Chew, January 9, October 29, 1764 and August 26, 1765: White, I, 445-456, 485.

45. New London *Gazette*, September 18, 1772; November 1, 1771; May 1, 1772; November 8, 1771; November 20, 1772; December 28, 1770; November 29, 1771; September 13, 1771; November 16, 1770; November 13, 1772.

46. Caulkins, pp. 409-410.

47. Curtis, pp. 72-73; Jennifer F. Goldsborough, *An Exhibition of New London Silver 1700 to 1835*, p. 8.

48. Letter from Gurdon Saltonstall to Roger Wolcott, December 13, 1753, *Wolcott Papers*, 402-403; Hempstead, pp. 620, 622, 624, 625; Caulkins, pp. 464-468.

Chapter III   New London's Role in the American Revoltuion

1. New London *Gazette*, November 18, November 25, 1763; January 6, 1764.

2. Charles McArthur Destler, *Joshua Coit: American Federalist 1758-1798*, p.5; Martin, p. 33; Chapelle, *Sailing Ships*, p. 31.

3. Martin, pp. 21-30; Rogers, p. 8; Zeichner, p. 83; letters from Nathaniel Shaw, Jr., to Peter Vandervoort, February 5, 13, 1767; Thomas and Isaac Wharton, June 12, 1771.

4. New London *Gazette*, May 4, June 15, 1764.

5. *Leading Business Men of New London;* Zeichner, pp. 54, 65; letter from Nathaniel Shaw, Jr. to Jos. and Wm. Packwood, January 20, 1766, Shaw Collection, Yale.

6. Letter from Nathaniel Shaw, Jr., to Jos. and Wm. Packwood, January 20, 1766, Shaw Collection, Yale.

7. Letters from Nathaniel Shaw, Jr., to Jos. and Wm. Packwood, January 20, 1766; to Peter Vandervoort, July 22, 1766.

8. New London *Gazette*, November 11, 1766, January 23, 1767; C.R., XIII, 126, 422.

9. New London *Gazette*, June 2, 1769.

10. Destler, p. 4.

11. New London *Gazette*, May 6, July 1, 1768.

12. New London *Gazette*, February 10, 1769.

13. New London *Gazette*, July 14, 1769. Letter from Nathaniel Shaw, Jr., to John Stoddard, May 15, 1759, Shaw Collections, Yale; letter from Nathaniel Shaw, Jr., to Peter Vandervoort, May 15, 1769, Shaw Collection, Yale.

14. Letter from Nathaniel Shaw, Jr., to John Stoddard, May 15, 1769, Shaw Collection, Yale; Zeichner, p. 83; *Pitkin Papers*, 200-201; letter from Nathaniel Shaw, Jr., to John and George Erving, September 14, 1769, Shaw Collection, Yale.

15. New London *Gazette*, August 25, September 8, 1769.

16. *Ibid.*, April 7, 1769.

17. Sanford, *Connecticut*, p. 182; New London *Gazette*, August 11, 18, 1789; June 15, July 6, 1770; C.R., XIII, 236.

18. New London *Gazette*, March 2, May 11, 1770.

19. *Ibid*, July 13, August 10, October 5, 1770; Caulkins, p. 502.

20. New London *Gazette*, April 10, 1772.

21. *Ibid.*, January 24, February 28, October 25, December 4, 11, 1772.

22. *Ibid.*, April 10, 1772, October 23, 1772.

23. Letter from Nathaniel Shaw, Jr., to Peter Vandervoort, October 22, 1773, Shaw Collection, Yale.

24. The Parade was an open area at the foot of State Street; *Connecticut Gazette,* July 1, 1774; Rogers, p. 23; Caulkins, p. 503; *Leading Businessmen of New London;* New London *Day,* September 18, 22, 1926.

25. Caulkins, pp. 501-512 *passim;* Van Dusen, p. 133; *Latest Views of New London,* n.p.

26. Christopher Ward, *The War of the Revolution,* I, 248; letter from Nathaniel Shaw, Jr., to Jonathan Trumbull, August 7, 1776, Shaw Collection, Yale.

27. Middlebrook, I, 3.

28. New London *Day,* October 4, 1893.

29. C.R., XIV, 264, 323, 346, 434; XV, 86, 233, 238-240; "Trumbull Papers," M.H.S., IV, 182; V, 4; William H. Starr, *Centenial Historical Sketch,* p. 16.

30. C.R., XV, 246; S.R., I, 83; Caulkins, pp. 520-524; Starr, p. 161.

31. Sir William James, *The British Navy in Adversity,* pp. 16-18, 427; Caulkins, pp. 516, 517, 525.

32. Christopher Ward, *The War of the Revolution,* I, 248; letter from Nathaniel Shaw, Jr., to Jonathan Trumbull, August 7, 1776, Shaw Collection, Yale.

33. Middlebrook, I, 3.

34. S.R., I, 184, 328-329, 388-389; Martin, p. 34; letter from Nathaniel Shaw, Jr., to Captain Handy, May 31, 1775, Shaw Collection, Yale.

35. C.R., XV, 99-100, 109.

36. C.R., XV, 111, 117, 200, 481, 488, 492; Francis H. Parker, "The Connecticut Navy in the Revolutionary War", pp. 9-10; Middlebrook, I, 9-10; II, 169-170; Caulkins, pp. 538-539; "Revolutionary Captains." 51.

37. S.R., I, 188, 318, 321-322, 334, 556; Middlebrook, I, 10, 214; Parker, p. 22.

38. Thomas S. Collier, "The Revolutionary Privateers of Connecticut", R. & P., I, pt IV, 6; Middlebrook, II, 11; Harold C. Bailey gives an excellent description of Connecticut privateering in "Connecticut's Share in Winning Independence at Sea", Unpublished MS, C.H.S.

39. Bailey, "Connecticut's Share," p. 2, 16; Edgar S. Maclay, *A History of the American Privateer,* pp. 9-10; letters from Oliver Wolcott to George Wyllys, April 17, 1777, *Wyllys Papers, 1590-1796,* XXI 452; Middlebrook, I; Connecticut *Gazette,* June 9, June 30, 1778.

40. Middlebrook, I, IX; II, 258.

41. "Connecticut Merchant Marine, "MS; Collier, pp. 7, 8, 13; Papers of the *Hancock* MSS, R & P; New London *Repository,* November 8, 1860.

42. Appendix X.

43. Bailey, "Independence at Sea," p. 3.

44. *Connecticut Gazette,* November 20, 1778.

45. Collier, 10.

46. Rogers, pp. 54-55, 61-62; Collier, 60.

47. Connecticut *Gazette,* June 3, 1779; Collier, pp. 10, 11, 25.

48. Letters from Benedict Arnold to Nathaniel Shaw, Jr., June 8, July 10, 1777, March 2, August 19, 1780, Shaw Papers, Yale.

49. "Memoirs of Captain Richard Law", R. & P., I pt I, 112; Fletcher Pratt, *The Compact History of the United States Navy,* p. 31; Samuel Chew received the vessel from the Continental Naval Agent, Nathaniel Shaw, Jr., August 26, 1777, Shaw Papers, Yale; Chapelle, *Sailing Navy,* p. 95; Middlebrook, II, 267; Pratt, *History,* p. 43.

50. Rogers, p. 23; letter from John Hancock to Nathaniel Shaw, Jr., April 23, 1776, Shaw Papers, Yale; Commission appointing Nathaniel Shaw, Jr., as Naval Agent, Shaw Papers, Yale; *Journals of the Continental Congress,* IV, 301; C.R., XV, 240, 474, 528; S.R., II, 136; Caulkins, p. 520.

51. Rogers, pp. 7-8, 54; C.A., Revolutionary War, Series I, 1783-1789, IX, 303-336, XIII, 11, 141; C.R. XV, 126, 240, 327.

52. Letters from Nathaniel Shaw, Jr., to Samuel Solly Wentworth April 6, 1775, Shaw Collection, Yale.

53. Letter from Nathaniel Shaw, Jr., to Peter Vandervoort, April 8, 1775, Shaw Collection, Yale.

54. Letter from Nathaniel Shaw, Jr., to Peter Vandervoort, April 25, 1775, Shaw Collection, Yale.

55. Letters from Nathaniel Shaw, Jr., to Ebenezer Pomproy, April 6, 1775; John Lawrence, May 25, 1775 ——, December 14, 1774; Thomas and Isaac Wharton, December 15, 1774 and April 8, 1775; Peter Vandervoort, April 25, 1775, Shaw Collection; Yale; William Bell Clark, identifies the recipient of the Dec. 14, 1774 letter as Eliphant Dyer in *Naval Documents of the American Revolution,* I, 21, U.S. Gov.

56. Receipt of "Powder and Ball" delivered to Lieutenant Nathan Hale, August 30, 1775, Shaw Collection; letter from Nathaniel Shaw, Jr., to Governor Johnathan Trumbull, February 3, 1776, MS in Misc. Correspondence Transcripts, Library of Congress.

57. New London *Repository,* November 24, 1858; letters from George Washington to Nathaniel Shaw, Jr., July 10, July 31, August 8, August 16; 1708 receipt for two horses signed by Marquis LaFayette, Major General, September 3, 1778, Shaw Papers, Yale Location of Tower Hill not indicated.

58. Letter from Nathaniel Shaw, Jr., to Governor Jonathan Trumbull, February 21, 1775, "Trumbull Papers," Mass. Bound Vol. 14, M.H.S.

59. Connecticut *Gazette,* April 12, 1776; Middlebrook, I, 11-13.

60. Alverda L. Beck (ed.), *The Letter Book of Esek Hopkins* pp. 58, 115; letters from Esek Hopkins to Nathaniel Shaw, Jr., May 21, June 5, 1776, January 20, January 27, 1777, Shaw Papers, Yale; *Journals of Continental Congress,* VII, 177; X, 207; XI, 589, 690; XII, 1101.

61. S. R., I, 418, 580; II, 357; III. 514; IV, 251-252; C.A. Revolutionary War 1763-1789, 1st Series, XXXI, 136; the *Connecticut Gazette* reports eighty escaped and that only nine were able to elude capture, June 7, 1782; letter from Nathaniel Shaw, Jr. to Joshua Huntington, January 4, 1779, Huntington-Wolcott Papers, M.H.S.; Order from Admiral Hopkins to Guy Richard, January 1, 1781, Shaw Papers, Yale.

62. S.R., I, 157, 347-348; Florence S. Crofut, *Guide to the History and the Historic Sites of Connecticut,* II, 728; *Connecticut Gazette,* July 25, August 1, August 8, August

22, 1777, December 18, 1778, August 25, 1779; Flag of Truce Document, Shaw Collection, Yale; Henry R. Stiles, *Letters from the Prisons and Prison Ships of the Revolution,* p. 30.

63. Connecticut *Gazette,* January 1, 1779; S.R., II, 190-191; letter from Joshua Mersereau to Nathaniel Shaw, Jr., February 27, 1779.

64. Rogers, p. 9; Caulkins, p. 512.

65. Letter from John Giddis to Nathaniel Shaw, Jr., August 27, 1777; letter from Nathaniel Shaw, Jr., to John Giddis, December 17, 1775; letter from Nathnaiel Shaw, Jr., to (?) Sargenton, December 17, 1775, Shaw Collection, Yale.

66. C.R., XI, 486; Caulkins, pp. 502-503; Destler, pp. 3-5, 17-18, 20.

67. C.A., Revolutionary War, 1st Series, 1763-1789, XXVI, 375; XXVII, 26, 1806, XXXVI, 53; Zeichner, p. 45; Insolvent Debtors, 1762-1787, 205-214.

68. Sherman W. Adams, "Revolutionary Naval Officers," R. & P. I, pt. II, New London, 47, 48; W.P.A. Federal Writers Project, *Connecticut, A Guide to its Roads, Lore and People,* p. 255; Caulkins, pp. 502-531.

69. Rogers, p. 55; Caulkins, p. 531; Middlebrook, II 99, 101, 144, 212.

70. Caulkins, pp. 527, 537-538.

71. Letter from Nathaniel Shaw, Jr., to Captain Charles Handy, May 31, 1775, Shaw Collection, Yale.

72. Letter from Nathaniel Shaw, Jr., to Samuel Solly Wentworth, January 16, 1776, Shaw Collection, Yale.

73. Letter from John de Nowfville & Son to Nathaniel Shaw, Jr., May 30, 1781, Shaw Papers, Yale.

74. Letter from Meredith Steward to Joshua Hempstead, 1776, Misc. MSS, Mystic Seaport.

75. Letter from Nathaniel Shaw, Jr., to Captain John Mackibbins, July 12, 1775, Shaw Collection, Yale; letter from Gerard Beekman to William Beekman, November 10, 1778, White, III, 1317.

76. Letter from Gerard Beekman to Abraham Beekman, October 18, 1778, White II, 1314.

77. Thomas S. Collier, "Brief Biographies of Connecticut Revolutionary Naval and Privateer Officers", R & P, I, pt. IV, 70; Caulkins, pp. 117, 131-139; Middlebrook, II, 48.

78. Middlebrook, II, 48, 49, 265; Collier, "Brief Biographies." 70; Rogers, pp. 126-128.

79. Collier raises some doubt as to the exact role and vessel of Hinman during the first naval expedition, "Brief Biographies," 66-67; Caulkins, p. 537; Morgan, *Connecticut* I, 194; Middlebrook, I, 12; "Captain Elisha Hinman" (Cedar Grove Cemetery), *Publications,* I, 3, New London; The New London Cemetery Society, 1941, 169-172; G.B.R., pp. 705-706.

80. Middlebrook, II, 150-153; Caulkins, p. 537; Collier, "Revolutionary Privateers," 26.

81. Middlebrook, I, 80-82, 87; II, 98, 166, 212; Caulkins, p. 624; C.R., XV, 508-509; S.R., I, 192.

82. Epaphroditus Peck, *The Loyalists of Connecticut,* No. 31, p. 3; Shepard, "Tories", 259; C.R., XIV, 264, 323, 346; Blanchard, *Long Island,* p. 100.

83. S.R., I, 333.

84. Pratt, *History of U.S. Navy*, p. 11; letter from Nathaniel Shaw, Jr., to Peter Vandervoort, April 25, 1775, Shaw Collection, Yale.

85. Caulkins, pp. 522-523, Todd, p. 22; Blanchard, *Long Island*, p. 100; *Annals of St. James*, pp. 53-54.

86. *Ibid.*, pp. 524-530.

87. Notice of British activity sent to New London, MS, Heath Collection, M.H.S., Revolutionary War, XXLL, Doc, 332; Charles Allyn, *The Battle of Groton Heights*, pp. 14-18.

88. Caulkins, pp. 549-550.

89. New London *Day*, October 28, 1893.

90. Allyn, *Groton Heights*, pp. 24-27; New London *Repository*, April 14, 1858; G.B.R., pp. 705-706; Rogers, pp. 21-22.

91. New London *Day*, October 14, 1893.

92. G.B.R., 705-706, R & C Voll. III, pt. II, p. 170.

93. Allyn, *Groton Heights*, pp. 53, 54, 92; Caulkins, pp. 564-565.

94. Letter from Jonathan Trumbull to Major-General Heath, September 7, 1781; letter from Major-General Heath to Jonathan Trumbull, September 10, 1781; letter from Major-Thomas Weeks to Major-General Heath, September 15, 1781, MSS at M.H.S; Barber, Historical Collections, p. 278; Rogers, pp. 73-74; *Connecticut Gazette*, October 5, November 17, 1781; S.R., III, 548-549.

95. New London *Day*, October 11, 1893.

96. Rogers, pp. 9-10; Elizabeth Gorton, "A Background Glances" R & P, III, pt. II, 172; Nathaniel Shaw's will, MS, C.S.L.; papers relating to Shaw's estate, MSS in Shaw Papers, Yale.

97. Middlebrook, II, 163-164; Rogers, pp. 10-11.

Chapter IV   New London Seeks Prosperity 1784 -1819

1. Destler, pp. 18-19.

2. Allyn, Groton Heights, pp. 147-156; Caulkins, p. 574.

3. Martin, p. 54; C. A., Trade and Maritime Affairs, II, 162; S. R., V., 325-326; Harwood, II 449.

4. Caulkins, pp. 581-582.

5. *Ibid.*, p. 581.

6. C. A., Insolvent Debtors 1762-1787, I, 186-187.

7. Letter from Richard Platt to Thomas Shaw, August, 1787, in Wadsworth Correspondence.

8. Rogers, p. 21; letter from Joseph Pernnell for Robert Morris to Thomas Shaw, May 29, 1782, Shaw Papers, Yale.

9. Letter from Thomas Shaw to Doctor Silvester Gardener, September 26, 1785; letter from Doctor Silvester Gardener to Thomas Shaw, November 15, 1785; letter from Thomas Shaw to Textier, June 15, 1784; letter from Thomas Shaw to Dousset, n.d.; Document of Attachment, Shaw Papers, Yale.

10. Letter from John Chenward to Thomas Shaw, July 20, 1787; letter from Esek Hopkins to Thomas Shaw, April 28, 1788; document of Power of Attorney to Samuel Eddy, January 2, 1792, Shaw Papers, Yale.

11. Will of Thomas Shaw, Probate Records, New London County, MS 4790, C.S.L.; Will of Temperance Shaw, Probate Records, New London County, MS 4788, C.S.L.

12. New London *Day*, 1923.

13. *Ibid.*, January 5, 1922.

14. S.R., I, 333,335.

15. Ibid., I, 346,572; V, 102; III, 549-550.

16. Caulkins, p. 575.

17. Destler, pp. 37-143 Passim.

18. Caulkins, p. 662.

19. Decker, "The Merchants", p. 272.

20. Misc. MS, VFM 621, Mystic Seaport.

21. "Memoirs of Captain Law", 119-125.

22. Sloop *Lovina*, Court of Claims, Lists of Vessels with Docket II, French Spoilation Claims, Record Group 36, Washington, D. C.

23. Connecticut *Gazette*, March 12, 1806.

24. Edward Bacon, "New London and the War of 1812", R&P, I, pt. I, 99-100, New London.

25. *Ibid.*

26. *Ibid.*, 100-107; *Connecticut Gazette*, January 12, 1814; letter from General Henry Burbeck to D. T. Brainard, December, 1813, MS in Doctor D. T. Brainard Letters, New London.

27. Connecticut *Gazette*, May 5, 1813.

28. Caulkins, 633.

29. Bacon, 101, 107; Rogers, p. 125; George Coggeshall, *History of American Privateers and Letters of Marque, 1812-1814*, p. 456; Collier, 70-71.

30. *Connecticut Gazette*, October 14, 1812, January 13, 1820, February 3, 10, 24, March 3, 17, April 14, 21, May 5, 1813.

31. *Ibid.*, June 2, 27, 1813.

32. *Ibid.*, April 28, 1813.

33. *Ibid.*, March 15, 1813.

34. Bacon, 101, 107; Rogers, p. 125; Coggeshall, p. 456; Collier, 70-71.

35. Decker, "The Merchants," p. 273.

36. *Ibid.*, p. 278.

37. *Ibid.*

38. *Ibid.*

39. Ibid. pp. 274-277.

Chapter V   New London in Whaling Days

1. New London *Day*, January 23, 1926.

2. Harwood, II, 494.

3. Caulkins, p. 136.

4. Hempstead, p. 72.

5. MS material of Edouard A. Stackpole, then Curator, Marine Historical Association, Mystic Seaport, plus a personal interview with Mr. Stackpole at the

Stillman Library, Mystic Seaport, July 11, 1962.

6. Williams, *Early Whaling,* p. 6.

7. Appendix XII.

9. *Ibid.*

10. Details of the worldwide commercial activities of General Williams can be found in the Williams Correspondence, MSS in the Manuscript Room of the New York Public Library. One letter in particular gives many details of the family business—Letter of William Williams, Jr., to Thomas W. Williams, August 20, 1867; D. Hamilton Hurd, *History of New London County,* pp. 236-237; Decker, *Whaling,* Appendix I, II.

11. Henry Clay Trumbull, *A Model Superintendent,* pp. 8-10.

12. New London *Gazette,* May 9, 1838.

13. Appendix XII.

14. Charles G. Woodward, *The New London, Willimantic & Palmer Railroad Company,* p. 5.

15. Marshall, *Modern History,* I, 78; Hurd, *New London County,* p. 239; GBR, p. 62; Billings Papers; Appendix XII.

16. Decker, *Whaling,* Appendix I; *The Financial Digest,* April, 1925.

17. GBR, pp. 755-756, Lawrence Collection.

18. New London *Day,* July 28, 1892.

19. Appendix XII; Shaw Papers at the N.L.C.H.S. contain deeds, letters and other MSS dealing with business activities of Elias Perkins. Starbuck, I, 264-378.

20. New London *Gazette,* April 25, 1838.

21. *Daily Chronicle,* July 16, 1851; *New London Gazette,* July 31, 1833.

22. *People's Advocate and New London County Republican,* March 19, 1848; New London *Day,* April 25, 1914.

23. *Daily Chronicle,* January 30, 1851; *New London Gazette,* May 17, 1837; *People's Advocate and New London County Republican,* January 26, 1848.

24. Nathaniel Taylor, *Life on a Whaler,* pp. vi-vii, 8-9, 116-118, 192; Starbuck, II 602-603; New London *Day,* April 13, 1935; Henry Clay Trumbull, A Model Superintendent, p. 106.

25. Harwood, II, 543; New London *Day,* March 30, 1935; Starbuck, I, 244-245.

26. Appendix XII; New London Day, October 19, 1921; April 21, 1923; Bernard Colby, *New London Whaling Captains,* pp. 7-8; Smith Estate Papers, Shaw Perkins papers, Shaw Mansion, New London.

27. Although Colby, p. 31, states that John O. Spicer became a captain on his second voyage in 1854, it appears that he made three voyages 1851-1861, at no higher than third mate, and then was in the merchant service 1861-1863, before becoming a whaling captain in 1863; New London *Day,* March 14, 15, 16, 1911; July 28, 1921.

28. *Ibid.*

29. Colby appears to be in error when he states that Captain Buddington farmed for ten years, p. 17 as Buddington was master of the *William C. Nye* in 1846 and of the *Georgiana* in 1853; Starbuck, I, 406-407; II, 510-511; The weather was so terrible that 13 vessels had given up the attempt to enter Davis Straits while the *George Henry* worked its way in at the rate of 1½ miles a day. Long Island Sound was frozen over for almost seven weeks that winter. New London *Day,* November

6, 1894; Sidney Withington, *Two Dramatic Episodes of New England Whaling,* pp. 18-37; Letter from Henry Grennell to the British Government, March 1, 1856, letter from John H. Clifford to Perkins and Smith, February 25, 1856, letter from Sir John Crampton to Perkins and Smith, May 20, 1856, letter from Edward E. Hale to Elias Perkins, January 21, 1856, letter from Lafayette S. Foster to Perkins and Smith, July 5, 1856, letter from J. A. Thomas, U. S. Department of State, to Perkins and Smith, September 19, 1856, documents concerning Captain James M. Buddington and his claims against Perkins and Smith, Shaw-Perkins Papers, New London; *The* (Washington, D. C.) *Daily Globe,* June 11, 1856, June 25, 1856; New London *Day,* February 23, 1935, blamed Henry Haven for the non-payment.

    30. Colby states J. M. Buddington went out as mate on the *Lizzie P. Simmons* in 1887; however, that vessel was lost the winter of 1881-1882. It would appear that the vessel was the *Palmetti* and later the *Sarah W. Hunt;* Colby p. 18; Reginald Hegarty, *Returns of Whaling Vessels Sailing From American Ports* pp. 13, 19, 22; New London *Day,* February 23, 1935; Colby mistakenly reports that Buddington was 90 when he returned from his last voyage and retired, p. 18.

    31. Starbuck, II, 616-617, 654-655, 658-659; Colby, pp. 35-36; Hegarty, pp. 4, 6, 8, 13, 40; New London *Day,* January 19, 1935.

    32. James A. Rogers, *Journal of Whaling Voyage of Ship Mentor of New London,* January 26, 1841.

    33. New London *Day,* April 4, 1918.

    34. Business correspondence between T. W. Williams and Augustus Durand & Co., Welles & Co., J. & H. Rose; Letter from J. Bradlee & Co. to T. W. Williams, June 23, 1826, Williams Papers, N.Y.P.L.

    35. Various advertisements in newspapers 1819-1892.

    36. *Weekly Chronicle,* May 27, 1858.

    37. People's Advocate, March 24, 1847; *Weekly Chronicle,* January 27, 1858.

    38. Letter from John Ross to Lawrence & Co., October 1, 1857, Lawrence Collection, Mystic Seaport.

    39. *People's Advocate,* February 2, September 15, 29, 1847; New London *Day,* October 2, 1926.

    40. *Weekly Chronicle,* March 24, 1859.

    41. New London *Day,* August 28, 1926.

    42. *Ibid.,* February 11, 1920.

    43. *People's Advocate,* May 13, 1846.

    44. Decker, *Whaling,* Appendix I.

    45. Clifford W. Ashley, The Yankee Whaler, p. 52; Colby, *Whaling Captains,* p. 5n.

    46. Letter from W. Williams to T. W. Williams, August 21, 1867, Williams Papers; Starbuck, I, 102. The *Peril* was not listed as a whaler and probably was on a sealing voyage to Desolation Island when destroyed.

    47. New London *Day,* October 1, 1927.

    48. *Ibid.,* April 13, 1896.

    49. Letter from Jestin Martin to Charles Martin, November 29, 1844, MS Whaling Collection, Mystic Seaport.

    50. New London Customs Records; Taylor, p. 8; *Whale Masters,* p. 17.

51. New London *Day,* October 20, 1921.

52. *Ibid.,* April 6, 1887.

53. *Ibid.*

54. New London *Day,* January 31, 1924; January 19, 1935; Williams, *Early Whaling,* p. 18; Starbuck, II, 430-431, 440-441, 448-449.

55. Whalemen's Shipping Articles,*Quickstep,* June 28, 1866, George and Mary, April 17, 1866. New London Customs Records.

56. New London *Repository,* May 18, June 8, July 6, 1859.

57. *Ibid.,* July 6, 1859.

58. *Weekly Chronicle,* December 9, 16, 1858; May 26, 1859; New London *Day,* June 25, 1895.

59. Starbuck, II, 594-595.

60. Starbuck, I, 102, 103n, II 556-557.

61. Decker, *Whaling,* Appendix VI.

62. E. Keble Chatterton, *Whales and Whaling,* pp. 173-176; Starbuck, I, 103-109. The *Paira Kohola,* a Williams & Haven vessel appears to have been a New London vessel transferred to the Hawaiian flag during the Civil War.

63. Trumbull,*Model,* pp. 102-103; Douglas L. Oliver,*The Pacific Islands,* p. 309; Caulkins, p. 685; New London *Repository,* March 15, 1860; Hurd, p. 229.

64. Charles M. Scammon, *The Marine Mammals of the Northwestern Coast of North America,* pp. 105-107, 149-151, 155, 160, 162;Trumbull, *Model,* pp. 102-107.

65. Daily *Chronicle,* August 16, 1855.

66. New London *Day,* July 6, 1931; Decker, *Whaling,* Appendix I.

67. New London *Day,* October 6, 1926.

68. *Ibid.,* October 9, 1930.

Chapter VI   Financial and Insurance Institutions

1. Harwood, II, 638-639. Incorrectly refers to the Union Bank as being the fifth bank chartered in the United States; New London *Day,* October 29, 1927 makes error over number of banks established in United States by 1792; Hasse, pp. 2-3.

2. C. A., Finance and Commerce, 2nd Series, 1689-1820, II, 22-30; S.R., VII, 338n, 384-391, 491-494; Caulkins p. 662; Parsons, pp. 1-3.

3. S.R., VII, 384n; Hasse, p. 3; Parsons, pp. 1-3; Caulkins, p. 662; Joseph Gurley Woodward, *Currency and Banking in Connecticut 1635-1838,* pp. 21-23.

4. Hasse, p. 14.

5. Marshall, II, 425-428.

6. *Weekly Chronicle,* April 9, 1857; August 4, 1859.

7. Notes of Elisha Denison and Captain Edward Chappell that they intended to apply to the General Assembly for charter of second bank in New London and that the Union Bank would not oppose it, Shaw Perkins Papers, New London; "C. A. Finance and Currency, 2nd Series, 1689-1820," I, 22.

8. Benjamin T. Marshall (ed.), *A Modern History of New London County,* II, 428-431; Caulkins, p. 662; C.A., Finance and Currency, 2nd Series, II, 23-26;

New London *Day,* October 29, 1921.

   9. Connecticut *Gazette,* September 25, 1811.

  10. *Daily Chronicle,* November 22, 1855.

  11. *Weekly Chronicle,* April 25, 1861.

  12. Hasse, p. 12; Woodward, p. 30.

  13. The others were in Hartford, 1819; Norwich, 1824; and Middletown, 1825, *Century of Banking,* p. 3; Hasse, p. 25; New London *Day,* October 29, 1921.

  14. Caulkins, p. 662; Marshall, II, 436-438.

  15. *A Century of Banking,* pp. 13-15.

  16. *Ibid.*

  17. Connecticut *Gazette,* January 19, March 2, 30, September 28, 1877.

  18. *A Century of Banking,* pp. 1-52, *passim;* New London *Day,* July 2, 1927.

  19. New London *Day,* May 27, 1971, January 3, 1972.

  20. *Ibid.,* January 19, 1924.

  21. *Ibid.,* October 29, 1921.

  22. G.B.R., p. 14.

  23. *Leading Businessmen of New London,* p. 54.

  24. *New London Chronicle,* February 7, 1851.

  25. Caulkins, p. 662; New London *Day,* October 29, 1921; New London *Telegraph,* June 25, 1908; Marshall, II, 438-439.

  26. Marshall, II, 438-439.

  27. New London *Day,* April 24, 1920; August 3, 1921.

  28. *Ibid.* January 18, 1972.

  29. *Weekly Chronicle,* March 15, 1855; July 9, 1857.

  30. *Ibid.,* April 12, 1855.

  31. Bray Hammond, *Bank and Politics in America,* pp. 731-734; Hasse, pp. 48-51; The First National Bank of New Haven received "Charter No. 2" after agreeing to allow a later application to receive "Charter No. 1" Rollen G. Osterweis, *Charter Number Two: The Centennial History of the First New Haven National Bank,* p. 1.

  32. Connecticut *Gazette,* April 13, 1877; New London *Day,* December 13, 1924; Hasse, pp. 49-58.

  33. Hasse, pp. 58, 63, Parsons, p. 2.

  34. Harwood, II, 557; Hasse, p. 53; Marshall, II, 447-450; New London *Telegraph,* June 25, 1908.

  35. New London *Day,* May 15, 1946.

  36. Hasse, p. 56; Parsons, p. 24.

  37. New London *Day,* December 30, 1904.

  38. *Ibid.,* March 8, 1922; December 8, 1971.

  39. *Ibid.,* August 24, 1942; February 15, 1972.

  40. C.A., I, Public Acts.

  41. *Ibid.*

  42. *Weekly Chronicle,* May 27, 1852.

Chapter VII   Leading Businesses and Industries

  1. Excellent accounts of all can be found in Curtis, *Silver.*

2. Connecticut *Gazette,* May 27, 1818.
3. New London *Day,* January 4, 1922.
4. Connecticut *Gazette,* December 19, 1873.
5. New London *Day,* February 13, 1904.
6. "Major-General George C. Wilson 1814-1841", *Cedar Grove Cemetery Publications,* I, No. 3, pp. 173-175.
7. New London *Day,* February 13, 1904; Hurd, p. 237.
8. Connecticut *Gazette,* December 19, 1873.
9. *Ibid.,* February 6, 1874.
10. *Ibid.,* New London *Day,* June 25, 1895.
11. New London *Day,* December 6, 1917; October 29, 1921.
12. New London *Telegram,* December 27, 1873.
13. *Ibid.*
14. *Ibid.*
15. New London *Gazette,* July 29, 1839.
16. Todd Burr, *Connecticut Labor,* pp. 7-20.
17. New London *Gazette,* July 9, 1828.
18. *Ibid.,* January 3, 1827.
19. New London *Gazette,* January 3, 1827; May 2, 1838; December 20, 1840; Daily *Chronicle,* February 11, 1851; New London *Day,* April 12, 1889.
20. People's *Advocate,* November 20, 1844.
21. Weekly *Democrat,* June 23, 1849.
22. People's *Advocate,* August 5, 1846.
23. Weekly *Democrat,* December 23, 1848.
24. *Ibid.,* January 27, 1849.
25. American Men of Affairs Magazine, I, Vol. 1, (1912) 35-36.
26. New London *Day,* November 4, 1897; August 2, 1899; October 29, 1921; October 6, 1971.
27. *Ibid.,* November 30; Weekly *Chronicle,* February 19, 26, 1852.
28. New London *Telegram,* December 4, 1873.
29. New London *Gazette,* January 7, 1881.
30. *Ibid.,* January 6, 1882.
31. New London *Day,* March 24, 1924.
32. Starr, pp. 77-78; New London *Gazette,* April 22, 1881.
33. Weekly *Chronicle,* December 26, 1861; January 30, February 6, 1862.
34. *Ibid.,* February 20, 1862.
35. *Ibid.,* July 10, August 14, 1862.
36. *Ibid.,* April 11, 1861.
37. *Ibid.,* September 11, 1862.
38. *Ibid.,* July 31, 1862.
39. John Nivins, *Connecticut for the Union,* pp. 90, 326, 345; *Hartford Courant,* December 22, 1862.
40. Henry J. Raymond, *The Life and Public Service of Abraham Lincoln,* p. 524.
41. New London *Day,* April 26, 1888.
42. Connecticut *Gazette,* March 20, 1874.
43. New London *Day,* February 4, 1899; April 7, 1900; March 31, 1927.
44. *Ibid.,* April 26, 1888.

45. Daily *Star,* July 12, October 27, 1871; New London *Telegram,* May 23, September 27, 1873.

46. Daily *Star,* December 11, 1871; Connecticut *Gazette,* July 31, 1874; New London *Day,* December 11, 1971; May 10, 1972.

47. New London *Day,* March 22, 1922; May 6, 1929.

48. John Bolles, *New London, A Seaport for North and West,* pp. 14, 15; Connecticut *Gazette,* February 20, 1874.

49. New London *Day,* March 18, 1895.

50. *Ibid.,* October 21, 29, 1929; *American Men of Affairs,* p. 35.

51. New London *Day,* November 13, 1893.

52. *Ibid.,* October 27, 1919; January 28, 1920; November 18, 1921; April 9, 22, 1930.

53. New London *Telegram,* April 28, 1884; May 31, 1902.

54. New London *Day,* November 16, 1896; September 16, 1902; November 3, 1914; July 19, 1921; May 9, 1947; November 22, 1971.

55. *Ibid.,* June 4, 1904.

56. *Ibid.,* March 30, 1892.

57. New London *Day,* November 18, 1893.

58. *Ibid.* May 3, 1894.

59. Morning *Telegraph,* December 3, 1894.

60. *American Men of Affairs,* p. 36.

61. New London *Day,* December 17, 1924.

62. *Ibid.,* December 13, 1895; February 17, 20, 22, May 25, 1922; December 26, 1925.

63. *Ibid.,* April 24, May 7, June 24, 1898; March 22, November 15, 1899.

64. *Ibid.,* December 15, 1914.

65. *Ibid.,* December 11, 1928.

66. *Ibid.,* September 14, 1918, November, 1918, *passim.*

67. *Ibid.,* March 26, 1920; March 29, April 11, 1918.

68. *Ibid.,* October 7, 1919; July 28 1920.

69. *Ibid.,* September 24, 1920.

70. New London *Day,* July 26, 1921.

71. *Ibid.,* September 2, 1921.

72. *Ibid.,* March 10, 1923.

73. *Ibid.,* August 24, 1942.

74. *Ibid.,* August 31, November 5, 1943.

75. *Ibid., August* 17, 1945; October 16, 1946.

76. *Ibid.,* October 19, 1945; February 8, 1972.

77. *Ibid.,* October 12, 1971.

Chapter VIII　Some 19th Century Business Figures

1. Robert G. Albion, *Square Riggers on Schedule,* p. 221; Captain Francis Allyn, *Cedar Grove,* I, No. 1, 9-11.

2. *Providence Sunday Journal,* June 25, 1939; Connecticut *Gazette,* April 10, 17, 1874.

3. New London *Gazette*, February 25, 1824; Weekly *Democrat*, December 4, 1969.

4. Charles G. Woodward, *The New London, Willimantic & Palmer Railroad Company*, p. 5; Hurd, pp. 234-236; New London *Gazette*, May 1, 1839; Weekly *Chronicle*, November 27, 1862.

5. New London *Day*, February 15, 1886.

6. *Ibid.*, July 21, August 26, 1902.

7. Weekly *Chronicle*, November 18, 1852.

8. Richard A. Wheeler, "The First Organized Church in New London County", *R&P* I, pt. III, 243.

9. New London *Gazette*, October 12, 1825; Peoples *Advocate*, October 14, 1846; Probate Records, State Library.

10. Hurd, p. 239; Williams, I, pt. III, 7; GBR, p. 62; New London *Day*, June 30, July 6, 1887.

11. "Richard H. Chappell", *Cedar Grove*, I, No. 2, 77-78; Daily *Chronicle*, August 11, 1855; Daily *Star*, November 7, 1867; New London *Telegram*, July 1, September 8, 1873; Connecticut *Gazette*, September 4, October 2, 1874.

12. GBR, p 12; Connecticut *Gazette*, October 17, 1921; *Century of Banking*, pp. 23-24.

13. GBR pp. 13-14; New London *Day*, January 21, 1881; November 12, 1893; June 30, 1904; *Hartford Evening Post*, January 6, 1880.

14. GBR p. 14; New London *Day*, February 10, 1915; New London *Gazette*, March 21, 1879.

15. New London *Day*, September 21, 23, 1920; July 1, 1922.

16. GBR, pp. 749-750; "Chappell", 80; *Connecticut Gazette*, April 3, 1874; New London *Day*, June 18, 1907.

17. New London *Day*, March 10, 1903.

18. New London *Gazette*, June 14, 1837.

19. Williams, I, III, 7; Daily *Star*, June 20, 1867.

20. Weekly *Chronicle*, May 12, 1859; New London *Repository*, May 18, 1859; Weekly *Democrat*, March 13, 1859.

21. New London *Day*, December 16, 1891.

22. "Harris—, 85.

23. New London *Day*, October 19, 1896.

24. Daily *Star*, November 18, 1871.

25. "Will of J. N. Harris", *Cedar Grove*, I, No. 2, 91-93.

25. New London *Day*, October 19, 1896; "Harris", 85-91.

26. Hurd, pp. 229-230; "Honorable Henry P. Haven", *Cedar Grove*, I, No. 2, 83; Trumbull, *Superintendent*, pp. 3-4.

27. Hurd, pp. 228-230; Trumbull, *Superintendent*, pp. 8-10.

28. Trumbull, *Superintendent*, pp. 117-118.

29. Connecticut *Gazette*, May 5, 1876.

30. "Henry Haven", 42; Trumbull, *Superintendent*, pp. 105-108.

31. Trumbull, *Superintendent*, pp. 102-104.

32. *Ibid.*, pp. 115-116.

33. Hurd, p. 230; Trumbull, *Superintendent*, pp. 123-142; Weekly *Chronicle*, April 1, April 8, 1852; Daily *Star*, January 23, 1869.

34. "Henry Haven", 84; Hurd, pp. 228-232; Trumbull, *Superintendent,* pp. 6-122 *passim.*

35. Trumbull, *Superintendent,* pp. 123-128; Weekly *Democrat,* January 23, 1869; New London *Telegram,* July 16, 1873.

36. "Henry Haven", 83; New London *Repository,* July 27, 1859; Hurd, p. 229; Trumbull, *Superintendent,* pp. 16, 41-44.

37. Trumbull, *Superintendent,* pp. 169-170.

38. Connecticut *Gazette,* May 5, 1876.

39. "Henry Haven", 83.

40. Weekly *Democrat,* August 6, 1870.

41. New London *Day,* April 14, 1896; Woodward, pp. 4-5; GBR, p. 775.

42. Lawrence Papers, Yale.

43. New London Vital Records, III, 157.

44. New London *Day,* April 14, 1896.

45. Log of Ship *Hindoo,* Lawrence Collection, Yale.

46. J. J. Lawrence, Cedar Grove Cemetery Records.

47. GBR p. 756; Lawrence & Company Papers, Mystic Seaport.

48. Lawrence & Company Papers, Mystic Seaport.

49. *Ibid.*

50. New London *Day,* October 26, February 8, July 4, 1898.

51. New London County Probate Records, State Library; New London *Day,* June 4, 1909.

52. GBR, 274.

53. New London *Telegram,* November 7, 1873.

54. Hurd, pp. 241-242; GBR, pp. 273-275; *Biographical Review,* pp. 9-10.

55. Rogers, pp. 80-82.

56. Letter of Oliver Ellsworth, November 3, 1788, Shaw-Perkins Papers, Shaw Mansion.

57. *Ibid.,* Letter from Jonathan Trumbull to Elias Perkins, appointments as judge, 1807-1821.

58. *Ibid.,* appointment as Boundary Commissioner, 1800.

59. Peoples *Advocate,* October 1, 1845.

60. Weekly *Democrat,* June 4, 1870.

61. Consular Appointments, Shaw Perkins Papers, Shaw Mansion.

62. Peoples *Advocate,* January 22, 1845.

63. Weekly *Chronicle,* February 13, 1862; January 8, 1863; Daily *Star,* March 4, 1871.

64. "Memoir of Honorable William H. Starr", I, pt. I, 82-84.

65. Hurd, p. 234; New London *Telegram,* October 22, 1873. New London *Day,* December 4, 1893.

66. Hurd, p. 700; Weekly *Democrat,* November 5, 1870.

67. Letter of William Williams, Jr. to Thomas Williams, August 21, 1867, Williams Papers, New York Public Library; Wheeler, pp. 675, 677-678; New London *Gazette,* January 8, 1912; Harwood, II, 763-764.

68. Hurd, pp. 347-350.

69. *Ibid.*; Weekly *Democrat,* November 5, 1870; Daily *Star,* January 11, 1871.

70. Connecticut *Gazette,* September 18, 1811; Daily *Chronicle,* September 20,

1855; New London *Day*, November 15, 1911; Hurd, pp. 236-237; Woodward, p. 4.

71. Hurd, p. 350.

72. Connecticut *Gazette*, June 28, 1815; Daily *Star*, May 9, 1867.

73. "Memoir of Honorable Charles Augustus Williams", *R&P*, I, pt. IV, 367-368; New London *Telegram*, May 30, 1873.

74. "Honorable Charles Augustus Williams", *Cedar Grove*, I, No. 1, 15.

75. "Williams", I pt. IV, 369-370.

76. New London *Day*, December 4, 1903.

77. *Ibid.*, September 27, 1889; August 15, 1893; January 1, 1900.

Chapter IX   Maritime New London

1. Carl Cutler, *The Story of a Small New England Seaport,* pp. 137-138.

2. Weekly *Chronicle*, November 24, 1853; New London *Day*, May 31, 1900; March 24, 1923.

3. BR, pp. 18-21.

4. New London *Day*, October 19, 1896; October 16, 1923; New London *Repository*, February 24, 1858; Weekly Chronicle, September 10, 1863.

5. Connecticut *Gazette*, August 22, 1810.

6. New London *Gazette*, July 30, 1828.

7. Weekly*Chronicle*, September 2, 1852; New London*Day* July 6, 1900; May 12, 1904.

8. Connecticut *Gazette*, March 6, 1822.

9. New London *Telegram*, October 2, 1883; New London *Day*, January 21, 1887; April 20, 1896; November 11, 1891; May 12, 1904.

10. *Ibid.*, September 16, 1893.

11. *Ibid.*, October 9, 1907; October 29, 1921.

12. Peoples *Advocate*, April 22, 1846; February 23, 1848.

13. New London *Day*, May 29, June 6, November 28, 1902; October 15, 1926.

14. *Ibid.*, September 27, 1919.

15. New London *Gazette*, April 25, 1838.

16. New London *Day*, November 14, 1925.

17. New London *Day*, February 17, 1896.

18. BR., p. 133; New London *Telegraph*, June 25, 1908; Roger Williams McAdam, *Salts of the Sound*, p. 99.

19. Daily *Star*, October 28, November 22, 1867; New London *Telegram*, June 5, 1873.

20. New London *Telegram*, September 5, 1873.

21. New London *Day*, July 17, 1888; April 11, 1890; November 26, 1898; July 15, 1895.

22. *American Men of Affairs*, p. 48; New London*Day*, October 27, 1891; January 16, May 12, 1904; New London *Telegraph*, September 22, 1894.

23. New London *Day*, November 16, 20, March 19, 1894.

24. *Ibid.*, March 9, 10, 19, April 7, 16, June 30, August 18, 1902; April 16, June 30, 1903; April 30, June 11, 1904; January 16, 1923.

25. New London *Day*, November 11, 1924; *American Men of Affairs*, p. 46.

26. New London *Day*, April 19, 29, 1926; February 10, 1928; July 6, 1931.

27. *Ibid.*, March 16, April 1, 1920; October 29, 1921; March 18, 19, 1924; July 6, 1931.

28. New London *Day*, May 3, 1946.

29. *Ibid.*, April 25, 1946.

30. *Ibid.*, April 25, 1946.

31. New London *Day*, November 4, 1971; February 11, March 4, December 16, 1972. In December of 1972 4 acres of waterfront were sold by the General Services Administration to the shipyard.

32. *Ibid.*, November 14, 1891; New London *Telegram*, January 4, 1883.

33. Connecticut *Gazette*, October 2, 1876; December 14, 1877.

34. New London *Day*, December 17, 1889; October 13, 1895.

35. *Ibid.*, May 22, 1925.

36. New London *Day*, December 19, 1922.

37. *Ibid.*, May 29, 1919.

38. New London *Telegraph*, June 25, 1908; New London *Day*, July 2, 1896; January 19, 1915; *American Men of Affairs*, pp. 40-41.

39. *Ibid.*

40. *American Men of Affairs*, pp. 37-38.

41. Clearance papers of schooner *Betsey*, Gurden Allyn, Master, April 6, 1838; bark *Condon*, Edward G. Farber, Master, October 19, 1839; brig *Hyder Ali*, Thomas Demik, Master, October 20, 1840, New London Customs Records.

42. Clearance papers of New London vessels for the West Indies, Benjamin Banell, 31 January 1805, New London Customs Records.

43. *Ibid.*, Clearance Records of Boston No. 143, Box 16 Clearance papers of schooner *Hero*, Theo. Eaton, Master, May 19, 1848, New London Customs Records; Papers of ship *Atlanta*, Lawrence Collection.

44. Billings Papers; Lawrence Collection, Papers of New London vessels engaged in coastal trade, New London Customs Records; Shipping Collection Papers, Sterling Library.

45. Business correspondence between T. W. Williams and Augustus Durand & Co., Welles & Co., J. & H. Rose; Letter from I. Bradlee & Co. to T. W. Williams, June 22, 1826, Williams Papers, N.Y.P.L.

46. Papers of the sloop *Joseph Lawrence*, L. Rogers, Master 1857, Lawrence Collection.

47. Billings Papers; Lawrence Collection; New London vessels registered for the foreign trade, New London Custom Records.

48. Clearance papers of New London vessels for foreign ports, New London Custom Records; Lawrence Collection; Letter from William Williams to Thomas ' W. Williams, August 21, 1867, Williams Papers, N.Y.C.P.L.

49. Cargo manifest of *Iris*, George Tauile, Master, 1840; cargo manifest of *Atlantic*, Lamb, Master, 1858, New London Custom Records.

50. Crew list of schooner *Ellen*, Joseph Comstock, Master, 1853; New London Custom Records.

51. Papers of various vessels, 1819-1909, Lawrence Collection; Shipping papers of various New London vessels, 1819-1909, New London Custom Records.

52. *Bolles,* p. 12.
53. Register of New London Fishing Vessels, New London Custom Records.
54. New London *Repository,* October 13, 1858.
55. Daily *Chronicle,* August 23, 1851.
56. Weekly *Chronicle,* July 25, 1852.
57. New London *Day,* December 1, 1889.
58. Connecticut *Gazette,* February 27, 1874.
59. *Ibid.,* November 22, 1878.
60. New London *Day,* July 18, 1920.
61. "Ninth Census of the United States, Original Returns of the Assistant Marshals, Industry for the Year 1870 in the State of Connecticut", pp. 425-434.
62. Connecticut *Gazette,* November 13, 1874.
63. *Ibid.,* February 27, 1874.
64. New London *Day,* November 28, 1891.
65. *Ibid.,* November 25, 1892.
66. *Ibid.,* May 22, 1893.
67. *Ibid.,* March 27, 1893.
68. *Ibid.,* March 2, 1896.
69. *Ibid.,* August 31, 1893.
70. *Ibid.,* February 12, 1923.
71. *Ibid.,* June 23, 1930; September 21, 1971.
72. *Ibid.,* October 29, 1921; October 23, 1930; July 6, 1931.
73. *Ibid.,* January 1, 9, March 5, 6, 15, 1929; January 8, July 6, 31, 1931.
74. *Ibid.,* June 19, 1942.
75. *Ibid.,* August, 1971; November 20, 1971.
76. *Ibid.,* May 12, 1972.
77. *Ibid.,* November 15, 1921.
78. *Ibid.,* August 27, 1926.
79. *Ibid.,* August 21, 1921.
80. *Ibid.,* August 4, 1921.
81. *Ibid.,* January 1, 1927.
82. *Ibid.,* December 29, 1924; January 1, 1926; January 1, 1931.
83. *Ibid.,* October 13, 21, 1924.
84. *Ibid.,* January 14, 1930.
85. *Ibid.,* April 10, 1922.
86. *Ibid.,* May 6, 1946.
87. *Ibid.*
88. *Ibid.*
89. Connecticut *Gazette,* June 5, 1799.
90. Bolles, pp. 1-24, *passim.*
91. *Ibid.,* p. 16.
92. *Ibid.,* pp. 15-16; Fletcher Platt, *The Compact History of the United States Navy,* p. 13.
93. Bolles, pp. 18-19.
94. Daily *Star,* June 30, 1871; Connecticut *Gazette,* September 25, November 27, 1874.
95. New London *Day,* October 19, 1895.

96. *Connecticut Guide*, p. 255; New London *Day*, November 13, 1903; October 29, 1921.

97. New London *Day*, October 29, 1921.

98. *Ibid.*, January 5, 12, 1940.

99. *Ibid.*, May 6, 1946.

100. Albert E. Van Dusen, *Connecticut*, p. 417.

101. New London *Day*, September 11, 1896.

102. *Ibid.*, September 20, 1917; October 20, 1920; October 29, 1921.

103. *Ibid.*, September 11, 1922.

104. *Ibid.*, January 5, 1920; September 7, 1928; Connecticut *Gazette*, July 31, August 7, 1974.

105. New London *Day*, April 13, 1972.

106. *Ibid.*, December 13, 1971.

Chapter X   Transportation

1. Isabel S. Mitchell, *Roads and Roadmaking in Colonial Connecticut*, pp. 19-20; Frederick J. Wood, *The Turnpikes of New England and Evolution of the Same Through New England, Virginia and Maryland*, p. 390.

2. Caulkins, p. 375.

3. In 1785 the first turnpike in America was authorized in Virginia to connect Alexandria to Snicker's Cap in the Blue Ridge Mountains. It opened to traffic in 1785. Wood, pp. 7, 9, 10, 334-336.

4. C.A., Travel, Highways, Ferries, Bridges and Taverns, 1700-1788, "1st Ser., II, 78-82; Caulkins, pp. 658-659; S.R. VII, 394-395; XI, 50-51.

5. Harwood, p. 370; S.R., VII, 511; Wood, p. 335.

6. S.R., VIII, xxv, 395; X, xxxii, 134-137; Wood, pp. 359-360; Caulkins, p. 659.

7. Caulkins, pp. 658-659; S.R., IX, 268-269, 269n; XI, 276; Wood, pp. 379-380; 391-392.

8. Wood, pp. 316, 390.

9. Mitchell, p. 18; Wood, pp. 390-391; Caulkins, p. 401.

10. Mitchell, p. 18.

11. "New London Town Records 1651-1660", p. 11; Connecticut *Gazette*, December 25, 1874.

12. Connecticut *Gazette*, December 25, 1874; Caulkins, pp. 89, 664.

13. Wood, pp. 390-391; Caulkins and the New London *Day* put the advent of a steam ferry as 1849, Caulkins, p. 660 and New London *Day*, October 29, 1921; January 26, 1923. Connecticut *Gazette*, December 25, 1874.

14. New London *Gazette*, August 14, 1833; August 21, 1839.

15. *Ibid.*, July 24, 1839; Weekly *Democrat*, August 25, 1849; Weekly *Chronicle*, May 29, 1858.

16. Weekly *Chronicle*, February 3, 1859; New London *Telegram*, May 27, 1873.

17. Connecticut *Gazette*, July 3, 1874; New London *Day*, October 29, 1921.

18. Connecticut *Gazette*, September 17, 1875; New London *Day*, October 29, 1887; New London *Telegram*, May 16, 1885.

19. New London *Day*, September 23, 27, October 1, 1901.

20. *Ibid.*, April 26, 1947; August 20, 1971.

21. *Ibid.*, August 3, 1929, February 7, 1923; November 29, 1924; November 16,

1926; September 20, 1928; March 6, 11, 1929.

22. Robert G. Albion, *The Rise of New York Port*, p. 146, Weekly Chronicle, July 3, 1850; September 20, 1860; Daily Chronicle, July 9, 1851.

23. Harwood, II, 404; McAdam, *Salts*, p. 31; Caulkins, p. 652.

24. "Captain Stevens and Moses Rogers", *Cedar Grove*, I, No. 2, pp. 112-113; Richard B. Wall, "Captain Steven Rogers", *R&P*, II, pt. V, 493-495.

25. Wall, II, pt. V, 495; Caulkins reports that the Savannah steamed for fourteen days and sailed for eight, p. 653; while Robert G. Albion states that steam was used for only eighty hours on the whole of the trip, *The Rise of New York Port*, p. 314.

26. Martin, p. 196.

27. Harwood, I, 404-407.

28. Harwood, II, 419.

29. Wall, "Rogers", p. 495.

30. McAdam, *Salts*, p. 97.

31. The Peoples *Advocate*, February 9, 1848.

32. *Ibid.*, May 26, 1847.

33. Weekly *Chronicle*, July 3, 1850.

34. New London *Day*, February 27, 1923.

35. New London *Gazette*, May 2, 1827.

36. Harwood, II, 408.

37. *Ibid.*

38. *New London Directory*, 1855; Weekly *Chronicle*, June 8, 1954.

39. Harwood, II 414.

40. *Ibid.*, pp. 414-417.

41. *Ibid.*, p. 417; Weekly *Chronicle*, January 12, 1860.

42. Connecticut *Gazette*, January 27, 1882; New London *Day*, June 2, 1893; August 28, 1922; July 6, 1931.

43. McAdam, *Salts*, pp. 97-99, 102, 105-109; Everett Barns, *History of Pawcatuck River Steamboats*, pp. 1-54 *passim*; B.R. p. 148.

44. Albion, *Ports*, p. 160.

45. Harwood, II 414; Caulkins lists forty-two as the number lost, p. 651; Harwood and Harwood, *Poets of New London*, p. 34.

46. Harwood, II pp. 103-105, 414-417.

47. New London *Day*, January 31, 1890.

48. New London *Gazette*, January 29, 1840.

49. Harwood, II, p. 418.

50. *Ibid.*, p. 417.

51. New London *Day*, February 11, 1922.

52. Caulkins, pp. 650, 652-653, 675.

52A. People's Advocate, August 21, 1844; January 29, 1845; Harwood, II, 386-387.

52B. Connecticut *Gazette*, September 18, 1874.

52C. New London *Day*, May 6, 1919.

52D. *Ibid.*, April 9, 1901.

52E. *Ibid.*, August 14, 18, 1892; August 28, 1922.

53. Sidney Withington, *The First Twenty Years of Railroads in Connecticut* pp.

13-14; Peoples *Advocate,* August 21, 1844; New London *Day,* March 7, 1893.

54. Bolles, p. 5; Connecticut *Gazette,* September 18, 1874; November 7, 1879.

55. Thelma M. Kistler, "The Rise of Railroads in the Connecticut Valley", XXIII, 66, 67; Kathryn Hulme, *Annie's Captain.*

56. Letter to John C. Holland, President of the Norwich & Worcester Railroad Company from Thomas W. Williams, *et. al.,* March 22, 1847, N.Y.C.P.L.; New London *Day,* May 6, 1919.

57. New London *Day,* June 1, 1895; August 28, 1922; New London *Telegraph,* January 11, 1894.

58. New London, Willimantic & Springfield Railroad Company, *Engineer's Report and Charter,* p. 38.

59. *Eighth Annual Report* of the Directors of the New London, Willimantic and Palmer Railroad Company, pp. 68-69; Charles G. Woodward, *The New London Willimantic & Palmer Railroad Company,* p. 4.

60. Kistler, 121-122n; Woodward, p. 3n; George Rogers Taylor, *The Transportation Revolution,* 1815-1860, p. 97; Decker, "Merchants", Appendix XXV and XXVI.

61. Peoples *Advocate,* February 2, 1848.

62. *Ibid.,* February 9, 1848.

63. Withington, pp. 13, 17, 25-26.

64. Kistler, pp. 69-70, 120-121, 171, 180, 209.

65. Weekly *Chronicle,* January 4, 1855.

66. Kistler, pp. 69-70.

67. New London *Day,* June 27, 1896.

68. Weekly *Chronicle,* August 5, 1852; January 13, October 8, 1860; Harlow, p. 275; Kistler, pp. 159-160.

69. Weekly *Democrat,* December 18, 1869.

70. Connecticut *Gazette,* March 12, 1880.

71. Caulkins, p. 682; Harlow, p. 195; E. C. Kirkland, *Men, Cities and Transportation, A Study in New England History* 1820-1900, I, 439; New London Telegraph, June 25, 1908; Daily *Star,* October 29, December 8, 1871; May 29, 1874.

72. Connecticut *Gazette,* June 15, 1877.

73. New London *Day,* January 8, 1940.

74. New London *Day,* July 9, 1946.

75. Daily *Chronicle,* March 15, 1851; Withington, pp. 27-28.

76. Woodward, pp. 3-4; Alvin F. Harlow, *Steelways of New England,* pp. 184-185.

77. Weekly *Chronicle,* December 9, 1858.

78. New London *Day,* February 9, 1893; Caulkins p. 682.

79. Weekly *Chronicle,* March 18, July 26, October 21, 1852; New London *Day,* October 29, 1921.

80. Connecticut *Gazette,* November 13, 1874; October 15, 1875; February 18, 1881.

81. New London *Telegram,* April 30, 1884; May 7, 1885; New London *Day,* March 16, May 11, 1886.

82. New London *Day,* May 13, 1886; April 19, July 15, 1887.

83. New London *Telegram,* April 21, 1883; New London *Day,* February 7, 1890; August 7, 1895.

84. New London *Day,* May 11, 1888; September 15, 1889; December 28, 1903.

85. *Ibid.,* June 29, 1883; October 11, 1895; June 3, 1899.

86. *Ibid.,* January 9, 1891.

87. New London *Day,* February 1, 1972.

88. New London *Day,* April 24, 1888; April 25, 1971; Hartford Times, April 25, 1871.

89. New London *Day,* February 1, 1972; October 18, 1971.

90. Weekly *Chronicle,* September 2, 1852.

91. New London *Day,* February 12, 1886; April 13, 1892; October 1, 1885.

92. *Ibid.,* April 12, 13, 1892.

93. *Ibid.,* June 21, October 11, November 22, 1892; Harwood II, 386.

94. New London *Day,* June 16, 1899; May 11, 1900.

95. *Ibid.,* April 4, 1921.

96. *Ibid.,* October 29, 1921.

97. *Ibid.,* July 16, August 8, 1918.

98. *New London Plan,* p. 48.

99. New London *Day,* October 20, 29, 1921.

100. *Ibid.,* March 22, 1921; July 6, 1931.

101. *Ibid.*

102. *Ibid.,* May 13, 1940.

103. Ibid., August 8, 1920; March 16, 1925.

104. *Ibid.,* August 29, November 2, 1928.

105. *Ibid.,* May 21, 1918; July 7, 1919; September 2, October 22, June 5, 1971.

106. *Ibid.,* May 25, 1971.

107. *Ibid.,* December 13, 1971.

Chapter XI   Health and Charities

1. Connecticut *Gazette,* June 18, 1784; New London *Day,* October 9, 1893.

2. Connecticut *Gazette,* February 7, 1816; August 13, 1817; New London *Day,* July 23, 1823; Caulkins, p. 671.

3. New London *Telegraph,* April 4, 30, 1883; April 30, 1892; New London *Day,* August 19, 1895.

4. Daily *Star,* May 7, 1867; Peoples *Advocate,* April 21, 1847.

5. New London *Gazette,* April 26, 1826; March 29, 1848; Peoples *Advocate,* April 16, 1845.

6. Connecticut *Gazette,* September 13, 1806; Peoples *Advocate,* July 8, 1846.

7. New London *Day,* August 26, 1904.

8. New London *Gazette,* July 9, 1828; September 18, 1839; Weekly *Chronicle,* April 29, May 20, 1858.

9. New London *Gazette,* August 21, 1839; Connecticut *Gazette,* September 22, 29, 1819.

10. Caulkins, pp. 583-584.

11. *Ibid.*

12. Connecticut *Gazette,* September 4, 1822.

13. *Ibid.,* September 11, 1798; January 9, 1799.

14. *Ibid.,* May 21, June 4, 1784; November 21, 1810; New London *Gazette,* May 13, 1840.

15. New London *Day,* March 6, 1883; December 21, 1886; November 23, 1891; May 18, 1904.

16. Weekly *Chronicle,* January 4, 1855; New London *Telegram,* May 13, 1884.

17. Connecticut *Gazette,* January 9, February 6, 1880.

18. New London *Telegram,* June 26, 1883.

19. New London *Day,* December 16, 1891; April 1, 12, 1892; December 4, 1893.

20. *Ibid.,* November 21, August 1, 1893; August 15, 1894; March 3, 1896.

21. *Ibid.,* January 20, 1897; February 13, 1899.

22. Weekly *Chronicle,* May 27, 1858, New London *Telegraph,* March 6, 1894; New London *Day,* April 16, 1901, March 1, 1901; March 3, October 10, 1902; October 10, 15, 1903.

23. New London *Day,* March 23, April 1, 1918.

24. *Ibid.,* September 5, 25, 27, 28, 1918; January 31, October 24, 1920.

25. *Annual Reports,* Lawrence & Memorial Associated Hospitals, 1943-1946; New London *Day,* October 21, 1946; August 20, 1918; July 6, 1931; January 7, 1942; July 10, 1942.

26. New London *Day,* May 15, 1922; *Annual Report,* 1945.

27. *Annual Report,* 1945, p. 12; New London *Day,* October 25, 1943.

28. New London *Day,* May 15, 1917; July 8, 1942; November 29, 1971; February 7, 1972.

29. *Ibid.,* November 15, 1918; May 14, 1921; August 8, 1924; November 24, 1928.

30. New London Day, September 21, 1971.

31. Hartford *Courant,* December 20, 1972.

32. The New London *Day,* August 6, 1920; July 9, 1923; March 4, 1929; *Annual Report,* 1945, p. 11.

33. Caulkins, p. 475; New London *Day,* September 8, 1917.

34. Connecticut *Gazette,* March 2, 1877; New London *Day,* January 31, 1922; March 22, 1927; January 14, 1928.

35. Caulkins, p. 663; *Lewis Female Cent Society,* pp. 4-5.

36. Peoples *Advocate,* April 29, 30, 1845; April 29, June 3, 1846; Weekly *Chronicle,* April 26, 1850; April 24, 1856; February 10, 1859; Weekly *Democrat,* May 1, 1869; New London *Day,* May 19, 1920.

37. New London *Day,* November 8, 1893; December 4, 1899; January 29, 1921; November 17, 25, 1924; January 2, 1925; February 19, December 10, 1927; January 20, 1928.

38. *Historical Sketch,* pp. 92-93; Weekly *Chronicle,* January 9, 1850; February 28, 1861; Connecticut *Gazette,* October 16, 1874; New London *Telegram,* January 29, 1884; New London *Day,* December 24, 1921.

39. New London *Day,* April 9, 1920; July 10, November 19, March 30, 1921; August 17, 1925; November 7, 1930; May 6, June 17, 1972.

40. *Ibid.,* September 21, 1925.

41. Ester Sulman, *A Goodly Heritage–The Story of the Jewish Community in New London 1860-1955.*

42. New London *Day,* May 6, 1946; October 15, 1971.

Chapter XII   Religion

1. Wheeler, p. 11; S. Leroy Blake, *The Early History of the First Church of Christ, New London, Connecticut,* pp. 2-3.
2. Charles M. Andrews, *The Colonial Period of American History,* II, 118; Blake, *Early,* pp. 13, 25, 55; Caulkins, p. 69.
3. Blake, *Early,* pp. 70-73.
4. *Ibid.,* pp. 43, 73, 78-79, 82; Wheeler, I, pt. III, 15-16.
5. Blake, *Early,* p. 93.
6. *Ibid.,* pp. 25, 91, 110-111.
7. *Ibid.,* pp. 124, 136, 142.
8. New London *Repository,* June 28, 1860; Caulkins, p. 376.
9. Blake, *Early,* pp. 201-206.
10. *Ibid.,* pp. 206-208.
11. *Ibid.,* pp. 175-180; John R. Bolles and Anna B. Williams, *The Rogerenes,* p. 173.
12. Bolles and Williams, p. 8; Blake, pp. 180-181.
13. Blake, *Early,* pp. 182-185; Crofut II, 734.
14. Blake, *Early,* pp. 213-215.
15. S. Leroy Blake, "Curdon Saltonstall, Scholar, Preacher, Statesman", *R&P,* I, pt. IV, 10-11.
16. S. Leroy Blake, *The Later History of the First Church of Christ, New London, Connecticut,* pp. 28-30, 38-41; Caulkins, p. 450.
17. Hempstead *Diary,* March 31, May 5, 1743.
18. Crofut, II, 734; *Connecticut Guide,* pp. 63, 263.
19. *Ibid.*
20. Blake, *Later,* p. 5.
21. *Ibid.,* pp. 53-54; Caulkins, p. 436.
22. Robert A. Hallam, *Annals of St. Jame's Church, New London for 150 Years,* pp. 15-23.
23. *Ibid.,* pp. 32, 50-51.
24. *Episcopal Church–St. James* (pamphlet); Hallam, p. 17; Crofut, II, 734.
25. Hallam, pp. 34-49.
26. *Contributions to the Ecclesiastical History of Connecticut,* II, 233; Blake, *Early,* pp. 8, 95.
27. Blake, *Early,* pp. 3-4; New London *Repository,* July 19, 1860.
28. Blake, *Later,* pp. 137, 142.
29. *Ibid.,* pp. 152-156, 161-163, 179.
30. *Ibid.,* pp. 164, 171, 173.
31. Hallam, pp. 20, 29, 55-57, 60.
32. New London *Day,* March 22, 29, 1902; Caulkins, p. 598.
33. New London *Day,* July 13, 1904.
34. Denison, pp. 293-294; Weekly *Chronicle,* March 29, 1855; New London *Day,* March 11, 1889.
35. Denison, p. 293.
36. New London *Day,* May 6, 1946.

37. Hallam, pp. 16, 106-107.
38. *Episcopal Church.*
39. Blake, *Later,* p. 226.
40. *Ibid.,* p. 207.
41. *Ibid.,* pp. 288-289.
42. *Ibid.,* .
43. *Ibid.,* pp. 298, 305, 323.
44. Blake, *Later,* pp. 304-307.
45. Contributions, II, 346-347.
46. Peoples *Advocate,* February 9, 1848; Weekly *Chronicle,* September 4, 1850.
47. New London *Day,* November 9, 1971.
48. Connecticut *Gazette,* March 14, 21, 1879.
49. New London *Telegram,* May 5, 1885.
50. *Ibid.,* May 25, 1885.
51. Richard B. Wall, *Dr. Ulysses Dow and His School,* p. 5.
52. Connecticut *Gazette,* January 6, 1882; New London *Day,* May 6, 1946, July 6, 1931.
53. New London *Day,* September 18, October 23, 1893; November 18, 1921; Caulkins, pp. 596, 678; *Historical Sketch–Baptist; Historical Sketch and Directory Federal Street M.E. Church.*
54. New London *Day,* July 14, 1903.
55. Blake, *Later,* pp. 356-365.
56. New London *Day,* May 20, 1901.
57. *Ibid.*
58. *Ibid.,* May 12, 1890; May 8, September 25, 1926; June 16, 1971.
59. *Ibid.,* March 17, 1892; May 1, 1895.
60. *Ibid.,* February 3, 1892; August 17, 1920; Daily *Star,* June 1, 1867; New London *Telegram,* September 29, 1873; New London *Gazette,* May 12, 1876.
61. New London *Day,* August 16, 1920; May 10, December 3, 1921; November 25, 1929; July 6, 1931; October 9, December 17, 1971.
62. Sulman, pp. 1-7, 10.
63. *Ibid.,* pp. 9-10, 13.
64. *Ibid.,* pp. 13-15, 31.
65. *Ibid.*
66. *Ibid.*
67. New London *Day,* July 6, 1931.
68. *Ibid.,* May 6, 1946.

Chapter XIII   Education

1. C.R., I, 520-521.
2. Benjamin Stark, *Historical Sketch of the Schools of New London,* II, pt. II, 115.
3. Caulkins, p. 395.
4. Stark, II, 115.
5. *Early Connecticut Probate Records,* I, 178-179.
6. Caulkins, p. 253.
7. Crofut, II, 732.

8. Caulkins, p. 397.

9. Stark, II, pt. II, 116-117.

10. *Ibid.*, 118-119; Connecticut *Gazette*, March 16, 1872.

11. Stark, II, pt. II, 123; New London *Gazette*, July 20, 1770.

12. Stark, II, pt. II, 117-118.

13. New London *Day*, July 16, 1883.

14. Wall, *Dow*, pp. 4-5.

15. *Ibid.*, p. 27.

16. New London *Telegram*, November 29, 1873; New London *Day*, September 19, 1895.

17. Stark, II, pt. II, 123; C.R. XIV, 382-384; Crofut, II, 732; Elias B. Sanford, *A History of Connecticut*, p. 285.

18. New London *Gazette*, April 27, 1836.

19. Stark, II, pt. II, 123, 130.

20. Various advertisements 1797-1848 in New London newspapers for "female" education.

21. Stark, II, pt. II, 124-125; New London *Gazette*, January 26, 1825.

22. Stark, II, pt. II, 130.

23. *Ibid.*

24. *Ibid.*, 126-128.

25. *Ibid.*

26. New London *Day*, May 23, 1901.

27. Stark, II, pt. II, 139; Connecticut *Gazette*, March 21, 1879.

28. New London *Day*, June 20, October 15, 1927.

29. *Ibid.*, October 14, 1902; August 17, 28, 1903; September 6, 1943.

30. New London *Day*, January 2, 1928, June 21, July 8, 1930.

31. New London *Day*, October 16, 1923; January 6, 1972.

32. Stark, II, pt. II, 131-140; Benjamin T. Marshall, *A Modern History of New London County*, I, 258-259; Connecticut *Gazette*, March 26, 1880; New London *Day*, September 14, 1892; September 23, 1920; September 10, 1970.

33. Weekly *Chronicle*, January 29, June 4, 1857; New London *Day*, March 25, 1919; November 13, 1920; January 12, 1947.

34. New London *Day*, September 19, 1917; September 29, 1928; October 13, 1945.

35. Stark, II, pt. II, 130-131.

36. Ibid., 131; Daily *Star*, October 12, 1867; Connecticut *Gazette*, March 6, 1874.

37. New London *Day*, June 1, 1921; May 6, 1943; March 11, 1944.

38. *Ibid.*, October 1, 5, 1920.

39. *Ibid.*, April 19, 1946.

40. *Ibid.*, July 21, 1924.

41. *Ibid.*, January 2, 1928; August 30, 1924.

42. Connecticut *Gazette*, December 6, 1878; April 11, 1879; New London *Day*, October 4, 1923.

43. *Municipal Records*, 1892, City of New London, P. 12.

44. *Ibid.*

45. New London *Day*, January 18, 1972.

46. Numerous advertisements each issue all newspapers.

47. New London *Day*, January 7, 1886.

48. New London *Oracle*, November 18, 1797; New London *Gazette*, November 10, 1841, New London *Day*, August 31, 1888.

49. Connecticut *Gazette*, March 9, 1825; Weekly *Chronicle*, March 26, 1863; New London *Day*, September 18, 1892; January 17, 1898.

50. New London *Day*, October 19, 1914; November 2, 1921; September 11, 1943.

51. *Ibid.*, April 23, 1902.

52. *Ibid.*, April 1, 1920, Irene Nye, *Connecticut College*, pp. 17-20.

53. *Conn. College*, pp. 17-20.

54. *Ibid.*

55. *Ibid.;* New London *Day*, June 11, 1924.

56. *Conn. College*, pp. 26.

57. *Ibid.*, 41, 49; New London *Day*, July 24, 1917; February 10, March 23, May 11, 1928.

58. *Conn. College*, p. 69.

59. *Ibid.*, pp. 70-75; New London *Day*, January 21, 1972.

60. Admiral Billiard Academy, *Catalogue* 1942-1947.

61. New London *Day*, November, 1939; July 10, 1942; September 17, 1945; June 18, 1971; September 11, 1971; New London Junior College, *Catalogue*, pp. 1-7, 12.

62. New London *Day*, June 2, 25, September 17, 1946.

63. *Ibid.*, September 21, 1971.

64. *Ibid.*, November 16, 1971.

Chapter XIV   Politics, The Arts and Leisure

1. Connecticut *Register and Manual*, pp. 71-77.

2. *Ibid.*, pp. 79-80.

3. *Ibid.*, pp. 89-91.

4. *Ibid.*, pp. 65-70.

5. *Ibid.*, pp. 63-64.

6. MSS, Shaw Perkins Papers, Shaw Mansion; Weekly *Chronicle*, February 26, July 30, 1863; Weekly *Democrat*, August 1, 1868; New London *Day*, July 6, 1889; November 22, 1893; November 1, 1922.

7. City Charter, 1784.

8. *Ibid.*, 1874.

9. *Ibid.*, 1921.

10. New London Day, June 15, 1899.

11. Caulkins, p. 670.

12. Charles W. Butler, "Commemorative Sketch of John P. C. Mather", III, pt. II, pp. 217-219.

13. Weekly *Chronicle*, August 7, 1850; Connecticut *Gazette*, January 11, 1878; New London *Telegram*, August 8, 1884; New London *Day*, March 29, 1923.

14. New London *Telegram*, October 15, 1873; New London *Day*, June 7, 1888;

November 1, 1922; January 25, 1924.

15. New London *Day,* July 2, 1889; July 22, 1893.

16. *Ibid.,* March 10, 1903; GBR pp. 52-53.

17. GBR pp. 53-54; New London *Day,* November 11, 1904.

18. New London *Day,* January 17, April 10, 1923.

19. *American Men of Affairs,* p. 15; New London *Telegram,* June 3, 1873; New London *Day,* August 14, 1924, March 29, 1927.

20. *American Men of Affairs,* pp. 26-27; New London *Day,* September 28, 1896; November 16, 1923.

21. *American Men of Affairs,* p. 40; New London *Day,* May 4, 1921; November 5, 1924; January 3, June 4, 1925; August 28, November 7, 1928.

22. New London *Day,* October 2, 1945; November 6, 1971; October 2, 1971.

23. *Ibid.,* February 8, 1947, September 8, 16, October 4, 1971.

24. *Ibid.,* August 26, November 4, 1971.

25. *Ibid.,* September 16, 1971; April 1, May 4, 1972.

26. *Ibid.,* December 27, 1922.

27. *Ibid.,* September 26, October 19, 1920; June 25, 1946.

28. Caulkins, p. 660.

29. New London *Day,* January 29, 1904.

30. Daily *Star,* January 25, 1871.

31. Wall, *Dow,* p. 26; Peoples *Advocate,* October 21, 1846; Weekly Chronicle, April 24, 1856.

32. *New London Hurricane,* pp. 22-32; New London *Day,* September 15, 1944.

33. "Historical Sketch of the New London County Historical Society," I, pt. I 11, 16, 25.

34. Rogers, *Connecticut's Naval Office,* pp. 152-158.

35. *Ibid.*

36. Connecticut *Gazette,* January 23, 1874; New London *Day,* March 13, 1894; December 18, 1917; February 26, 1927.

37. Harwood, I, 225-227.

38. Hempstead, p. 311.

39. *Ibid.,* p. 219.

40. New London *Gazette,* June 16, 1769.

41. *Ibid.,* May 26, 1824; May 11, 1825.

42. *Ibid., July 22,* 1835; June 2, 1837; Peoples *Advocate,* June 3, 1846; Weekly *Democrat,* May 12, 1849; Daily *Star,* May 31, 1851; Weekly *Chronicle,* April 8, 1858.

43. Weekly *Chronicle,* February 14, 1856; December 25, 1862; New London *Day,* November 22, 1921.

44. New London *Day,* November 29, 1921.

45. New London *Gazette,* June 4, 1784; Caulkins, p. 663.

46. New London *Day,* June 11, 1887.

47. Connecticut *Gazette,* January 14, 1881.

48. *Ibid.,* November 14, 1838.

49. George Parsons Lathrop, "Description of the Public Library at New London", I, pt. I, 90-91.

50. Providence Sunday *Journal,* June 25, 1939; New London *Day,* November 6, 1930.

51. Weekly *Chronicle*, January 6, 1853.

52. Connecticut *Gazette*, January 7, 1881; New London *Telegram*, February 28, 1883.

53. Henry P. Cody, "How to Retire Comfortably on Six Columns a Week", Yankee (September 1972) 84-89, 179-190.

54. New London *Day*, October 7, 1971.

55. *Ibid.*, January 21, 27, 1972.

56. *Ibid.*, October 29, 1921; December 28, 1922; September 21, 1943.

Chapter XV   Town Services

1. Richard B. Wall, *New London Police Department.*

2. Hempstead, p. 28.

3. *Ibid.*, p. 261.

4. *Ibid.*, p. 120.

5. *Ibid.*, p. 37.

6. *Ibid.*, pp. 94, 195, 263, 272, 411.

7. *Ibid.*, pp. 126-127.

8. *Ibid.*, p. 619.

9. Caulkins, p. 410.

10. *Ibid.*, pp. 576-577.

11. *Ibid.*, p. 629.

12. Hempstead, pp. 139-141.

13. C.A. VI, Crimes, 241-242.

14. Wall, *Police.*

15. Peoples *Advocate,* April 2, 1845.

16. New London *Telegram*, May 12, 1873.

17. Wall, *Police.*

18. *Ibid.*

19. *Ibid.*

20. *Ibid.*

21. *Ibid.*

22. *Ibid.*

23. *Ibid.*

24. New London *Day*, February 27, 1880.

25. *Ibid.*, September 3, 1888.

26. Wall, *Police.*

27. New London *Day*, July 12, 1899.

28. Wall, *Police.*

29. New London *Day*, August 12, 1917.

30. *Ibid.*, December 26, 1923.

31. *Ibid.*, November 1, 1927.

32. *Ibid.*, February 20, 1929; May 9, 1922.

33. *Ibid.*, April 2, 1929.

34. *Ibid.*, February 10, 1923.

35. *Ibid.*, December 7, 1920.

36. *Ibid.*, November 17, 1924.

37. *Ibid.*, May 26, 1925.

38. *Ibid.,* June 13, 1925.
39. *Ibid.,* April 9, 1946.
40. *Ibid.,* March 21, 1930.
41. Wall, *Police.*
42. New London *Day,* April 1, 1946.
43. *Ibid.,* April 3, 1972.
44. *Ibid.* December 1, 1971; Salaries represent overtime and extra-duty time.
45. *Ibid.,* August 19, December 14, 1971; April 4, 1972.
46. Lila Parrish Lyman, *One Hundred Years of Niagara Engine Company No. 1,* p. 10.
47. Caulkins, pp. 475-476.
48. Lyman, p. 12.
49. *Ibid.,* pp. 12-13.
50. *Ibid.,* pp. 7-8, 13.
51. *Ibid.,* p. 14.
52. New London *Gazette,* August, 1838.
53. *Ibid.,* January 6, 1841; Caulkins, p. 658.
54. Lyman, pp. 9, 11, 14-15.
55. New London *Day,* November 17, 1891; Lyman, pp. 12-13.
56. Lyman, pp. 10, 14-16, 46-47; New London *Day,* November 12, 1900; September 23, 1903; October 29, 1904.
57. Weekly *Chronicle,* December 1, 1853; New London *Day,* February 17, 1896.
58. Lyman, pp. 16-17; New London *Day,* December 30, 1891.
59. New London *Day,* February 1, 1926.
60. New London *Telegram,* September 17, 1873.
61. New London *Day,* January 18, 1892; Connecticut *Gazette,* December 11, 1874.
62. New London *Day,* January 11, 14, 1895; August 14, 1924.
63. *Ibid.,* December 17, 1920; August 14, 1924.
64. *Ibid.,* October 29, 1921; Lyman, p. 19.
65. Lyman, pp. 14-16.
66. *Ibid.,* pp. 24-28; Connecticut *Gazette,* June 26, 1874.
67. New London *Day,* May 16, 1927.
68. Lyman, p. 29.
69. New London *Day,* August 8, 1923; January 9, 1926.
70. Connecticut Gazette, January 7, 1881.
71. *Ibid.,* June 7, 1878.
72. New London *Day,* January 26, 1922.
73. *Ibid.,* January 9, 1922; Peoples *Advocate,* January 26, 1848.
74. Weekly *Democrat,* January 27, 1849.
75. Weekly *Chronicle,* November 24, 1853.
76. *Ibid.,* November 9, 16, 1854.
77. *Ibid.,* January 22, 1857; November 3, 1861; October 14, 1871.
78. Lyman, p. 20; Connecticut *Gazette,* November 6, 1874.
79. New London *Day,* November 30, 1888.
80. *Ibid.,* January 15, 1889.
81. *Ibid.,* September 20, December 20, 1901.

82. *Ibid.*, December 31, 1924; February 19, December 31, 1924; January 13, 1923; January 1, December 4, 1926; January 28, 1928; January 1, 1929.

83. *New London City Directories,* 1946-1971.

84. S.R., X, 29-31.

85. Weekly *Democrat,* September 9, 1848.

86. Daily *Star,* June 6, 1871; August 12, 13, September 8, 14, 19, November 14, 15, 1873.

87. Starr, *Historical Sketch,* pp. 89-90; New London *Telegram,* June 5, 1873; New London *Day,* October 29, 1921.

88. New London *Telegram,* January 29, 1885; New London *Day,* October 6, 1900.

89. New London *Day,* December 4, 1888; September 19, 1902; October 21, 1920; March 14, 1929.

90. New London *Day,* June 11, 12, September 25, 1888; May 9, 1897; December 12, 1919; October 29, 1921; September 19, 1928; July 6, 1931.

91. Caulkins, p. 664; Peoples *Advocate,* February 2, 1848; Weekly *Democrat,* June 12, 1869.

92. Weekly *Chronicle,* July 21, 1859.

93. New London *Directory,* 1876-1877.

94. Connecticut *Gazette,* January 16, April 23, 1880.

95. J. Leigh Walsh, *Connecticut Pioneers in Telephone: New Haven Telephone Pioneers of America,* p. 106; Connecticut *Gazette,* January 13, 1882; New London *Telegram,* March 29, 1883; New London *Day,* July 6, 1931.

96. New London *Day,* July 5, 1888.

97. *Ibid.*, April 3, 1900; Walsh, p. 213.

98. New London *Day,* October 28, 1914; May 22, 1920.

99. *Ibid.*, October 1, 1925; January 7, 1928.

100. *Ibid.*, July 6, 1931.

101. *Ibid.*, February 8, 1897.

102. *Ibid.*, February 20, 1897.

103. *American Men of Affairs,* p. 44; Glenn Weaver, *The Hartford Electric Light Company,* p. 128.

104. "The Green Family of Printers", *Cedar Grove,* I, No. 3, 177-188.

105. Peoples *Advocate,* October 15, 1845.

106. Weekly *Chronicle,* January 26, 1865.

107. GBR pp. 324-325; New London *Day,* February 8, 1921.

108. New London *Day,* June 27, 1922.

109. "New London's Community Burial Ground", *Cedar Grove,* I, No. 3, 191, 192, 209-210.

110. New London *Day,* September 29, 1902.

111. *Ibid.*, December 2, 1925.

112. "Burial Grounds", *Cedar Grove,* I, No. 3, 193.

113. *Ibid.*

114. Daily *Chronicle,* January 2, March 29, August 26, 1851.

115. New London *Day,* August 4, 1925.

Conclusion

1. New London *Day,* January 4, 1972.
2. *Ibid.,* December 13, 1971.
3. *Ibid.*
4. *Ibid.*
5. *Ibid.*
6. *Ibid.,* November 5, 1971.
7. *Ibid.,* February 8, 1972.

SOURCES CONSULTED
(Bibliography)

The raw materials for a study of New London, e.g. business records, court records, church records, diaries, government documents, monographs, newspapers and pamphlets, constituted an almost unlimited source of history. Unfortunately, the material had not been organized beyond very generally for storage or shelving purposes. The researcher's problem has been to make use of the materials, selectively deciding what will best tell the story of New London in the limited space available.

Following are the major materials utilized from those consulted. While this is not intended as a definite history of all the materials, it should prove useful for those interested in the source material.

Manuscripts

Among the federal government manuscripts the most useful were the French Spoilation Claims, Record Group 36, in the National Archives and the Shaw Manuscripts, Miscellaneous Correspondence, Force Transcripts at the Library of Congress. A valuable collection, the New London Customs Records, has been relocated at the Federal Records Center, Waltham, Massachusetts.

Connecticut's State Library at Hartford contains the most extensive collection of manuscripts pertinent to this study. The voluminous Connecticut Archives have been catalogued under a number of headings such as Trade and Maritime Affairs, Insolvent Debtors, Revolutionary War, Towns and Lands, Travel, Highways, Fences, Bridges and Taverns, and Finance and Currency, which proved most valuable to this book. The New London Probate Records, Collection of Shipping Papers, Papers of Jeremiah Brainard and Joshua Coit, as well as "Census of the United States, Original Returns of the Assistant Marshals in Connecticut," the Book of Insurance Risks, Washington Insurance Company, and the William Hale "Diary" are all pertinent to this study.

The New London County Court Records at the State Library include the Supreme Court of Errors, Superior Court, County Court, Maritime Court, Court of Common Council and Court of Common Pleas while the City Court Records there include those of the Justice Court of the Peace and City Court.

Church records are always excellent sources and the State Library contains: First Congregational Church, First Congregational Society, Second Congregational Church, First Baptist, Federal Street Methodist Episcopal Church and St. James Church.

The Connecticut Historical Society possesses several individual items which proved of use in its manuscript collection. The General Jedidiah Huntington Letters, the John Winthrop, Sr. and Jr., Letters, Wadsworth Correspondence, various account books of New London merchants, and the Aaron Bull Diary were consulted. In addition, several manuscripts provided valuable information: Harold C. Bailey, "Connecticut's Share in Winning Independence at Sea," Eva L. Butler, "Colonial Letters of our Ancestors, 1653-1733," "Joseph Coit Personal History," and Francis H. Parker, "The Connecticut Navy in the Revolutionary War."

At the G. W. Blunt White Library, Mystic Seaport, the N. and W. W. Billings Collection, the Lawrence & Co. Papers, the John K. Pimer Papers and the John Turner Papers proved useful. Other excellent collections include Logs and Journals, Whaling Documents, and a Miscellaneous Collection. Not to be overlooked is the T. A. Scott Company Papers 1889-1927 which detail the case of the *Deutschland,* a commercial submarine, which carried a cargo to the United States during World War I and entered New London harbor.

At the Shaw Mansion, the New London County Historical Society possess several manuscripts of value. The Shaw Papers rank as the most valuable, but also preserved are the Dr. D. T. Brainard Letters, the Hancock Papers, the Shaw-Perkins Papers, Winthrop Papers, N. & W. W. Billings Papers, and a Dr. S. P. H. Lee Account Book and Papers. Dr. Lee established an early New London whaling company.

The Sterling Library, Yale University, contains several items of interest concerning New London. Of the material here the Shaw Collection is the most important, containing thirty-five account books and ledgers, and many individual documents totaling 8,832 items, which have been placed on microfilm. Yale also possesses the Frink Papers, the Lane Collection, the Joseph J. Lawrence Collection (four boxes), Leffingwell Papers, 1734-1810, and the Shipping Collection. Letters of Coddington Billings, Noyes Billings and William Williams Billings can be found in the Miscellaneous Manuscript Collection. New London Deeds in the Connecticut Collection, and the Whaling Logs yield information about merchant activities. Yale preserved, but recently moved to the G. W. Blunt White Library, Mystic Seaport, the National Whaling Bank Collection of sixty-five boxes and one hundred volumes.

At the Baker Library, Harvard Graduate School of Business, Harvard University, valuable items contained are the Letterbook of Matthew Howland and the Mercantile Marine Insurance Company's Risk Book.

The Massachusetts Historical Society houses several collections of interest, the Heath Collection, Huntington-Wolcott Papers, and the Miscellaneous Bound Collection. A number of Nathaniel Shaw, Jr. Letters have been collected by the Society.

The Manuscript Division of the New York Public Library possesses two collections useful for a study of New London, the Miscellaneous Connecticut Boxes and the Thomas W. Williams Papers.

The Stonington Historical Society has preserved a shipping paper of the *Blackstone* under Captain Fordham, 1780, indicating a whaling voyage of that date.

Government Publications

Among the public documents of value are W. C. Ford and Gaillard Hunt, eds., *Journals of the Continental Congress, 1774-1789* (34 vols., Washington, D.C.; Government Printing Office, 1904-1937) which contain references to Nathaniel Shaw's work as Continental Naval Agent. *The American State Papers; Commerce and Navigation* (2 vols., Washington, D.C.; Gales & Seaton, 1832-1834) list the tonnage of American ports in the coastal trade, fishing, foreign trade and whaling from 1794 to 1819. Seamen registered at the ports are also noted. William Bell Clark, ed., *Naval Documents of the American Revolution* (3 vols., Washington, D.C.; Government Printing Office, 1964-1968) contain several letters to Shaw and deal with naval and privateering events during the Revolution.

The Public Records of the Colony of Connecticut 1636-1776 (15 vols., Hartford: Brown & Parsons, F. A. Brown, and Case, Lockwood and Brainard 1850-1890), edited by James Hammond Trumbull and Charles J. Hoadly proved invaluable for a study of Connecticut. Equally valuable are the *Public Records of the State of Connecticut 1775-1803* (3 vols., Hartford: The Case, Lockwood & Brainard Co., 1884-1922, and 8 vols., Hartford: The State, 1942-1967 edited successively by Charles J. Hoadly, Leonard Woods Labaree, Albert Van Dusen and Christopher Collier.

The annually issued *Connecticut State Register and Manual* and Charles Manwaring William, ed., *A Digest of the Early Connecticut Probate Records* (Vol. I, Hartford District, 1635-1700) proved useful.

Newspapers

Newspapers are always a very valuable source. The editorials, Marine Lists and Historical Sketches proved particularly interesting. New London has been especially blessed in this area with the large number and varied views represented by its press. Among the newspapers consulted were the following: *New London Summary* (1758-1763); *New London Gazette* (1763-1844), called the *Connecticut Gazette* (1775-1823); *Weekly Oracle* (1795-1800); *New London Bee* (1797-1802); *The Republican Advocate* (1818-1828); *Connecticut Centinel* (1828-1830); *(Working Man's Advocate* (1830-1831); *The People's Advocate and New London County Republican* (1840-1848); *Morning News* (1844-1848); *Weekly Chronicle* (1848-1868); *Daily Chronicle* (1848-1868); *New London Weekly Democrat* (1845-1873); New London Daily Star (1848-1873); *New London Repository* (1858-1862); New London Press (1868); *New London Daily Times* (1871); *New London Evening Telegram* (1873-1909); *Connecticut*

Gazette (1873-1909); The New London *Day* (1881-still being published); *New London Morning Telegraph* (1885-1920).

General Works

For information on the exploring of the area before settlement John Bartlet Brebner, *The Explorers of North America 1492-1806* (New York: World Publishing Company, 1964) proved useful. Oliver P. Chitwood, *A History of Colonial America* (New York: Harper and Brothers, 1948), discusses early shipbuilding colonial America.

Fessenden S. Blanchard, *Long Island Sound* (New York: D. Van Nostrand, 1958) contains an excellent section on the early history of the New London area, and Samuel Adams Drake, *Nooks and Corners of the New England Coast* (New York: Harper & Brothers, 1876) provides some general information on the port.

Connecticut history has attracted many authors and several of their works offer material of value. Marguerite Allis, *Connecticut Trilogy* (G. P. Putnam's Sons, New York, 1934) deals mainly with the folklore of the state, while John Warner Barber, *Connecticut Historical Collections* (New Haven: John W. Barber, 1836), is a collection of others' works and newspaper articles. Richard L. Bushman, *From Puritan to Yankee: Character and the Social Order in Connecticut, 1690-1765* (Cambridge, Mass.: Harvard University Press, 1967), examines the Connecticut trade centers and their rivalry; an older account, George Clark, *A History of Connecticut, Its People and Institutions* (New York, G. P. Putnam's Sons, 1914), gives some attention to merchant activity at New London. A brief look at New London is provided by the Federal Writers Project, *Connecticut, A Guide to Its Roads, Lore and People* (Boston: Houghton Mifflin Company, 1938). Dorothy Deming, *The Settlement of the Connecticut Towns* (New Haven: Yale University Press, 1939), presents a short account of New London's beginnings. Forrest Morgan, ed., *Connecticut As a Colony and State* (4 vols., Hartford; The Publishing Society of Conn., 1904), Elias B. Sanford, *A History of Connecticut* (Hartford: S. S. Scranton and Company, 1889), Iveigh Hunt Sterry and William H. Garrigus, *They Found a Way* (Brattleboro, Vt.: Stephen Daye Press, 1933) and Benjamin Trumbull, *A Complete History of Connecticut* (New London: H. D. Utley, 1898), 2 vols., all provide a few items of information about New London. Samuel A. Peters, *General History of Connecticut* (London, 1781), presents an anti-American view and takes note of New London's dependence upon Boston and New York. Charles Burr Todd, *In Olde Connecticut* (New York: The Grafton Press, 1906) describes the beginning of West Indian trade at New London and the whaling industry. Albert Van Dusen, *Connecticut* (New York: Random House, 1961) covers the merchant trade and history of New London more extensively than any other history of Connecticut. Benjamin T. Marshall, ed., *A Modern History of New London County* (5 vols., New York: Lewis Historical Publishing Company, 1922) provides much information on newspapers, P. Leroy Harwood, *History of Eastern Connecticut* (3 vols., Chicago: The Pioneer Publishing Company, 1931), appears deeply indebted to Caulkins, *History of New London*. No local study could be complete without consulting Florence S. Crofut, *Guide to the History and the Historic Sites of Connecticut* (2 vols., New Haven: Yale University Press, 1937.

New London

Only one adequate history of New London exists, Frances Manwaring Caulkins, *History of New London* (New London: H. D. Utley, 1895). Of use are the New London Town Records especially for the Seventeenth Century which have been made quite readable in a transcript prepared by Eva L. Butler (1946). Several short histories of the town provide additional insight into its development. Among these are Catherine B. Avery, *A Brief History of New London, Connecticut* (n.p.;n.d.), John Rogers Bolles, *New London, A Seaport for North and West* (New London: George E. Starr, 1877), Augustus Brandagee, *Some Incidents in the Early History of New London* (n.p.; 1896), W. R. Starr, *A Centennial Historical Sketch of the Town of New London* (New London: Press of George Starr, 1876) and Carl Jay Viets, *A Brief History of New London* (New London: Viets, 1896). Three volumes intended to extol the virtue of the port, *Leading Businessmen of New London* (Boston: Mercantile Publishing Company, 1890, *Pictorial New London and Its Environs at the Commencement of the Twentieth Century* (Providence: Journal of Commerce Company, 1901), and *Pcituresque New London* (Hartford: American Book Exchange, 1901) do provide facts about the port after the high point of whaling had long passed and the town hoped to develop an industrial base. Hildegarde Hawthorne, *Old Seaport Towns of New England* (New York: Dobb, Mead Co., 1916) provides a good description of early New London as a West Indian port. Richard A. Wheeler, "The First Organized Church in New London County" (N.L.C.H.S. *Recs. and Papers,* I, pt. III, New London: N.L.C.H.S., 1891), 11-25, describes the early settlement of the New London area.

New London, Connecticut And the Adjacent Sea-Shore (New London: New London Businessmen's Association, n.d.), presents brief information and pictures of the area. For a more detailed study concerning the failure of the town to reach its potential as a major port see Robert O. Decker, "The New London Merchants: The Rise and Decline of a Connecticut Port" (Unpublished Ph.D. Thesis, University of Connecticut, 1970). An interesting account of New London in the second half of the nineteenth century is contained in Charles B. Jennings, *Recollections of New London of Seventy Years* (n.p.:n.d., 1921). For those interested in the labor movement in The Town *The Early Labor Movement in Connecticut: 1790-1860* (West Hartford: privately printed, 1972) by Nelson R. Burr is valuable. An early business organization, forerunner of the town's Chamber of Commerce, can be traced in John Humphrey's *A Brief History of the New London Businessmen's Association* (New London: n.p., 1913). Two volumes of value are Ernest E. Rogers, *New London's Participation in Connecticut's Tercentenary* (New London, 1935) and S. Leroy Blake's, "Two Hundred and Fiftieth Anniversary of the Settlement of New London" (*R&P,* II, pt. III, N.L.C.H.S., 1897), 187-298.

American Men of Affairs Magazine (Vol. I, No. 1, 1912), provides brief history of businesses and businessmen as well as some general knowledge of the town. Several special studies of New London provide knowledge of areas not available elsewhere. These include J. Harvey Kerns, "A Study of the Social and Economic Conditions of the Negro Population of New London, Connecticut" (October-November, 1944, The National Urban League), *New London 1646-1946* (Technical Planning Associates, 1946), Herbert S. Swan, *The New London Plan* (New

London, 1929) and Bessie Bloom Wessel, "The Ethnic Survey of New London, Connecticut, 1938-1944" *(The American Journal of Sociology,* Vol. I, No. 2, Sept. 1944). The latter is a re-study of an earlier project "Ethnic Factor in Population of New London" (Vol. XXXV, No. 1, July 1929).

A delightful picture of pleasant days and scenes now long past is given in James Lawrence Chew, "Old Buildings of New London" *(R.&P.,* I, pt. IV, N.L.C.H.S., 1893), 77-96, "Historical Sketch of the New London County Historical Society" *(R.&P.,* I, pt. I, N.L.C.H.S., 1890), 16-19, *Latest Views of New London* (New London, 1906), George Parsons Lathrop, "Description of the Public Library" *(R.&P.,* I, pt. 1, N.L.C.H.S, 1890), 90-91, and Richard A. Wheeler "Memories" *(R.&P.,* II, pt. V, N.L.C.H.S., 1904), 474-478. Carlotte M. Holloway, "A Daughter of Puritans" *(Connecticut Quarterly,* Vol. III, No. 1, 3-18) provides an excellent sketch of the port with pictures of homes, men and vessels. Another fine short description of the port town is in *Towns of New England . . .* (Boston, 1921, pt. II). Also of value is Mary E. Perkins, *Chronicles of a Connecticut Farm* (Boston, 1905). New London Directories help in location of homes, businesses, schools and institutions.

Biographies, Diaries, Journals and Papers

Biographies of New London merchants are few in number. Nathaniel Shaw, Jr., lacks a full length biography but has a short item in the *Dictionary of American Biography,* XVII (New York), 45-47, and more information in Ernest E. Rogers, *Connecticut's Naval Office at New London* (N.L.C.H.S., Collections, II, N.L.C.H.S. 1933). Other information about the Shaws can be found from Caulkins, *History of New London* and from the New London Probate Records containing the wills of Nathaniel, Jr., Temperance and Thomas Shaw.

Several works concern the New London Coit's of shipbuilding and merchant fame; *Martha Coit Letters* (Norwich, Bulletin, 1895), Mehetabel Coit, *Her Book* (Norwich: Norwich Bulletin, 1895), Frederick Chapman, *The Coit Family* (Hartford: Case, Lockwood & Brainard Company, 1874), and Chester Destler, *Joshua Coit, American Federalist* (Middletown: Wesleyan University Press, 1962).

For this paper a number of other works proved useful. Daniel Deshon receives a short sketch in George Munson Curtis, *Early Silver of Connecticut and Its Makers* (The Barta Press, 1913). Three works concern Henry P. Haven: Henry Clay Trumbull, *A Model Superintendent* (Philadelphia: John D. Walters, 1880), Ernest E. Rogers, "Henry P. Haven" Cedar Grove Cemetery *Publication,* I (New London: New London Cemetery Association, 1936), 284, and "Henry P. Haven" (N.L.C.H.S. *Recs. and Papers,* I, pt. II, New London: N.L.C.H.S., 1890) 41-44.

Joshua Hempstead's diary, *Diary of Joshua Hempstead, 1711-1758* (N.L.C.H.S. Collections, I New London: 1901) shows colonial New London in its everyday activities. Another work which helps with the Hempstead family is Mary Branch, *The Old Hempstead House* (New London: 1896).

Of value also is "Captain Elisha Hinman" (Cedar Grove Cemetery Society, *Publications,* I, No. 3, New London, 1941), Alverda L. Beck, ed., The Letter Book of Esek Hopkins (Providence: Rhode Island Historical Society, 1932), Francis Caulkins "Memors of Captain Richard Law" (N.L.C.H.S., 1890), and the diary of one of New London's founders, Thomas Minor, *The Diary of Thomas Minor* (New London: The Day Publishing Co., 1899).

S. Leroy Blake, "Gurdon Saltonstall, Scholar, Preacher, Statesman" (N.L.C.H.S., *R.&P.*, I, pt. V, New London: N.L.C.H.S., 1894), 3-28.

New London's Winthrop family has several useful items, the Winthrop Papers (MSS, N.L.C.H.S.), the *Winthrop Papers* (5 vols., Boston: M.H.S., 1929-1947) and James Kendall Hosmer, ed., *Winthrop Journal* (2 vols., New York: Charles Scribner's Sons, 1908). Most useful of the secondary works include Robert C. Black, III, *The Younger John Winthrop* (New York: Columbia University Press, 1966). Richard S. Dunn, *Puritans and Yankees: The Winthrop Dynasty of New England, 1630-1717* (Princeton, Princeton University Press, 1962), and Lila Parrish Lyman, *The New London Homestead (1754-1892) of the Winthrop Family* (Stonington: Pequot Press, 1957). The Winthrop activity in King Philips War is best covered in Douglas Edward Leach, *Flintlock and Tomahawk: New England in King Philip's War* (New York, 1958).

Some very excellent biographical sketches can be found in the Cedar Grove Cemetery booklets. Francis Allyn, William Albertson, Rial Chaney and Charles Augustus Williams are discussed briefly in I, No. 1, while Charles Butler, Richard H. Chapell, Herbert Crandall, J. N. Harris, Henry P. Haven, Stevens and Moses Rogers are in I, No. 2. The final issue No. 3 contains sketches of General George C. Wilson and the Green Family.

Further sketches of importance are in *R.&.P.* of N.L.C.H.S. These include Charles W. Butler "Commemorative Sketch of John P. C. Mather", III, pt. II (1912), 217-219; Thomas S. Collier "Frances Manwaring Caulkins", I, pt. I (1890), 30-32; John McGinley, "Memoir of Hon. Benjamin Stark", II, pt. IV (1901), 371-376; Same author, "Memoirs of Captain Charles Augustus Williams" II pt. IV (1901), 367-370; Maria F. Starr, Memoir of Hon. William H. Starr", I, pt. I, (1890), 82-84; and Richard B. Wall "Captain Stevens Rogers", II, pt. IV (1904), 493-499.

The Connecticut Historical Society has published the papers of several Connecticut leaders important to this study in the collection; *Fitch Papers,* Vols., XVII (1919) and XVIII (1920), *Pitkin Papers,* Vol. XIX (1921), *Talcott Papers,* Vols. IV (1892) and V (1896) and *Wyllys Papers,* Vol. XXI (1924).

The following contain a number of biographical sketches which prove useful: *Biographical Review* (Boston: Biographical Review Publishing Co., 1898), Vol. XXVI, *Geneological and Biographical Record of New London County, Connecticut* (Chicago: J. H. Beers and Co., 1905) and D. Hamilton Hurd, *History of New London County* (Philadelphia: J. W. Lewis & Co., 1882).

Banking

The most valuable work on New London banking is William F. Hasse, Jr., *A History of Money and Banking in Connecticut* (New Haven: Privately Printed, 1957). Of help in rounding out the financial operations are Francis Parsons, *The History of Banking in Connecticut* (New Haven: Yale University Press, 1934), and Joseph Woodward, *Currency and Banking in Connecticut* (Boston: D. H. Hurd & Co., 1857). G. W. White Blunt Library, Mystic Seaport, possesses the National Whaling Bank

Collections. *A Century of Banking in New London* (New London: The Savings Bank of New London, 1927) which provided some general information. For a discussion of the national banking system and New London, Bray Hammond, *Banks and Politics in America* (Princeton: Princeton University Press, 1957) and Rollen G. Osterweis, *Charter Number Two: The Centennial History of the First New Haven National* (New Haven: Yale University Press, 1963), are useful, as is *The Savings Bank of New London, Connecticut* (New London: n.p., 1952). Mr. Ralph E. Wadleigh was kind enough to share his time, material and knowledge of his banking career and study on the "History of Banking in New London".

Maritime

The colonial development of the port of New London can be traced in the Shaw manuscripts, Francis Caulkins and R. R. Hinman, *Letters from the English Kings and Queens* (Hartford: John B. Eldredge, 1836). Roland M. Hooker, *The Colonial Trade of Connecticut* (New Haven: Yale University Press, 1934), Margaret Martin, *Merchants and Trade in the Connecticut River Valley, 1780-1820 (Smith College Studies in History,* Vol. XXIV, Nos. 1-4 October, 1938-July 1939), and John Stoughton, *A Corner Stone of Colonial Commerce* (Boston: Little, Brown and Company, 1911), present a general discussion of colonial trade and New London's role in the overall picture. One of the important families is covered by Chester McArthur Destler, *Joshua Coit: American Federalist* (Middletown: Wesleyan University Press, 1962). Two studies deal with the ill-fated New London Society for Trade and Commerce, Andrew McFarland Davis, "A Connecticut Land Bank" (Publications of the Colonial Society of Massachusetts, V, *Transactions, 1897-1898,* 96-111; VI, *Transactions,* 1899-1900, 6-11), and N. Shaw Perkins, "New London Society for Trade and Commerce" (N.L.C.H.S. *R.&P.* II, pt. II, New London; N.L.C.H.S., 1896), 145-152. Destler's Account and Albert E. Van Dusen's "The Trade of Revolutionary Connection" (Unpublished Thesis, University of Pennsylvania, 1948) provide the best coverage of the Revolutionary Trade of the port.

Robert G. Albion, *The Rise of New York Port* (New York: Charles Scribner's Sons, 1939) is a classic study of merchant initiative in the development of a major port. A look at the individuals and families who are responsible for New London's Maritime History is provided by Robert O. Decker, "New London, Connecticut: Its Maritime Story" (Stamford Genealogical Society *Bulletin,* Vol. 15, Nos. 1, 2, 3), and *Annie's Captain* (Boston, 1961), Kathryn Hume's fictionalized account of a New London captain.

Bernard Bailyn, *The New England Merchants in the Seventeenth Century* (New York: Harper & Row, 1964) is one of the best accounts of colonial merchant development. Vessels and their rigs are identified in Charles G. Davis, *Rigs of the Nine Principal Types of Sailing Vessels* (Salem: Peabody Museum, 1962) and Romola and R. C. Anderson, *The Sailing Ship: Six Thousand Years of History* (New York: W. W. Norton, 1963).

Several aspects of New London trade and the vessels used is discussed in A. P. Brigham, *Geographical Influences in American History* (Boston: Ginn & Co., 1913), Howard I. Chappelle, *The History of the American Sailing Ship* (New York: Bonanza

Books, 1935), Carl Cutler, *Queens of the Western Ocean* (Annapolis: United States Naval Institute, 1961) and Roger Williams McAdam, *Salts of the Sound* (New York: Stephen Daye Press, 1957). The most valuable business records prove to be the Shaw materials, the Billings Papers, the Lawrence Collection and the *Beekman Mercantile* Papers 1745-1799 (3 vols., New York: The New York Historical Society, 1956), edited by Philip L. White.

Insurance rates which indicate the dangers of trade in peaceful time and the threat of capture in war can be studied in the *Risk Book of the New London Union Insurance Company*, Boston (2 vols., MSS, Baker Library). A good general treatment of war risks can be found in Robert G. Albion and Jennie B. Pope, *Sea Lanes in Wartime* (New York: W. W. Norton, 1942).

Privateering

Four sources prove of particular value in tracing the history of New London privateers during the American Revolution: Thomas S. Collier, "Brief Biographies of Connecticut Revolutionary Naval and Privateers Officers," and "The Revolutionary Privateers of Connecticut" (N.L.C.H.S., *R.&P.*, I, pt. IV, New London N.L.C.H.S. (1893), 1-74, Louis F. Middlebrook, *Maritime Connecticut During the American Revolution, 1775-1783* (2 vols., Salem: The Essex Institute, 1925) and Harold C. Bailey "Connecticut's share in Winning Independence at Sea" (MS, C.H.S.). The Shaw Papers (N.L.C.H.S., the Connecticut *Gazette* and William Bell Clark, ed., *Naval Documents of the American Revolution* (3 vols., Washington, D.C.: United States Government Printing Office, 1964-1968), provided additional privateering information. A general account of American privateering is provided by Gardner Allen, *Naval History of the American Revolution* (New York: Russell & Russell, 1962), and Edgar S. Maclay, *A History of American Privateers* (New York: D. Appleton & Co., 1899).

Revolutionary War

Oscar Zeichner, *Connecticut's Years of Controversy: 1764-1775* (Chappel Hill: University of North Carolina Press, 1949), describes the land of steady habits as being unsteady and gives a background to the Revolution by dealing with the issues creating the lack of stability. For merchant activity during the conflict the Shaw Collection at the Beinecke Library and the Shaw Papers at the Shaw Mansion are the most valuable. Also, Francis Caulkins, *History of New London,* New London *Gazette,* Connecticut *Gazette* and the *Colonial Records* and *State Records* are useful.

F. H. Parker, "The Connecticut Navy in the Revolutionary War" (MS, C.H.S.), and Sherman W. Adams, "Revolutionary Naval Officers" N.L.C.H.S. *R.&P.*, I, pt. II, New London, N.L.C.H.S. 1890), 47-51, deal with the Connecticut navy. Fletcher Pratt, *The Compact History of the United States Navy,* (New York: Hawthorne Books, 1962), relates an incident of a mutiny in New London harbor by a Continental naval vessel. Howard I. Chappelle, *The History of the American Sailing Navy*

(New York: Bonanza Books, 1942), presents plans and conditions of detail of American naval ships during the Revolution. Conditions of New London prisoners of war on prison ships at New York are described in Henry R. Stiles, *Letters from the Prisons and Prison Ships of the Revolution* (New York: Privately Printed, 1865). Christopher Ward, *The War of the Revolution* (2 vols., New York: The MacMillan Co., 1952), covers the military events involving New London and its people. The burning of New London is described in Caulkins, Charles Allyn, *The Battle of Groton Heights* (New London: Houghton and Company, (1882), and Christopher Leffingwell's "Account of the Burning" MS, Beinecke Library). Useful for the Tories of New London are Epaphroditus Peck, *The Loyalists of Connecticut* (New Haven: Yale University Press, 1934), and James Shepard, "The Tories of Connecticut" (*Connecticut Quarterly*, vol. 4, 1898), 139-151, 257-263. The British naval side of the war is given in Sir William James, *The British Navy in Adversity* (London: London Press, 1926). Two informative accounts of Arnold's raids are to be found in *Battle of Groton Heights: A Story of the Storming of Fort Griswold and the Burning of New London . . .* (New London, 1931) and E. E. Rogers (ed.) *Sesquicentennial of the Battle of Groton Heights and the Burning of New London . . .* (Hartford, 1932).

Transportation

Although the most important information on turnpikes can be found in the State Records, Isabel S. Mitchell, *Roads and Roadmaking in Colonial Connecticut* (New Haven: Yale University Press, 1933), Philip Elbert Taylor, "The Turnpike Era in New England" (Unpublished thesis, Yale University, 1934) and Frederic J. Wood, *Turnpikes of New England* (Boston: Marshall Jones Company, 1919) are of use. Frances Caulkins has the most entensive coverage of the steamship history of New London. Richard B. Wall, "Captain Stevens Rogers" (N.L.C.H.S. *R.&P.*, II, pt. V, New London: N.L.C.H.S., 1904), 493-499, recounts New London's link to the first transAtlantic crossing of a steamboat, New York—New London steamboat service is covered in detail by Roger Williams McAdam, *Salts of the Sound* (New York: Stephen Daye Press, 1957).

By Far the best account of New London's railroads is Thelma M. Kistler, *The Rise of Railroads in the Connecticut Valley* (*Smith College Studies in History*, vol. XXIII, Nos. 1-4/October, 1937/ July, 1938). An introduction to the railroad era in Connecticut is provided in Sidney Withington. *The First TWENTY Years of Railroads in Connecticut* (New Haven: Yale University Press, 1935). Charles G. Woodward, *The New London, Willimantic & Palmer Railroad Company* (Hartford: Case, Lockwood & Brainard, 1941) traces the establishment of the road by whaling interests and its problems which finally led to its demise.

The Sterling Library, Yale University, has a number of helpful pamphlets on New London and Stonington Railroad; New London, Willimantic and Palmer Railroad Company; and New London Northern Railroad Company; and also several annual reports of the New London, Willimantic and Palmer Railroad Company. General information on New London railroads is provided by Webb's *New England Railway and Manufacturing Statiscal Gazetteer* (Providence: Providence Press Co., 1896), Alvin F. Harlow, *Steelways of New England* (New York: Creative Press, 1946) and Edward C. Kirkland, *Men, Cities and Transportation* (2 vols., Cambridge, Harvard University Press, 1948).

Whaling

No single source presents a complete picture of New London whaling. The New London Customs Records in Record Group 45 at the Federal Records Center, Waltham, Massachusetts, are a "gold mine" of information on firms, vessels, crews, cargoes and areas visited. The most helpful material concerning operations of whaling firms can be found at the G. W. Blunt White Library, Mystic Seaport, Mystic Connecticut. Only two collections deal with whaling firms, the Lawrence & Co. Papers, 1822-1904, which consist of eleven boxes with 5,700 items and 133 volumes, and the more comprehensive but less voluminous source the N. and W. W. Billings Collection, containing thirteen volumes of records covering the firms' operations during the 1830's and 1840's. Of value also are the John K. Primer Papers of 1,841 pieces including thirty-one volumes. Primer supplied sails for many of the whaling vessels and often received reimbursement in the form of shares in the voyages. His records present a picture of costs of whaling operations. and value of returns. The John Turner Papers, concerning shipbuilding also prove of value as he built and rebuilt whaling vessels and often received a share in whaling ventures in lieu of cash payment. Of interest, is the Erastus Brewster Kimball, "Journal, June 8, 1828 to March 13, 1832," which relates day-to-day experiences of Brewster while on two New London whalers, the *Wabash*, 1828-1829 and the *Mentor*, 1831-1832. The Whaling Collection of documents has several interesting items, among them a letter from Jestin Martin to brother Charles Martin warning about the conditions of a whaling life.

The Sterling Library, Yale University, possesses several useful items. A number of logs of whalings vessels can be found in the Whaling Log Collection while the Miscellaneous Manuscript Collection contains the Coddington Billings Letters, Noyes Billings Letters, the William Williams Billings Letters and the Frink Papers. At the Baker Library, Harvard Graduate School of Business Administration, a valuable item is the Letterbook of Matthew Howland which contains letters to whaling captains of the firm from 1858 to 1879. It relates much information concerning the whaling business. Also at the Baker Library is the Mercantile Marine Insurance Co.'s Risk Book which lists rates and values of whaling vessels and outfits.

The Manuscript Division of the New York Public Library possesses the Miscellaneous Connecticut Boxes which contain several items about New London whaling and the Thomas W. Williams Papers, twenty-two boxes of material. At the Connecticut State Library the William Hale "Diary" provides a day-to-day account of whaling.

Primary printed sources are represented best by the works of Eva L. Butler, who edited several accounts by seamen of voyages on New London whalers. These include *Journal of Whaling Voyage in the Ship Onward of New London* (n.p.:n.d.), *Journal of a Whaling Voyage in the Ship Bengal of New London* (n.p.:n.d.), *The Journal of the Barque Harmony of New London* (n.p.:n.d.). *A Short Account of Whaling and Excerpts from the Journal of a Whaling Voyage in the Ship Bengal of New London* (New

York: Industrial Art Cooperation Service, n.d.). A seaman has left a readable account of his experience, James A. Rogers, *A Journal of a Whaling Voyage of the Ship Mentor of New London* (New Bedford: Reynolds Printing, n.d.). Nathaniel W. Taylor served as doctor on the *Julius Caesar* from 1851 to 1853. He wrote an excellent description of his adventures concerning whaling in *Life on a Whaler* (New London: N.L.C.H.S., 1929).

Among the secondary works the standard whaling history is Alexander Starbuck, *History of the American Whale Fishery from its Earliest Inception to the Year 1876* (New York: 1964). Reginald Hegarty, *Return of Whaling Vessels Sailing from American Ports* (New Bedford; The Old Dartmouth Historical Society, 1959) continues the Starbuck work to 1928. Unfortunately, these lists of voyages are far from complete. *The Whalemen's Shipping List and Merchant's Transcript* was the weekly newspaper of the Industry from 1843 to 1914 published at New Bedford. To help in tracing the captains, the Work Progress Administration of Massachusetts produced the *Whaling Masters* (New Bedford: Old Dartmouth Historical Society, 1936) which lists all captains who sailed on whalers from 1725 to 1925.

Elmo P. Hohman, *The American Whaleman* (New York: Longmans, Green & Co., 1928), Frances Deane Robotti, *Whaling and Old Salem* (New York: Bonanza Books, 1962). C. M. Scammon, *Marine Mammals of the Northwestern Coast of North America, with an Account of the American Whale Fishery* (New York: Dover Publication, 1969), Edouard A. Stackpole, *The Sea Hunter* (Philadelphia: J. B. Lippincott Co., 1953) and W. S. Tower, *A History of the American Whale Fishery* (Philadelphia: University of Pennsylvania, 1907) collectively present a picture of all aspects of the whaling industry. For New London whaling, C. A. Williams, "Early Whaling Industry" (N.L.C.H.S. *R&P.*, II, pt. I, New London: N.L.C.H.S., 1895), 3-22, presents a short but valuable account of the ports activity. Barnard L. Colby, *New London Whaling Captains* (Mystic, Connecticut: The Marine Historical Assoc., 1936), has selected a number of leading masters and relates the highlights of their careers.

Two unusual events involving New London whalers are recounted in Sidney Withington, *Two Dramatic Episodes of New England Whaling* (Mystic, Connecticut: Marine Historical Assoc., 1958). Norman R. Bennett and George Brooks, Jr., *New England Merchants in Africa* (Boston: Boston University Press, 1965) demonstrate New London whalers picking up supplies and trading with Africans while Eldon Griffin, *Clippers and Consuls: American Consular and Commercial Relations with Eastern Asia 1845-1860* (Ann Arbor: Edwards Brothers, 1938) deals with New London whaling voyages to Japan.

Whaling activities in the Pacific Islands is covered in C. Hartley Grottan, *The Southwest Pacific to 1900* (Ann Arbor: The University of Michigan Press, 1963), Douglas L. Oliver *The Pacific Islands* (Cambridge: Harvard University Press, 1951), Rex and Thea Rienits, *The Voyages of Captain Cook* (London: The Hamlyn Publishing Group, 1968).

Whalemen's Memorial (n.p.n.d.) gives a brief description of highlights of New London whaling. *Daboll's Almanac* (1844-1892), lists the firms and returns of whaling year by year. Hamilton Cochran, *Blockade runner of the Confederacy* (Indianapolis: Bobb-Merrill Co., 1958), relates the destruction of whalers by the

Confederate raiders, E. Keble Chatterton, *Whales and Whaling* (London: Unwin Ltd., 1926), covers the Arctic disaster of 1871. The opening of Arctic grounds and Bowhead whaling is described by Albert Cook Church, *Whale Ships and Whaling* (New York: W. W. Norton & Co., 1939). Clifford W. Asheley, *The Yankee Whaler* (Boston: Houghton Mifflin Company, 1938) gives an excellent picture of whaling life.

Edmund Burke's speech to Parliament about the widespread operations of the American whaling by 1775 is reproduced in Thomas Beale "The Natural History of the Sperm Whale" *(The London Quarterly Review,* April, 1838), 177-190. Henry M. Kendale, Robert Glendening and Clifford H. MacFadden, *Introduction to Geography* (New York: Harcourt, Brace & Co., 1952), describes the conditions at Desolation Island.

Two interesting articles by Charlotte M. Holloway, "The Old Whaling Port" *(The Connecticut Quarterly,* Vol. III, No. 2), 206-221 and "The Last Shot in the Arctic" *(The Connecticut Quarterly,* Vol. IV, No. 2, 1898), 163-174 provide information about New London's whaling fleet. The only full scale account of the port's whaling industry is contained in Robert O. Decker, *New London Whaling Industry* (York, Pa., Shumway, 1973). Of some value by the same author "The New England Whaling Industry" *(Wethersfield Post,* March 10, 1971). Another first hand account is Francis Allyn Olmsted, *Incidents of a Whaling Voyage* (New York, 1969). Stan Hugill, *Stanties and Sailors Songs* (New York, 1969), presents a number of whaling songs.

Religion

A wealth of material exists both published and unpublished for those seeking the religious history of the town. As cited above, the State Library has extensive records of the churches as has United Church House, Hartford.

As is to be expected, the Congregational Church has done especially well in the amount of published material available. S. Leroy Blake's works, *The Early History of the First Church of Christ, New London* (New London: Day Publishing Co., 1897); *The Later History of the First Church of Christ, New London* (New London: Day Publishing Co., 1900) and "Gurdon Saltonstall Scholar, Preacher, Statesman" *(R.&P.,* N.L.C.H.S., I, pt. V,1894,3-28; trace the founding of the church and its history to the end of the nineteenth century. Also helpful are Paul F. Laubenstein (ed.), *The First Church of Christ in New London . . .* (New London: New London Printing Co., 1946), *Contributions to the Ecclesiastical History of Connecticut* (I, New Haven: William Kingsley, 1861, II, Hartford: Connecticut Conference of United Church of Christ, 1967), Richard A. Wheeler, "The First Organized Church in New London Country", *R&P.,* I, pt. III, N.L.C.H.S., (1891) 11-25, and *The Second Congregational Church.*

For other religious groups numerous newspaper articles outline their history. Also the following were of use: *Historical Sketch of the Huntington Street Baptist Church* (New London, 1899), *Historical Sketch and Directory: Federal Street M. E. Church,* Robert A. Hallam, *Annals of St. James Church, New London for 150 Years* (Hartford, 1873). *Episcopal Church–St. James* (n.p.: 1964), *First Baptist Church of New London* and Ester Sulman, *A Godly Heritage: The Story of the Jewish Community in New London 1860-1955* (New London: 1957).

F. Denison (ed.) *The Evangelist: or Life and Labors of Rev. Jabez Swan* (William Peckham, 1873) presents an interesting account of a man who was a minister at all three New London Baptist churches. The story of a seamen's entrance to the ministry is related in "Ira R. Steward's Autobiography" (MS, Yale).

Education

Most valuable for a view of the educational development of the area is Benjamin Stark's "Historical Sketch of the Schools of New London" (*R.&P.*, II, pt. II, N.L.C.H.S., 1846), 115-144. A highly entertaining account of an early school master can be found in Richard B. Wall's *Doctor Ulysses Dow and His School* (New London, 1907). Of interest are the yearly catalogues of the institutions of higher education: Admiral Billard Academy, Coast Guard Academy, Connecticut College, Mitchell College and Mohegan Community College. In addition of use was *New London Junior College* (n.p.:1939), Riley Hughes, *Our Coast Guard Academy* (New York: 1944) and Irene Nye, *Connecticut College* (New London: 1943).

Special Studies

A clear picture of the physical setting of New London can be gained from Richard Foster Flint, *The Glacial Geology of Connecticut* (Hartford: State Geological and Natural History Survey, 1930), Wilbur G. Foye, *The Geology of Eastern Connecticut* (Hartford; State Geological and Natural History Survey, 1949, William North Rice and Herbert Ernest Gregory, *Manual of Geology* (Hartford: The Case, Lockwood & Brainard Co., 1906) and Henry Staats Sharp, *The Physical History of Connecticut Shoreline* (Hartford: State Geological and Natural History Survey, 1929).

Charles M. Andrews, *The Connecticut Intestacy Law* (New Haven: Yale University Press, 1933), covers a subject which caused a strain between England and New London. An event which had international repercussion is covered by Roland M. Hooker, *The Spanish Ship Case* (New Haven: Yale University Press, 1934). Edward Bacon, "New London and the War of 1812" (N.L.C.H.S. *R.&P.*, I, pt. I, New London: N.L.C.H.S., 1890), 94-109, gives an excellent account of the conditions of the port during the war. The little privateer activity of the War of 1812 is covered in George Coggeshall, *History of American Privateers and Letters of Marque, 1812-1814* (New York: George Coggeshall, 1850). Indian affairs are adequately covered in Alden T. Vaughan, *New England Frontier, Puritans and Indians 1620-1675* (Boston: Little, Brown and Company, 1965) and Caulkins, *New London*.

The story of an arctic expedition in which New London played a leading role is told in William H. Cunnington's, *The Polaris Expedition* (Philadelphia: Philadelphia Book Co., 1873).

No better material on the cemeteries of New London can be found than in the excellent Cedar Grove three volumes. A complete history of the different burial grounds can be found in I, No. 3, 189-235 which includes War Veterans listing;

additional lists of War Veterans can be found in I, No. 2, 139-158. The history of Cedar Grove Cemetery appears in I, No. 1, 27-66.

For the names, work and some biographical information concerning New London's excellent silversmiths George Curtis Munson, *Early Silver of Connecticut and its Makers* (Meridan: 1913), Henry N. Flynt and Martha Gandy Fales, *The Heritage Foundation Collection of Silver: With Biographical Sketches of New England Silversmiths, 1625-1825* (Old Deerfield, 1918) and Jennifer F. Goldsborough, *An Exhibition of New London Silver, 1700 and 1835* (New London: 1969). *Tercentenary Exhibition* (Lyman Allyn Museum, 1946) is excellent.

Other special studies of interest include: *Thamses Club* (n.p.:n.d.), C. M. Holloway, *History of the Niagara Steam Fire Company No. 1* (New London: 1900), Lila Parrish Lyman, *One Hundred Years of Niagara Engine Co., No. 1* (New London: 1950), Alice Chew, *Lewis Female Cent Society* (New London, 1910), J. Leigh Walsh, *Connecticut Pioneers in Telephone* (New Haven, 1950), Glenn Weaver, *The Hartford Electric Light Company* (Hartford, 1969, and *New England Hurricane* (WPA, Boston: 1938).

ILLUSTRATION CREDITS

All photo copies made by Louis S. Martel, Waterford, Conn.

Philip A. Biscuti, p. 275
Harold Cone Collection, pp. 43, 73, 81, 85, 88, 171, 173, 180, 186, 188, 195, 198, 202, 212, 215, 217, 219, 222, 225, 283, 288, 301
Edgerton Collection, Public Library, New London, pp. 4, 8, 14, 45, 59, 93, 115, 119, 122, 126, 128, 131, 133, 138, 144, 147, 148, 157, 165, 174, 178, 184, 191, 205, 207, 221, 222, 223, 230, 233, 247, 251, 252, 254, 261, 263, 266, 268, 269, 272, 279, 280, 286, 290, 292, 293, 296, 297, 299, 300, 302, 303, 304, 305, 306, 311, 313, 327, 331
General Dynamics, Groton, pp. 175, 190
Lyman Allyn Museum, Frontispiece, pp. xvi, 3, 7, 15, 35, 63, 96, 98, 122, 151, 153, 169, 181, 284, 299, 329
Louis S. Martel, pp. 19, 43, 248, 25 ` 258, 269, 270, 293, 332, 333, 334
Mitchell College, p. 277
U.S. Navy, p. 189
New London County Historical Society, pp. 38, 65, 78, 79, 144
Ruth Newcomb, pp. 303, 305
Savings Bank of New London, p. 99
Lou Silverstein, p. 174
State Library, Hartford, p. 45

INDEX

CPSIA information can be obtained
at www.ICGtesting.com
Printed in the USA
BVHW022104080523
663793BV00009B/115